A Concise History of Poland

The second edition of *A Concise History of Poland* has been revised
to shed more light on the highly complex past of this state prior to
1795, as well as to include most recent developments, notably its
accession to the European Union. Once a dominant force in central
and eastern Europe, home to a remarkable experiment in consensual
politics in an area covering not only its present-day borders, but also
Lithuania, Ukraine and Belarus, in 1795 its neighbours excised it
from the map. Resurrected in 1918, partitioned afresh during the
Second World War, it survived to become a satellite of the Soviet
Union. Yet in the 1980s, it was Poland which blazed the trail in
casting off communism, and it was finally able to reassert its
Christian and European heritage. This book is the ideal companion
for all looking for a clear and comprehensive survey of this fascinating country.

JERZY LUKOWSKI is Reader in Polish History at the University of
Birmingham. His previous publications include *The partitions of
Poland 1772, 1793, 1795* (1999) and *The European nobility in the
eighteenth century* (2003).

HUBERT ZAWADZKI teaches history at Abingdon School. His
publications include *A man of honour: Adam Czartoryski as a
statesman of Russia and Poland 1795–1831* (1993).

236-245

CAMBRIDGE CONCISE HISTORIES

This is a series of illustrated 'concise histories' of selected individual countries, intended both as university and college textbooks and as general historical introductions for general readers, travellers and members of the business community.

For a list of titles in the series, see end of book.

A Concise History of Poland

SECOND EDITION

JERZY LUKOWSKI

and

HUBERT ZAWADZKI

CAMBRIDGE
UNIVERSITY PRESS

CAMBRIDGE UNIVERSITY PRESS
Cambridge, New York, Melbourne, Madrid, Cape Town, Singapore, São Paulo

Cambridge University Press
The Edinburgh Building, Cambridge CB2 8RU, UK

Published in the United States of America by Cambridge University Press, New York

www.cambridge.org
Information on this title: www.cambridge.org/9780521618571

First published 2001
Second edition 2006
Reprinted 2007

Printed in the United Kingdom at the University Press, Cambridge

A catalogue record for this publication is available from the British Library

ISBN 978-0-521-85332-3 hardback
ISBN 978-0-521-61857-1 paperback

For

Lesley and Francesca

CONTENTS

ILLUSTRATIONS

MAPS

PREFACE TO THE SECOND EDITION

We are delighted to be able to bring out a second edition relatively soon after the original and are grateful to Cambridge University Press for allowing us both to expand the text and to add further illustrative materials. Most of the expansion has gone into the pre-1795 section of the book. A number of reviewers felt, rightly, that there was too dense an accumulation of materials (though some also appear to have failed to appreciate this belongs to a series of 'Concise Histories') and we trust that our additions will help readers come to grips more comfortably with what was one of the most complex states of Europe. The present day adds its own complexities and we have tried to take these on board at least to the extent of showing readers the challenges and problems that face today's republic and member of the European Union.

Our thanks to Steven Rowell for his generous insights into the history of the medieval and early modern Lithuanian state, and to Michael Laird for his very useful comments on chapters 6–8. Isabelle Dambricourt at Cambridge University Press has been a model of editorial tact and assistance.

PREFACE TO THE FIRST EDITION

Writing Concise Histories is an activity more rewarding than satisfactory. The begetters know how much has been omitted; readers, no matter how much or how little they know, have to put up with those omissions. This present offering in the Cambridge Concise Histories series is no exception. It is, however, the first to have been written by two authors, one an eighteenth-century specialist, the other more at home in the nineteenth century. Neither of us felt quite up to the undertaking of an all-embracing treatment of Poland's entire past; if some of the difficulties which such an undertaking might have created become apparent to our readers, then we will have achieved something.

For there have been at least two 'Polands'. One disappeared from the political map of Europe in 1795. For over one hundred and twenty years afterwards, it either did not exist, or did so in the form of spluttering, half-formed entities, which had a kind of relationship with what had gone before, but a relationship so uncertain, be it at a wider political level or be it at that of the individual 'Pole', that it is almost impossible to define it in any satisfying detail. The state that emerged in the aftermath of the First World War was very different indeed from the one which met its end in the late eighteenth century; these differences are even more striking in the state which appeared after the Second World War, following an excision from the political map more brutal than anything the country had endured before.

The links between the two 'Polands', the one pre-1795, the other post-1918, remain indissoluble. Poles have always had to rebuild their past, not least because of the systematic attempts to deprive them of it. The most tangible sign of that of course is Warsaw itself: the so-called Old and New Towns are bijou replicas not just of structures destroyed by the Germans during the Second World War but of buildings going back to the old, pre-1795 state and to the Middle Ages. And similar extensive reconstruction has taken place in Gdańsk, Wrocław and Poznań – to mention only the most notable examples.

Here historians enter very treacherous waters. To say that there are two Polands is not so much a necessary simplification as a gross distortion. Indeed, virtually anything that can be said about 'Poland' by one observer can be plausibly demonstrated to be false by another. Its territories in their length and breadth have been the abode not only of the Slavonic people who call themselves 'Poles' but also of (among others) Germans, Jews, Armenians, Lithuanians, Ukrainians, Belarusians, Tatars – and these, in turn, have often intermarried, absorbed each other's cultures and faiths, become one another. As late as the 1850s, one in five marriages in the city of Poznań (or, as it was known to its then Prussian rulers, Posen) was between Poles and Germans. Across wide stretches of territory, for much of their history, the degree of intermarriage between Poles and Lithuanians/Ukrainians/Belarusians was at least as high. It remains reflected today in the frequent incidence in the Polish population of surnames of diverse linguistic-ethnic origins (a comparable diversity can, of course, be found among Poland's neighbours). In the great and bloody ethnic untanglings that have blighted the twentieth century, these people were often forced to choose their 'ethnic identity', whatever this concept (scientifically bizarre but conventionally indispensable) is understood to mean.

For much of its history, Poland was very much a border region of more or less peacefully co-existing peoples and cultures. From the late Middle Ages onwards, its elites evolved a remarkable consensual political culture, without which the Polish state would probably have fallen apart under the strains of accommodating its differences. These divergences and the less than satisfactory mechanisms of consensus brought the Polish state close to disintegration during the seventeenth century and, we can see with hindsight, contributed massively to its destruction by the end of the eighteenth. While there is much to criticize in that failed political and constitutional experiment, it is worth pointing out that the governance of multi-ethnic political entities in our own times has left at least as much to be desired. The ruling elites' consensual commitments translated into a strong attachment to 'liberty', which, in turn, helped those who considered themselves to be Poles to survive the nineteenth century, yet also helped to bring about the catastrophically unsuccessful insurrections of 1830–1 and 1863–4.

By the late nineteenth century, amid universally burgeoning nationalisms, the old notion of the Pole as a nobleman who could readily accommodate more than one 'ethnic' identity showed itself to be unsustainable romantic nostalgia. Some within the diverse ethnic groups living on territories which once formed part of the Polish state would indignantly deny that they ever shared a common homeland. Poland's current homogeneity is very much an enforced product of the Second World War and its immediate aftermath. It is also something not seen in Poland since at least the middle of the fourteenth century. The pasts of Poland and its neighbours are too intertwined for easy, compartmentalized analysis. The nation-state is not yet dead, but, if it were, a reading of Poland's history might be much facilitated. It may not matter very much to a Briton or American (not that these labels are without their own pitfalls) that a Pole will refer to the city of L'viv (in Ukraine) as Lwów; it would probably not matter to a Ukrainian. But it might matter to a Ukrainian if the label Lwów is applied to L'viv in a book such as this, aimed at a wider, non-Polish or non-Ukrainian readership. In such a context, 'Lwów' might say something which 'L'viv' does not (and vice versa): a descriptor with a baggage of Polish overtones and belongings; whereas to a Pole, in the same context, 'L'viv' might well appear a denial of the Polish character of a great trading city which was once part of Poland. Seemingly innocuous 'Lemberg' – how Lwów/L'viv was labelled by Austrian bureaucrats – is a hopeless anachronism. Comparable alarms and suspicions can still be generated over other descriptors: Gdańsk/Danzig; Toruń/Thorn; Wilno/Vilnius; Grodno/Gardinas/ Hrodna; even Oświęcim/Auschwitz. If this is a particularly acute problem for historians of Poland (even if born in Britain) seeking to project their past for the benefit of others, it is a problem found throughout much of eastern Europe and bedevils the writing of any history of the region. In this context, the early part of this book is careful to use the term Rus' (not Russia) for the regions to Poland's east – if we cannot avoid the charge of furthering Polish terminological imperialism, we would certainly wish to avoid that of abetting its Muscovite variant.

We appreciate that our approach to such sensitivities will satisfy few who have any emotional involvement in or even substantial knowledge of eastern Europe's past. There are too many of these pasts to be quietly reconciled. We have therefore eschewed consistency in the naming of parts: we are conscious that this will only lead to historical absurdities; we have sometimes avoided the issue altogether. We have used terminology which seems right for the period. Thus, in chapter 2, Vilnius appears as Vilnius; as Wilno in chapters 3, 4 and 5; as both Wilno and Vilnius in chapter 6; 'Thorn' and 'Danzig' in the early modern period are labels meant to reflect the Germanic character of their elites, integral components of the late Jagiellonian state and Polish-Lithuanian Commonwealth. English is insufficiently acquainted with east European toponymy to permit the consistent use of anglicized, and therefore neutral(?), descriptors such as Warsaw or Kiev. Even where such descriptors exist, current usage tends to the adoption of Polish forms (Kraków, rather than Cracow; even British football commentators have been known to struggle with Łódź, rather than Lodz). We are only too happy to encourage this development. We have listed some alternative versions in the index. Readers should feel at liberty to argue among themselves as to what form we should really have used. At a hopefully less contentious level, we have chosen to retain some established anglicizations of Polish proper names (thus, John Casimir, as opposed to Jan Kazimierz); and drop other anglicizations in favour of the Polish (Bolesław, Władysław or Stanisław, rather than Boleslas, Ladislas, or Stanislaus/Stanley). Once again, we have been guided by our own instincts rather than any spurious consistency, though we accept that what feels right to us will not seem so to others.

This is primarily a political history. It is here that we feel the need for a coherent narrative to be most pressing. This has meant some regrettable sacrifices: economic and social developments receive comparatively limited attention, particularly in the first three chapters. The Jews, so important in Poland's past life, receive far too little acknowledgement. To do them justice, and the many others who have received altogether too short shrift in these pages, would mean abandoning all hope of conciseness. For those who want their histories sprawling and expansive, we cannot do other than point them in the direction of Norman Davies' *God's playground: a history of Poland* (2 volumes, Oxford, Clarendon, 1981 and 2005).

Numerous persons have helped and encouraged us, not least by pointing out our shortcomings. Our thanks for their advice and apologies for not always having followed it to Danuta Manikowska, Robert Frost, Robert Swanson, Chris Wickham, Jūratė Kiaupienė, Michael Laird and Richard Hofton. Graeme Murdock has provided pleasurably clear illumination of the darker crevasses of late medieval and early modern Hungarian and Balkan politics. Will Zawadzki and Anna Zawadzki have helped with the search for illustrations in the second half of the book. Will has also provided invaluable advice on the design of the maps, while Meg Zawadzki has removed some stylistic infelicities from the text. Our mistakes remain ours alone. We both owe a particular debt of gratitude to William Davies at Cambridge University Press: he has been a model of forbearance, patience, understanding and all-round helpfulness.

A NOTE ON POLISH PRONUNCIATION

The pronunciation of Slavonic languages, not least Polish, can be something of a problem for the uninitiated. The following can only be a very simplistic guide; it is not meant for philological or phonetic perfectionists.

ą	similar to the French 'on' if crossed with the 'o' in 'dome'
ę	similar to the French 'on', if crossed with the 'e' in 'get'
ó	u, as in 'shook'
y	i, as in 'bit'
ci	short 'chee', as in 'chit'
si	short 'she', as in 'ship'
Ć, ć	'ch', as in 'chop'
cz	as the above, but harsher
c	'ts' as in 'pots', except in the combinations 'ci' and 'cz'
Ł, ł	'w' as in 'wet'
ń	slighty softened 'n' – as in Spanish 'ñ'
Ś, ś	'sh' as in 'shut'
sz	as the above, but harsher
rz, Ż, ż	as the above, but with a 'z' sound (zh as in 'Zhukov')
w	'v' as in vile
zi	pronounced as first two letters of French 'gîte'
Ź, ź	pronounced as first letter of French 'gîte'

CHRONOLOGY

1387	Conversion to Latin Catholicism of the Grand Duchy of Lithuania begins
15 July 1410	Polish and Lithuanian victory over the Teutonic Knights at the battle of Grunwald/Tannenberg
1422–30	Privileges of Czerwińsk and Jedlnia: *Neminem Captivabimus nisi iure victum*
6 Mar. 1454	King Casimir IV decrees the annexation of the Prussian lands to the Polish Crown
1454	The 'Thirteen Years War' with the Teutonic Knights begins; the 'Nieszawa privileges' issued
19 Oct. 1466	The 'Thirteen Years War' is ended by the peace of Thorn: Royal Prussia is incorporated into Poland
1505	Privilege of *Nihil Novi*
1514	Lithuania loses Smolensk to Muscovy
1525	The Lutheran faith is formally established in the duchy of Prussia and the lands of the Teutonic order are secularized
8 April 1525	Treaty of Kraków: Albrecht of Hohenzollern accepts rule of the duchy of Prussia as a Polish fief
1561	Livonia is incorporated into Poland; establishment of the duchy of Courland as a Polish fief
4 July 1569	Polish–Lithuanian Union of Lublin
7 July 1572	Death of Sigismund II and extinction of the Jagiellonian dynasty
1573	The Confederacy of Warsaw: formal admission of the co-existence of different religious denominations in Poland; Henri of Valois becomes the first king to be fully elected by the body of the Polish nobility
1578	Creation of the Tribunal of the Crown
1581	Creation of the Tribunal of Lithuania
1596	Union of Brest: union of Catholicism and Orthodoxy
1610–11	Polish occupation of Moscow during the 'Time of Troubles'
1619–29	Polish–Swedish conflict which sees the loss of most of Livonia to Sweden
1620–1	Polish–Turkish war
1632–4	Smolensk war between Poland and Muscovy
1648	Ukrainian revolt erupts under the leadership of Bohdan Khmel'nytskyi
1652	Władysław Siciński is the first individual envoy to disrupt a Sejm through the liberum veto
18 Jan. 1654	Union of Pereiaslav between the Ukraine and Muscovy
1655	Muscovite and Swedish invasions of the Commonwealth: the 'Deluge' begins

19 Sept. 1657	Treaty of Wehlau: Poland abandons its sovereignty over the duchy of Prussia
8 May 1660	Peace of Oliva ends the Polish–Swedish war
30 Jan. 1667	Truce of Andrussovo brings an end to the Polish–Muscovite war: Poland cedes eastern Ukraine to Muscovy (confirmed by the treaty of Moscow, 6 May 1686)
18 Oct. 1672	Treaty of Buczacz: Poland cedes Podole and Kamieniec Podolski to Turkey
12 Sept. 1683	Polish participation in the relief of Vienna: defeat of the Turks
1697	Election of Frederick Augustus I, elector of Saxony, as Augustus II of Poland
26 Jan. 1699	Peace of Carlowitz: Poland recovers Podole and Kamieniec Podolski
1700	Beginning of the Great Northern War (ends 1721)
12 July 1704	Election of Stanisław Leszczyński, as Swedish-backed anti-king
8 July 1709	Peter the Great defeats Charles XII at the battle of Poltava
1 Feb. 1717	The 'Silent Sejm'
1733	Divided royal election between Stanisław Leszczyński and Frederick Augustus II, elector of Saxony
1733–6	War of the Polish Succession: Russian intervention secures the Polish throne for Frederick Augustus II as Augustus III
1740	Foundation of the *Collegium Nobilium* by Stanisław Konarski
1756–63	The Seven Years War: neutral Poland serves as a 'wayside inn' for the armies of Prussia, Russia and Austria
5 Oct. 1763	Death of Augustus III
May 1764	Reforms of the Convocation Sejm
6 Sept. 1764	Election of king Stanisław August Poniatowski
Feb. 1768	Confederacy of Bar inaugurates civil conflict in Poland
5 Aug. 1772	Conventions of St Petersburg between Russia, Prussia and Austria: First Partition of Poland
14 Oct. 1773	Establishment of the Commission for National Education
1788–92	The Four Years Sejm
3 May 1791	Enactment of a reformed constitution
May 1792	Russian invasion of Poland, supposedly at the invitation of the Confederacy of Targowica
23 Jan. 1793	Treaty of St Petersburg: Russia and Prussia agree on the Second Partition of Poland
Mar.–Oct. 1794	Kościuszko's Insurrection

3 Jan. 1795	Treaty of St Petersburg: Russia and Austria agree on the Third Partition of Poland (accepted by Prussia, 24 October)
25 Nov. 1795	King Stanisław August Poniatowski abdicates
12 Feb. 1798	Death of Stanisław August Poniatowski
1798–1800	Polish legions in Italy under French aegis
1803	Tsar Alexander I reopens a Polish university in Wilno (Vilnius)
1805	Collapse of Czartoryski's plan for restoration of Poland in union with Russia (October)
1807	Creation of the Napoleonic duchy of Warsaw (July); abolition of serfdom in the duchy of Warsaw
1809	Duchy of Warsaw enlarged (October)
1812	Napoleon's expedition to Moscow with Polish participation
1813	Russian forces occupy the duchy of Warsaw
1815	Russo–Austrian–Prussian treaties on Poland (3 May); Final Treaty of Vienna (9 June): creation of the 'Congress' Kingdom of Poland with Tsar Alexander I as king; creation of the Grand Duchy of Posen (Poznań) and of the Free City of Kraków; introduction of Alexander I's constitution for his Polish kingdom (24 December)
1816	University of Warsaw founded by Tsar Alexander I
1818	Opening of the first session of the Sejm of 'Congress' Poland (27 March)
1820	Opening of the second session of the Polish Sejm (13 September): Alexander I warns against the abuse of liberty; Adam Mickiewicz's 'Ode to Youth'
1821	Alexander I bans all secret societies in 'Congress' Poland (November)
1823	Czartoryski dismissed as curator of Wilno university (October)
1825	Tsar Nicholas I succeeds Alexander I as Polish king (1 December)
1827–8	Trial of the Polish 'Decembrists'
1830	November Insurrection against Russian rule (starts 29 November)
1831	Deposition of Nicholas I by the Polish Sejm (25 January); Russo-Polish war; fall of Warsaw (September); beginning of the 'Great Emigration'
1832	Nicholas I's Organic Statute abolishes the Polish Constitution (February); Polish Democratic Society founded in Paris (March)
1834	Publication in Paris of Mickiewicz's *Pan Tadeusz*

1839	Greek Catholic Church absorbed by the Russian Orthodox Church
1840	Russian law replaces the Lithuanian legal code in the western governships of the Russian Empire
1846	Revolution in Kraków (February); Polish nobles massacred by peasants in western Galicia (February–March); Austria annexes Kraków (16 November)
1848–9	Polish participation in the 'Springtime of Nations'; insurrection in Poznania and in Kraków and Lwów; abolition of serfdom in the Austrian Empire
1850	Abolition of customs barrier between Russia and 'Congress' Poland
1861	Abolition of serfdom in the Russian Empire (February); unrest in Warsaw; Marquis Wielopolski appointed head of civilian administration in 'Congress' Poland (March); Jews granted equal rights in 'Congress' Poland
1863	Outbreak of insurrection against Russian rule in Russian Poland (22 January)
1864	Tsar Alexander II grants generous property rights to the Kingdom's peasants (March); execution of last insurgent leader Romuald Traugutt (5 August)
1869	Introduction of provincial autonomy in Austrian Poland (Galicia)
1872	Compulsory German-language schooling introduced in Prussian Poland
1873	Bismarck's *Kulturkampf* against the Catholic Church extends to Prussian Poland
1882	First Marxist society on Polish soil founded by Ludwik Waryński
1886	Bismarck creates a special fund to buy out Polish-owned estates in Prussia
1888	Poles in Prussia found a Land Bank
1892	Polish Socialist Party (PPS) founded in Paris (November)
1893	Social Democratic Party of the Kingdom of Poland (SDKP) formed by Rosa Luxemburg in Warsaw (July); becomes the Social Democratic Party of the Kingdom of Poland and Lithuania (SDKPiL) in 1900
1895	Polish Peasant Party founded in Rzeszów (August)
1897	National Democratic Party ('Endecja') founded by Roman Dmowski
1905	Revolution in the Russian Empire (and in Russian Poland); October Manifesto promises liberalization within the Russian Empire
1906	Opening of the First Duma in St Petersburg; Polish Socialist Party splits (November)

1907	Universal male suffrage introduced in Austria
1911	Introduction of elected local councils (*zemstva*) in the western governorships of the Russian Empire
1912	Region of Chełm detached from 'Congress' Poland and incorporated into the Russian Empire
1914	Outbreak of the First World War; Piłsudski's legions enter Russian Poland with little success (6–9 August); Russian commander-in-chief issues manifesto promising a reunified Poland under the tsar (14 August)
1915	Russian forces expelled from Poland by the Central Powers (August)
1916	Restoration of the Kingdom of Poland by German and Austrian emperors (5 November)
1917	Creation of a Polish army in France (June); Dmowski establishes the Polish National Committee in Paris (15 August); Regency Council created in German-occupied Warsaw (15 October); Lithuanian 'Taryba' calls for Lithuanian independence (11 December)
1918	Woodrow Wilson's Fourteen Points include an independent Poland with access to the sea (8 January); treaty of Brest-Litovsk (3 March); Belarusian National Council in Minsk proclaims the independence of Belarus (25 March); start of Polish-Ukrainian fighting for control of Lwów and east Galicia (31 October); declaration of Polish Independence in Warsaw (11 November): Piłsudski assumes power in Warsaw; creation of the Polish Communist Party (16 December); start of successful anti-German uprising in Poznania (27 December)
1919	Elections to the first Sejm of re-born Poland (26 January): National Democrats the largest party; France, UK and Italy recognize the independence of Poland (24–27 February); treaty of Versailles transfers Poznania and West Prussia (the so-called 'Polish Corridor') to Poland (28 June); Polish forces occupy Wilno (19 April) and Minsk (8 August); Poles establish complete control over east Galicia (June–July); 'Curzon Line' proposed by the Great Powers as Poland's provisional eastern demarcation line (8 December)
1920	Polish–Ukrainian alliance (21 April); Polish forces enter Kiev (8 May); plebiscite in southern East Prussia (11 July); coalition Government of National Defence formed under Witos (24 July); Bolshevik counter-offensive turned back at the battle of Warsaw (16–18 August); 'mutinous' Polish forces seize Wilno (9 October)

1921	Franco–Polish alliance (9 February); Polish–Romanian defence treaty (3 March); adoption of a new constitution (17 March); treaty of Riga with Bolshevik Russia (18 March); plebiscite in Upper Silesia (20 March); Witos' centre-left government toppled (June); German–Polish partition of Upper Silesia (20 October)
1922	Incorporation of Wilno by Poland (24 March); assassination of president Narutowicz (16 December)
1923	Conference of Ambassadors in Paris recognizes Poland's eastern border (15 March); centre-right coalition government under Witos (May–December); non-party government under Władysław Grabski (19 December)
1924	Monetary reform: Polish *złoty* introduced (April)
1925	Construction begins of a new port in Gdynia; Concordat with the Catholic Church (10 February); German–Polish tariff war starts (15 June); a grand coalition government under Aleksander Skrzyński replaces Grabski's administration (20 November)
1926	Skrzyński resigns (5 April); centre-right government under Witos (10 May); Piłsudski's coup d'état (12 May): beginning of the 'Sanacja' regime
1928	Creation of the Non-Party Bloc of Co-operation with the Government (BBWR); parliamentary elections (3 March): eclipse of the National Democrats
1929	Parties of the centre and the left form alliance against the 'Sanacja' (September); the Great Depression hits Poland
1930	Piłsudski becomes prime minister (August–December); incarceration in Brześć of political opponents of Piłsudski's regime (10 September–29 December); pacification of eastern Galicia (September–November); BBWR largest party in the November elections
1931	Formation of a single Polish Peasant Party (PSL)
1932	Polish–Soviet Treaty of Non-Aggression (25 July); Colonel Józef Beck becomes foreign minister (2 November)
1933	Polish–German tension over the Free City of Danzig (February–March)
1934	Polish–German Treaty of Non-Aggression: end of Polish–German tariff war (26 January); Polish–Soviet Treaty of Non-Aggression extended for ten years (12 February)
1935	New Polish constitution strengthens presidential powers (23 April); death of Marshal Piłsudski (12 May)
1936	Centrist opposition politicians form the 'Morges Front'

	(February); General Edward Rydz-Śmigły becomes Marshal of Poland (10 November)
1937	Launching of the four-year state investment plan and of the Central Industrial Region (COP) (February)
1938	Polish ultimatum to Lithuania (17 March) leads to the establishment of diplomatic relations (31 March); Stalin dissolves the Polish Communist Party (March); Polish ultimatum (30 September) leads to the surrender of Teschen by Czechoslovakia (1 October)
1939	Polish government declines Hitler's offer of alliance (26 March); British guarantee of Polish independence (31 March); Hitler repudiates the Polish–German treaty of 1934 (28 April); Franco-Polish military agreement (19 May); Poland declines consent for the transit of Soviet forces through its territory (19 August); Nazi–Soviet Pact (23–24 August); Anglo-Polish treaty of alliance (25 August); Nazi Germany invades Poland (1 September); Soviet forces invade Poland (17 September); Polish government and High Command cross into Romania (17–18 September); Warsaw surrenders to the Germans (27 September); Nazi–Soviet demarcation line established across partitioned Poland (28 September); Polish government-in-exile formed in Paris under General Sikorski (30 September)
1940	Deportations of Poles to the Soviet interior begin (February); Sikorski's government moves to London (June); Polish pilots in action during the battle of Britain (August–September); creation of the Warsaw ghetto (October)
1941	Nazi invasion of the USSR (22 June); Polish–Soviet treaty signed in London by Sikorski and ambassador Maisky (30 July)
1942	Wannsee conference (January): gradual liquidation by the Nazis of Jewish ghettoes in occupied Poland; creation of the communist Polish Worker Party (PPR) (January); creation of the Home Army (AK) (14 February)
1943	Union of Polish Patriots formed in USSR (March); Jewish insurrection in the Warsaw ghetto (April–May); revelation of the Katyn massacre (April); Stalin suspends diplomatic relations with the Polish government-in-exile (25 April); General Sikorski killed off Gibraltar (4 July); decisions of the Three-Power conference at Teheran on Poland's future frontiers (November–December)
1944	Creation of the Soviet-backed Polish Committee of National Liberation (PKWN) (22 July); Polish forces in

action at the battles at Monte Cassino (May), Falaise (August) and Arnhem (September); Warsaw Uprising (1 August–2 October); Mikołajczyk resigns from the premiership of the government-in-exile (24 November); PKWN declares itself the 'Provisional Government of the Republic of Poland' (31 December)

1945   Yalta Conference (February); communist-led Polish 'provisional government' signs 20-year treaty of friendship with USSR (21 April); UK and USA withdraw their recognition of the Polish government in London (5 July); Potsdam Conference establishes the Oder–Neisse line as the western limit of Polish administration (July–August); Polish–Soviet frontier agreement (16 August)

1946   Decree for the nationalization of industrial enterprises (3 January); start of systematic deportation of the German population from Poland (14 February); rigged referendum (30 June); anti-Jewish pogrom in Kielce (4 July); Polish armed forces in the West dissolved (3 September)

1947   Communists and their allies win rigged elections in Poland (19 January); elimination of anti-communist opposition; government in Warsaw declines participation in the Marshall Plan (9 July); Mikołajczyk flees to the West (21 October)

1948   Stalinist regime introduced; Polish Socialist Party unites with the communists to form the Polish United Workers' Party (PZPR) (15–21 December)

1949   Creation of a central economic planning office (10 February); pro-communist United Peasant Party created (27–29 November); start of collectivization of farms

1950   Launch of the Six Year Plan for rapid industrialization (21 July)

1951   Gomułka arrested (2 August)

1952   First Polish-language broadcast from Munich by Radio Free Europe (3 May); introduction of the Stalinist constitution: proclamation of the Polish People's Republic (22 July)

1954   Józef Światło's revelations on Radio Free Europe (December)

1955   Central Committee of the PZPR condemns Stalinist repression (21–24 January); formation of the Warsaw Pact (14 May)

1956   Workers uprising in Poznań (28–29 June); Gomułka becomes leader of the PZPR (21 October): end of

	Stalinism in Poland; Cardinal Wyszyński released from detention (29 October)
1965	Polish–Soviet friendship treaty renewed for another 20 years (8 April); Polish bishops' letter of reconciliation to German Roman Catholic episcopate (18 November)
1966	Rival State–Church celebrations of the millennium of Polish statehood and of Poland's baptism (April and June)
1967	Arab–Israeli war (June) leads to communist condemnation of 'Zionists' in Poland
1968	Student protests across Poland (March); anti-Semitic purge of the PZPR (March): forced emigration of intelligentsia of Jewish origin
1970	West Germany recognizes *de facto* the Oder–Neisse Line as the western border of Poland (7 December); strikes in Gdańsk and along the coast (14–19 December); Edward Gierek replaces Gomułka as communist leader (20 December)
1971	Strikes in Szczecin (22–24 January)
1972	Vatican recognizes the post-war Polish ecclesiastical administration in the ex-German territories (June)
1975	Helsinki Final Act signed (1 August): recognition of post-war borders and of human rights
1976	Workers' demonstrations in Radom (25 June); creation of the Committee for Defence of Workers (KOR) (23 September)
1978	Cardinal Karol Wojtyła is elected Pope John Paul II (16 October)
1979	Pope John Paul II visits Poland (2–10 June)
1980	Strikes spread across Poland (July): the creation of Solidarity with Lech Wałęsa as leader (16 August); Miłosz's Nobel Prize for literature (9 October)
1981	Rural Solidarity recognized by the authorities (12 May); General Jaruzelski replaces Kania as PZPR leader (18 October); Jaruzelski introduces martial law (12–13 December)
1983	Martial law formally suspended (22 July); Wałęsa receives the Nobel Peace Prize (5 October)
1985	Warsaw Pact renewed for further 20 years (26 April)
1987	President Reagan ends sanctions against Poland (19 February)
1988	End of jamming of Radio Free Europe (1 January)
1989	Round table talks between the communist government and the opposition (6 February–5 April); semi-free elections (4 June); Gorbachev's consent for Poland to determine its own political future (3 July); Tadeusz

Mazowiecki becomes the first non-communist prime minister in the Soviet bloc (19 August); Poland ceases to be a so-called 'People's Republic' (29 December)

1990   Balcerowicz's economic reforms (January); PZPR dissolves itself (27–29 January) and is replaced by a social democratic party, labelled in 1991 as the Left Democratic Alliance (SLD); re-emergence of the Polish Peasant Party (PSL) (May); re-united Germany recognizes the Oder–Neisse frontier (14 November); Wałęsa succeeds Jaruzelski as president of the Third Republic (December)

1991   Polish–German treaty of friendship (17 June); dissolution of the Comecon (June) and of the Warsaw Pact (July); first fully democratic elections since the Second World War (October): Poland recognizes the independence of Ukraine (December)

1992   Poland signs treaties of good neighbourliness and co-operation with Ukraine (18 May), Russia (22 May) and Belarus (23 June); Hanna Suchocka forms a centre-right government (July)

1993   Remaining Russian troops leave Poland (18 September); Waldemar Pawlak forms a centre-left government (October)

1994   Polish–Lithuanian treaty (April)

1995   Revaluation of the Polish *złoty* (January); centre-left administration under Józef Oleksy (March): Aleksander Kwaśniewski elected president (November)

1996   Włodzimierz Cimoszewicz becomes centre-left prime minister (7 February)

1997   New liberal constitution endorsed by popular referendum (25 May); centre-right coalition with Józef Buzek as prime minister (September)

1998   Sejm ratifies Concordat with the Vatican (February)

1999   Poland, Hungary and the Czech Republic join NATO (12 March)

2000   Kwaśniewski re-elected as president (8 October)

2001   Parliamentary elections (September): implosion of Solidarity; centre-left government under Leszek Miller

2003   Poland joins the US-led invasion of Iraq (20 March); national referendum on joining the European Union (7 and 8 June)

2004   Poland formally joins the EU (1 May); Marek Belka forms a government of experts (June)

2005   Death of Pope John Paul II (2 April)

PART I

POLAND, TO 1795

I

Piast Poland, ?–1385

The Romans never conquered Poland: a source of pride to its first native chronicler, Bishop Vincent of Kraków, writing around 1200, but a nuisance to the modern historian. Since Rome neither subjugated nor abandoned Poland, there is no widely recognizable Year One from which to launch a historical survey. The year AD 966 has to serve, for in that year Mieszko, the ruler of what has come to be known as 'Poland', accepted (and imposed) Latin Christianity. We know as little about this event as we do about anything else that happened during the next hundred years or so. The written record begins to assume substantial proportions only in the fourteenth century. Some eighty years before Bishop Vincent, an unknown clergyman, possibly of French origin (he has come to be called Gall-Anonim, 'the anonymous Gaul'), produced the earliest chronicle emanating directly from the Polish lands. Archaeological and toponymic evidence, the accounts of foreign observers and travellers, inform the historian little better than the folk memory on which Gall relied to locate the founder of the ruling house in a successful peasant adventurer called 'Piast',* who had overthrown a tyrannical predecessor, Popiel (supposedly gnawed to death by some very hungry mice), at some point in the ninth century AD. Historians are more inclined nowadays to accept that Mieszko's immediate forebears, Siemowit, Lestek and

* The label 'Piast' was attributed to the ruling dynasty only in the late seventeenth century by Silesian antiquarians. Medieval sources used formulae such as 'the dukes and princes of Poland' ('duces et principes Poloniae').

Siemomysł, were real persons, not just figments of Gall's imagination; and that it was under them that the early foundations of the future *Regnum Poloniae* were laid, with commercial and administrative centres in Gniezno and Poznań. Echoes of Lestek's realm are to be found in contemporary Byzantine and Germanic chronicles.

The later twentieth century has added its own myths. In the forty or so years after the Second World War, Polish historiography was wont to depict a 'Piast Poland' whose boundaries were curiously congruent with those of the post-1945 state. This reflected more than an attempt by a deeply unpopular communist regime to legitimize itself by appeal to an original past. It was also symptomatic of a genuine need for stability after a thousand years of a history when borders were rarely fixed, but could contract and expand, twist and disappear within the span of a lifetime, taking in or discarding groups of people some of whom even today cannot wholly decide on their own identity: 'Poles'? 'Germans'? 'Ukrainians'? 'Jews'? 'Belarusians'? 'Lithuanians'?

'Polak' (*polonus*, *polanus*, *polenus* were the commonly used medieval Latin forms) derives from *pole*, plain or clearing – the land of the *Polanie*, living in the basin of the middle Warta river, in the western part of modern-day Poland. Remote though these territories may have been, they were not isolated. Even in Roman times, a well-established trade route joined the southern shores of the Baltic and its much-prized amber resources to the Europe of the Mediterranean. By the ninth, tenth and eleventh centuries, in the shadow of the fortified strongholds, the *grody*, which housed garrisons and princely officials, and which preserved the ruler's authority, small commercial communities, even a scattering of Jewish trading centres, grew to service the arduous overland routes connecting the Rhineland, Germany and Bohemia with Kiev, Byzantium and the Orient. The primacy of these western lands came to be acknowledged in the thirteenth century with their designation as 'Old' or 'Great' Poland (Wielkopolska, *Polonia Maior*) – as opposed to 'Little' Poland (Małopolska, *Polonia Minor*) to the south and south-east. What linked the *Polanie* to their neighbours and to so many peoples of the great Eurasian plain was language – *słowo* – the word: those who spoke intelligibly to one another were *Słowianie*, *Sclavinii*, Slavs – as opposed to the 'Dumb Ones' (*Niemcy*) who spoke no tongue intelligible to 'Poles' or 'Czechs' or 'Russians'. The 'Dumb Ones' were mainly from the Germanic world – Saxons, Franks, Bavarians, Lotharingians. The Dumb Ones were little bothered by such linguistic insults. The pagan Slavs, whether living east of the Elbe or north of the Danube, were fair game as slaves. It was in Venice, one of the great entrepôts of the early medieval world, that the word *Sclavus* first came to be synonymous with both 'Slav' and 'slave' – so many were the numbers of southern, Balkan Slavs sold on by its merchants.

Linguistic community did not mean political solidarity. The Slav tribes of the lands between the Elbe and the Oder were as likely to be in conflict with their Polish/Silesian/Czech neighbours of the east as with incomers from the west. In 965, the *knez*, the prince of the Polanie, Mieszko I, thwarted a troublesome alliance between the Christian Czechs and his pagan, Slav neighbours to the west by his marriage to Dobrava, daughter of Duke Boleslav I of Bohemia. Conversion in the following year allowed Mieszko to tap into the manpower, military technology and politics of the German Empire in a way that would have been inconceivable if he had remained a heathen. Most of the early clergy who came to Poland were German; Mieszko and his successors were as willing to conclude marriage alliances with the great families of the Empire as with the ruling dynasties of Scandinavia, Hungary and the Rus' lands. They were quite prepared to furnish the emperors with tribute and warriors in return for recognition of their lordship over the borderlands that they disputed with the German marcher lords. Mieszko's marriage to Dobrava was something of an aberration – the Piasts and the Bohemian Přemyslids had too many conflicting interests for family ties to take root.

Political contacts with German potentates must have existed for a long time before Mieszko's accession. It was probably Mieszko's father, Siemomysł, who first pushed across the river Oder around Lubiąż (Lebus), and north-west into Pomerania. This westward drive was bound to lead to clashes with the rulers of the 'Northern Mark', a political unit of undefined borders established by the German emperor Otto I east of the middle Elbe. Its rulers had a free hand to convert the Slavs and annex their territories, which they did with genocidal gusto. Christian German and pagan Slav rulers could, as occasion demanded, form alliances. Mieszko was clearly well informed of the feuding and power struggles within the German empire. Even before his conversion, he agreed in 964 to pay tribute to Otto I for at least some of his lands. For his part, the Emperor saw in rulers such as Mieszko a useful counterforce against the excessive ambitions of his own marcher lords. Conversion was also likely to strengthen the ruler's own position: among the *Polanie*, there was almost certainly no one central cult, but a variety of localized beliefs. Christianity could provide a central, unifying religious force, which of its very nature was bound to strengthen the ruler's authority.

Byzantium was too far away for its version of 'Orthodox' Christianity to be convenient, and similarly Kiev, which adopted Christianity in 988, saw 'Latin' Rome as distant and unimpressive. Mieszko preferred to receive his new faith from the Bohemians, perhaps to escape possible subordination to the planned new archdiocese for the North Mark, Magdeburg (established two years after Poland's conversion, in 968). The unstable German politics of the time required some deft footwork: Bohemia at this time fell within the jurisdiction of the Bavarian bishopric of Regensburg. It has even been speculated that Mieszko and his immediate entourage may have been christened in Regensburg, early in 966, before the missionaries came to Poland. There was a strong Bavarian connection, so much so that in 979, Otto II launched a punitive expedition against Mieszko for the support he gave to his opponents in Bavaria. The experience seems to have convinced the Polish ruler not to go too far. He loyally supported the young Otto III in the troubles which shook his early reign, not least in the great East Elbian pagan Slav revolt of 983. His second marriage to a German princess, Ode, daughter of Dietrich of the Northern Mark, around 980, signified that his Christianity and connections with Germany were there to stay.

According to the Arab-Jewish merchant, Ibrahim ibn Yakub, Mieszko had 3,000 heavily armed cavalry and infantry at his call. Even if this is a very flattering assessment (the emperor Otto I, ruling over lands perhaps five times as populous, had an army of 5,000 mounted knights), Mieszko's retinue of warriors was an impressive instrument, which enabled him to annex Silesia from his former Bohemian in-laws. His son, Bolesław I Chrobry, 'the Valiant' (992–1026), deprived them of the burgeoning commercial centre of Kraków and its southern hinterland, extending the Piast realm to the Carpathian mountains. The two rulers brought under their sway the Pomeranian lands between the Vistula and Oder deltas. It was probably Mieszko who founded the port town of Gdańsk around 980 to consolidate his grip on lands at the mouth of the Vistula. Bolesław's western forays, into lands still peopled by fellow Slavs, took him to the Elbe. In 1018, Emperor Henry II reluctantly acknowledged his rule over Militz and Lusatia, west of the Oder. In 1018, too, Bolesław intervened in Kiev, to secure his brother-in-law, Sviatopolk, on its throne. He was even briefly able to impose his rule over Bohemia, Moravia and much of modern-day Slovakia.

Almost annual expeditions for human and material plunder were essential to the 'economy' of the early medieval state. But Piast Poland, with a population of well below a million in lands densely tangled by forests, swamps and heaths, could not sustain such efforts indefinitely. The aggressive reigns of Mieszko II (1025–34), Bolesław II (1058–81) and Bolesław III (1102–38) were interwoven with periods of revolt, foreign invasion and recovery. Even Chrobry faced serious rebellions in 1022 and 1025. He had to pull out of Bohemia and his successors had to abandon Moravia and Slovakia. His protégé, Sviatopolk, was driven out of Kiev by his brother, Yaroslav 'the Wise', as soon as Polish forces withdrew. Mieszko II had to abandon Militz and Lusatia; he lost his kingdom and his life to domestic revolt. Between 1034 and 1039, Poland may have been without a ruler at all (some chroniclers tried to fill the gap with a Bolesław the Forgotten, but he is just as likely to have been a Bolesław the Non-Existent), as it threatened to disintegrate under the pressures of pagan reaction and Bohemian invasion. Mieszko II's son, Casimir (Kazimierz) 'the Restorer' (1039–58), needed at least fifteen years to stitch his lands back together with Imperial and Kievan help. It was during his reign that Kraków began to establish itself as Poland's capital: the old political and metropolitan centre of Gniezno was so devastated by the disorders as to be temporarily uninhabitable.

1   One of the earliest surviving Polish churches: the collegiate church of
the Blessed Virgin and St Alexis, *c.* 1150–61, at Tum, near Łęczyca, in
western Poland.

Few, if any, of the Slav tribes east of the Elbe accepted Christianity gracefully. It was only in the course of the twelfth century
that their marcherlands were effectively brought under the authority of German rulers. Only in 1157 did Slav Brunabor become
German Brandenburg. The Polanie and their associated tribes were
no exception. Christianity was the price that had to be paid to
escape the fate of their more obdurate fellow Slavs to the west,
such as the Wends, who kept faith with the pagan ways and
suffered one murderous Christian onslaught after another, until
they lost their gods, their independence and their identity. Today,
between the Elbe and the Oder, some 50,000 Sorbs survive with
their language, an ethnic and linguistic reminder that the peoples
who lived in these lands were once not German but Slav.

To the bulk of the populace, Christianity brought burdens which
only exacerbated those imposed by the ruler's war bands and
garrisons. Bolesław I took his role as Christian ruler sufficiently
seriously to be regarded by the young emperor Otto III as his

partner in the conversion of Slavonic Europe. In the person of Vojtěch (Adalbert) of Prague, Bolesław furnished Poland with its first, albeit adopted, martyr – in 997 Vojtěch was slain by the heathens of Prussia whom the king hoped he would convert. He was canonized two years later. Like Vojtěch, most of the early clergy came from abroad. They were supported with tributes and tithes exacted by a brutal ruling apparatus. A significant native clergy did not begin to emerge until at least three or four generations after Mieszko I's conversion. The deeper Christianization of Poland began only with the coming of the monasteries and friars in the twelfth and thirteenth centuries. Until then, the Church remained an alien, unpopular institution, foisted on the people by a ruling elite in pursuit of its own political and expansionist ambitions. But it differentiated Poland from its eastern Slav neighbours in one crucial respect. The new bishops, with their dioceses and synods, with their political and economic privileges, with their ties to Rome, came eventually to open a door to the differentiation and variegation of political authority, limiting the ruler's monopoly on power. Further east, the traditions of Orthodoxy and Byzantine caesaropapism were to direct the lands of Rus' along a very different path of political development.

The new institution of kingship which accompanied Christianity found little wider echo. The Polish word for king, *król* – a corruption of 'Karol' (Charles, Charlemagne) – reflects its alien character. Bolesław I, Mieszko II and Bolesław II were Poland's only crowned monarchs before 1296. All faced revolts almost immediately after their coronations (1025, 1026 and 1076). Opposition came not just from the lower orders. Mieszko II was murdered by a disgruntled courtier. Bolesław II emulated Chrobry in his forays into Kiev, Bohemia and Hungary; he backed the pope against the emperor in the Investiture Conflict; he was a generous benefactor of the Church – but it was an ecclesiastic, Bishop Stanisław of Kraków, who appears to have headed a reaction among the king's own notables against his demanding foreign policy, not least because the strains it imposed threatened their authority over their own peasantry. In 1078, Bolesław had Stanisław tried by a compliant synod, and hacked to pieces, a traitor's death. According to the chronicle of bishop Vincent, the king himself administered the

punishment. Whatever the facts of the matter, the king inadver-
tently produced Poland's first native martyr (Stanisław was to be
canonized in 1253). Within a year, Bolesław was deposed, exiled
(he died in Hungary in 1081) and replaced by his younger brother,
Wodzisław Herman (1079–1102). Real power was exercised by the
palatinus, Sieciech, head of the war bands and of the network of
garrison-towns, the *grody*.

Wodzisław's elevation highlights a key weakness of the Piast
state (though hardly one peculiar to it) – the absence of a secure
means of succession. It is widely accepted (though the evidence is
limited) that shortly before his death in 992, Mieszko I placed
Poland under direct papal jurisdiction. It may well be that he
nourished the hope that ecclesiastical influence might preserve the
rights of his sons by his second marriage to the German princess
Oda. Bolesław I settled the matter in his own way: he either exiled
his rivals or had them blinded. Bishop Vincent's chronicle suggests
a society in which any form of hereditary claim had to be reinforced
with a more general acceptance of the individual ruler: Mieszko's
lineal descendants may not have been wholly assured of their
position until the full consolidation of Christianity, in the late
twelfth century. The presence of a younger brother provided a
figurehead for a revolt against Bolesław II; the availability of
Wodzisław's sons, Zbigniew and Bolesław, facilitated revolts
against their father and his over-mighty palatine, Sieciech, in 1097
and 1100. When the emperor Henry V invaded in 1109, it was in
support of Zbigniew (who also had the backing of the Church
hierarchy) against his ruthless younger half-brother. Despite a
formal reconciliation, Bolesław III had Zbigniew blinded and killed
in 1111. Bolesław's nickname, 'Wrymouth', may well refer to the
ease with which he broke his oaths rather than to any physical
deformity. He, too, tried to solve the problem of the succession, this
time in more civilized fashion, in his testament of 1138, by a
borrowing from Kievan practice: overall political authority would
be vested in the *princeps*, the eldest of his five sons. The fertile and
populous southern provinces of Kraków and Sandomierz would
form the territorial basis of the *princeps'* power, but he would also
retain the right to make appointments to all the leading lay and
ecclesiastical offices of the Piast patrimony. The younger brothers

would be his viceroys in different provinces; the position of *princeps* would always be held by the eldest survivor.

The expedient proved no more successful than in the Kievan state. In 1202, there were five Piast duchies; by 1250, nine; and by 1288, seventeen, at least ten of them in Silesia. Almost immediately after his death, the sons of Wrymouth's second wife, Salomea of Berg, egged on by their mother and by an understandable sense of self-preservation, banded together against the designated senior ruler – the only son of Wrymouth's first marriage, Władysław. The lay and ecclesiastical notables by and large supported the younger children – they could sell their services in return for concessions and favours from them. The expulsion of Władysław 'the Exile', in 1146, from Poland and his hereditary duchy of Silesia not only created a huge chasm of mistrust between the elder and the younger Piast lines, but it encouraged fresh outside interference in Poland's affairs. For Władysław was married to the half-sister of the German king, Conrad III; and although that connection did not secure his reinstatement, Conrad's successor, the emperor Frederick I Barbarossa, was able in 1163 to impose Władysław's son, Bolesław the Tall, on Silesia; and, in the process, to secure acknowledgement of imperial suzerainty from all the Piast princes.

Nor was unity preserved among Wrymouth's younger sons. In the first generation, the efforts of the most energetic of this brood, Mieszko III (ruling periodically during the sixty-four years between 1138 and 1202 – hence his sobriquet, 'the Old') to impose authoritarian rule provoked chronic revolts. In 1177, his siblings, nephews and his own son joined forces to assign the position of *princeps* to the youngest of Bolesław Wrymouth's sons, Casimir 'the Just'. He could still exercise real authority outside his own Kraków–Sandomierz lands, through his patronage of the Church and his power to appoint bishops. As canonical elections increasingly took hold, his successors were less well placed. Kraków retained a prestigious and symbolic role – no one could credibly lay claim to the title of *princeps* without control over it. Casimir the Just and his successors in the principate were, in effect, elected rulers. The idea that the *princeps* should always be the eldest Piast did not long survive. The position was filled by unanimous or majority agreement among the different Piast dukes. But, ever

Map 1   Early Piast Poland, *c.* 1000.

more, the consent of the Kraków–Sandomierz notables was sought. Ecclesiastical support was critical. So too, by the second half of the thirteenth century, was that of the wealthy, largely German-speaking Kraków urban elite.

Fragmentation may, paradoxically, have facilitated economic and cultural development. Rulers and their leading subjects had little choice but to expand their resources by intensive means, just like the lords of Germany's thinly populated eastern marches. From the early twelfth century, the lords of these territories began to attract new colonists with the promise of collective and individual exemptions from dues and services and the prospect of lighter burdens in the future. West of the Elbe, the bulk of the peasantry remained closely tied to their lords – unless they broke loose and made the difficult decision to settle in the east on more generous terms, albeit under harsher physical conditions. In Silesia, dukes Bolesław the Tall (1163–1201) and his son, Henry the Bearded (1201–38), both of whom had spent many years in Germany as a result of the expulsion of the elder Piast line in 1146, were particularly well positioned to observe the progress of such settlement drives. A strong, prosperous Silesia could provide an ideal platform for the realization of their claims to the principate. Through their German wives and through their patronage of religious orders such as the Cistercians, they were able to launch the expensive tasks of recruiting settlers from Germany, Wallonia and the Rhineland. These *hospites*, 'guests', brought with them technical innovations in the form of mills, heavier ploughs and more compact field systems. By 1229, Henry the Bearded was beginning to accept the need to set up Polish settlements, perhaps not on the same terms as the newcomers, but certainly with degrees of exemptions and immunities from 'Princely Law' – the near arbitrary demands of the ruler's service. These were the beginnings of the process of settlement under 'German law', *ius teutonicum* – not the laws in Germany, but the more-or-less standard package of terms under which colonists from the German lands, and, with time, from elsewhere in Poland, were settled east of the Elbe and Oder rivers.

The settlement of the east Elbian lands developed into a major enterprise, as entrepreneurs and speculators, *locatores*, looked to enrich themselves by the provision of human capital to landowners desperate for the manpower without which even the most extensive estates were useless. Other lords, dukes and ecclesiastics followed suit. By the middle of the fourteenth century, if not earlier, the bulk of the Polish peasantry, including a largely assimilated German element, could regard themselves as in some sense 'free'. But assimilation worked both ways. By the end of the thirteenth century, in central and northern Silesia, the more fertile areas most attractive to new settlers were becoming German, rather than Polish. By 1300, the once Polish village of Wleń, near Wrocław, had become the German Lähn; and Wrocław itself, to increasing numbers of its inhabitants, was becoming Breslau.

Parallel influences were at work in Polish towns. Most were very small. The largest, Kraków and Wrocław, are unlikely to have numbered more than 5,000 inhabitants each in 1200. This was not enough to generate the wealth that Poland's rulers wanted. Seeking to attract merchants and craftsmen, they looked to the German lands, where, in the course of the eleventh century, more and more towns had succeeded in wresting a degree of genuine autonomy from their overlords: they appointed their own judges, administrators and magistrates. The towns' new status found legal expression in charters of rights and privileges. Magdeburg, the closest significant German urban centre to Polish lands, had secured effective self-rule in 1188. Its pattern of an elected or co-opted bench of aldermen, sitting as magistrates, assisting a mayoral figure, the Vogt (in Poland, *wójt*), administered under its own municipal law, was to become almost universal in the Polish lands. In 1211, Henry the Bearded conferred Magdeburg law on the little Silesian town of Złotoryja; in 1258, Bolesław 'the Bashful' did the same for Kraków. Judicial appeals and other delicate questions were usually referred to Magdeburg itself for advice and adjudication. Before the thirteenth century was over, around one hundred Polish towns had Magdeburg-style municipal institutions.

The governing classes in these towns were increasingly German and German-speaking. Indigenous Polish peasants were forbidden (ineffectively) to live in Kraków, since princes and landlords feared the drain of manpower from their own estates. In Silesia, by the end of the Middle Ages, Polish was above all the language of the peasantry, although even in the countryside it began to go into stubborn retreat. In larger towns, Germans, or Poles assimilated as Germans, made up a majority. Those most likely to resent germanization were, to begin with, the native Polish clergy, who, as they found their feet, increasingly opposed the intrusion of Germans into their ranks. At the synod of Łęczyca in 1285, Archbishop Jakub Świnka of Gniezno warned that Poland might become a 'new Saxony' if German contempt for Polish language, customs, clergy and ordinary people went unchecked.

The local rulers of Silesia and western Pomerania were particularly exposed to German wealth and culture, whose charms outshone those of the impoverished Polish lands. It was only towards the later thirteenth century, encouraged by clerics like Archbishop Świnka, that Polish developed enough sophistication to be suitable for the delivery of sermons. As a literary medium, it could scarcely compare with German before the early 1500s. Henry the Bearded of Silesia had enjoyed listening to the fireside tales of Polish peasant storytellers; his great-grandson, Henry IV Probus 'the Honourable' (1257–90) spoke German by preference and was proud to compose and perform poetry and song in the language, a princely *Minnesänger*. Further east, German communities in the towns tended to be isolated islands. In the countryside, even in much of Silesia, German peasants were more likely to be assimilated by native elements. The same went for German knights and adventurers attracted to the courts of Polish rulers.

The twelfth and thirteenth centuries also witnessed the transformation of the old Piast rulers' erstwhile warrior-bands into 'knights', *milites*, in the western European mould. The old warbands had been ruinously expensive. And, at a time when rulers accepted that there was little prospect of enrichment by the old plundering expeditions of the early Piasts, there was little point in trying to maintain them. Instead, those who served in a military capacity were increasingly expected to keep themselves from their own lands, conferred by the prince; but that, of necessity, both reduced the size of these forces and also gave the beneficiaries of ducal land grants a new interest in attracting settlers. Those who obtained enough land and peasants for themselves from their ruler to maintain a warhorse, weapons and armour, or who were sufficiently well placed to take part in the process of *locatio*, came to form a western-European style of military aristocracy. The less well-endowed, the *włodycy*, tended to be absorbed into the peasantry.

In principle, the knights held land in return for service (although the kinds of feudal homage ceremonies widespread in France and England were little practised). But as the Piast states fragmented, their rulers found they had to concede immunities and jurisdictional rights to their mounted fighting-men, just as they had had to to the Church. Those with enough chutzpah and resources simply appropriated these rights, so that by the turn of the thirteenth and fourteenth centuries, anyone who could plausibly claim to hold land by *ius militare*, that is, any *rycerz*, exercised jurisdictional rights over it (the terminology hints at the strength of German influences in the thirteenth century – *rycerz* derives from *Ritter*, German for knight). The dukes reserved, at best, the right to hear appeals. As the dukes gave away, or were obliged to give away, their powers of jurisdiction, they found they had to resort to co-operation and collaboration with their leading subjects. When, in 1228, Władysław 'Spindleshanks' (1202–28) issued the Privilege of Cienia to the bishop of Kraków and the local *barones*, according them the right to be consulted at assemblies, *wiece*, which made laws and heard judicial cases, he was formalizing a situation that had been in the making at least since Wrymouth's reign, in the early twelfth century.

The Catholic Church contributed significantly to the survival of a sense of unity in the Polish lands. Gniezno, given metropolitan status in 1000, was able to preserve its ecclesiastical authority over the five other sees of the old Piast state and ultimately to back the programmes of political unification which emerged. After all, the Church itself was one of the chief victims of political disorders. The hierarchy made strong efforts in the thirteenth century to deepen the parish and schools network and to tighten their links to the populace. As the largest landowner after the dukes, the Church had an urgent material interest in halting the processes of political fragmentation – which, in the final analysis, counterbalanced the positive social and economic developments of the twelfth and thirteenth centuries.

The rag-bag of Piast duchies could not hope to aspire to the forceful political role of Mieszko I and his immediate successors. Before a number of external threats, they found themselves on the retreat or on the defensive. Conrad, duke of Masovia (Mazowsze) (1202–47), found himself unable to protect his north-eastern borders against the incursions of still-pagan Prussian and Yatwingian tribes, who seriously threatened the integrity of his possessions. To contain them, in 1227, he settled the crusading order of the Teutonic Knights on the lower Vistula. Elsewhere, the Poles stood no chance against the devastating Mongol onslaught which wreaked havoc across eastern and central Europe and which swept across Poland in 1241. Duke Henry the Pious of Silesia was slain at the battle of Legnica on 9 April. Only news of the death of their Great Khan Ögödei caused the Mongols to withdraw from their Polish and Hungarian conquests in December. Their destruction of much of Kraków in 1241 remains part of the city's collective memory, even today. They remained in the Crimea and in the steppe-lands of the Black Sea and the eastern Balkans, a new and long-lasting menace to all within reach of their plundering expeditions.

Historians have traditionally painted a grim and lurid picture of this period. Silesia and Masovia went furthest down the road of fragmentation. The local princes through whom the Piasts had ruled in western Pomerania broke loose. Only the core lands of Wielkopolska and the principate lands of Kraków and Sandomierz remained more or less intact. But it was also in the period after the Tatar onslaught that the new settlement processes reached their peak and the freedoms granted spread to the indigenous population. The assemblies of the different duchies, the *wiece*, where the prince dispensed justice, heard appeals and issued decrees, where notables, officials, knights and townsmen were grouped together, acted as a school of political and judicial instruction. Nobles and urban patricians acquired a sense of entitlement to be consulted and that they should have a say in the running of the judicial and administrative business which most affected them.

The Polish duchies were able by and large to resist efforts to impose the vassalage and dependency that successive German emperors had tried to impose on the Polish lands – lands whose rulers had often welcomed that overlordship to advance their own interests. With the disintegration of political authority after the death of the emperor Henry VI in 1197, Germany began to slide into the same sort of fragmentation as Poland. When, at the beginning of the thirteenth century, bishop Vincent of Kraków was chronicling the mythical successes of the ancient Poles against the Roman emperors, he was not simply engaged in a flight of whimsy: he was asserting the independence of the Polish duchies, no matter how weak they may have been, against the claims of the ideological successors to the mantle of Roman imperial authority, the emperors of the German lands.

The road to even partial reunification was a tortuous one. In 1289, the nobles, knights and the bishop of Kraków chose as *princeps* Duke Bolesław II of Płock, in Masovia. Bolesław transferred his rights over the principate to his cousin, Władysław 'the Short' (Łokietek, literally 'Elbow-High'), ruler of the little duchies of Łęczyca, Kujawy and Sieradz. This princely thug found that his penchant for brigandage won much support among knights and squires on the up. He was quite unacceptable in Kraków, whose townsmen handed over the capital to Henry IV Probus, the Honourable, duke of Wrocław/Breslau. It was Henry who took the first serious steps towards what would be so symbolically important for any reunification of the Polish lands. He began to negotiate with the papacy and with his patron, the emperor-elect Rudolf, for agreement to his coronation. Just before his childless death in June 1290 he bequeathed the duchy of Kraków to Duke Przemysł II of Wielkopolska. Przemysł was already suzerain of the port of Gdańsk and of eastern Pomerania. On paper, he had a stronger territorial power-base than any of his predecessors for over a century. The idea of a crowned head was much more attractive to a more latinized Poland than it had been in the early Piast state. Archbishop Świnka was all in favour: the canonization in 1253 of Bishop Stanisław of Kraków, whose dismembered body had undergone a miraculous regrowth, provided an irresistible metaphor for Świnka's aspirations. Przemysł's only serious Polish rival was Łokietek, clinging on in the duchy of Sandomierz. Both men were, however, overshadowed by an ambitious and powerful foreign ruler, Vaclav II of Bohemia.

Vaclav was one of the Middle Ages' most successful territorial stamp-collectors. His father, Přemysl Otakar II (1253–78) – Přemysl to his Slav subjects, Otakar to his Germans – had built up a glittering court at Prague. Bohemia's mineral, commercial and agricultural wealth enabled him to support an ambitious programme of expansion, until his bid for leadership of the German Empire came to an abrupt end when he fell at the battle of Durnkrütt on 26 August 1278, against the closest he had to a German rival, Rudolf of Habsburg. The petty rulers of the disintegrating Piast lands looked abroad for protection: one such focus of attraction was the Přemyslid court of Bohemia; the other was its rival, the Arpad court of Hungary. After the death of Henry Probus, Vaclav's own ambition to acquire Kraków was abetted by the local barons and patricians. In terms of security, prestige and economic prospects, he offered far more than either Przemysł or Łokietek. Vaclav secured the crucial support of Małopolska by the Privilege of Litomyšl of 1291. He promised its clergy, knights, lords and towns the preservation of all their existing rights, immunities and jurisdictions; he would impose no new taxes on them and fill all existing offices from their ranks. Łokietek's position collapsed. His unruly soldiery and knightly followers spread alienation everywhere they went. By 1294, he had not only to sue for peace but to receive his own remaining lands back from Vaclav as a fief. It may have been to pre-empt the almost certain coronation of Vaclav that Archbishop Świnka persuaded the pope to consent to Przemysł II's coronation in Gniezno cathedral on 26 June 1295. The machinations behind this decision are as obscure as anything in Polish history; nor is it clear whether Przemysł regarded himself as ruler of the whole of Poland, or just of Wielkopolska and eastern Pomerania. He did not survive long enough to test his real support. In February 1296 he was murdered, almost certainly on the orders of the margraves of Brandenburg, whose territorial ambitions were blocked by the new king's lands. He left Poland one enduring bequest, in the shape of the crowned eagle which he adopted as the emblem of his new state.

The nobles of Wielkopolska opted at first for Łokietek as his successor – but his continued inability to control his own men, his readiness to carve up Przemysł's kingdom with other petty dukes, and a military offensive from Brandenburg drastically eroded his support. In 1299, he once again acknowledged Vaclav as overlord. Even Archbishop Świnka, conscious that the Kraków clergy were behind Vaclav, accepted the inevitable. In September 1300 he crowned him king – although he could not refrain from complaining at the 'doghead' of a priest who delivered the coronation sermon in German.

Unity, of a kind, was restored. Łokietek was forced into exile. His quest for support took him as far as Rome, where he won the backing of Pope Boniface VIII, hostile to the Přemyslids. Vaclav's last serious opponent, Henry, duke of Głogów/Glogau (1273–1309), nephew of Henry Probus, recognized his suzerainty in 1303. Much of Poland, however, remained under the rule of territorial dukes. Vaclav's direct authority covered mainly Kraków–Sandomierz, Wielkopolska and eastern Pomerania. He left an enduring administrative legacy in the office of *starosta* (literally 'elder'). Its holders acted as viceroys in and administrators of royal estates, although his preference for Czechs in this role provoked growing resentment. To Vaclav, of course, the Polish lands were simply a subordinate part of a greater Přemyslid monarchy. Polish reunification for its own sake was of little interest to him.

In January 1301, King Andrew III of Hungary died, leaving no male heirs. Vaclav found the temptation irresistible. His attempts to impose his 11-year-old son, another Vaclav, on Hungary and, in the process, massively expand Přemyslid power, were too much for the Hungarians, the papacy, Albrecht of Habsburg and the rulers of south Germany. By 1304 a Hungarian–German coalition had been formed. To gain the support of the margraves of Brandenburg, Vaclav promised to hand over to them eastern Pomerania and the port city of Gdańsk. His supporters in Wielkopolska, already seething at the harsh rule of Czech *starostowie*, could not accept this. Early in 1305, revolt shook the southern part of the province. Those not reconciled to Czech rule would have preferred to turn to Henry, duke of Głogów. Vaclav's Hungarian and German enemies declared for his exiled rival, Łokietek. Hungarian forces supporting Charles Robert of Anjou's bid for their throne helped Łokietek seize control of almost all the territories of Małopolska, except for Kraków itself. Vaclav II made peace with the coalition, just before he died on 21 June 1305. He agreed to withdraw from Hungary. But to keep the margraves of Brandenburg on his side, the young Vaclav III renewed his father's undertaking to cede Gdańsk and Pomerania and prepared to enter Poland at the head of an army. If Vaclav had not been murdered at the instigation of discontented Czech lords on 4 August 1306, he and Łokietek might well have divided the Polish territories between themselves. Instead, Bohemia was plunged into rivalries over the succession, until the election of John of Luxemburg in 1310. In Poland, although the townsmen of Kraków reconciled themselves to Łokietek, most of Wielkopolska preferred to recognize Henry of Głogów.

In 1307, disaster struck Łokietek in Pomerania. The German patriciates of the two chief towns, Tczew and Gdańsk, gravitated towards the margraves of Brandenburg; the Polish knighthood of the countryside remained loyal to Łokietek. In August 1308, the castle of Gdańsk was besieged by the troops of margraves Otto and Waldemar. Łokietek called on the help of the Teutonic Knights. The arrival of their forces lifted the siege of the castle – which on the night of 14 November they proceeded to seize for themselves, massacring Łokietek's men in the process. By the end of 1311, most of Polish Pomerania was in the Knights' hands.

Founded in the late twelfth century as an offshoot of the Order of St John of Jerusalem, just in time to be forced out by Islam's counter-attack against the Crusader states of the Middle East, the Teutonic Knights had relocated their military-proselytizing operations to Hungary and Transylvania. King Andrew II threw them out once their ambitions to carve out their own independent state revealed themselves. In 1227, Conrad I, duke of Masovia, settled them in the county of Chełmno on the Vistula in order to defend his eastern borders against the pagan tribes of Prussia, while he devoted himself to feuding with his Piast relatives and meddling in the politics of the Rus' principalities. Backed by emperors and popes (the Knights proved adept at playing one off against the other), patronized by the rulers and knighthood of Christian Europe (not least by individual Piast princes), they built up a *de facto* independence. Their most enthusiastic supporters included Přemysl Otakar II (in whose honour they named the new port of Königsberg in 1255), Vaclav II and John of Bohemia. By the late

1270s, they had subdued the Prussian tribes; they could embark on the process of colonization which gave the area its Germanic character for almost 700 years. The Order was also able – precisely because it was a religious organization, bound by a rule, dedicated to the higher goal of the spread of the Catholic faith and the conversion of the heathen – to organize its territories on lines very different from those of contemporary medieval territories. The Order represented the impersonal state – something higher than a dynastic or patrimonial entity. The command structures of what has come to be known as the *Ordensstaat* were less subject to the whims and favouritisms of individual monarchs. Its Grand Masters were elected from the tried and the tested by an inner circle of superiors who had shown how to combine prayer and aggression, faith and brutality. They and their fellow northern-Crusaders, the Knights of the Sword further along the Baltic coast, in what are now Latvia and Estonia, could suffer setbacks, but, constantly renewed by fresh recruits and enthusiastic part-timers, they could always rise above them. The actual fighting monks, the German Knights of the Blessed Virgin, were, however, few in numbers – this was their weakness. Control of Gdańsk and its hinterland permitted a steady flow of settlers, soldiers, recruits and allies from the German lands. In 1309 the Grand Master, Conrad von Feuchtwangen, moved his principal headquarters from Venice to Marienburg (now Malbork) on the lower Vistula. This was the *Ordensstaat*'s new capital, rapidly built up into one of the most formidable fortified complexes of medieval Europe, a mirror of the Knights' power and pride. The fragile entity ruled by Łokietek and his successors could do little more than rail and complain at the Order's perfidy and brutality – but its rulers could not subdue what they had nurtured.

Łokietek had no realistic hopes of recovering Pomerania. Most of Wielkopolska remained alienated. The dukes of Masovia mistrusted him. In May 1311, only Hungarian help enabled him to subdue a major revolt of German townsfolk in Kraków. Poles replaced Germans in key positions on the town council, Latin replaced German as the official language of town records. True, it was not many years before German burghers and merchants regained their old influence, but the town itself ceased to be the

2   The Teutonic Knights' castle and principal administrative seat, at
Malbork (Marienburg). Fourteenth century. The castle underwent
extensive restoration in the 1820s by the Prussian authorities, who used it
as a showcase for the Teutonic Knights' (and, by extension, Prussia's)
'historic mission' in the east.

political force it once had been. The repression did little to enhance
Łokietek's appeal to townsmen elsewhere.

   In 1309, his rival in Wielkopolska, Duke Henry of Głogów died,
leaving five young sons, all more German than Polish. The knights
preferred Łokietek to fragmentation and German rule, but it was
not until the submission of the town of Poznań in November 1314
that serious opposition was eliminated. In control of Wielkopolska
and Kraków, Łokietek could realistically aspire to the royal dignity
– were it not for the rival claims of the new king of Bohemia, John
of Luxemburg, who had cheerfully taken over the claims of his
Přemyslid predecessors. Most of the Silesian and Masovian dukes
looked to him. Brandenburg and the Teutonic Knights endorsed
him as the supposed heir of the Vaclavs in Poland, in the expectation of satisfying their own titles and claims. Pope John XXII,
whose approval was necessary to a coronation in what was tech-

nically a papal fief, was reluctant to offend either party. He gave his consent in terms so ambiguous as to suggest that he considered both men to have a legitimate royal title. When Łokietek's coronation did finally take place on 20 January 1320, it was not in Gniezno but, for the first time, in Kraków. The new venue was dictated not only by a recognition of the greater economic importance of the southern provinces but by a tacit acknowledgement of the still limited extent of Łokietek's territorial support. He controlled less than half of the territory which Bolesław Wrymouth had ruled: Wielkopolska in the west, Kraków and Sandomierz in the south, the two regions linked in the central Polish lands by his own duchies of Łęczyca and Sieradz. Łokietek was more king of Kraków than king of Poland. He was fortunate that John of Bohemia had his own difficulties with the Czech nobility.

Łokietek sought security through marriage alliances: in 1320, he cemented his long-standing alliance with the Angevins of Hungary when his daughter Elizabeth (1305–80) married King Charles Robert (1308–42). In 1325, the king secured his son's marriage to Aldona (d. 1339), daughter of the Lithuanian prince Gediminas – at the cost of driving the Masovian dukes, perpetually feuding over their eastern borderlands with the Lithuanians, into an alliance with the *Ordensstaat*. His only recourse against the Knights lay in persuading the papacy to issue legal pronouncements enjoining them to restore Pomerania. Such pronouncements (never definitive) were indeed made, but the Knights paid no attention. John of Bohemia prepared, in 1327, to attack Kraków – and had he not been kept in check by Charles Robert from Hungary, Łokietek's monarchy might not have survived. Most of the dukes of southern Silesia declared themselves John's vassals. Łokietek's offensive against Duke Wacław (1313–36) of Płock only precipitated incursions by his allies, Brandenburg and the Knights. Łokietek bought Brandenburg off in 1329 with the county of Lubusz (Lebus), at the confluence of the Warta and the Oder. In the winter of 1328–9, John of Luxemburg and the Knights undertook a 'crusade' against Łokietek's Lithuanian allies. The Polish military diversion into the county of Chełmno backfired: John and the Knights conquered the northern Polish territory of Dobrzyń, which John, by virtue of his claims to the Polish throne, generously awarded to the Knights. Duke Wacław of Płock declared himself to be his vassal. So did most of the remaining Silesian dukes.

The Knights followed up with an offensive into Wielkopolska in July 1331. They comprehensively sacked Gniezno, although, as a religious order, they felt it politic to spare the cathedral. On 27 September, the Polish and Teutonic armies met at Płowce. The battle lasted most of the day; if, on balance, this pyrrhic encounter was a Polish victory, it resolved nothing. It marked the limit of Łokietek's military endeavour. The king could raid, but not re-conquer; above all, he lacked the resources and the organization to take on the Knights' strongholds. Had John of Luxemburg also invaded – as he had promised the Knights – Płowce might have been even more irrelevant than it was. In 1332, the Knights more than made up for Płowce by occupying Łokietek's old patrimonial duchy of Kujawy. In August, he had to agree to a truce which left them in possession of all their recent gains. Through sheer, murderous persistence, he had semi-reunited Poland. But at his death, on 2 March 1333, he left an even smaller kingdom than the one which had acknowledged him at his coronation in 1320. His successor, Casimir III, began his reign by renewing the truce with the Teutonic Knights.

Domestically, Poland needed stability, which could only come about by strengthening royal authority. Externally, the new king had not only to resolve relations with the *Ordensstaat* and the House of Luxemburg, he had to deal with a power vacuum on Poland's south-east borders, which threatened to embroil him with the Tatars and with Lithuania. Poland continued to lie in the shadow of the Hungarian Angevins, first, of Casimir's brother-in-law, Charles I Robert, and then his nephew Louis the Great (1342–82), both of whom had their own designs on the Polish throne. The realm, the 'Crown' as it was styled by his jurists – *Corona Regni Poloniae* – that Casimir ruled, a narrow and irregular lozenge of territory, spilled from north-west to south-east on either side of the Vistula; with probably fewer than 800,000 inhabitants, it contained less than half the territories and popu-lation that might plausibly have been called Polish. Against the Knights, Casimir was largely on his own. The Angevins wanted good relations with them in their own struggles against the

Wittelsbachs and the Luxemburgs. Poland was to be kept in its subordinate place. The treaty of Kalisz of 8 July 1343 was a 'compromise' which benefited the Knights. They restored the vulnerable border territories of Dobrzyń and Kujawy lost by Łokietek, but kept what they really wanted – Gdańsk and Pomerania. Casimir also had to face up to the loss of Silesia. In 1348, John of Bohemia's successor and heir-elect to the Empire (he was to succeed Louis the Bavarian in 1349), Charles IV, decreed its incorporation into the kingdom of Bohemia. He even contemplated the incorporation of the duchies of Płock and Masovia, by virtue of the claims he had inherited from the Vaclavs and his father. With only faltering support from Louis of Hungary and with a storm brewing in the south-east, Casimir resigned himself. By the treaty of Namysłów (Namslau) of 22 November 1348, he abandoned his claims to the Silesian principalities. There was some consolation in the north-east, where in 1355, Duke Ziemowit III (1341–70), who succeeded in reuniting (albeit briefly) most of the Masovian lands, acknowledged Casimir's overlordship. He stipulated, however, that the preservation of the relationship after Casimir's death was contingent on the king's siring a legitimate male heir.

The troubled situation in the south-east, in the lands of Rus', helps explain Casimir's retreat in the west. After the reign of Yaroslav I the Wise (1019–54), the once-great principality of Kiev had undergone its own dynastic fragmentation. The Mongol onslaughts of 1237–40 had savaged these lands far more viciously than Poland. The successor-states of Kievan Rus' were largely reduced to tributaries of the Golden Horde, established in the Eurasian steppes. The continued raids of the Mongols, or Tatars as they were widely known, carried them periodically into Polish territory. In 1340, Bolesław-Iurii, the childless ruler of the two westernmost principalities of Halych and Vladimir, and a scion of the Masovian Piasts, was poisoned by his leading boyar-advisers, thoroughly alienated by his open contempt for them and his over-enthusiastic support for Roman Catholicism.

No credible claimant to Halych-Vladimir emerged from among the other Rus' princes. Casimir seized the moment. These fertile Rus' principalities, straddling the great east–west overland trade route from Germany to the Black Sea, offered pleasing prospects of

Map 2 Poland under Casimir the Great (1333–70).

GRAND

DUCHY

OF

LITHUANIA

RUS' LANDS

- Vilnius
- Krėva

Nieman

- Warsaw

Bug

Vistula

San

- Sandomierz

- Vladimir

Kiev ●

MAŁOPOLSKA

- L'viv

PODOLE

Halych ●

Dniester

- Košice

MOLDAVIA

SCALE

0   50   100   150   200   250 km

0   50   100   150 miles

enriching both the nobility of southern Poland and the merchants of Kraków. They could serve as a buffer zone against Tatar raids. They offered some compensation for the lands renounced in the west and north. They also aroused the appetite of Lithuania and the Hungarian Angevins. If Casimir did not annex them, others would. His invasion of 1340 may have been prompted by the very real fear that the Tatars would impose their direct rule in the 'regnum Galiciae et Lodomeriae', the 'kingdom of Halych and Vladimir'.

It took twenty years of intermittent struggle to impose even partial Polish authority. The Lithuanians established themselves in the north. Casimir satisfied himself with acknowledgement of his suzerainty by Lithuanian princelings. Casimir held the south, centred on the town of L'viv (Lwów/Lvov/Lemberg). But even here he owed his position to Hungarian support. Poland's Rus' lands remained separate from the rest of the Crown: in return for Louis of Hungary's assistance in their subjugation, Casimir agreed in 1350 that they would pass to him on his demise. Divisions in Lithuania, where Duke Gediminas' seven sons quarrelled among themselves after his death in 1341, worked to Casimir's advantage. Even the Black Death helped: it left a sparsely populated Poland largely unscathed, but in 1346 it devastated the Golden Horde. Despite all this, the venture cost Casimir dear. In 1352, to raise money for his war effort, he plundered the archiepiscopal treasury in Gniezno. He borrowed from all and sundry, even from the Teutonic Knights, to whom he assigned the county of Dobrzyń as security. Impoverished Dobrzyń could scarcely begin to compare with Rus' potential prosperity.

Casimir's principal achievement was to restore strong monarchic rule at home, within the narrow limits open to any medieval ruler. His deliberate patronage of talented lay and ecclesiastical advisers from southern Poland, the advancement of their careers by service on the royal council, created a generation of new men, ready to aid and abet fresh fiscal and administrative initiatives. The king was more aware than his predecessors of the value of more formal means of government. In 1364, he set up, in Kraków, a partial university or *studium generale*, teaching mainly law, with some medicine and astronomy (the papacy would not agree to instruction in theology). The new institution above all aimed at producing the jurists and lawyers increasingly indispensable to the government of a self-respecting monarchy. Casimir introduced written regulation of judicial procedure and criminal law. In the 1360s, he began to widen the bases of his support to Wielkopolska. He never sought to put an end to the established divisions and differences between his two chief provinces, but instead played their elites off against each other. An extensive programme of revindication of usurped royal lands, often by arbitrary royal fiat, recovered hundreds of properties, though it led to revolt in Wielkopolska in 1352. Casimir made some tactical concessions. In 1360, after the troubles had died down, the revolt's leader, Maćko Borkowic, was arrested, chained in a dungeon and starved to death, though it seems that his involvement with local brigandage rather than his political past was more responsible – not so much a royal act of revenge as a warning to powerful men not to get above themselves.

It may be that Casimir wished to build up new elements on which he could base royal power. For the first time, the non-knightly administrators of peasant villages, the *wójtowie* and *sołtysi*, were expected to turn out in their own right on military campaigns. His confiscational programme was matched by an extensive settlement of peasants under 'German law' on royal domain. The king encouraged Jewish settlement, mainly of Ashkenazim from the Empire. While the same baggage of prejudices and misconceptions found across Christendom was reflected in Poland, it was clearly not enough to put a stop to such immigration. He took a Jewish mistress. And although the merchants and guilds of many towns, fearful of competition, secured bans on Jewish residence inside the town walls, they were almost invariably able to settle in the suburbs or in privileged enclaves beyond municipal jurisdiction. Whatever reservations his Christian subjects had about them (and there were occasional anti-Jewish riots), Casimir appreciated that they represented an invaluable asset. The 1338 coinage reform helped boost the circulation of small-denominational silver monies. All this, combined with a flourishing north–south and west–east trade, with Kraków at its crossroads, enabled Casimir successfully to pursue a harsh fiscality. He subjected peasant holdings on lay and ecclesiastical estates to an annual land ('plough', *poradlne*) tax of 12 *groszy* per *łan* (about 18.5 hectares). Only land worked directly for the lords was exempt. Such taxation, combined with a reform of the administration of the lucrative royal salt-mines at Bochnia and Wieliczka, first exploited in 1251, enabled him to finance a major defence and reconstruction programme. He built some fifty castles across Poland, and provided twenty-seven towns with new curtain walls (or, rather, they did so on his orders). It was enough to contain the incursions of the Tatars and the ever more frequent raids of the Lithuanians; but none of Casimir's new fortresses could match the Teutonic Knights' defensive marvel at Marienburg. The Kraków patriciate was kept sweet by the king's successful commercial policies and by the enhanced prestige it enjoyed from his ban on all municipal appeals to Magdeburg: two appellate urban courts were set up in the capital.

For all the difficulties that Casimir experienced in Halych-Rus', it was in his reign that the processes took off which were to give the area its variegated ethnic character for almost the next six centuries. The campaigning devastated the countryside; but the area's fertility made it a magnet for the dispossessed, impoverished and adventurous from all over Poland and beyond. The boyar aristocrats of the area either died out during the wars or preferred to migrate to Rus' lands under Lithuanian lordship: the surviving lesser nobility was in no shape to stand up to the influx of immigrants. The great trading centre of L'viv continued to attract a vigorous mix of settlers. Germans formed the largest number of incomers, then Poles and Czechs – though by the end of the fifteenth century, most of these elements were to be polonized and L'viv/Lwów itself became something of a Polish island in a sea of Rus', Orthodox peasantry. The first Jews established themselves in 1356, alongside a thriving Armenian community. During Casimir's last years and over the next decades, petty and not-so-petty Polish nobles were granted extensive land rights in the area. Casimir and his successors preferred to govern through an alien, non-boyar, non-Orthodox class on whose loyalty they could rely. The process was made easier in that even the Rurikid princes of Halych-Rus' had shown considerable interest in accepting union with the Latin Church, as a channel for securing help against the Mongols. The

petty Orthodox boyars who clung on, loaded with service obligations, uncompensated by any rights or liberties on the Polish or
Hungarian models, found that polonization and Catholicization
offered the easiest route to preserving and advancing their status
and fortunes. It was in these lands of western Rus' that the process
of the separation and alienation of the elites from the mass of the
local population first began and proceeded furthest.

Casimir's greatest failing was dynastic. He had four wives: the
first, Aldona-Anna of Lithuania, produced two daughters. The
second, Adelaide of Hesse, was pious, unexciting and possibly
barren. Casimir despised her and ensured that she spent a miserable
marriage confined in remote castles until a divorce came through
around 1356 – in scandalous circumstances. The king's lust for
Krystyna, the widow of a patrician of Prague, got the better of him.
He contracted a bigamous marriage with her even before his
divorce from poor Adelaide. No children were produced. In a race
against time, he put Krystyna aside to marry, in 1363, Jadwiga,
daughter of Duke Henry of Żagań. Four children followed – all
girls. Casimir could not produce legitimate sons. He may, nevertheless, have had second thoughts about letting the Angevins get their
hands on his lands. In 1368 he adopted as his heir his grandson
Kaźko, heir to the duchy of Słupsk in Pomerania. Days before his
death on 5 November 1370, he bequeathed his patrimony of
Łęczyca, Sieradz and Kujawy to Kaźko. The Rus' lands, Wielkopolska and the territories around Kraków and Sandomierz were to
pass to Louis of Hungary. Casimir had clearly not shaken off the
sense that this was a family, patrimonial monarchy, ultimately his
and his alone to dispose of. But this was not a view shared by the
lawyers, clergy and barons who had helped him rule. His thirty-
seven-year reign had persuaded them that their political arena was
more than a local or regional one: that the 'Crown', the *Corona
Regni Poloniae*, was a real political entity that had to be preserved.
A freshly divided Poland was unlikely to hold on to the potential
riches of the hard-won Rus' lands. At the same time these notables
had an unmissable opportunity to return to the politics their
predecessors had practised at the height of Poland's fragmentation,
of playing off one potential ruler against another, albeit now on a
scale that went beyond Poland's borders. The county court of

Sandomierz ruled the will invalid. Kaźko settled for compensation in the shape of the county of Dobrzyń, to be redeemed from the Knights, as a fief to be held of Louis of Hungary, who was to inherit the Crown.

Even in his own lifetime, Casimir III's attainment of a relative peace and prosperity, his legal and administrative reforms earned him the title 'the Great' (the only Polish monarch so honoured). Yet Poland remained a lesser power, too weak to assert its claims to its old territories in the west and north. Casimir probably did as much as could have been done with some unpromising materials. For better or worse, he paved the way for a new course of eastwards expansion. He restored strong monarchic rule, although nothing that he did could compensate for the lack of a legitimate son.

Whatever the vagaries of Casimir's policies, he had been a strong, at times even brutal, ruler. The nobility had good reasons for welcoming Louis' accession. An absentee king (he ruled in Poland largely through his mother, Casimir's sister, Elizabeth) would almost inevitably be less demanding. He had made promising concessions in return for acceptance of his succession. In 1355, by the Privilege of Buda, Louis had solemnly assured the nobility and clergy that he would exempt them from any new taxation. His uncertain health, and the gratifying inability he shared with Casimir to father sons, opened up even more favourable prospects. In 1374, the nobility agreed that he could designate one of his three daughters as successor in Poland. In return, from Košice in northern Hungary, Louis promulgated a Privilege, reducing in perpetuity the *poradlne* tax paid by peasants on noble and knightly estates from 12 to 2 *groszy* per *łan*. He went on to promise that he would pay his knights for any military service beyond Poland's borders. In 1381, he extended these provisions to the clergy.

In retrospect, these concessions can be viewed as the beginning of a linear process which was to give the nobility a dominant and domineering position within the state. At the time, they were more an attempt to secure protection against royal fiscal arbitrariness. The 'nobility' were the beneficiaries because they held a near-monopoly of military force. But the Polish 'nobles' at this time

3   Interior view of the cathedral at Gniezno, as rebuilt after 1342 in the gothic style, replacing the earlier romanesque building. This can be seen as part of a general programme of renovation which contributed much to the reputation of Casimir III.

were simply all those who held land carrying the obligation – even if it was in many cases notional, rather than real – of performing military service. Those affected ranged from lords of the royal council to backwoods squires barely able to afford a horse and military accoutrement. The driving force consisted of a core of some twenty families, most of whom had risen under Casimir III and were determined not to lose their standing in the state. These were the primary beneficiaries of the Privileges of Buda and Košice. That their lesser fellow-*rycerze* also gained was a useful bonus which enabled the great families to build up followings and clienteles – it was to be at least another century before these junior knights/nobles became a serious political force in their own right. Louis' Privileges also applied to the townsmen – their existing rights were confirmed – but they enjoyed only local and *ad hoc* concessions, grants and favours. The towns, divided by commercial rivalries, failed to show a common front. Members of the Kraków patriciate, who might even sit on the royal council, were concerned only with the well-being of their own city, not that of other towns; in any case, they could reasonably aspire to a niche among the aristocratic core. The clergy followed on the coat-tails of the 'communitas nobilium'.

While Louis accepted that he had to make concessions in order to secure the throne for his daughters, like Vaclav II barely two generations previously, he felt no compunction at truncating Polish territory. In 1377 he incorporated Polish Rus' into Hungary, a step already agreed on with Casimir and made easier by its separate status of a royal *dominium*. He confirmed the cession of Silesia to the Luxemburgs. He transferred disputed border territories to Brandenburg. These measures and the behaviour of Hungarian officials caused immense resentment, culminating in the massacre of dozens of Hungarian courtiers during riots in Kraków in 1376. In 1380, Louis judged it prudent to relinquish rule in Poland to a caucus of Małopolska potentates, which did nothing for his wavering support in Wielkopolska. When he died, in September 1382, the question of the succession was almost as vexed as ever. The Polish elites had promised to accept his daughter, Maria – but jibbed when Louis, in an attempt to unite the Angevin and Luxemburg houses, insisted that she should marry the unpopular

Sigismund of Luxemburg. The Hungarians compromised and suggested that a younger daughter, Jadwiga (she was barely 10 years old), could be substituted. Małopolska agreed, but Wielkopolska wanted Duke Ziemowit IV of Płock as king. Angevin support in the south proved too strong for him. The entry of pro-Jadwiga troops obliged Ziemowit to withdraw.

Wielkopolska's leaders were prepared to accept Jadwiga if her long-standing betrothal to Wilhelm of Habsburg could be broken off in favour of Ziemowit. She was crowned 'king' (this was not an age which discarded law and custom lightly) in Kraków on 15 October 1384. The southern lords had little truck with Wielkopolska's provincialism. They, too, could play the dynastic card as well as any Luxemburg or Angevin. Jadwiga's engagement was broken off – not in favour of Ziemowit, but of the illiterate heathen, Jogaila, ruler of Lithuania. At Krėva, in Lithuania, on 14 August 1385, Jogaila confirmed a deal his representatives had struck with Louis' widow, the queen-dowager Elizabeth, and with Małopolska's lords: he and his Lithuanian subjects would convert to Catholicism; he would marry Jadwiga, provide money to pay off the disappointed Wilhelm of Habsburg and annex to Poland his vast principality, stretching from the Baltic to the Black Sea. Małopolska's elite had embarked on a spectacular exercise in corporate dynasticism, well worth the price of a 12-year-old's feelings. Former Piast Poland stood on the threshold of a bizarre and unexpected new career.

2

Jagiellonian Poland, 1386–1572

Jogaila of Lithuania was received into the Catholic Church in Kraków cathedral on 15 February 1386. His baptismal name, Władysław, harked back to Łokietek, re-unifier of the 'Crown', the kingdom of Poland – reason enough for Ernst von Zöllner, Grand Master of the Teutonic Knights, to decline the invitation to stand as godfather. In the autumn of 1387, Peter I Mushat, *hospodar* of Moldavia, transferred allegiance and homage for his lands from the rulers of Hungary to Władysław and Jadwiga of Poland. He and Zöllner recognized that a new power had arrived. Barely a hundred years later, not only Poland and Lithuania, but Hungary and Bohemia had come under Jagiellonian rule. It was the greatest dynastic concatenation of territory Europe had yet seen.

Appearances flattered to deceive. In 1386, it was the Teutonic Knights who menaced the existence of Lithuania. Only three years before, they had capped over a century of bloody, unremitting effort by sacking much of the Lithuanian capital of Vilnius and destroying the great stronghold of Trakai. Lithuania was riven by civil war; western, 'lower' Lithuania, Žemaitija, had been ceded to the Teutonic Order by Jogaila's cousin and rival, Vytautas, in return for its support. The union with Poland and the acceptance of Latin Christianity were a desperate gamble by Jogaila to avert a seemingly inevitable subjugation.

Lithuania, stretching from the Baltic in the north to the Black Sea in the south, to the upper Volga and beyond the Dnieper in the east, was a highly unstable political entity. Its rulers had imposed themselves on these vast lands in the the wake of the Mongol invasions of the 1230s. In the late fourteenth century, the Lithuanians proper are unlikely to have numbered more than 300,000. Mainly pagan, they would have been outnumbered sevenfold by the Christian Orthodox inhabitants. Many of the descendants of the ruling house of Gediminas had converted to Orthodoxy, a deliberate policy to facilitate the dynasty's rule over the Rus' lands. What linguists call 'Middle Belarusian' prevailed in the government's chancelleries, albeit with admixtures of native Lithuanian and Latin. Lithuanian began to receive written form only in the mid-sixteenth century. To the majority of his subjects, Lithuania's 'Grand Duke' was *hospodar* rather than *didysis kunigaikštis*. The formally untrammelled powers of the ruling house allowed for enormous bursts of political and military energy. A practice of more or less collaborative rule by brothers and close relatives developed, although periodically the inevitable blood rivalries erupted. Jogaila himself had come to power in 1382 with the murder of his uncle Kestutis. When, in February 1387, Jagiełło (to use the polonized form) instituted the bishopric of Vilnius and ordered his armed followers, his 'boyari sive armigeri', to convert to Catholicism, he aimed to deny the Knights any further justification for their onslaught on his homeland. As co-monarch with Jadwiga of Poland, he hoped for Polish support against both them and Kestutis' dangerous son, Vytautas.

The reasons for Jogaila's acceptance of the Polish crown went beyond a quest for an alliance against, or protection from, the Teutonic Knights. The rapid expansion of Lithuania under Gediminas (1315–41) and then under the partnership of his sons, Algirdas (1345–77) and Kestutis (1345–82), brought its own difficulties. The vastly outnumbered Lithuanians would, under any circumstances, have had real difficulties in preserving their authority over the Rus' lands. Algirdas' victory at Sine Wody over the Mongol Golden Horde in 1363, consolidating his grip on Kiev itself, had given a huge boost to Lithuanian prestige. The nobles – the boyars – of these empty territories were prepared to accept those of the ruling Gediminid dynasty who russified and converted to Orthodoxy. How long an over-extended ruling House could preserve its authority on such sufferance was an open question.

Russification, of course, meant the loss of Lithuanian cultural identity. It would not solve the very real threat posed by the Teutonic Order, to whom heathens and schismatics were equally fair game. Moreover, the fourteenth century saw the consolidation of a new Rus' power in the east, beyond the reach of the Lithuanian rulers – the principality of Moscow. Frictions between the two reached back to the 1330s. Dmitrii Donskoi's defeat of a Mongol force at Kulikovo Pole in 1380 – a victory made possible in part because the Lithuanians were unable to furnish Khan Mamai of the Golden Horde with the support they had promised – did not secure the removal of Mongol overlordship from Moscow: but it did establish Moscow, alongside Lithuania, as a credible alternative claimant to the heritage of Kievan Rus'. Where individual Lithuanian princes sought to break away from Vilnius' domination – as did Jogaila's russified half-brother, Andrew the Hunchback, prince of Polotsk, in 1377–8 – they received every encouragement from Moscow. Indeed, in 1383–4, serious if ultimately unsuccessful negotiations took place with Dmitrii Donskoi for Jogaila's marriage to his daughter, Sophia. Donskoi insisted on the conversion of Jogaila to Orthodoxy. Had the union come to pass, one can only speculate how different the course of eastern European history might have been.

Embracing Catholicism at least offered the prospect of containing the threat from the Teutonic Knights; and union with Poland the prospect of a firm alliance against them. Catholicization – which was aimed not at Orthodox Rus' subjects, but at pagan Lithuanians – also offered the prospect of preserving Lithuanian identity – provided, of course, it did not come at the price of polonization. But prospects were all that at first could be offered. Jogaila's nobles went along because they were promised that they would have a share in ruling Poland, just as they ruled Rus'. In February 1387, Jagiełło promised his boyars the same rights and privileges as his Polish nobles enjoyed. The reality was very different. Jogaila/Jagiełło saw in the Poles allies as much against the machinations of his cousin Vytautas and his supporters, as against the Knights. No Polish office went to a Lithuanian; but a series of plum Lithuanian offices went to the leading nobles of Małopolska; and a series of Lithuanian strongholds were garrisoned by Polish forces. The 1387 concession of rights was meaningless – Lithuania lacked the machinery of local assemblies, judicial institutions and cultural traditions which alone could give life to such a measure.

The man most frustrated by this was Vytautas. He was much more than a proud and ambitious princeling. Deeply imbued with the destiny of the House of Gediminas, determined to preserve and even extend its mastery over the Kievan inheritance, he was as conscious as Jagiełło of Lithuania's many dilemmas. He accepted that paganism was unsustainable. He was indifferent as to which form of Christianity he adopted (he had 'converted' to Catholicism in 1383, when aligned with the Teutonic Knights; to Orthodoxy in 1384, once more to Catholicism in 1386; and in later life, showed an unhealthy interest in Bohemian Hussitism), provided it helped wrong-foot his enemies, preserve the rule of his dynasty and the dominance of Lithuania over Rus'. His political choice in 1385–6 was Catholicism – but not at the cost of subordination to Poland. It is this which explains the twists and turns of his policies, which drove friend and foe alike (the two were often indistinguishable) to a mixture of fury, despair and dazzled admiration. The same fear of subordination to Poland also helps explain the tangled relationship between the two states over the subsequent centuries of their relationship.

The decision by the barons of Małopolska to offer the throne to a pagan ruler was one of the most remarkable in the annals of medieval Europe. While the agreement of Krèva of 14 August 1385 obliged Jagiełło, in very general terms, to undertake the recovery of 'all the lands stolen from . . . the kingdom of Poland', the territories annexed by the *Ordensstaat* were a secondary issue. The lords of Małopolska were more concerned to neutralize the dangers from Lithuania itself and to secure the fertile territories of Halych-Rus' subdued by Casimir the Great, to which not only Lithuania, but also Hungary laid claim. As recently as 1376, Jogaila himself had participated in a savage raid which had laid waste the rich lands between the San and the Vistula. The Krèva Act seemingly promised that he would incorporate Lithuania into Poland. For over 150 years the Poles were to insist on this. A series of further enactments (the so-called 'unions' of Vilnius, 1401; Horodło, 1413; Grodno, 1432; and Vilnius, 1499) continued to stress

Lithuania's incorporation or subordination. The term used for 'incorporate' in 1385 – 'applicare' – has given rise to much acrimonious discussion between Polish and Lithuanian historians, but the Poles had no doubt of what it meant at the time. On the other hand, Jagiełło and his successors had no intention of implementing these purely tactical promises.

These different 'unions' represented attempts to redefine and regulate relations between Poland and Lithuania in the light of changing circumstances. The Catholicized Lithuanian elite increasingly came to appreciate the value of a purely dynastic union, while at the same time they sought to preserve the maximum degree of political power for themselves. The Poles pushed for the maximum degree of influence and power over the Grand Duchy; and the final results, as expressed in these enactments, were often messy, even contradictory compromises, open to the most varied interpretations, and over which historians continue to argue. The 1499 Union of Vilnius, for example, reiterated the act of Union of Horodło, of 1413 (which, in its preamble, explicitly enjoined the incorporation of Lithuania into the Crown, but then went on to treat the two as separate polities), but in such a way as to ignore the incorporation; and went on to suggest a common election, by Crown and Lithuanian lords, of the king of Poland and Grand Duke of Lithuania, without providing any formal machinery for doing so. This seemingly confused relationship suited the ruling Jagiellonian dynasty well. For they enjoyed hereditary status in the Grand Duchy (even if the Polish side in some of these acts maintained, explicitly or implicitly, that they did not), and saw in that a guarantee that they would continue to be elected as kings in Poland proper, whose great nobles continued to look enviously at the prospect of acquiring lands and offices in Lithuania's vast expanses. Almost all concerned – Catholic and Orthodox, Polish, Lithuanian and Rus' (or 'Ruthenian') – came to appreciate the benefits of some kind of connection; the real and ultimately never fully resolved disputes were over what form that connection should take.

With Lithuania, Poland meant much; without it, little. It remained perilously fragile. To the suspicious nobility of Wielkopolska, Jagiełło's elevation was a bid for political dominance by the

4   Effigy of king Władysław Jagiełło in the cathedral of Wawel castle, Kraków. The first lifelike representation of a Polish monarch to survive.

baronage of Małopolska. The two provinces were physically
separated by a belt of fiefs granted by Louis the Great to his
helpmate, the Silesian Piast, Władysław of Opole, who, in 1392,
floated a scheme to divide the Crown between the *Ordensstaat* and
Sigismund of Hungary. Only in 1396 were his lands forcibly
annexed by Jadwiga and her husband. In 1387 disorders in
Hungary helped Jadwiga to recover the Rus' territories transferred
by her father from Poland. The Crown's narrow lands were painfully slowly bulked out with the extinction of the ruling lines of
minor Piast branches, especially those associated with the duchy of
Masovia. Its final incorporation with its capital, Warsaw, came
only in 1526. Silesia and, even more so, western Pomerania,
remained out of reach. The Crown lacked the strength to enforce
its annexationist claims on the Grand Duchy, whose leading lords
remained wary of such aspirations, even after the extinction of the
Jagiellonian dynasty. After 1422, Poland and Lithuania pursued
different, if often complementary, foreign policies, with Poland
looking to the north and south and Lithuania to the east. Chronic
strains dogged their relationship, not least over the possession of
the southern Rus' territories of Podole and Volhynia. The unilateral
recognition in 1440 by the great lords of Lithuania of Jagiełło's
second son, Casimir, as their Grand Duke, marked a technical
sundering of the union, until his election as king by the Poles in
1446. Likewise, in 1492, the separate, independent accessions of
Jagiełło's grandsons, John Albert (Jan Olbracht) in Poland, Alexander in Lithuania, had, strictly speaking, the same effect. The
union was stitched together once more in 1501, when Alexander
succeeded his childless elder brother in Poland.

The relationship survived its early years because Jagiełło and
Vytautas were able to compose their differences in what was, in
effect, a partnership of equals, reminiscent of the glory days of the
harmony between Algirdas and Kestutis. In 1392, Jagiełło acknowledged his cousin as 'dux' of Lithuania, while maintaining a
formal overlordship as 'supremus dux'. Each clung to the hope of
siring legitimate sons who would succeed to both Crown and
Grand Duchy. It was Jagiełło who finally scored, at the impressive
age of seventy-two and on his fourth marriage (Jadwiga died in
1399). In 1424, Władysław was born, in 1426 Casimir. The latter's

unilateral acclamation as hereditary *hospodar* by the great families of Lithuania in 1440 put an end to a decade of strife between rival, stop-gap successors nominated by Jagiełło after Vytautas' death in October 1430. Casimir IV's accession to the Polish throne in 1447, following his election by Polish notables the previous year, restored a measure of stability in relations between the two states.

Vytautas was encouraged by the crushing defeats inflicted by Tamerlane on the Mongols of the Golden Horde to try to wrest from it mastery of the old Rus' lands. But he overestimated the Horde's disarray. His grandiose hopes ended in disaster in 1399 with the destruction of his army on the Vorskla river. In the previous year, he had had to recognize the consequences of his own folly in dallying with the *Ordensstaat* when, by the peace of Salin, he had been obliged to confirm its possession of Žemaitija. The Teutonic Knights and their associated Order, the Knights of the Sword in Livonia, now had a perfect springboard against Vilnius. Vytautas began to scheme for Žemaitija's recovery almost as soon as he had surrendered it. He could count on Jagiełło's support. Officially, neither the king nor his Polish subjects were involved in Vytautas' wars. Yet many Poles served him in their private capacities: on the Vorskla in 1399, in the uprisings which he fomented in Žemaitija between 1401 and 1404 and again in 1409. They helped garrison Lithuanian strongholds. The Order's purchase from Sigismund of Luxemburg in 1402 of the Neumark, flanking Wielkopolska's north-west border, alarmed its nobility. But it was only in July 1409 that Jagiełło was able to persuade his Polish subjects openly to oppose any attack by the Knights on Lithuania. In August, Grand Master Ulrich von Jungingen responded with an attack on northern Poland.

So began a long conflict which Poland eventually 'won' but never truly resolved. Not until 1466 were the territories the Order had seized during Łokietek's reign recovered. The stunning victory which the forces of the Polish-Lithuanian lands won over the Knights on 15 July 1410, near the villages of Grunwald and Tannenberg, failed to deliver the capital, Marienburg. Behind their fortifications, the Knights were impregnable, for their enemies lacked the resources for sustained siege warfare. A series of debilitating wars (1409–11, 1414, 1422, 1431–5) gave the Crown

Map 3   Poland under Jagellonian rule, 1386–1572.

almost nothing in territorial terms. Lithuania at least secured the
unconditional restoration of Žemaitija at the peace of Melno in
September 1422. Vytautas and his successors concentrated their
attention on Rus'. Their co-operation with Poland against the
Knights largely ceased.

The inconclusive, periodic fighting caused immense devastation
in and around the Teutonic Knights' Prussian lands. Germany's
parallel political and demographic crisis led to severe recruitment
shortages for the Order, which tried to compensate by increasingly
brutal fiscal policies. When, on 6 March 1454, the Crown chancellery issued an act of incorporation of Prussia, it did so in response
to growing agitation and rebellion among the Order's own subjects,
with the nobility and the great towns of Danzig, Thorn and Elbing
in the van. Such was the massive scale of initial defections that it
might have seemed the Order would be swept away almost without
a fight. Its nerve held. The Polish treasury was empty. To begin
with, Casimir IV was barely able to afford the services of 2,000
mercenaries. The Polish *levée en masse*, the *pospolite ruszenie*, was
routed at Chojnice on 18 September 1454. The war dragged on for
thirteen years. Though Poland taxed itself heavily (Piotr Świdwa,
castellan of Poznań, complained that 'the war cost the king more
than all of Prussia is worth'), the chief burden was borne by the
Prussian lands themselves. But the Knights had their own financial
problems. Marienburg castle was delivered into Polish hands in
June 1457 by the Knights' Czech mercenaries in return for payment
of their wage arrears. The peace of Thorn of 19 October 1466
showed just how badly hit the Order was. Its rich, western
territories along the lower Vistula passed under Polish suzerainty
as 'Royal Prussia'. The rich see of Warmia (Ermeland) was
detached from the Order as a separate *dominium* under the Polish
Crown. The Order retained the hinterland of the port of Königsberg, poorer lands for which its Grand Masters now had to
perform homage to the kings of Poland.

The success came at a price. Despite the incorporation of 1454,
Royal Prussia received, in law, enough autonomy for its elites to
regard it as a distinct political unit. Successive Grand Masters did
their utmost to ditch their vassal status or even to reverse the peace
of Thorn altogether. Frederick of Saxony, Grand Master from 1497

5   The town hall of Danzig/Gdańsk, 1379–80. Note the sixteenth-century Flemish-style buildings, much influenced by Danzig's commercial contacts. Extensive post-1945 restorations.

to 1510, managed to evade paying homage completely. The Grand Masters' support for the fractious bishops of Warmia brought about the short-lived conflict of 1478–9 known as 'the padres' war', *wojna popia* or *Pfaffenkrieg*. Only the death of king John Albert in 1501 prevented military reassertion of its sovereignty by Poland. The continued refusal to do homage by Frederick of Saxony's successor, Albrecht of Hohenzollern-Ansbach, finally led to a resumption of open conflict in 1519, ending in an inconclusive truce in April 1521. That *Deus ex machina*, Martin Luther, helped resolve the situation. In March 1525, Grand Master Albrecht proposed to King Sigismund I the secularization of the Order in its Prussian lands. He had been openly backing the Reformation in Königsberg since at least 1523. He was also bankrupt: the secularization of the Order's lands would enable him to claw his way out of a financial hole. The few remaining members of the Order were content to share in the spoils. The treaty of Kraków on 8 April 1525 reaffirmed that of Thorn of 1466, but delivered eastern, now 'Ducal', Prussia to the Grand Master as his hereditary possession and a fief of the Polish Crown. Two days later, outside the Kraków cloth-hall, Albrecht of Hohenzollern, the first territorial Lutheran ruler, swore his oath of fealty. The duchy was to revert to Poland on the extinction of his line. Contemporaries criticized Sigismund for not embarking on outright annexation. Experience showed, however, that such a course might well have led to more prolonged warfare – and Poland and Lithuania had to face up to the constant prospect of fighting elsewhere on their far-flung borders. A secularized, Lutheran Ducal Prussia would be utterly reliant on the Crown and might yet revert to it.

The difficulties in the north seemed to be counterbalanced by advances in the south. In Hungary and Bohemia at the turn of the fourteenth and fifteenth centuries, royal authority crumbled. The Jagiellonians sought to acquire these lands because that was what kings were supposed to do, and because they wished to prevent them from falling into the hands of hostile rulers. The memory of the machinations of the Luxemburg dynasty, and even of Angevin collaboration with the Teutonic Knights, spurred the Poles to extend their own influence into these lands. But the regency council which ruled Poland after Jagiełło's death in 1434 gravely miscalculated in trying to foist young Władysław III on Hungary in 1440. The civil war which erupted between his supporters and opponents was provisionally resolved in a misguided crusade against the Turks. At the battle of Varna in November 1444, Władysław was among the dead. Only John Hunyadi's generalship prevented the total destruction of the Christian army.

The tortuous road to Hungary turned out to lie through Bohemia. There, the chronic feuds between nobles and magnates, between Hussites and Catholics, their jockeyings for outside support, led, in 1469, to the election of Casimir IV's eldest son, Władysław, as king-designate. He ascended the throne two years later, on the death of George of Poděbrad. However, his elevation brought him into conflict with the energetic king Matthias Corvinus of Hungary, who, by 1474, succeeded in wresting Moravia, Silesia and Lusatia from him. Casimir IV's efforts to support his son foundered on lack of money.

Matthias died without a legitimate heir in April 1490. Władysław/Vladislav/Ulászló, the notoriously easy-going King 'Bene', King 'Fine' (reputedly, his stock response to any request) was just what the Hungarian nobility wanted after the late king's harsh rule. They chose him as king in February 1491. Casimir IV had hoped they would choose his second, favourite son, John Albert. He even undertook a disastrous military intervention, which ended in John's defeat at Eperyes in January 1492. But it was John Albert, not Władysław, who secured election to the Polish throne on Casimir's death in June of that year. A younger brother, Alexander, was recognized as separate *hospodar* by the Lithuanian nobility: partly in deference to the old king's wishes to provide for his youngest son; partly out of concern to block Polish annexationist hopes.

The Jagiellonian family firm had made its greatest gains, but emphatically by invitation only. The separate successions of John Albert in the Crown and Alexander in the Grand Duchy showed that it was a highly fractured dynastic enterprise. Their rule in Bohemia and Hungary was faced with continuous internal opposition, much of it encouraged by the Austrian Habsburgs who, especially under that most elastic of politicians, Maximilian I, had their own designs on those territories. Maximilian stirred up trouble for the Polish Jagiellonians wherever and whenever he could: he encouraged the Teutonic Knights in their refusal to abide by the treaty of Thorn. He even gave encouragement to the tsars of Muscovy in their conflicts against Lithuania.

Troubled as relations with the Habsburgs were, they were as nothing compared to the problems posed by the rise of the Ottoman Empire. Poland had only a limited role in Władysław III's disastrous Varna campaign, primarily a Hungarian undertaking. With the fall of Constantinople to Mehmet II in 1453, it was clear that the Ottoman empire had become an established, permanent fixture of the European scene. Both he and his successors were eager to extend their European possessions and to build up their hold on the Black Sea basin. In 1475, the Tatars of the Crimea acknowledged Turkish sovereignty, accepting Turkish garrisons in their coastal towns. While difficulties of supply, terrain and distance made it difficult for the Turks to annex outright the Danubian principalities of Wallachia and Moldavia – the latter a vassal state of Poland since Jagiełło's accession – it was clear that they had little hope of maintaining their independence intact.

Moldavia's *hospodars* could preserve a degree of freedom of action only by manoeuvring between their more powerful neighbours of Poland, Turkey and Hungary: in practice, this meant siding with whichever of these powers appeared to be the strongest at any given moment. Casimir IV gave his tacit approval to the annual tribute of 2,000 ducats which Stephen the Great of Moldavia (reigned 1457–1504) paid to the Sultan as a token symbol of Turkish suzerainty – after all, Polish and Lithuanian rulers, too, paid such sums to the Tatars of the Volga and the Crimea in order to persuade them (with only limited success) not to raid their lands. Poland and Hungary were both rivals for influence in Moldavia – and the rivalries prevented them from co-operating. With Hungarian help, Stephen was able to thwart Turkish efforts in 1475 and 1476 to annex his Black Sea ports of Kilia and Akerman (Belgorod), but he was unable to stop them falling to a huge Turkish–Tatar army in 1484. Polish help allowed him to recover some lost ground in 1485, but both ports remained in Ottoman hands. The Poles infuriated Stephen by agreeing to a truce which preserved the new status quo, and deprived him of the two ports, and which also allowed their own merchants freedom to trade in them; he had to continue to acknowledge Polish suzerainty, pay tribute to Turkey and suffer the loss of two of his most important commercial centres.

It was a deep humiliation. Stephen and his successors took their fury out by attempting to wrest from Poland the border territory of the Pokucie (Pokutija). In 1497, John Albert, in yet another of his ill-considered forays, led a major expedition into Moldavia, ostensibly to try once more to throw the Turks out of Kilia and Belgorod, but in reality to place his younger brother, Sigismund, on the principality's throne. The siege of Stephen's capital, Suçeava, was a dismal failure and John Albert's retreating army suffered heavy losses. Though the disaster meant the effective abandonment of Polish claims to suzerainty, Moldavian raids into Pokucie intensified and relations with Moldavia remained a thorn in Poland's side until Suleiman the Magnificent asserted a much closer control over his (no longer Poland's) vassal state after 1538.

The Moldavian imbroglio was, in turn, overshadowed by the far more fraught relationship with the Tatars of the Crimea. During the fifteenth century, the old Mongol realm of the Golden Horde had broken up into separate Khanates based in the Crimea and around the lower Volga. The Jagiellonians, as Grand Dukes of Lithuania, generally sought good relations with these Mongol groupings and tried as far as possible to manoeuvre them, when they were not fighting one another, against an increasingly powerful Moscow. After the Crimean submission to Ottoman overlordship in 1475, the Sultans had only a limited interest in restraining Tatar raids. If nothing else, they were a constant reminder to friend and foe alike of how great the Ottoman Porte's reach could be. Plunder, primarily the seizure of captives for sale in the slave markets of Kaffa and Constantinople, was the mainstay of the Tatar economy. The damage their expeditions wreaked was far greater than anything that Turkey's other unruly vassals, the Barbary pirates, inflicted on the coastlines of Mediterranean and Atlantic Europe. In the last quarter of the fifteenth century, Tatar incursions depopulated huge swathes of Lithuania's Rus' territories. In 1482, they sacked and burned much of Kiev. In 1505, they reached the outskirts of Vilnius. In 1490, they plunged deep into Poland itself, to within a few miles of Lublin. A decade later, they threatened Warsaw, capital of Masovia. One of the reasons why Poland was unable to give Moldavia more help was because of the constant need to divert forces against these intruders. Mobile and extremely hardy, the Tatars were an almost impossible foe to pin down, except after they had done their worst, as they returned home with their booty and their captives. Polish and Lithuanian forces won individual victories, but were unable to staunch the blizzard of raids. During the 1480s and 1490s, Lithuania lost its always tenuous control over the northern shores of the Black Sea. The devastation the Tatars wreaked in the last decades of the fifteenth century put an end to settlement and colonization efforts on the east bank of the Dnieper for two generations. Khan Mengli Gerei himself acknowledged that these lands along the borders, this 'Ukraine', had been turned into an empty wasteland. The only way in which the raids could be restricted was by the payment of 'gifts' – protection money – to the Crimean Khans, although even they admitted that they could not control the freebooting of many of their own subjects.

If, in Sigismund II's reign, the intensity of Tatar raids into Polish and Lithuanian territory diminished, this owed much to the improved state of garrisons and fortifications in the Ukrainian lands and to the establishment of 'cossacks' – runaways, petty (and some not so petty) nobles, adventurers, or those who just wished to be free – on the fringes of more populated areas. The word 'cossack', of Turkic origin, meant, appropriately, both 'watcher' and 'brigand'. Patronized by the kings and grand dukes and their officials, cossacks were a kind of Christian counterweight to the Tatars, giving as good as they got, raiding deep into Tatar territory and the Crimea itself. They were a volatile force, controllable (if at all) only by those who held their respect – the well-born, the ruthless and the daring, who cared as little for the commands of their own rulers as for the truces periodically negotiated between Poland, Lithuania, the Crimea and the Porte. Cossack activity did much to deter Crimean raids (and to strain relations with Constantinople). Probably an even more important factor in toning down Tatar raids was the appreciation by the Khans of the growing power of Moscow, especially in the wake of Ivan IV's subjugation of Kazan and Astrakhan in 1552 and 1556. Provided the kings of Poland remained ready to furnish them with generous gifts, the Crimean Mongols preferred to raid the territories of Moscow, rather than of Poland and Lithuania, whose further weakening could only encourage Muscovite expansion southwards, towards their own lands.

The last Jagiellonian kings, Alexander (1501–6), Sigismund (Zygmunt) I (1506–48) and Sigismund II (1548–72) all sought good relations with the Turks. Conscious of dynastic over-stretch, they resigned themselves to letting the Habsburgs take over their position in southern Europe. Sigismund I sent no help to his nephew, Louis II of Hungary, in the ill-fated Mohacs campaign: not only was Poland exhausted by its recent campaigning in Prussia, but, in 1524, Turkey had fired a warning shot against any such involvement when Turkish (as opposed to merely Tatar) forces had raided Polish territory, penetrating as far as L'viv. When Louis II, Władysław/Vladislav/Ulászló's son and successor, was killed at Mohacs in February 1526 and the Hungarian army annihilated, it was the Habsburgs who scooped up the Jagiellonian inheritance south of the Carpathians. Under the terms of the treaty of Prague of 1515, Louis' sister, Anna, married to the emperor Charles V's brother, Ferdinand, was to inherit Louis' lands if, as he did, he remained childless. The Czechs duly elected Ferdinand, the Hungarians split between him and a native contender, John Zápolya. Though Sigismund kept up a residual interest in Hungary – in 1529 his daughter, Isabella, married Zápolya – the once ambitious Jagiellonian policy was reduced to a delicate balancing act between the Zápolyas, the Habsburgs and the Turks. It was Turkish protection, not Polish influence, which allowed John Zápolya's and Isabella's son, John Sigismund, to hang on in Transylvania as an Ottoman client after 1547.

In Lithuania, the adoption of Latin Christianity drove a wedge between native Lithuanians – who gravitated towards Catholicism – and the majority of their Rus' subjects. The gradual percolation of Polish-style rights and privileges ought to have had its own attractions for the Rus' nobility; however, the Union of Horodło of 1413 had barred non-Catholics from the leading dignities of state. This was part of a deliberate policy, especially on Vytautas' part, to assert the rule of a Catholicized, Lithuanian elite, over the lands of Rus'. The only Orthodox, russified nobles to whom he was prepared to entrust major responsibility were close Gediminid relatives. This policy of favouring Catholic Lithuanians was pursued even more intensively after his death. When in 1470, for the first time in its history, a non-princely, Catholic official was named governor of Kiev, he had to be imposed by force on the city and its inhabitants. To Orthodox nobles, especially in the distant eastern borderlands, taking service with Moscow often seemed to offer a more promising path of advancement, even if many more preferred to argue for an extension of the rights and liberties of their Catholic counterparts to themselves. To the grand princes of Moscow, Catholic rule in Lithuania provided the perfect pretext for seeking to 'recover' the Rus' lands ruled from Vilnius. Casimir IV managed, by and large, to preserve good relations with Muscovy, but, towards the end of his reign, this was only by turning a blind eye to repeated border violations, and to the constant encouragement by Moscow of Tatar raids. On Casimir's death in 1492, Ivan III unleashed open war.

The comparatively loose military organization of the Grand Duchy, composed of the retinues of great magnates and princes, the *pospolite ruszenie* and all too few mercenaries, could not cope with the forces the much more centralized Muscovite state could mobilize. A series of dogged conflicts (1492–4; 1498–1503; 1507–8; 1512–22; 1534–7) left Lithuania on the ropes. In 1503, it had to cede about a third of its territory to Moscow. These were, admittedly, lands over which the Grand Duchy had always exercised very loose control; and in subsequent campaigns, the distances involved made military operations much more difficult for the Russian tsars. But this was of little consolation to the Lithuanian elite, not least because it only served to indicate to others, notably the Tatars (and, for that matter, the Poles), the extent of their military weaknesses. Lithuania's eastern border in 1492 was less than 100 miles from Moscow, but some 400 from Vilnius; after the catastrophic loss of Smolensk in July 1514, it was pushed back to around half that distance. While Polish volunteers and mercenaries fought in the Lithuanian ranks, it was not until 1508 that king Sigismund I was able to persuade the Polish

6 The battle of Orsha, 1514: view by an unknown painter, but almost certainly a participant in the battle, fought on the north-eastern marches of Lithuania. A feigned cavalry retreat brought the Russian forces onto the Polish and Lithuanian artillery. The victory, however, was not enough to recover over two decades' territorial losses (including the town of Smolensk) to Muscovy.

Parliament to vote any funding for the nebulously remote fighting in
the east. Polish troops and money helped the Lithuanians to victory
on the river Orsha in September 1514 and to contain further
Russian gains, but Smolensk remained in Russian hands for almost
another century. The lands around Homel, restored by Moscow in
March 1537, were little more than a fleabite in Lithuania's losses.
Respite came largely as a result of Ivan IV's internal preoccupations
and his distractions against the Tatar Khanates of Kazan and
Astrakhan.

It was on Lithuania's northern and eastern borders that the most
ambitious and most fateful of Jagiellonian foreign policy initiatives
was to unfold. The enfeoffment of Ducal Prussia in 1525 had
settled, at least for the time being, the Crown's most vexatious
problem. To the north of Lithuania lay the Livonian lands controlled by the Teutonic Order's sister organization, the Knights of
the Sword. By the 1550s, these territories were largely Lutheran
and the Knights virtually a secular institution, acknowledging a
vestigial allegiance to the Holy Roman Emperors. Though Livonia
grew rich on trade and tolls from Lithuania and Muscovy, the
Knights' endless quarrels with the archbishop of Riga made for
political weakness. It was all very tempting for Ivan IV, who
regarded Livonia as part of his Rurikid inheritance. Should it fall
into his grasp, he would have a boulevard to the Baltic and be
placed to threaten Lithuania from the north as well as the east.
Sigismund Augustus showed great interest in Livonia, not just for
its strategic importance, but because its wealthy cities might
provide new resources for his chronically hard-up monarchy.

Sigismund initially hoped to impose some form of vassal relationship, which would secure him what he called 'dominium maris
Baltici' – 'mastery of the Baltic Sea'. Yet his Polish and Lithuanian
lands were ill prepared for the sustained, large-scale warfare that
conflict in the region was to demand. For a start, Polish military
and fiscal support was very fitful: the Poles were only interested in
providing continuous support at the price of the full incorporation
into Poland of Livonia. That, of course, remained anathema to
most of the Grand Duchy's elite, who saw in Livonia a purely
Lithuanian prize, compensation for the loss of Smolensk. Sigismund
would have liked to have got his way by a combination of military

bluff and diplomatic wheeling and dealing, but real warfare was impossible to avoid. By massive alienations of royal domain, loans, by occasional, inadequate tax grants from the Polish and Lithuanian parliaments, by calling on the retinues of individual magnates or even the *pospolite ruszenie*, he was able to put together an impressive artillery park and to mass substantial numbers of troops for individual campaigns, but never to keep them on the constant war-footing required (though his enemies had the same problems). A series of understandings between the Livonian Masters, the archbishop of Riga and Sigismund between September 1557 and November 1561 progressed from an agreement on mutual assistance to the outright incorporation of Livonia into the Polish Crown. The Order was secularized. Its last Grand Master, Gotthard Kettler, received the territory of Courland, running along the southern bank of the Dvina river, as a hereditary duchy and fief of Poland.

Sigismund was powerless to deflect the ferocious invasions which were Ivan IV's response. In 1558, the Russians captured Narva and Dorpat, and in 1560 the centrally located town of Fehlin, although they failed to take the strategically crucial port of Riga. Distractions against the Crimean Tatars and Ivan's decision in 1563 to switch his main war effort directly against Lithuania helped stave off outright conquest. Ivan was also wary of the involvement of other parties. Denmark showed a close interest in the area. In 1561, the port of Reval, mistrusting the shortcomings of Sigismund's military efforts, submitted to the ambitious Erik XIV of Sweden, whose forces began to extend Swedish rule throughout Estonia.

Ivan's diversion against Lithuania eased the pressure on the luckless Livonian lands, but it cost the Grand Duchy the fortress of Polotsk, which fell in February 1563. It was not, however, the Lithuanian victory over the Russians on the river Ula in 1565 which led to a prolonged lull in the fighting. Rather it was renewed Tatar onslaughts (which, in 1570, saw much of Moscow destroyed by fire), and Ivan's disastrous inauguration of the *Oprichnina*, the reign of terror against his domestic enemies, real and imagined, in January 1565. From July 1566, a kind of truce prevailed between Moscow and its Polish-Lithuanian protagonists. Sigismund Augustus' forward policy had foundered: more Lithuanian terri-

tory than ever was under Russian occupation; Livonia was torn
between chaos with Swedish occupation in the north, Polish and
Lithuanian garrisons in the south and west and Russian forces in
the centre. The repercussions went further: fishing for support in
the Empire, Sigismund had, in March 1563, agreed that, should
Albrecht of Prussia's line fail, Ducal Prussia could revert to the
electoral, Brandenburg branch of the Hohenzollerns. Thus did the
1525 treaty of Kraków begin to be jeopardized by the Jagiellonians' own brand of imperial overstretch.

The problems facing the dynasty were on a physical scale scarcely
to be found elsewhere in Latin Christendom. In 1490, Poland and
Lithuania covered vast expanses, getting on for twice the size of
France, yet numbering fewer than 8 million people. From Kraków
or Poznań to Viazma or Briansk on Lithuania's eastern marches
was over 700 miles – almost as far as to Paris. East of the Vistula,
agriculture scarcely rose above subsistence level in a landscape
dominated by forest, swamp and steppe. These distances and the
paucity of resources, especially in Lithuania, help to explain much
of the passive, or at least reactive, nature of foreign policy. Polish
magnates saw in the Grand Duchy a kind of Jagiellonian dowry,
which should, by rights (the various acts of Union), be theirs. The
abandonment by Sigismund the Old of any kind of forward policy
in Bohemia, Hungary and against the Ottomans encouraged them
to look with interest at the prospects of new wealth in Lithuania
and Rus'. As for the Lithuanians, they feared Polish pretensions,
were unwilling to accept that Vytautas' era of predominance over
Rus' belonged to the past and, when and if they did receive military
help from Poland, always found it wanting. In these conditions, the
preservation of the link between the Polish Crown and the Grand
Duchy of Lithuania was an achievement in itself. Only the
Ottoman Porte and Muscovy faced comparable difficulties. Their
solutions – sustained, brutal centralism with little or no regard for,
nor even conception of, their subjects' rights and privileges, were
utterly impracticable in Poland.

Władysław II Jagiełło was made king not just to bring territory,
but to consolidate the dominance of an elite of 'prelates et
barones'. In 1426, when Jagiełło refused a fresh confirmation of

privileges, his leading nobles slashed their document of assent to the succession of his baby son to pieces in front of him. He relented and issued the confirmation four years later. His successors were never allowed to forget their elective position. His second son, Casimir IV, had to wait almost three years after the death of his elder brother, Władysław III 'of Varna', before he was accepted as king and had to be threatened with deposition before he would confirm his subjects' privileges in 1453.

The 'prelates et barones' or 'proceres' were, in the first instance, members of the royal council, which, in the early sixteenth century, assumed the name of Senate: the Catholic bishops and great officers (chancellor, treasurer, marshal); the palatines (*wojewodowie*) and castellans, heading the hierarchy of counties (*terrae*) and palatinates (*palatinatus*) which had coalesced out of the old Piast duchies. Of these approximately seventy dignitaries, those who took key decisions of state with the king numbered some half-a-dozen. Membership of the council depended on talent and patronage (especially through the royal chancellery). Its members took further royal favour for granted – and could be relied upon to cause trouble if they did not receive it. Once made, appointments were regarded as irrevocable.

Lower down the scale, participation in the feudal levy, the *pospolite ruszenie*, might be enough to ensure acceptance as a knight/gentleman/noble – a *szlachcic*. Even this was not always necessary. To ease the incorporation into the Crown of the duchies of Płock and Masovia in 1495 and 1526, John Albert and Sigismund I confirmed the supposedly noble status of thousands of impoverished smallholders – illiterate, uncouth and eager to be distinguished from what were, in reality, other peasants. The result, by the second quarter of the sixteenth century, was social inflation, with a 'noble' estate making up perhaps some 6 per cent of the 5 million or so inhabitants of the Crown – a proportion largely maintained until the end of the eighteenth century.

The *szlachta* of the wider 'communitas nobilium' voiced their hopes and fears at the local assemblies, *sejmiki*, which had their roots in the judicial and administrative activities of the Piast era. During the fifteenth century, the practice grew of the holding of larger, regional assemblies, a development which nurtured the emergence of representatives or 'envoys' – *nuntii terrarum*. The nobility were largely free to attend in person more important sessions of the royal council. Their attendance converted its sessions into a 'conventio generalis' or 'Sejm Walny'. Those present tended to be drawn from the ranks of councillors' clienteles. During the 1490s, these *nuntii* gained their own separate chamber at the Sejm, probably as a deliberate move by John Albert to keep a check on over-mighty councillors. The Sejm was never able to disencumber itself of its original character of an outgrowth of the faction-ridden royal council, mistrusted by the *szlachta* at large. Envoys rarely felt confident of being able to speak for their electors on matters not directly put to them. Tax grants were often accompanied with the rider that their payment depended on final approval by individual constituencies. *Sejmiki* felt able to advise, enjoin or even restrain their envoys' activities. The growing number of envoys, from around forty in 1500 to almost eighty by mid-century, brought the Sejm, at best, only increased moral authority. Given the resort, especially by John Albert and Alexander, to a common front between monarch and nobles against over-mighty magnates, some kind of more lasting constitutional partnership might have evolved; but the clear preference of Sigismund I and II for working with their senatorial lords put an end to the prospects (insofar as they existed) of any such compact. The Chamber of Envoys regarded itself as a forum for local emissaries, rather than as part of a sovereign legislative body in its own right. No monarch felt confident enough seriously to attempt to impose discipline and order on its frequently chaotic proceedings, nor did the Chamber feel sufficiently assured of its own role to do so for itself. There was not even a formal voting procedure – laws were passed by acclamation and if sufficient agreement could not be mustered, the whole parliament might disperse without any conclusive measures.

Poland's cash-strapped monarchs had no alternative but to look to the *szlachta* for support. In 1422 and 1454, the *pospolite ruszenie* refused to move against the *Ordensstaat* until its grievances were addressed. In 1496, John Albert, in return for backing for his expedition to Moldavia, not only confirmed all existing privileges but went on to grant the nobility exemption from customs duties on all commodities of domestic production and consumption. He even agreed that townsmen should be barred from owning land and to making it almost impossible for peasants to leave their seigneurial estates. Yet this was not just constitutional extortion – the monarchs, too, were bidding for wider support against their over-mighty subjects – usually members of the royal council who sought, unavailingly, to distance themselves from their lesser fellow-nobles. The Chojnice–Nieszawa Privileges of 1454, binding the king not to levy taxes, enact new laws or even call the *pospolite ruszenie* without the prior consent of the *sejmiki*, were designed to enable Casimir IV to appeal over more powerful magnates to the nobility at large. Ironically, these concessions were made to a *pospolite ruszenie* which otherwise threatened not to fight against the Teutonic Knights. It was promptly defeated, but the concessions remained.

To begin with, the nobility did not seek to share power with the monarchy, but protection against oppression. The post of justiciar, with its virtually unlimited powers of arrest, which Jagiełło had promised to abolish in 1386, was wound up by John Albert only in 1496. The Privileges of 1422 (Czerwińsk) and 1430 (Jedlnia) had supposedly safeguarded the nobility from confiscation of property and arrest, save after due process – *Neminem captivabimus nisi iure victum*. Yet complaints against the abuse of power by royal officialdom continued to increase. The bulk of the 1454 Privilege addressed *szlachta* concerns at judicial abuses and arbitrariness by councillors and royal officials, or the monarchy itself. Among its provisions was confirmation of the nobles' right to run their own civil judicial affairs, a point regarded as crucial to their platform of 'liberties': they could elect the key offices of judge and deputy-judge to the county courts, the forum of civil disputes within the *szlachta* estate. Such concessions generated their own momentum. Increasingly, even justice was noble, as opposed to royal.

Royal councillors, alarmed by the progress of ordinary nobles in carving out their liberties, seized the opportunity of John Albert's death to secure a whip-hand. At Mielnik, in November 1501, they warned his brother, Alexander, ruling in Lithuania, that they would elect him king only if they themselves received the right to determine the Senate's membership and appoint to lesser offices of state. Should the king refuse to follow policies which they were to propose, he would forfeit their obedience. Alexander, distracted by war with Muscovy, agreed – only to turn the tables at the Sejm which met in Radom in 1505. Many officials simply found it unacceptable to take orders from a senatorial council whose membership they mistrusted. The king used the resentments generated by the senators' self-seeking misrule to rally the *szlachta* behind the statute known as 'Nihil Novi', 'Nothing New': 'We have hereby affirmed for all time to come that nothing new may be enacted by Us and our Successors save by the common consent of the senators and the envoys of the constituencies.' The place of the gentry within the parliamentary system was confirmed, as a check on the Senate. 'Nihil Novi' laid the cornerstone of *szlachta* freedoms for almost three centuries. The Mielnik concessions became a dead letter. Even so, it was not until the 1550s that the open nomination by great lords and royal dignitaries of envoys supposedly mandated by the *sejmiki* ceased.

The king had to work within the limitations imposed by the *szlachta*. Sigismund I was able to resume much alienated royal domain by more careful administration. He extended the range of customs duties, albeit at the cost of extensive *szlachta* exemptions. In the late 1520s, he was able to reform the currency. His actions lay within the acknowledged royal prerogative and could rely on wider noble support. It was otherwise when kings attempted policies which threatened noble interests directly. Sigismund I's hopes of commuting the obligation to serve in the *pospolite ruszenie* to a regular cash levy were rebuffed. The election by the Senate-dominated Sejm of 1529–30 of his nine-year-old son, Sigismund Augustus, provoked such an outcry among the *szlachta* that the Sejm of February 1530 banned future royal elections *vivente rege* – during the reigning monarch's lifetime. Sigismund I's second wife, Bona, daughter of Gian Galeazzo Sforza of Milan, was widely suspected to be behind Sigismund Augustus' premature elevation. As a foreigner, a woman and a representative of a wholly different political tradition, she attracted much suspicion during the reigns of her husband and son, whose clear preference for working with the lords of the Senate only heightened fears of kingly absolutism. The scandalously damaging affront to royal authority in 1537, when the *pospolite ruszenie*, assembled near Lwów for a punitive expedition into Moldavia, went on strike, threatened royal ministers and had to be sent home, demonstrated just what monarchs could expect if they failed to show due regard for noble sensibilities (or failed to control mischief-making senators behind the scenes). In pursuing his ambitious Baltic policies, Sigismund II Augustus had to rely on the dangerous expedient of creating facts and then hoping that the Sejm would vote the funds. It did not always do so.

Their organization and military muscle gave the lesser nobility, or 'ordo equester' as its more learned members styled themselves, a major advantage over other social groupings. In the course of the fifteenth century, most of the *szlachta*'s privileges were extended to the clergy. Senior Church positions were largely reserved for the nobility. A community of interest was produced which constant quarrels over tithe and jurisdiction shook, but could not undermine. The periodic alignments of king and *szlachta* prevented the emergence of a legally distinct higher nobility (seats in the Senate were not hereditary, but came only through specific offices) and, instead, helped give birth to a fiction of equality among all nobles – but which more canny over-mighty subjects learned to manipulate to their own advantage. Kings could, at best, manoeuvre between noble groupings.

Kings had no alternative sources of effective support. Major towns were pitifully few. Kraków, Lwów or Poznań were content with their individual privileges. Their town halls, markets and churches (most spectacularly, Veit Stoss of Nuremberg's dazzling altar-piece in Kraków's Lady-Church) bespeak a real prosperity, founded mainly on overland transit trade and raw material exports. But there were no centres of manufacture capable of competing with the Rhine valley, Flanders or northern Italy. Even the capital, Kraków, at the end of the sixteenth century, numbered around 14,000 inhabitants – barely the size of a secondary provincial centre in France. Piotrków, the usual venue for the Sejm Walny, numbered only some 3,000 inhabitants. The fastest-expanding group within the towns was the Jews who, by 1600,

7   The church of the Blessed Virgin Mary, Kraków. Completed 1397.
Kraków was unique among the major cities within the post-1945
borders of Poland in suffering only minimal structural damage during the
Second World War.

8   The great altarpiece by Veit Stoss (Polish, Wit Stwosz) of Nuremberg (died 1533) in the church of the Blessed Virgin Mary, Kraków. Stoss lived in Kraków between 1477 and 1496. He spent many years, between 1477 and 1489, working on his masterpiece. In 1484, he was granted full citizen rights in Kraków. In 1939, the Germans removed Stoss' triptych to Nuremberg. It was recovered by the Poles in 1946, but prolonged restoration work meant that it was reinstated in its rightful place only in 1957.

may have numbered over 200,000 through immigration and
natural increase. Of course, they played no direct political role
(though isolated individuals might rise high in the royal or magnate
administration) and many towns legally excluded them from
permanent residence. For that reason they were much favoured by
the nobility whose 'protection' was bought by creaming off the
profits of their trading and banking activities.

The one concentration of urban wealth allied to real political
power lay in Royal Prussia. Danzig in 1500 counted over 35,000
inhabitants; Thorn and Elbing over 10,000 each; their commercial
wealth allowed them to dominate the local nobility. Yet although
the 1454 'Letters of Incorporation' proclaimed Royal Prussia's
return 'to the body of the realm', they simultaneously conceded
such extensive autonomy that the province regarded itself as
virtually distinct from the Crown proper. Before 1569, the Prussian
estates sent only observers to the Sejm and rarely, if ever, were
prepared to vote tax monies unless their own immediate interests
were served. The Jagiellonians courted individual towns (although
Sigismund II, unlike his father, loathed Kraków and never visited it
after 1559) for their goodwill and money. Towns sent representatives to assist in royal elections throughout the fifteenth century;
leading patricians might even take a seat on the royal council.
Wealthy townsmen and merchants had little difficulty in obtaining
ennoblement, either by royal favour or by securing court judgements 'confirming' their new status. In 1492, Kraków took this to
its logical extreme when it secured noble status and the right to
send its own representatives to the Sejm, to exercise their influence
on Kraków's behalf.

The nobility extended their advantages into the economic
sphere. Under the Statute of Warka of 1423, noble landlords were
permitted to buy out, against independently assessed valuations,
the rich hereditary holdings (*sołectwa*) of negligent or recalcitrant
village administrators (often *szlachta* themselves). Price controls
were imposed on towns; guilds were declared abolished; peasants
were forbidden to migrate to towns without their seigneurs'
consent. Most of these provisions were unenforceable. They were
reaffirmed and sharpened in 1496 and 1520. It was only from then
that the restrictions on the peasantry began to take on real force, as

an agrarian boom, fuelled by grain exports through Danzig, brought about a shift from cash rentals to revenues derived from the direct exploitation of peasant labour services. Free peasants became enserfed because there was no way of stopping the process, although for much of the sixteenth century agrarian prosperity cushioned the worst effects of the restrictions on their freedom. Save for its Baltic rim, Poland remained overwhelmingly agrarian, even by contemporary European standards. The price revolution made manufactured imports much cheaper relative to raw material exports. If artisanal activity in Poland's own towns suffered, most nobles were unconcerned.

It was middling and great nobles, those wealthy enough to own at least one or two villages with good access to ports and navigable rivers (principally the Vistula and its tributaries), who benefited most from the exports of raw materials, fuelled by growing demand from western and Mediterranean Europe. It is unlikely that more than 2.5 per cent of total Polish grain production was exported, even at its height at the turn of the sixteenth and seventeenth centuries. Most grain was sold on the internal market. But this, coupled with the extension of seigneurial demesne and their growing powers over the peasantry, the lack of strong central government, the remarkably peaceful conditions which prevailed in most of Poland proper (that is, excluding the Rus' territories exposed to Tatar incursions), all induced a sense of well-being, prosperity and self-confidence, which in popular *szlachta* mythology was to mark out the sixteenth century as a kind of Golden Age. The principal beneficiary, in material terms, was the port of Danzig, through which the great bulk of Polish exports went. Indeed, Danzig, dealing mainly with Dutch traders from Amsterdam, may have accounted for some 70 per cent of the Baltic grain trade as a whole. The city had a network of agents buying up, arranging credit and taking orders for luxury goods throughout much of the Crown. Most nobles however, showed little interest in commerce or maritime ventures *per se*: they were quite content for the world's merchants to beat a path (as they saw it) to their farms and demesnes. All they had to do was to squeeze more out of their peasants. And if grain could not be sold, timber and cattle could be.

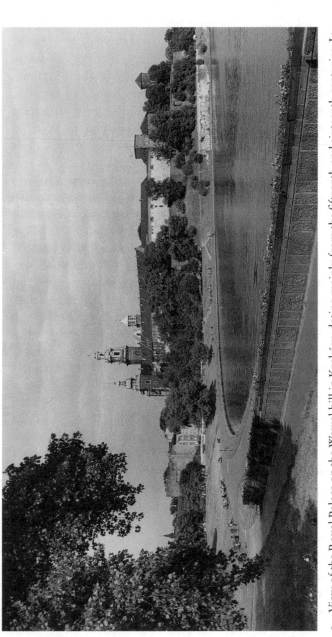

9   View of the Royal Palace on the Wawel hill in Kraków, dating mainly from the fifteenth and sixteenth centuries. In 1596 Sigismund III decided to transfer the court to Warsaw (the move was only completed in 1611), much more favourably placed for communications with Lithuania and the Baltic region. Polish kings continued to be crowned in the small cathedral attached to the Wawel palace until 1764, when the last king of Poland, Stanisław August Poniatowski, concerned at its ruinous condition, chose to have his coronation ceremony in Warsaw.

10 Sigismund I's Renaissance courtyard in the Wawel palace, Kraków
(early sixteenth century). Sigismund enjoyed the benefit of a humanistic
education. His second wife, the Milanese princess Bona Sforza,
contributed to the deepening of Italian cultural influences.

During the reign of Sigismund I, the tensions within the noble
estate took on more definite contours with demands by the lesser
nobility for 'Executio Legum', the 'Execution of the Laws', or full
implementation of old laws supposedly designed to protect the
szlachta. As a bonus, the same laws allowed them to strengthen
their own position vis-à-vis non-nobles. The movement waxed and
waned throughout the sixteenth century, to reach a sustained
crescendo during the 1550s and 1560s. The starting point was
legislation enacted by the Sejm of 1504, insisting that all alienations and pledging of royal demesne should cease; the competence
of the great offices of state was more distinctly defined and the first
steps were taken against multiple office-holding by individuals. A
prominent demand was that the king should provide for the
defence of the realm out of his own resources, if necessary by
resuming royal demesne alienated to great magnates and royal
creditors. This ought, conveniently, to spare the *szlachta* the

burdens of taxation. These restrictions on alienation of demesne and multiple office grants (the so-called *incompatibilia*) aimed to curb the ability of royal councillors to enrich themselves and accumulate excessive political influence.

Particularly in its early phases, 'Executio Legum' was driven, as much as anything else, by in-fighting among the great nobles themselves – as individuals such as bishop Jan Łaski, chancellor of the Crown after 1503, sought to do down their rivals and to bolster their own position by playing to the *szlachta* gallery. Notionally, as much as one-fifth of the Crown and Lithuania counted as the Jagiellonians' direct patrimony. Jagiełło, almost from the moment he was chosen king, began alienations on a huge scale, to win political support and to raise cash for his wars. There was some justification for *szlachta* suspicions of misuse of their monies. They rightly suspected that their grants of the extra-ordinary land tax, the *pobór*, were actually spent on ends other than military (barely 10 per cent of the 1485–6 military subsidy was spent on troops; most of the rest went on court and adminis-trative outlays). On the other hand, the diversion of such funds testified to the parlous state of the royal finances.

The nobility's capacity to be obstructive was stoked by the cultural efflorescence of the sixteenth century. The way was well paved. In 1400, Jagiełło had re-founded Kraków University with a Theology Faculty to assist in the conversion of Lithuania. It was, however, during the Council of Constance that the university's jurists, especially Paweł Włodkowic (Paulus Vladimiri), came to the attention of an international audience with their views on the rights of nations and international relations. Their rejection of the validity of Christian rule imposed by force sought to refute the propaganda of the *Ordensstaat*. The presence of humanists such as Filippo Buonaccorsi (1437–96) and Conrad Celtis (1459–1508) at the turn of the fifteenth and sixteenth centuries made the university, if briefly, one of the most exciting in Europe. Nicholas Copernicus (1473–1543) represented the apogee of a well-established astro-nomical tradition at the university, critically respectful of Aristotle. Polish developed into a sophisticated literary medium through the works of writers and poets such as Mikołaj Rej (1505–69), Łukasz Górnicki (1527–1603) and, above all, Jan Kochanowski

(1530–84). Much of the literature of this 'Golden Age' was produced in Latin – but it was very rapidly translated into Polish and disseminated throughout literate *szlachta* and urban society. The first printing-press had been set up in Kraków in 1476. It was not only Latinate, 'western' culture which benefited: as early as the 1490s, a Kraków printer, Szwajpolt Fiol, had produced the very first Old Church Slavonic/Cyrillic texts in print for the Orthodox cathedral in Przemyśl. The first Polish work aimed for wider circulation, the 'Paradise of Souls', appeared in 1513. The publication in 1506 of a chronological collection of Polish laws was intended by its compiler, Crown chancellor Jan Łaski (hence its popular name of 'Łaski's Statute') to raise the awareness of the Executionist movement of their own legal entitlements. The earliest vernacular versions of the Sejm's statutes were published, to meet *szlachta* demand, in 1543 (the same year as the posthumous publication in Nuremberg of Copernicus' *De revolutione Orbium Coelestium*).

Increasingly strong contacts with Italy helped the *szlachta* elite create a culture modelled (at least in their own minds) on the values of Republican Rome. Sigismund I and Queen Bona transformed the royal castle on Kraków's Wawel hill into a Renaissance showpiece. In the north, Königsberg formed a centre of Polish learning and humanism second only to Kraków. It was in the interests of its Lutheran rulers to produce bibles, books and Protestant literature both in Latin and in Polish to cultivate support in the Crown and Lithuania. It was in Königsberg that Martynas Mažvydas' reformed catechism, the first printed text in the Lithuanian vernacular, was published in 1547, followed, four years later, by the first Polish translation of the New Testament. The first complete Polish translation of the Bible was printed in Kraków in 1561. The whirlpool of foreign and national influences found concrete expression in the welter of different dress styles adopted by the nobility, with native, western and oriental influences (the latter arriving largely through Hungary) combining to produce a distinctive couture of caftan, boots, belts and breeches around the mid-century.

In this bubbling cultural atmosphere, a combination of prosperous, ambitious, educated gentry and great lords drove the Exe-

11   The great cloth-hall ('Sukiennice') in the main square of Kraków, rebuilt after a fire in 1555. The architect was Giovanni Il Mosca of Padua (hence his sobriquet, 'Padovano'). Kraków owed its original prosperity to its situation at the junction of two major trade routes: east–west, between the Black Sea hinterland and Germany; and north–south between the Baltic and Bohemia/Hungary. Kraków's importance declined with the departure of the royal court for Warsaw and the wars and recessions of the seventeenth century.

cution movement. It had no single leader, although by the 1550s, its most distinctive personalities were closely associated with the Reformation; the disgorging of ecclesiastical wealth and land would reduce the need for extraordinary taxation and consolidate the nobility's pre-eminence in the realm. Since Lithuania increasingly called on the support of the Crown against Moscow, the Execution movement took up old calls for its full incorporation. All parts of the body politic, including Royal Prussia, were to contribute towards its defence. It was not a programme bereft of positive aspects, but torchbearers such as Andrzej Frycz Modrzewski, who sought to extend its scope beyond sectional self-interest, were few and far between. In 1538, the 1496 law barring townsmen from acquiring landed property was reaffirmed; in 1550 guilds were again banned. Such restrictions, notwithstanding their ineffectiveness, also belonged to the old laws which the *szlachta*'s virtuous forebears had secured.

Sigismund I and Sigismund II Augustus were sceptical. Both felt that matters of state were not for debate with 'ploughmen', as they were ready to call *szlachta* agitators. They were, unsurprisingly, alarmed by some of the more extreme claims pumped out by the Execution movement. In 1507, Stanisław Zaborowski, protégé of chancellor Łaski, published his *Tractatus de natura iurium et bonorum regis* (*A treatise on the nature of royal rights and property*) in which he argued for the social and political supremacy of the *communitas* of nobles, to whom the king answered for the condition and disposition of crown property as a steward to his master. The pendulum had swung too far in the favour of small-minded squires who had little understanding of politics and who sought to restrict the monarchical right to reward faithful servants as they deserved. For most of their reigns, disputes over 'Executio' inflamed domestic politics. The inexorable accumulation of noble rights made reversing the trend practically and ideologically impossible. Those who wanted strong government argued for more effective Sejmy, better collaboration between monarch and nobles or, if all else failed, moral reformation. Polish political literature was almost wholly bereft of any arguments for absolute monarchy.

Sejmy were called almost annually, even in time of supposed peace, to pay for measures against the seemingly endless Tatar raids. Most Sejmy did vote funds for the *obrona potoczna*, the 'general defence' force based around the fortress of Kamieniec Podolski on the Crown's south-eastern border. But the monies rarely sufficed to maintain this force at above some 2,000 men. Kings had to resort to a variety of expedients to keep their troops in being – negotiating with local *sejmiki*, calling on the local *pospolite ruszenie* or magnate retinues, alienating royal demesne or even establishing quasi-military colonists in the border areas – lawless settlements of Cossacks, who gave the Tatars as good as they received. The Sejm of 1508 agreed, for the first time, to financial help for Lithuania against Moscow. For a few months, the Crown and the Grand Duchy put some 25,000 troops into the field. The *szlachta* of the Crown were prepared to vote (though not, when it came to the crunch, necessarily to pay) sustained taxation for the wars on the frontier with Muscovy – but only if the Grand Duchy were prepared to accept full incorporation into Poland proper, a price that most of the Lithuanian elite were not willing to contemplate. Even the most vigorous *ad hoc* efforts were no substitute for regular taxation which alone would have permitted the long-term maintenance of large armies – but then of course, these were still the exception, rather than the rule, throughout most of Europe.

Agitation for the Execution of the Laws (*Egzekucja*) reached a noisy height soon after Sigismund II's accession in 1548. Inevitably, it fused with religious passions. Poland's western borders lay only a day's ride from Saxony across Silesia. Reformed ideas and writings began to circulate immediately after Luther's first protests, finding their strongest support in the towns of Royal Prussia. Sigismund I's one serious attempt at a crackdown took place in Danzig in 1525, occasioned mainly by his fears of the unruly pretensions of the lower orders. Once a few ringleaders had been executed and the authority of the city council restored, Sigismund did not interfere: Lutheranism, shorn of social radicalism, won over the German-speaking patriciates. His son confirmed their confessional freedoms in 1557 and 1558. If anything, it was Catholicism which was on the defensive in Prussia.

Among the *szlachta*, reformed ideas – not only Lutheran but, increasingly, Calvinist and even antitrinitarian – fused with long-standing disputes over tithe with the Church and with the drive for political dominance. The core of reformed support came from wealthy families in Wielkopolska, such as the Górkas, Leszczyńskis and Sienickis – all of them, by the mid-century, highly active in the Egzekucja programme. The Reformation had to insinuate itself into the movement, for there was never any other possibility of its attracting mass political support. Freedom of religion was seen as an extension of political liberties. But the decision by the Sejm of 1562–3, forbidding royal *starostowie* from using their police powers to carry out the judgements of ecclesiastical courts, was as much a triumph for *szlachta* anticlericalism as a success for the reformers. Significantly, the number of Protestant envoys began to fall off after this Sejm. Once Egzekucja had run its course, the Polish Reformation found itself reliant on the uncertain protection and attitudes of individual noble patrons.

Exponents of Reformation could be found virtually anywhere from the Silesian border to the depths of the Ukraine. Attempts to form a common front foundered on doctrinal differences between Calvinists and Lutherans on the one side and the antitrinitarians, or Aryans, as they came to be called, on the other. The last two Jagiellonians tolerated religious diversity (which, after all, sprang from the very bones of the lands they ruled) out of necessity and good sense. The alternative, Sigismund II recognized, was probably internal disintegration, as in France or Germany. While he showed a proper humanist interest in the new doctrines, he had no intention of abandoning Catholicism.

By the late 1550s, Sigismund II had to face up to the real prospect that he might be the last of his line. He married three times, to no avail. In May 1543, it was Ferdinand of Habsburg's daughter, Elizabeth. She died two years later. In July 1547, in Vilnius, he secretly married a young widow, Barbara, born into the powerful Radziwiłł family, a love-match which fuelled paranoid fears among the Crown nobility of Lithuanian domination. Their relations with the king were blighted for years. Barbara died in May 1551. Two years later, Sigismund reluctantly married his first wife's younger sister, Catherine. He loathed both his Habsburg consorts. The last marriage petered out in a humiliating separation and Catherine's return to Austria in 1566 (she died at Linz in February 1572). Sigismund's petitionings to the papacy for a divorce failed. Had he wished to emulate Henry VIII, as a Polish king he was in no position to do so. His failure to sire an heir and the manifest incapacity of Lithuania alone to withstand Muscovy undermined the rationale for maintaining the separation of the Crown and the Grand Duchy. The Executionists' calls for the resumption of royal demesne, restrictions on officials' abuses, and even for the annual summons of the Sejm offered scope for a platform of constructive reform. Their demands for the subordination of Lithuania and Royal Prussia to the Crown promised the chance of creating a new and formidable polity. In September 1562, Sigismund embraced their cause, but whether as anything more than a desperate tactical expedient to which, as a childless monarch, he had to reconcile himself, remains uncertain.

The Sejm which met at Piotrków from November 1562 to March 1563 attempted to secure peacetime revenues by the resumption and closer regulation of alienated royal demesne. The audits and surveys which the Sejm instituted were to be repeated at five-yearly intervals. The king could make land grants, but recipients were to enjoy only one-fifth of the income, while the remaining four-fifths were to cover the expenses of court and government. One-quarter (*kwarta*) of the monarch's share was specifically earmarked for the upkeep of the defence of the south-east against Tatar incursions. It could not, nor was it meant to, pay for the war with Muscovy. The *szlachta* voted an increased *pobór* (land tax), paid mainly by their peasants. They were, however, allowed to make up half of their amount from tithes due to the Church. The new *pobór* thus permitted indirect ecclesiastical taxation.

The *kwarta* eventually made available a regular source of monies for the defence of the south-eastern borders, but did little to increase the size of what was now known as the '*kwarta* army'. The survey commissions which completed their work by 1565 increased the returns from royal demesne to almost half a million zloties – an eightfold increase on the 1540s. Yet the commissions were so inadequately staffed, the task facing them was so enormous, that the new returns could scarcely have represented more than a fraction of the revenue potential. Certainly, individual magnate families lost extensive properties. The Executionists even succeeded in imposing the surveys and resumptions on Royal Prussia, on the grounds that royal demesne was involved. Once it became clear, however, that lesser *szlachta* were being drawn into the net of resumptions, interest rapidly diminished. After 1569–70, there was to be no full survey until 1660. Sigismund II himself connived at evading or softening the losses of some of the most badly affected senators. The returns of the new *pobór* proved disappointing because many *szlachta* simply did not want to pay. If it was true, as the historian Antoni Mączak has suggested, that in its supposed golden age, the Crown's economy was retarded by such shortages of specie that the nobility simply could not afford taxes on the scale necessary to meet Poland's needs, those needs remained. The Sejm of 1565 had to sanction the raising of fresh loans against the security of royal properties.

Sigismund II Augustus felt that only a new Union, on terms acceptable to both the Crown and Lithuania, would give the nobility of both a real stake in the survival of a reconstructed polity. The outright annexationism of the Executionists would not do. Convergence of a kind had long been under way. The Polish written and spoken word was, by the late fifteenth century, making rapid progress among Lithuania's elites, to produce a fascinating written and spoken linguistic hybrid of Belarusian, Lithuanian, Latin and Polish. By the 1560s, if not earlier, the Lithuanian nobility at all levels were predominantly Polish speakers and Lithuanian itself had been reduced to the language of the peasantry. Cultural polonization was certainly not opposed by Lithuanian elites: many, not least Rus' Orthodox, positively embraced it as a channel to a more sophisticated western European culture. The Radziwiłłs' conversion to and enthusiastic patronage of Calvinism was a means of combining integration with distinctiveness. But political polonization was a very different matter. The importation of distinct Polish-style courts, *sejmiki* and genuine elections to a central Sejm and to local offices threatened to overturn the patrimonial dominance of the members of the *hospodar*'s council. The resumption of grand-ducal domain threatened them with economic catastrophe. But irresistible pressures were building up. The constant presence during the Muscovite wars of Polish troops, drawn mainly from the *szlachta*, served to familiarize their Lithuanian counterparts with Polish ideas and institutions. Sigismund Augustus' Privilege of Vilnius of July 1563 aimed to win round Orthodox nobles by restoring their access to offices on the *hospodar*'s council. The Lithuanian magnates, led by the Radziwiłłs, offered concessions. The Vilnius Sejm of November 1565 to March 1566 sanctioned the introduction of distinct elective courts on the Polish model. A hierarchy of local officials patterned on Poland's followed in 1566 as part of a new codification of common law (the so-called Second Lithuanian Statute). The Lithuanian Sejm, hitherto largely a magnate mouthpiece, formally assumed the same legislative powers and procedures as the Crown's. Union was being administratively engineered from within.

The climax came at the Sejm which met in Lublin in January 1569. Sigismund insisted that the Lithuanian lords and envoys should attend. Prompted by Sigismund, the Poles declared their readiness to accept a separate hierarchy of great offices of state for Lithuania – but there would have to be a common Sejm; the Poles' right to settle and own land in the Grand Duchy would have to be conceded. This last demand led to fears that the generally wealthier Poles would swamp the Grand Duchy. When most of the Lithuanian representation walked out on 1 March, Sigismund angrily announced the incorporation of Volhynia and Podlasie, part of Lithuania's Rus' lands, into the Crown. The local boyars, comparatively few by the standards of the Polish lands proper – at most they may have accounted for some 3 per cent of the population of these territories – complied with little fuss. As far as most of them were concerned, it was their obligation to follow the dictates of their *hospodar*, Sigismund, heir to the rulers of old Rus' – a ruler, moreover, who had only recently lifted the restrictions imposed by Lithuanian Catholic Vilnius on Orthodox subjects' access to the great offices of state; incorporation into the Crown brought the promise of sharing in Polish-style rights, liberties and freedoms.

On 16 March, the king ordered the senators and envoys from Royal Prussia, attending as observers, to take their seats in the assembly – their separate status, too, would end. They caved in. On 6 June, the royal chancellery announced the incorporation into the Crown of the sprawling palatinate of Kiev, with the overwhelming approval of the local nobility. If the Lithuanian objectors persisted, there was every likelihood that the original annexationist demands of the Executionists would be carried. Sigismund still believed that 'voluntary' union was better: he even promised that the resumption of royal demesne would not apply to Lithuania (in fact, it did not even apply to the former parts of the Grand Duchy which were incorporated into Poland). The Poles agreed that Lithuanians could enjoy reciprocal rights of settlement in the Crown. On 28 June the last objections were overcome. The new Union was confirmed by the king on 4 July. A new entity, the Rzeczpospolita Obojga Narodów, Polskiego i Litewskiego, 'The Commonwealth of the Two Nations, the Polish and Lithuanian', had come into being.

The Union was Sigismund Augustus' greatest achievement and

greatest failure. Hard experience had taught him to make compromises whenever possible, perhaps too much so. Through the Union of Lublin he hoped to establish a realm based on partnership between the *szlachta* and a future monarchy. But the aftermath demonstrated what he must have always feared. To the overwhelming majority of the *szlachta*, 'Executio' was a means of securing their rights and privileges. Nothing was done to improve the workings of the Sejm. The balance between Sejm and *sejmiki* remained unsteady and, if anything, in favour of the latter. The Union probably made the problems worse. Magnates and *szlachta* may have been theoretically equal in law, but in practice the former could and did use their sheer wealth to dominate their 'lesser brethren'; the mutual opening up of the Crown and Lithuania meant that magnates on both sides could now acquire landed estates and the influence that went with them throughout the new Rzeczpospolita. Mikołaj Radziwiłł 'the Red' complained that a 'free' Lithuania had been buried 'for all time'. He need not have worried. His idea of freedom had a long career before it.

Despite formal unification and supposed closer integration of the Crown, Royal Prussia and the Grand Duchy, in practice the forces of local particularism remained strong. Regardless of Sigismund's lifting of obstacles to Orthodox nobles' advancement in 1563, a combination of Catholicization and polonization and the utter refusal of the Catholic Church hierarchy, increasingly gripped by the enthusiasms of the Counter-Reformation, to regard Orthodoxy as anything other than a schismatic faith, meant that its relationship with Catholicism remained as uneasy as it had been in the Grand Duchy after 1386. Lithuania bristled with resentment at its treatment at Lublin. For all the progress of cultural polonization, its nobility's sense of distinctiveness remained undiminished. Danzig remained *sui generis*. Right up to Sigismund's death it continued to sabotage his plans to build a Baltic navy, which it saw as a threat to its own position. Although Royal Prussia now sent envoys to the Sejm, it retained its own regional parliament, the so-called Prussian *sejmik*-general.

The Lublin Sejm itself and the Sejmy of 1570 and 1572 refused to discuss machinery for the regulation of royal elections after Sigismund's death. The *szlachta* feared a *rapprochement* between

Sigismund and the magnates and from that, a Habsburg succession. An ailing and disillusioned Sigismund may have felt that his new and fractious Commonwealth could best be preserved by the election of Ernest of Habsburg, Emperor Maximilian II's younger son. That might secure the Commonwealth some wider support against the dangers that beset it. The Habsburgs could always count on considerable support among the senators, who felt their rule could only strengthen their own position. But among the wider masses of the *szlachta*, Habsburg rule in Hungary and Bohemia had secured them a bizarre reputation, brokered largely by Habsburg opponents and demagogues, as enemies of freedom second only to the tsars of Muscovy. The Executionist leaders were content to protect the gains of 1569. Some, rewarded with royal demesne and new offices by the king, went over to the senatorial side; others shared the fears that a strengthened monarchy might ultimately pave the way to Habsburg tyranny. Rather than vote extraordinary subsidies for the Russian war, the *szlachta* settled for a three-year truce with Muscovy in June 1570. Polotsk remained in Ivan IV's hands.

Sigismund consoled his last years with a string of sexual liaisons, which did nothing to enhance his reputation. A daughter born to his mistress, Barbara Giżanka, in 1571, provoked grumbling that her mother was a whore and the king was not her father. The last Sejm of his reign had to be abandoned in May 1572 because of his poor health, broken by gout, gallstones, tuberculosis and frustration. At six o'clock in the afternoon on 7 July 1572, Sigismund II Augustus, Poland's last Jagiellonian king, died at the royal hunting-lodge at Knyszyn, where he had sequestered Giżanka, fearing his nobles might abduct her. The *szlachta* were on their own.

3

The Commonwealth of the
Two Nations, 1572–1795

In a field outside Warsaw on 10 May 1573, Henri, duke of Anjou, was elected king of Poland. His elder brother, King Charles IX of France, appreciated that a Valois-ruled Poland, bordering on Austria, could prove very useful. As for the *szlachta*, so confident were they in their constitutional defences that even Protestants were prepared to accept a ruler widely deemed responsible for the previous year's St Bartholomew's massacre.

At the 'Convocation' Sejm in January 1573, the gentry's leaders had blustered the senatorial elite into conceding that all nobles were entitled to vote for their king *viritim* – in person. The Sejm formed an association, the 'Confederacy of Warsaw', which drew up constitutional ground rules. The king would not secure a successor *vivente rege*, during his own lifetime; he would have to preserve interdenominational peace; he would decide matters of peace and war in conjunction with the Senate and the Sejm; parliament was to be called every two years for a six-week term, or as necessary; its consent would be required for all extraordinary taxation. The nobility's jurisdiction over their peasants would remain untouched. If a ruler failed to observe his sworn commitments, he would forfeit his subjects' obedience. These 'Henrician articles' were complemented by the *pacta conventa*, obligations crafted for individual kings. King Henri's ranged from the provision of scholarships at the Sorbonne for young nobles to extravagant promises of financial and military support for Poland-Lithuania in the Muscovite war.

The 1573 settlement remained basic to the structure of the Commonwealth of the Two Nations for most of its existence. Interregnums and 'free' royal elections were essential to correct the abuses and infractions of the previous reign. Warsaw's central location made it much more convenient as the election venue than Kraków (for the same reason Sigismund III made it his permanent place of residence from 1611). The formal procedures evolved during the first interregnum remained in place for two centuries. The archbishop-primate of Gniezno stood in for the king, as *interrex*. The Election Sejm heard representations from would-be monarchs' agents (foreign candidates were not allowed into the country before the election). The attendant *szlachta*, organized by palatinates and counties, camped around the huge barn-like struc-ture in which the senators and gentry leaders debated before proposing a candidate for general acclamation.

As many as 40,000 nobles may have attended Henri of Anjou's election. Only some 4,000 turned up for Władysław IV's election in 1632, because no one seriously doubted he would succeed his father, Sigismund III. Most elections saw several 'Piast' (native Polish) candidates, but a nation of supposedly equal noblemen disliked seeing one of its fellows elevated above the rest. When electors divided, as in 1576, 1587 or 1697, then readiness to move quickly and use force carried the day.

At his coronation, Henri refused final confirmation of the articles bearing his name. Monarchy in the French tradition was incompat-ible with Polish legalism. The extent of privilege, and its dissemina-tion among some 6 per cent of the population, gave so many an immediate, vested interest in the status quo as to make change enormously difficult. Wealthier, better-educated and more widely travelled nobles might be sufficiently mature (or cynical) to appre-ciate that their kind could do very well under strong monarchs, but even they were predisposed, by custom and outlook, to the preservation of extensive constitutional checks. On the night of 18 June 1574, four days after hearing of the death of his elder brother, Charles IX, a frustrated Henri III of France slipped out of Kraków's Wawel palace and made for the nearby frontier as fast as his horse could carry him.

The *szlachta* nation ran its own affairs: the *sejmiki* performed a huge range of tasks and gave men of even moderate wealth (even those who owned only a fraction of a village, if they had the education) an opportunity to engage in local government and self-advancement. The creation, in 1578 and 1581, of independent, annually elected supreme courts, the Crown and Lithuanian Tribunals, placed the bulk of judicial business affecting the nobility in its own hands. The Sejm's enactments, particularly on taxation, continued to require the electorate's further approval, amendment or even rejection at the *sejmiki*. Direct royal appeals to the constituencies for monies usually received a sympathetic response, but did nothing to enhance parliament's authority. Nevertheless, the extensive network of local institutions which the *szlachta* built up provided them with a machinery for dealing with most of the public business they deemed important – there was therefore little purpose served in building up the elaborate, centralized bureaucracies developing elsewhere in Europe.

The reforms of the Execution movement proved inadequate. Kings felt they alone should decide what use they made of royal domain lands. The *szlachta* acknowledged that they (or their peasants) would pay extraordinary taxes to deal with emergencies: mainly the traditional land tax, the *pobór;* they were ready to pay them at higher rates; they were even prepared to accept wholly new imposts – even the highly 'demeaning' poll tax. But supply was rarely voted for more than twelve months at a time. In 1620, in anticipation of a Turkish invasion, the Sejm voted to increase the regular army from 12,000 to some 60,000 men – impressive by the standards of the time, but in 1622 scaled back to under 12,000. Such fluctuations were all too characteristic. Recruitment and pay inevitably lagged. Signal victories such as Kircholm over the Swedes in 1605 or Cudnów over the Russians in 1660 went to waste as troops mutinied over arrears. A numerous *soldatesca* emerged, plundering its own taxpayers in order to survive. Kings, magnates, officers had to dig deep into their own pockets to keep troops in being and supplement them with their own private retinues. The feudal levy of the nobility, the *pospolite ruszenie*, usually a disastrous encumbrance, remained a significant feature of the military panoply well into the eighteenth century: if nothing else, it served as a rhetorical device which allowed the nobility to claim they were ready to sacrifice their lives and fortunes for their country, which required no other substantial form of military defence.

The Commonwealth was more a cumbersome federation than a unified state. The great magnate families who dominated Lithuania built on the compromises of the 1569 Union of Lublin to preserve a distinct political identity, even as cultural and linguistic differences crumbled. The revised codification of common law of 1588, the 'Third Lithuanian Statute', even contravened the Union of Lublin in barring those born outside the Grand Duchy from office – although as wide-scale Polish settlement proceeded, and as 'Lithuanian'/'Polish' magnates acquired land and positions across the Commonwealth, such restrictions became meaningless. In 1673, the Lithuanian magnates secured approval for every third Sejm to meet in Grodno, in Lithuania. Yet at the Election Sejm of 1697, the mass of Lithuanian gentry dealt a blow to magnate hegemony by extending the Crown's restrictions on multiple office-holding to the Grand Duchy. The adoption by that Sejm of Polish, in place of a hybridized Belarusian, as the Grand Duchy's official chancery language marked the progress of cultural unification. The origin myth of a common, 'Sarmatian' ancestry, assiduously propagated by humanist writers, allowed very different groups to merge their identities into a wider whole – provided they were nobles. To the disgust of later nationalists, Lithuanians and *Ruteni*, or Rusini (nowadays, Belarusians and Ukrainians) could regard themselves as 'Poles' because they were also 'Sarmatians'.

Integration had mixed success in the Ukraine. Pride in the traditions of Kievan Rus' could not always accommodate itself within the framework of the Rzeczpospolita. If the native nobility of these sparsely populated marches wished to get on, polonization and the adoption of 'Latin' faiths, Catholicism above all, offered the means. The great, practical, intellectual difficulty for those who wished to stay true to the Orthodox religion lay in its lack of any dynamic cultural centre on the lines of Catholic Rome or Calvinist Geneva. The Moscow patriarchate was adamantly opposed to any form of intellectual enquiry; the 'modernizing' reforms of the patriarch Nikon in the 1650s created a huge schism within the Church which persisted at least until the October Revolution. In the towns and monastic schools of the Polish Ukraine, it is true that a broader-based intellectual revival took off in response to increasing pressures from reformed Catholicism and Protestantism, but it did so just as the Orthodox social elite were going over to the Roman faith. Prince Konstanty Ostrogski founded an Orthodox academy in his town of Ostrih/Ostróg in 1576, reacting to the establishment, two years previously, of the first Jesuit college in the Ukraine at Jarosław. Giving the lie to the charges of Poland's most celebrated Jesuit preacher, Piotr Skarga, of Orthodox ignorance and backwardness, the Academy taught a humanist, liberal arts curriculum, with instruction in Old Church Slavonic, Latin and Greek. In 1581, it brought out the first scholarly edition of the Orthodox Bible. While it existed, it was a magnet for townsmen, nobles and Cossacks who were not ready to lose their cultural identity to the forces of latinity. Its weakness, reflecting the weaknesses of non-Catholic faiths in general in the Polish-Lithuanian state, was its total dependence on a great patron. Ostrogski, a grand aristocrat with a reputation for indolence, took no steps to secure its future through a royal charter or formal Sejm approval. By 1600, he had largely lost interest in his own creation. He had no son, and all his three daughters were married to Roman Catholics. After his death, his Catholic heirs shut the Academy down in 1608. It had been the one Orthodox establishment which could begin to compete with Jesuit colleges and Protestant gymnasia. No Orthodox nobles of comparable stature remained to take up the torch.

The decision, in 1596, by a majority of the Orthodox bishops at Brest, in Lithuania, to unite with Rome was prompted by more than Catholic pressure or fear of the increasingly hostile patriarchate of Constantinople or the new patriarchate of Moscow. To some, at least, of the 'Uniate' bishops, the only means of restoring spirituality and intellectual credibility to the Orthodox religious tradition, even, indeed, of the preservation of a distinct cultural identity, lay in borrowing from the Latin West. The Uniates kept their own liturgy and even their married parish clergy – but an obdurate Latin episcopate prevented their bishops from taking up the senatorial seats promised them. Orthodox clergy aspiring to higher education found that, of necessity, they were obliged to attend Catholic colleges, even that of St Athanasius in Rome, pretending to be Uniates, before reverting to their original faith.

Even the initially ardent defender of Orthodoxy, Meletii Smotritskii, came to throw in the towel and embrace Uniate Catholicism in 1627. This *trahison des clercs* among many of their spiritual leaders was not matched among townsmen and petty nobles for whom Orthodoxy represented a vital link with the glories of their Kievan Rus' *ethnie*. This might have been less significant, had not the Commonwealth's *Rusini* accounted for almost half its population; the many lesser nobles among them resented their *de facto* subordinate position on the *szlachta* spectrum. Among them and among the rank-and-file clergy the Union provoked enormous hostility. In 1620, the patriarch of Jerusalem, returning from a visit to Moscow, surreptitiously consecrated a number of Orthodox bishops. Sigismund III tactfully turned a blind eye and in 1632, Władysław IV officially acknowledged their reinstatement. Yet the mere presence of the Uniate church with its often heavy-handed proselytizing kept religious frictions in the expansive eastern marches on the boil.

The late sixteenth and early seventeenth centuries saw the creation of massive complexes of estates in these lands. Inter-marriage and royal favour allowed comparative newcomers such as the Potockis or Lubomirskis to measure up to the likes of established princely houses of Lithuania, the Radziwiłłs or the Wiśniowieckis. These great landowners soon learned to manipulate the values of 'Golden Liberty'. By the eighteenth century, Polish politics largely became centred on the acquisition of office and crown leaseholds. Kings gave rewards for service – or because they had to. Their power to punish was increasingly limited. King Stefan Batory (1576–86) had Samuel Zborowski executed in May 1584 for plotting his overthrow. His successor, Sigismund III (1587–1632), won praise for pardoning those who, in 1606 and 1607, had fomented armed revolt and sought his deposition. But he dared not press matters too far: even the army which defeated the rebellious 'rokosz of Sandomierz' in July 1607 suspected that their opponents had some justification in claiming that they were resisting 'absolutum dominium'. Attempts by John II Casimir (1648–68) in the 1650s and 1660s to rid himself of prominent opponents backfired, even when proofs of their dealings with hostile powers were palpable.

12   The town hall of Zamość, the centrepiece of the vast estate built up by Jan Zamoyski (1542–1605), grand *hetman* and grand chancellor of the Crown. Zamoyski was the principal collaborator of king Stefan Batory and, thanks to royal patronage, was able to build up a huge clientele and massive fortune. In Zamość, after 1580, he created a model Renaissance town, designed by the Paduan architect, Bernardo Morando (1540–1600).

The Sejm proved unable to cope with regional differences and magnate rivalries. It was these which underlay the emergence of the *liberum veto* – the right of a single individual to destroy the parliamentary session. No machinery for formally voting on legislation existed before 1768: acclamation remained the norm. The marshal, or speaker, of the Chamber of Envoys had virtually no real power to discipline, direct or control proceedings, which, amid intense factional rivalries, could all too easily degenerate into an undignified shambles. The primary role of the Sejm was not necessarily to pass laws at all. It was to protect noble freedoms and to restore them where they had been infringed. In the words of the historian, Anna Sucheni-Grabowska, 'Once the nobility had secured a legally privileged status within the state, legislation, in the fullest sense, became, in general, undesirable.' Thus, the occasional failure of Sejmy to produce any final enactments did not cause undue alarm – that was how the Commonwealth staggered along politically. 'It is nothing unusual, Your Majesty', explained the speaker of the 1606 Sejm to Sigismund III, 'for Sejmy to end in failure . . . There is something hereditary in Poland about these parliaments, one way or another they take place, but they do not always succeed.'

Bills became law only after a final reading in the closing days of the Sejm: Władysław Siciński's protest in March 1652 against any prolongation of the normal six-week term terminated the proceedings. Though the detailed circumstances of this first, formal disruption by a single protestor remain controversial, royalists and oppositionists allowed it to happen because both feared that prolongation would bring them political defeat. In November 1669, a Sejm was, for the first time, disrupted before the end of its normal term. The veto caught on at local level – *sejmiki* became liable to disruptions, wreaking administrative and judicial havoc. The *szlachta*'s attitude to the veto was ambivalent. It was the 'palladium of liberty', yet individuals who wielded it (though no one man would do so unless he was sure of strong support) were widely condemned. In the eighteenth century it was as common to talk proceedings out as to disrupt the Sejm outright. Three of the five Sejmy of Michael Wiśniowiecki's reign (1669–74) were broken; under John III Sobieski (1674–96), it was five out of eleven. Of thirty-seven Sejmy between 1697 and 1762, only twelve enacted legislation. The establishment of a Confederacy – a league with a common programme – was the only effective means of setting the veto aside, but such leagues, formed during wars or interregnums, invariably aimed to preserve cherished ancestral liberties. For all the opprobrium heaped on individuals who dared exercise the veto, it had become one of those liberties. Sejmy which met after 1763 were much more successful – but most met under the aegis of confederacies imposed on the nobility.

And yet the *Rzeczpospolita* showed itself capable of bursts of astonishing energy and resilience in the face of invasion and rebellion. The Union of Lublin of 1569 went a long way to opening up the Lithuanian lands to the Crown *szlachta*, restrictions in the 1588 Lithuanian Statute notwithstanding. And, of course, there was now no impediment to seeking new wealth in the Rus' lands incorporated into the Crown. The wars against Muscovy were no longer a Lithuanian preserve – they became of vital interest to the Commonwealth in its entirety. The campaigns of Stefan Batory between 1578 and 1582 reversed the territorial gains notched up by Ivan IV, securing Livonia and Polotsk. Batory owed much of his success to his close collaboration with Jan Zamoyski, grand chancellor and grand *hetman* (commander-in-chief) of the Crown, the richest magnate of all Poland, a highly cultured demagogue turned statesman, the closest that Poland produced to a royal 'favourite' in the mould of a Buckingham, a Richelieu or an Olivares. He had been one of the leading lights of the Executionist movement, and an increasingly close collaborator of Sigismund II. It was Zamoyski who had mobilized the nobility during the first interregnum to go for *viritim* royal election, not least because he felt this was the surest means of excluding the Habsburgs. He assured the *szlachta* that they were the foundation of a Commonwealth superior even to Republican Rome. He went down well. Instrumental in bringing about Batory's election, he was rewarded with almost limitless royal patronage and the highest offices in the land. His massive clientele was invaluable in maintaining support for the new king, in whose service he demonstrated military as well as political and administrative talent. Between them the two men oversaw the emergence of a veteran military cadre which was to render sterling service over the next generation.

Sigismund III's reign witnessed even more remarkable successes. Intervention in Russia during the later reign of Boris Godunov and the 'Time of Troubles' saw a Polish-backed pretender briefly placed on the Muscovite throne in May 1606. In 1610, Russian boyars elected Sigismund's 15-year-old son, Władysław, as tsar. Though the prince never entered Moscow, the city received a Polish garrison in September 1610, which, in the face of a massive uprising, held out in the Kremlin until October 1611. The election of Michael Romanov in March 1613 gave the Russians a ruler around whom to unite, but it was years before Polish troops and Cossack freebooters were cleared from Russian soil. In 1618, Russia ceded Smolensk to the Commonwealth. Michael Romanov's attempt to recapture it during the 'Smolensk war' of 1632–4 ended in humiliation. The 'Perpetual' peace of Polanovo of June 1634 left Smolensk in Polish hands. Nothing seemed more emphatically to proclaim the strength of the new state created by the Union of Lublin.

Some of these achievements pointed to shortcomings, as well as strengths, in the Polish-Lithuanian polity. The Russian adventure of 1606 was begun as a private initiative by irresponsible grandees seeking to exploit the disorders of Boris Godunov's reign. By the time the Sejm approved involvement in 1609, the opportunities seemed too good to ignore. Likewise, the semi-private initiatives of ambitious border magnates at the turn of the sixteenth and seventeenth centuries aimed to reassert Poland's dormant influence over Moldavia and Wallachia. This courted disaster, for such undertakings could only jeopardize the good relations established with the Porte by the Jagiellonians. Unofficial, destructive raids by Poland's Cossacks against Turkish possessions on the Black Sea aggravated matters. The 1620 expedition under Crown grand *hetman* Stanisław Żółkiewski, to keep a friendly *hospodar* on the Moldavian throne, suffered a crushing defeat at Turkish hands at Tutora. Poland was fortunate that domestic troubles in Turkey weakened its ability to launch a full-scale counter-offensive and facilitated the defeat of the Turkish punitive expedition of 1621 at Khotin, just inside Moldavia.

Even in victory, the *szlachta* were divided over these foreign ventures. The Sejm refused to endorse Stefan Batory's plans for resuming the Russian war in 1584 and to many, his unexpected death in December 1586 was a relief. His Vasa successors, Sigismund III and Władysław IV (1632–48) looked to Habsburg support, which they hoped would help clinch their plans for hereditary rule in Poland – and/or make good their claims against Sweden. Sigismund III, son of John III of Sweden and Sigismund Augustus' formidable sister Catherine, had been brought up a staunch Catholic in a Lutheran country. Elected king of Poland in 1587, he succeeded in Sweden as hereditary king in 1597, to be deposed within two years in favour of his uncle, the future Charles IX. Fishing for international support, the Vasas followed Batory in making concessions to the Hohenzollerns over Ducal Prussia, until in 1618 Sigismund III assigned the duchy's reversion to the collateral Brandenburg line.

The Vasas' Swedish preoccupations brought a chain of misfortunes on Poland-Lithuania. The Poles had elected Sigismund III partly with the expectation of 'recovering' Estonia, filched, as they saw it, by the Swedes during the wars with Ivan the Terrible. Sigismund only agreed to the transfer in 1600, after his dethronement in Sweden. Poland ground itself down in an unavailing effort to expel the Swedes. After 1626, Gustavus Adolphus carried the war into Polish Prussia. The six-year truce of Altmark of 1629 left Riga and the bulk of Livonia in Swedish hands and northern Poland devastated. Władysław IV modernized the army and then found the *szlachta* would not let him use it. In 1635 they insisted, over the king's objections, on extending the truce for another sixteen years.

A frustrated Władysław looked to the Cossacks of the Ukraine. Sigismund Augustus had used these lawless frontiersmen as a counterforce to the perpetual Tatar raids. Batory had made use of their sterling infantry. In their stronghold of Sicz, on the lower Dnieper, they elected their own military leader, or *hetman*, and their own army council. They fought the Tatars; they raided the Black Sea littoral. In 1614 they attacked Trebizond and Sinope; in 1615, they burned the suburbs of Constantinople. For all their reassurances to the Porte, Polish kings were simply unable to control these restless fighters. In an effort to curb their destabilizing raids, the Sejm had agreed to 'register' and pay those in the Commonwealth's direct military service, thereby removing the economic need for such activities. This, however, accounted for only a fraction of those who regarded themselves as Cossacks. The *szlachta* spurned the aspirations of those on the register, let alone those excluded from it, to be counted as nobles. The drive to exploit the fertile soils of the Ukraine, 'Poland's Indies', and the systematic imposition of labour-services provoked a series of uprisings, suppressed with increasing difficulty. After the defeat of the 1637 rising, the Cossacks were formally degraded to 'a commonality of peasants', save for a register of 6,000.

This treatment of a disaffected martial element was ill-considered, if understandable in the context of the times. Flushed with successes against Muscovy and the Porte, the *szlachta* were reluctant to admit that they owed much to the support of the Cossacks – at Khotin, in 1621, there were at least 20,000 of them, the bulk of the rank-and-file of the Commonwealth's army. Those petty nobles who chose to retain their religion, especially in the surroundings of Kiev and the trans-Dnieper territories, where polonization had made nothing like the progress it had further west, were indeed looked down on as second-rate citizens. There seemed little point, amid a vigorous Catholic Reformation, in according truly equal rights to the schismatics of Orthodoxy, particularly when the most truly powerful landowners had gone over to Catholicism. In the vigorous colonization drives which they pursued in the early decades of the century, sugh magnates preferred to give posts of responsibility to Polish, Catholic nobles, often incomers, rather than to their 'lesser' Orthodox confrères. These thus lost out twice over: by increasing exclusion from the offices of state and also by exclusion from the private enterprise which marked these territories around the middle and lower Dnieper. To many of the petty nobles of the area, descendants of the boyar servitors of the Rus' princes, the newcomers brought alien ways, political oppression, violence and instability, not least in the constant feuding between the great magnates who were trying to grab as much land as they could in the region and whom the monarchy was powerless to restrain.

13   The Royal Castle ('Zamek Królewski') in Warsaw; seventeenth and
eighteenth centuries, destroyed during the Second World War: the present
building has been reconstructed since 1971. The castle also provided
accommodation for Poland's Parliament (Sejm) when it met in Warsaw.
To the right of the picture is the column first erected in 1643–4 by
Władysław IV in honour of his father, Sigismund III, bearing a cross and
a drawn sword, the symbols of the militant Counter-Reformation. The
statue was raised despite the objections of the papal nuncio, Mario
Filonardi, who felt that this kind of honour belonged to religious, rather
than secular, figures.

In truth, the Ukraine had been like this for centuries, but the
sharpening cultural and religious divides enhanced the nostalgia
for a mythical Golden Age when the Kievan lands had been
harmoniously ruled by their own Orthodox princes. For their part,
the Catholic and Catholicized nobility saw in the Orthodox an
element of instability and rebellion. The Cossacks, including the
thousands of petty nobles or would-be nobles counted among their
ranks, were valuable in times of war; but in periods of peace, they
were deemed a menace, both to colonization and to liberty. There
were many among the Cossacks who looked naively to the
monarchy, especially Władysław IV, to improve their condition.
Władysław himself sympathized with the Cossacks and saw in

them a potent ally in his dreams of a strengthened kingship. He saw his chance in the outbreak of war between Turkey and Venice in 1645. If he could engineer Poland's involvement, he would leave the Sejm with no choice but to vote campaign monies. Success would allow him to strengthen the monarchy and assure his son of the throne. Instead, the Sejm got wind of his plans and forced him to promise to disband the troops he was raising. Undeterred, Władysław cut a secret deal with the Cossacks. He would double their register to 12,000 and grant near-autonomy to the Ukraine if only they would help provoke a conflict with Turkey's vassals, the Crimean Tatars.

This fantastic exercise was rendered meaningless by the deaths, first of the king's only son, Sigismund Casimir, in August 1647, then, the following May, of the king himself. The powder-keg of the Ukraine had already exploded. A private feud between a Polish official and Bohdan Khmel'nytskyi, one of those party to the clandestine dealings with the king, escalated beyond all control. Much of the Crown army was wiped out in May 1648; hurriedly reconstituted, bolstered by private militias, placed under the orders of a demoralisingly divided committee of squabbling nobles, it fled in panic before a joint Tatar–Cossack force in September.

Khmel'nytskyi, far from provoking the Tatars, looked to their support – though they were not prepared to allow him to become too powerful. His periodic bids to impose control over Moldavia were bound to suck in the Turks. Whether he wanted an independent Ukraine, or a looser relationship with his more powerful neighbours, remains uncertain. He could scarcely control the forces he had unleashed. At its height, his rebellion numbered some 150,000 armed men, mainly peasants who loathed their Polish masters and the Jews who dominated much of Ukrainian commerce as the *szlachta*'s economic agents. The swing of the pendulum in the Poles' favour, marked by the victory of Władysław's successor and half-brother, John II Casimir, at Beresteczko, in June 1651, was nullified by the massacre of most of the Polish regular army at Batoh a year later.

The hitherto cautious Russians now seized their chance. In January 1654, by the Union of Pereiaslav, the Ukraine placed itself under Tsar Alexei's protection. An irresistible Russian invasion

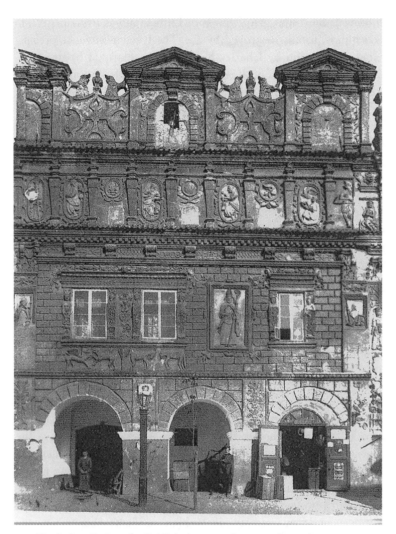

14   Kazimierz Dolny, the St Nicholas town house and warehouse
(kamienica pod św. Mikołajem), built by the Przybyła merchant family in
1615. Kazimierz Dolny on the middle Vistula grew rich as a staging-point
for Polish exports, mainly grain, in the late sixteenth and first half of the
seventeenth centuries. Like so many Polish towns, it never fully recovered
from the devastating impact of the 'Deluge', the invasions precipitated by
the Swedish onslaught of 1655. This photograph, taken in 1900, conveys
an impression of the decayed grandeur of the town. Today, the town, much
restored, is something of an artistic Mecca and a tourist trap.

followed. By August 1655, most of Lithuania was overrun. Wilno was almost totally destroyed by fire. The Russian advance precipitated an invasion by Charles X of Sweden, alarmed by its implications for his Baltic position. He also had a splendid opportunity to eliminate, once and for all, the Polish Vasas' claims on Sweden. With the fall of Warsaw in September to Charles; with mass defections among the Polish nobility; and with John Casimir's flight to Silesia, the Commonwealth seemed about to disintegrate. Indeed, at Radnot in Hungary, on 6 December 1656, Sweden and Transylvania agreed to carve up the Commonwealth between themselves, the Ukraine and Brandenburg. Brandenburg's ruler, Frederick William, the 'Great Elector', was awaiting his chance to cement Ducal Prussia to the Brandenburg heartland by acquiring Royal, Polish Prussia. All that would have remained would have been a small principality under Swedish protection, carved out of Lithuania for Bogusław Radziwiłł, protégé of Charles and the Elector.

Poland survived the 'Deluge' – *Potop* – of invasions. The brutality of the over-extended Swedish and Muscovite forces provoked a major national uprising, embracing every level of society. The successful defence of the fortified shrine of the Madonna at Częstochowa in December 1655 proved a legendary turning-point. The defections to Charles X went into reverse. His seemingly remorseless progress provoked Austrian, Danish and Russian attacks on him – though the 'help' the Austrian troops gave the Poles was almost as ruinous as their enemies' invasions. Polish and Tatar forces smashed a Transylvanian invasion in the summer of 1657. By the autumn, Polish troops were coming to the assistance of the hard-pressed Danes. Frederick William switched sides, but at a price: under the treaty of Wehlau of September 1657, the Commonwealth abandoned its suzerainty over Ducal Prussia – which, in 1701, was to be accorded the status of a kingdom in its own right by the emperor Leopold I. The unexpected death of Charles X in February 1660 paved the way for the end of the Northern War. The peace treaty of Oliva in May 1660 was concluded on the basis of the *status quo ante bellum* – and the surrender by the (childless) John Casimir of his dynastic claims on

15   The defence of the Pauline monastery of Jasna Góra against the
Swedes, in November–December 1655. The engraving commemorates
the miraculous intervention by the Blessed Virgin Mary to protect the
monastery, which housed an icon of the Black Madonna, supposed to
have been painted by St Luke the Evangelist (the icon dates from the
fifteenth century). The failure of the siege marked a turning-point in the
Swedish invasion, helping bring about a massive nationwide uprising,
uniting all social classes against the invaders. In fact, of the comparatively
small besieging force, only some 450 were Swedes. Most – around 1,000
– consisted of Polish troops who had defected in the early stages of
Charles X's invasion. This has done nothing to detract from the potency
of the legend, which has helped to make the monastery the most
celebrated religious site in Poland.

Sweden. After all the rivers of blood shed in the Swedish wars, he
was allowed to retain the courtesy title of king of Sweden.

With the Swedish conflict settled, the struggle with Russia
resumed. Khmel'nytskyi died in August 1657. His *de facto* successor, Ivan Vykhovskyi, himself of noble birth, judged that
'liberty' could have no future under the tsars' rule. The Accord of
Hadziacz which he made with Poland on 16 September 1658

would have created an autonomous principality of Rus', with its own hierarchy of ministers and officials, the equal of the Crown and Lithuania. Orthodoxy was to have the same status as Roman Catholicism – Greek Catholicism would be allowed to wither away as no new ecclesiastical appointments would be made. The Orthodox bishops were to sit in the Senate. The new principality would have its own army of 30,000 registered Cossacks and its own regional parliament. But it came a good ten years too late. Popular venom against the Poles made it unworkable. A new Commonwealth of Three Nations was not to be. In May 1659, although the Sejm reduced the very extensive scope in the Accord for the new principality to conduct foreign affairs, it largely ratified the agreement – but to no avail. In September, a year after it was first drawn up, a Cossack assembly rejected it outright as a sell-out by a self-seeking leadership.

Although it never received any chance to come into effect, the Accord made renewed war with Russia unavoidable, by challenging its mastery of the Ukraine. Inadequate taxation and renewed domestic unrest undercut the Poles' ability to exploit a string of military successes. At the little village of Andrusovo in 1667, the exhausted protagonists concluded an armistice, to run for thirteen years. Smolensk and its hinterland remained in Russian hands. The Ukraine was partitioned: the territories east of the river Dnieper, with the addition of Kiev – which the Russians promised to restore within two years (they never did) – remained under Russian control; the 'right bank' Ukraine remained nominally Polish.

During the wars, John Casimir and his queen, Louise-Marie de Gonzague, made no secret of their hopes of strengthening royal power. Though they dallied with the thought of reforming the veto, their attention focused on securing the succession. The childless couple looked above all to Louis XIV of France. The Great Condé; his son, the duke of Enghien; the French client Philip Wilhelm, duke of Neuburg – all were seriously considered. Once the immediate pressures of the 'Deluge' eased, the king and queen pushed for election in the king's own lifetime. The Polish nobility and Poland's neighbours were equally alarmed. The court's efforts to destroy its chief opponent, Jerzy Lubomirski, provoked rebellion. Its defeat at Mątwy on 12 July 1666 cost the royal army 4,000 casualties; the king barely escaped with his life. Only Lubomirski's own death the following year put an end to his plotting, but his memory lived on to the end of the Commonwealth – to most, an exemplary defender of noble liberties against royal absolutism. The embattled John Casimir abdicated on 16 September 1668, to die in France in 1672.

Even at John Casimir's election, prognosticators saw in his Latin title 'Ioannes Casimirus Rex' the legend 'Initium Calamitatum Regni' – the beginning of the calamities of the realm. The wars devastated huge swaths of the Commonwealth, inflicting damage to match anything in the Germany of the Thirty Years War. The *szlachta* greeted with suspicion the king's vow in April 1656 to alleviate the oppressions of the common people – the peasantry and townsmen fighting so vigorously in the guerrilla war. Pressures on the peasantry intensified as landlords tried to reconstruct their devastated properties; the ruined towns became an even feebler political and economic force.

The *szlachta* had borne the brunt of Khmel'nytskyi's fury. So too had their protégés, the Jews, who dominated the commerce of Ukrainian settlements, in the wake of the *szlachta*'s colonization drives. Though the figures remain hotly disputed, up to 10,000 Jews may have perished during the Cossack rebellion; many more would have been massacred without the protection of magnate militias. However, amid the decay of commercial and urban life, the Jews, unconstrained by medieval guild regulations, more entrepreneurial, and actively encouraged by their noble patrons, were able to consolidate and expand their already strong position in Polish commercial life, particularly in the smaller townships. Even in the many royal towns which forbade Jewish settlement, the Christian guilds found themselves frequently on the defensive, as Jewish traders settled in suburbs or noble-owned enclaves beyond municipal jurisdiction. Even in the Polish Ukraine, the Jews were rapidly restored. Nowhere in Europe were there so many Jews as in Poland-Lithuania (around a million by the 1770s). But their dominance of much of commercial and economic life, their distinctive faith and culture, also gave rise to resentment, envy and hatreds which have never fully been excised.

The wars eroded Poland's toleration, even if they did not destroy

Map 4   The Polish-Lithuanian Commonwealth in the later sixteenth and seventeenth centuries

Narva

Novgorod •

• Pskov

⌐, 1721)⌐

• MOSCOW

vina   • Polotsk
        [(to Russia, 1667)]
        •Vitebsk
          •Smolensk
        Andrusovo

RUSSIA

• Minsk

SCALE

0   50 100 150 200 250 300 350 km
0   50   100   150   200 miles

N

[(to Russia, 1667)]
•Kiev   Hadziacz •
  •Pereiaslav
óg   • Cudnów   *Dnieper*   • Poltava
        [(under Turkish rule, 1672–1699)]
iczacz
Kamieniec Podolski   [(to Russia, 1667)]
•Khotin   Batoh •
  Dniester   Sicz •
Tutora •
                Ochakov •
        Prut
MOLDAVIA
                            CRIMEAN
ɴIA   **TATARS**
OTTOMAN

LLACHIA   **EMPIRE**

Boundary between the Crown and the Grand Duchy of Lithuania after 1569

Border of Poland–Lithuania after 1629/34

Border of territories ceded to Russia in 1667

Territory under Turkish rule, 1672–99

it. The Swedish Lutheran and Russian Orthodox invasions were seen as a religious war. Protestants were convenient scapegoats. Although the treaty of Oliva safeguarded continued public Lutheran worship in Polish Prussia, elsewhere it was a different tale. Most great magnates had long converted to Catholicism – Bogusław Radziwiłł, the last great Calvinist patron, died in 1669. And although mainstream Protestantism was too deeply rooted to be eradicated, its lesser fringes could be picked off. After all, the Warsaw Confederacy of 1573 had been a compromise, a grudging safety valve to prevent civil collapse. The open-ended consensus to preserve peace 'among those who differ and dispute in religion and rite' had been matched by no specific commitments towards non-Catholics. The bishops remained overwhelmingly hostile to wider toleration; the vast majority of the *szlachta* remained Catholic. The 1573 agreement had had only limited effect in preventing sporadic religious violence in the towns. As the network of Jesuit colleges thickened (11 schools in 1599, 46 by 1700, 66 by 1773), as elected kings looked to the Church to provide them with support, so the Counter-Reformation began to take its toll. As early as 1638, the antitrinitarian school and printing-press at Raków in western Poland had been closed, following charges of blasphemy. Confessional war left little room for mutual tolerance. The 1658 Sejm ordered the exile of all antitrinitarians.

The Commonwealth's failure to reassert its position over the Ukraine combined with the opposition to the Vasas' supposedly absolutist intentions to break the back of Poland's pre-eminent position in eastern Europe. Domestic politics fused with the foreign policies of its neighbours. Opponents of strong monarchy, that is, defenders of noble liberties, saw nothing wrong in conniving with foreign rulers to thwart any moves towards more effective government. The treaty of Stockholm of 1667, between Sweden and Brandenburg, was the first in a long series of agreements between neighbour-states aiming specifically to block any political reform in the Commonwealth.

The effects appeared starkly under John Casimir's successors. The magnate families which had backed French or Austrian candidates would not forgive Michael Wiśniowiecki's elevation, forced on them by *szlachta* gathered in unprecedented numbers for the election (80,000 according to some observers). Disgusted by endless grandee rivalries, the nobility insisted on one of their own – the impoverished scion of a once great family, whose father had distinguished himself (more by brutality than effectiveness) in the wars against Khmel'nytskyi. A coterie centred around the primate, Nicholas Prażmowski, and the grand Crown *hetman*, John Sobieski, spent most of Wiśniowiecki's brief reign plotting his overthrow. When, in 1672, Poland was invaded by the Turks, it stood on the verge of civil war. Once Kamieniec Podolski fell and Lwów was besieged, Polish negotiators had little choice but to capitulate. By the treaty of Buczacz, Podole and Kamieniec were ceded outright to the Porte; the right-bank Ukraine was placed under its overlordship. The *Rzeczpospolita* agreed to pay an annual tribute to the Turks. The Sejm of February–April 1673 rejected the terms; it voted unprecedented sums for a new army; but it could not heal internal divisions. Sobieski's spectacular destruction, in November, of a Turkish army at Khotin could not be followed up, as Lithuanian forces, commanded by his rival, Michael Pac, refused co-operation; the unpaid Crown troops deserted in droves.

Yet the victory created a huge wave of euphoria, which secured the throne for Sobieski (King Michael died before news of the victory arrived). To Michael Pac, and to most magnate clans, every victory the new king gained would be one for Sobieski and his family (Wiśniowiecki at least had the good grace to be impotent) and promised to do nothing at all for the liberties that constituted the Commonwealth. Pac would not furnish the military support from Lithuania which Sobieski needed. At Żurawno in October 1676, the king had to settle for a renewal of the terms of 1672 – the Turks dropped only the demand for tribute.

Sobieski's plans for recovering Ducal Prussia for Poland (preferably as a hereditary Sobieski fief) were dashed by the same opposition. His hopes of building up support around the Sapieha family in Lithuania backfired as the Sapiehas exploited his patronage to tighten their own grip on the Grand Duchy and then turned against the king as virulently as had the Pac family. Monarchs would continue to be hamstrung by an opposition which elsewhere would have been viewed as treasonable; in Poland-Lithuania its mischief was genuinely seen as a defence of ancestral liberty.

When the Turks finally attacked Austria and besieged Vienna in 1683, Sobieski appreciated that he could recover lost territories only by alliance with the Habsburgs. The victory which the combined Polish and Imperialist forces won under his command at Vienna, on 12 September 1683, was – for Poland and its king – a mirage. Crucified by domestic politics, Sobieski was always in a position of weakness – made only worse by relations with Muscovy. Between 1676 and 1681, Tsar Feodor's government actually went to war against the Turks in an unsuccessful bid to push them from the right-bank Ukraine and impose Russian suzerainty. The Russians even warned that, unless the Poles finally agreed to convert the Andrusovo armistice into a definitive peace, they would realign with the Turks. The Poles had little choice but to give way. The treaty of Moscow of 6 May 1686 finally confirmed Andrusovo. Kiev was definitively lost. Moreover, the Russians secured the role of protectors of the position of the Commonwealth's Orthodox – in effect, giving the tsars the right to intervene in Poland's domestic affairs. For Sobieski, it was one of the worst humiliations of his reign – but so dire was Poland's situation, that he had no option but to ratify the treaty. At least it obviated a Russian invasion, but Moscow's ineffectual campaigns against the Crimean Tatars brought Poland no direct benefits. Polish military efforts for the rest of the war were largely restricted to unhappy thrusts into Moldavia. Their expeditions helped weaken Turkish resistance in the Balkans, but it was primarily thanks to Imperialist successes that the Poles finally regained Kamieniec, Podole and the right-bank Ukraine at the peace of Carlowitz in January 1699 – after Sobieski's death.

Sobieski sought solace during his last years in accumulating a massive private fortune and beautifying his private residences. He died on 17 June 1696, in his beloved palace of Wilanów, outside Warsaw, almost as despised as his two predecessors. The rivalries and unpopularity of his sons doomed their bids for the throne. The energy of the Wettin elector, Frederick Augustus I of Saxony, his cynical conversion from Lutheranism to Catholicism and his paying off of the army's arrears, assured him of the throne over his dithering French rival, the prince of Bourbon-Conti.

The new king, hereditary ruler of the wealthiest state of the Holy

Roman Empire, schemed to weld Saxony and Poland into a new northern power. Along with the young tsar Peter I, he envisaged relieving the teenage Charles XII of Sweden's Baltic empire. Swedish Livonia would become a Wettin principality. Augustus invaded Livonia in February 1700, using Saxon troops stationed in Lithuania supposedly to keep the peace between the Sapiehas and their opponents. In November 1700, the Sapiehas were resoundingly defeated by their rivals, but the hopes that Augustus had of exploiting their discomfiture were dashed by his own troops' miserable performance against the Swedes and the crushing rout of the Russian army at Narva by Charles XII in the same month. The Poles' attempts to persuade Charles that Augustus' attack was nothing to do with them found no sympathy. For five years, Charles pursued Augustus, hoping to terrorize the Poles onto his side. In January 1704, Charles even stage-managed the election, by a rump of a few hundred *szlachta*, of his own puppet king, Stanisław Leszczyński. Much of the time, Charles was fighting Saxon or Russian, rather than Polish troops, many of whom were kept waiting in the wings, living off the land, while their commanders, the *hetmani*, awaited the outcome of the conflict. Rival confederacies supported the two kings, and once more civil war took hold.

Only in 1706 did Charles judge the international situation right to strike Saxony itself and force Augustus to abdicate as king of Poland. He was reinstated by grace and favour of Peter the Great, following the Swedish disaster at Poltava in July 1709. While Charles had bogged himself down in Poland, Peter had rebuilt Russia's army. After Poltava, he used it to impose his protectorate over Poland, which was to remain a liberty-addicted, unreformed Commonwealth, a massive security buffer along Russia's western border. Peter was satisfied with what he extracted from Sweden at Nystad in 1721: Karelia, Ingria, Estonia and, most valuable of all, Livonia – once Poland's own. The *Rzeczpospolita* counted for so little that it did not even participate in the peace talks.

Throughout the war, extra-parliamentary assemblies struggled to maintain some kind of army and raise some kind of taxation. The 'General Assembly' of 1710 optimistically voted an army 64,000 strong. In fact, supply depended on a combination of looting and *ad hoc* decisions by local *sejmiki*. The *hetmani* acted as regional

16   A fat Polish noble (*szlachcic*); sketch (1776) by Jean-Pierre Norblin
(1745–1830). Norblin was active in Poland 1774–1804, benefiting
especially from the patronage of the Czartoryski family.

warlords, regarding the troops as their own private armies. The
exactions of Swedish, Saxon and Russian forces, famine and plague
compounded the miseries – as bad as anything suffered during the
'Deluge'. The devastation of the towns, the destruction of schools
and churches plunged literary and cultural life into a frozen torpor.

Augustus' quartering of Saxon troops in Poland provoked the
szlachta in November 1715 to form the Confederacy of Tarnogród
in defence of its liberties. The more disciplined Saxons might have

crushed the movement, had not Russian diplomats, backed by Russian arms, brokered a settlement profitable to Peter. The treaty of Warsaw of November 1716 gave Poland new constitutional and fiscal machinery. Most Saxon troops were to be evacuated. The army was fixed at 24,000 units of pay (in real terms, perhaps half that number of men) drawn from specified, permanent revenues – no longer under the control of the *sejmiki*. The troops themselves were dislocated across specific crown estates. A permanent budget was thus established – to support a pitifully small force utterly incapable of resisting any invader. The so-called 'Silent Sejm' of 1 February 1717 confirmed the deal, without debate, in a single day. The Commonwealth had been reduced to a *de facto* Russian protectorate. The threat of armed Russian intervention, encouraged by Peter's many clients in Poland, frustrated all attempts which Augustus was to make to restore his freedom of action. That his son was to succeed him would owe nothing to the king's efforts – it, too, would owe everything to Russia.

Above all the nobility wanted their liberties and freedoms preserved. Ever since the arrival of the Vasas on the Polish throne, almost every monarch seemed to have been plotting to destroy their privileges. The most recent and greatest threat had come from Augustus II and it had been checked. The Great Northern War was a traumatic, destructive event from which the Commonwealth had gained nothing – but it had, at least, emerged with its freedoms intact. Poland owed its physical survival above all to the protection of Divine Providence. The prime task of the nobility was to ensure that it maintained a perpetual vigilance against the monarchy, the sole real threat to its position.

Augustus II died in February 1733. An emotional reaction against foreign rulers and their dubious designs swept the country. A 'Piast', supposedly more attuned to the libertarian spirit of the nobility, was waiting in the wings – none other than the Stanisław Leszczyński pushed onto a temporary throne almost thirty years previously by Charles XII. In exile, his daughter, Marie, had in 1726 won the European marriage sweepstake by becoming bride to Louis XV of France. Around 13,000 nobles, confident of French support, enthusiastically elected Leszczyński in September 1733. But Russia and its Austrian ally had decided that continued Wettin

17   A thin Polish noble (*szlachcic*); sketch by Jean-Pierre Norblin, 1776.

rule in Poland was preferable to that of the king of France's father-in-law. Russia was anxious to maintain its new pre-eminence not only in Poland, but in fractious Sweden, a shadow of its old self. Leszczyński was too closely associated with the adventure of Charles XII to be acceptable in St Petersburg. Once Frederick Augustus II of Saxony promised to preserve the Polish constitution, Vienna and Petersburg went to war on his behalf. In December 1733, 4,000 nobles, 'protected' by Russian troops, elected him King Augustus III. Russian arms ensured his triumph. In Italy and on the Rhine, the French secured what they wanted from this War of the Polish Succession. In October 1735 the Preliminaries of Vienna delivered Austria's satellite duchy of Lorraine to France. Leszczyński would be allowed to rule over it as nominal duke; on his death, it would pass to France; meanwhile, he could keep his title, king of Poland. No one consulted the Poles about the terms – there was little point.

Amid the political degradation, Augustus III's reign saw a kind of healing. By the late 1740s, much of the worst damage after the Great Northern War had been repaired. Although Poland never regained its sixteenth-century pre-eminence as purveyor of grain to Europe, cereals and other commodity exports – timber, cattle, horses, naval stores – pump-primed prosperity for great and middling landowners. The Catholic Church, with its international connections, was in the forefront of a cultural reconstruction. The two teaching orders, the Piarists and the Jesuits, began to compete from the 1740s and 1750s to provide the kind of elite education they were offering in Italy and France. Dresden was a second home to many Polish nobles – and a channel for new ideas. 'Enlightenment' became chic. The most effective exponent of reinvigorating old traditions through new philosophies was the Piarist Stanisław Konarski, whose Collegium Nobilium, established in Warsaw in 1740, served as a model school for the more fashionable nobility. In 1733, as an active Leszczyński supporter, he had tried to persuade his countrymen that liberty without sovereignty was unsustainable. His *On the means to efficacious councils* of 1761–3 was a blistering demolition of the *liberum veto* and its evils. More than that, however, it was also a plea for something Poland had never had: a truly powerful parliament, which devised and decided policy, something far more potent than a tutelary body whose main function was to preserve noble liberties. It was to be, in its own right, an elected absolute ruler, more powerful even than the English parliament which Konarski admired so strongly. Those who saw in the veto a monstrous constitutional aberration could not praise Konarski enough; those for whom the veto was 'the palladium of liberty' could barely contain their vitriol at the presumption of a clergyman (even if nobly born) to lecture the ruling nation. Its recourse to new ideas, not least in its unprecedented exaltation of the English constitution, forced even conservative critics to look beyond their homespun sloganeering.

Konarski's ideas found favour with one powerful grouping – the Czartoryski family. Of ancient, princely Lithuanian stock, they had long languished in obscurity, until, under Augustus II, a combination of royal patronage and useful marriages built them up into a formidable political force. The Czartoryskis appreciated that if Poland were to be anything other than a passive victim of international circumstances, the whole shape of its politics had to be recast. Even under Augustus II they cautiously advocated restrictions on the *liberum veto*. They believed that they could both preserve liberty in the Commonwealth and run it themselves – in the manner of the Whig grandees of Britain, whom they so admired. The cultured, ruthless brothers August and Michael looked to Russia to break the impasse of domestic politics. To them, the worst danger came from Frederick II of Prussia. His conquest of Habsburg Silesia between 1740 and 1742 could only stimulate the traditional Hohenzollern appetite for Polish Prussia. Ties with Russia, the Czartoryskis felt, would offer some protection.

Under Augustus III, Poland periodically served as transit route for the warring armies of Prussia, Russia and Austria, even the Ottoman Porte. At least the full horrors of the past were not repeated. Exactions were localized, on occasion even orderly. To large landowners, insulated from the incidental damage which foreign armies caused, their custom furnished useful market opportunities. Poland was, technically, neutral during the Seven Years War of 1756–63, though quite unable to keep foreign troops off its soil. But it was neutral for the wrong reasons. Its army was pitiably weak, its parliaments paralysed and its leaders unable to formulate policy in the midst of a conflict which, as some of its politicians appreciated, was of vital strategic importance to it. At the very least, if Frederick the Great kept Silesia, Polish territories would surely be next on his menu. For most of the war, Austria's client, Saxony, was under Prussian occupation. Augustus III, who, like his father, always preferred the delights of Dresden, was forced into a prolonged residence in Warsaw. He returned to a devastated Saxony only in March 1763, to die that October. Russia again

18   A view of Polish political life: Jean-Pierre Norblin's sketch of a *sejmik* (local parliamentary assembly) meeting outside a church. Eighteenth-century English electors might have felt almost at home.

19　Another view of Polish political life: painting by Canaletto the Younger (Antonio Eugenio Bellotto, 1721–80) of the election of king Stanislaw August Poniatowski in 1764 (painted 1778). Canaletto was court painter to Augustus III and Stanislaw August Poniatowski.

settled the Polish succession – this time, single-handedly. Its troops had been stationed in Poland since 1757 – topping them up to ensure the return of the preferred choice of the new empress, Catherine II, was an easy matter.

The man elected king in September 1764 was Stanisław Ponia-towski, nephew to Michael and August Czartoryski. In St Peters-burg on diplomatic business in 1754–5, he had become the grand duchess Catherine's lover. He desperately wanted to reform Poland – he even adopted the coronation name of 'August' as a sign of his wish to be his country's renovator, just as Augustus had been of the Roman world. Catherine saw in him, however, not a reformer, but a pliant, accommodating puppet. Her ambitious plans to succeed where Peter the Great had failed – to thrust back the frontiers of the Ottoman Porte and to project Russian influence into the Holy Roman Empire – posited a manageable, not merely anarchic, Poland. A soft intellectual reliant on her financial bounty (she even paid for Stanisław August's coronation) seemed ideal.

The empress sought to further her control by reversing the disadvantaged position of Poland's Protestants. The 1733 Convo-cation parliament had barred them from the Sejm. But Protestants continued to be the recipients of crown estates, local offices, even army officerships, up to and including general rank. They played a key role in the public life of Royal Prussia and its towns. The execution of ten leading burghers in the aftermath of a religious riot in Thorn in 1724 barely dented the dominance of the town's Lutheran elite. That the overwhelming majority of the Polish nobility were hostile to the Protestants is unquestionable – yet at a time when Catholic nobles constantly complained at the lack of offices and rewards open to them, their Protestant counterparts continued to play a role in public life far more prominent than that enjoyed by religious minorities in countries such as Britain or the Netherlands which regarded themselves as the van of European civilization. Catherine counted on the Protestants to form a depend-ent, reliable agency. In a Europe whose intellectuals despised the backwardness of the Catholic Church, her supposedly enlightened intervention might even help cleanse the stigma of her murderous way to the Romanov throne. Of course, she went through the motions of improving the position of Poland's Orthodox – but

Orthodox nobles of any standing had almost disappeared. Her real
energies centred on the Protestants.

No Polish politician seriously dared endorse a massive, sudden
restoration of the old Protestant position. The empress's efforts in
this respect collided with those of Stanisław August to implement
his own reform agenda. Catherine could accept the shackling of
hitherto irresponsible ministers such as the military generalissimos,
the *hetmani* or the treasurers by collegiate boards; she could not
accept major restrictions on, let alone the abolition of, the *liberum
veto* – precisely what the king hoped to secure at the 1766 Sejm. The
Russian ambassador warned that his troops would tear Warsaw
down 'stone by stone' unless the assembly reaffirmed the veto in
full. Any form of military resistance with the feeble forces available
was out of the question. A reluctant and humiliated Sejm gave way,
conscious of what the full reaffirmation of the veto meant.

The *szlachta* could accept even the imposition of a king from
Russia. They had so far swallowed transit marches and occasional
military intervention. But Catherine's systematic, sustained appli-
cation of force to bend their constitution to her plans was something new. The last straw was the Russian treatment of the
confederated Sejm of 1767–8. It was only by the use of force, terror
and even the deportation of opponents to the Russian interior that
Catherine secured her aims: the opening up of the Sejm and Senate
to dissenters; a senatorial seat for the Orthodox bishop of
Mohylew (a Russian subject, imposed on the Poles); a restructuring
of parliamentary procedures, obviating its total disruption, but
retaining the veto for all but the most insignificant legislation. To
cap it all, the Poles were made to accept a Russian guarantee of
their laws and constitution, and even for their territory, binding
them hand and foot to their seemingly irresistible neighbour.

Even before the Sejm ended, a group of nobles gathered at Bar, in
Podole, in late February 1768, to set up a confederacy aiming
explicitly to reverse the new religious settlement. Their further, as
yet unstated, plans called for the overthrow of Poniatowski and a
restoration of the Saxon Wettins. The Russians easily crushed the
initial outbreak; but the Confederacy of Bar opened the way to
four years of civil and guerrilla warfare, with uncontrollable
international repercussions.

In October 1768, the exasperated Ottoman Porte declared war. It had long feared that Russia was set on reducing the Commonwealth to a supply base for a future reckoning with Turkey. The conflict brought Russia an almost unending string of military and naval victories. The peace of Kuchuk Kainardji of June 1774 was a dreadful humiliation for the Turks, not only costing them territory, but forcing them to abandon their lordship over the Crimea. Conducted over distances almost unimaginable in western Europe, the triumphant campaigning imposed a massive strain on Russia. It was to provoke the great Pugachev revolt. The resources to crush the guerrillas of Bar were not there. Neither Poniatowski nor the Czartoryskis were willing to assist the Russians; on the contrary, they hoped to use the Confederacy to secure, at the very least, a reversal of Russia's guarantee; even to escape its clutches altogether.

Russia's thrusts into the Danube basin alarmed Austria. Austria's ally and Turkey's friend, France, was equally anxious to roll back the Russian advance. France, Austria and Turkey each gave greater or lesser degrees of support to the Barists. The resulting tensions were brilliantly exploited by Frederick of Prussia. Russian power, which had so nearly destroyed him during the Seven Years War, had come as a shock. In April 1764, he had formed an alliance with Catherine and had seconded her activities in Poland. He appreciated that Russia's was the dominant role in Poland. He loyally (if querulously) supported Catherine's Turkish war with financial subsidies. Wary of direct military involvement, he realized that he could yet draw profit from the conflict. He constantly warned Russia that immoderate expansionism would provoke the Habsburgs. That, he claimed, would draw in their ally France – a new front would thus be opened up in western Europe, engulfing the whole continent in an uncontrollable conflagration. It was disinformation of the highest order – neither Austria nor France was in any condition to fight a major war. But it enabled him to achieve his ends. Catherine, egged on by advisers who saw in grabbing Polish lands opportunities for personal profit, was persuaded that an apocalyptic escalation could be averted only by desisting from outright gains in the Balkans. Instead, Russia should seek 'compensation' from the original cause of the trouble, the *Rzeczpospolita*.

Map 5   The Polish-Lithuanian Commonwealth in the eighteenth century.

Of course, Austria, too, had to be pacified – by taking matching territory from Poland; the disadvantage that Habsburg expansion would confer on Prussia could be countered only if Russia allowed its faithful ally to take its 'share of the cake'.

Russia had had its eyes on the Lithuanian lands west of the Smolensk area since the 1740s. Catherine's territorial guarantee of 1768 was elastically worded. And while the empress had never intended to share Poland with anyone (least of all Frederick), many in St Petersburg were persuaded that the road of all-round compensation offered the best exit from the imbroglio. Russia would, after all, still control what remained of Poland.

The precipitating factor was Austrian annexation of small strips of Polish highlands along the rugged Carpathian border. Frederick remorselessly played up the extent of this petty territorial larceny, warned of (non-existent) French preparations for war and, by 1772, had persuaded the Russians that a deal had to be cut. On 5 August, three bilateral conventions signed between Russia, Austria and Prussia in St Petersburg gave Catherine the territories along the headwaters of the Dvina and Dnieper; the Austrians received extensive lands along the upper Vistula and San rivers; and Frederick finally obtained Polish Prussia – without Danzig, deemed too valuable by Catherine to deliver to her all-too-clever friend. Even so, in economic terms, he was the biggest gainer, seizing Poland's most valuable lands and the economic jugular of the Vistula (which he proceeded to squeeze for all he could for the rest of his reign). Practical measures of occupation began in April 1772, in anticipation of the final agreements. Most Poles were astonished – rumours of Partition had circulated for years; their own kings had warned them of their likely fate. The protection so long afforded them by God and the European balance had finally run its course.

The humiliation was compounded by a prolonged Sejm, insisted on by the partitioning powers. It was bludgeoned into giving formal approval for the whole partition. Stanisław August's hopes, that in return for loss of territory the monarchy's powers might be strengthened or the *liberum veto* rescinded, were dashed. The 1768 constitutional settlement was reaffirmed, though the concessions to the dissenters were drastically scaled back – the great bulk of

20 Rejtan at the Sejm of 1773: an iconic painting of an emotional protest against the First Partition by Jan Matejko (1838–93). Painted 1866. The painting infuriated a number of Polish aristocrats who objected to this close identification of their ancestors with a less than happy turning-point in Polish history. One complained: 'The exploitation of an historical scandal for mere popularity's sake has never been the task of artistic masters.' On the other hand, the Emperor Franz Joseph was sufficiently taken with it to purchase it for 50,000 francs after its exhibition in the Paris salon of 1867.

Protestants were, in any case, now under Prussian rule. The bishopric of Mohylew, the last Orthodox see, had passed to Russia. A new administrative body, the 'Permanent Council', was set up to provide a minimum of day-to-day administrative continuity and coordination. The major innovation was the creation of a Commission for National Education, aimed at supervising and modernizing the curriculum in the secondary colleges and the two 'Principal Schools' (universities) of Kraków and Wilno. It was made possible by the papal abolition (under French and Spanish pressure) of the Jesuits in 1773: the Order's schools and properties furnished the backbone of the new educational regime. But it took a decade for the Commission to extricate itself from its teething troubles – longer still to overcome noble suspicions of its new-fangled ideas.

The Commonwealth was too weak to resist dismemberment. Its society and army were demoralized, bewildered, humiliated and divided. The most spectacular act of defiance, attaining near-mythological status in folk memory, occurred in April 1773, when Tadeusz Rejtan blocked access to the Sejm's debating-chamber in a vain protest against the inevitable. Although the demographic estimates can be only tentative, Poland may have lost getting on for 5 million of its 14 million inhabitants, with Austria taking the largest number, over 2.5 million. Poland was deprived of about a third of its territory, including its richest provinces. The frontiers of Austria and Prussia advanced towards the old Polish heartlands. Russia's gains were the most extensive, Prussia's the least, but they were economically and strategically the most valuable. The Austrians rued the day they had allowed themselves to be manoeuvred into a settlement which disproportionately strengthened their hated rival. All three powers extended their guarantees, as solemn as they were worthless, of the new constitutional and territorial order.

The king hoped against hope that the new educational reforms and his generous cultural patronage would eventually permit the emergence of a more mature and responsible citizenry. His reign did indeed see a cultural efflorescence, the culmination of patient efforts of a long generation of individuals, many of them clergymen, many of them foreign immigrants fascinated by the sheer libertarian weirdness of the Polish world, to rebuild the Renaissance grandeurs of its language and literary world. The poetry of Ignacy Krasicki (1735–1801) or Stanisław Trembecki (1740–1812) matched anything produced during the Renaissance. The output of major political and social commentators such as Józef Wybicki (1747–1822) or Hugon Kołłątaj (1750–1812) deliberately eschewed the latinisms of their predecessors and gave the Polish language a new force and sophistication. A cadre of Piarists in Warsaw and Wilno, pupils of Konarski, eagerly collaborating with the Commission for National Education, consciously sought to re-educate the nobility into accepting the need to abolish serfdom, revive the economy and build a new and fairer Commonwealth. The king saw in the Warsaw theatre a means of propagating new ideas. The capital's press was as free and exuberant as any in Europe. Yet all this was not enough. The great majority of the nobility had no time for new-fangled ideas of serf emancipation and were intensely suspicious of the reformed schooling their offspring were being given. The sole means of survival lay, Stanisław August was convinced, in keeping with Russia in the hope of persuading Catherine to countenance further reform. But the last thing Russia wanted was any form of Polish revival. St Petersburg confirmed itself as Poland's unofficial capital. Magnate coteries appealed to the Russian court to put them in positions of profit and power. The king was seen, even by his erstwhile allies, the Czartoryskis, as a Russian cipher, to be used, abused and circumvented. This was what Catherine wanted. So dependent did Poland seem that by 1780, she felt sufficiently confident to withdraw the great majority of her troops.

Some hoped the European diplomatic conjuncture might yet bring salvation. In 1781, Catherine effectively ditched her Prussian alliance, to realign with Joseph II of Austria. Only the Habsburgs, not the Hohenzollerns, could offer effective support for her grandiose ambitions of throwing the Turks out of Europe and establishing her grandson, Constantine, as ruler of a new Greek Empire. Russia's outright annexation of the Crimea in 1783 ultimately brought about a fresh Turkish declaration of war in August 1787.

The Russo-Turkish war of 1787–92 furnished a final interval for the reassertion of Polish sovereignty. Catherine's conviction that her interests were best served by preserving a tried, if not entirely trusted, Poniatowski on the throne led a frustrated opposition to cast about elsewhere for support – Prussia. At the same time, Prussia's new king, Frederick William II, and his chief minister, Friedrich von Hertzberg, hoped to round off earlier gains with the acquisition of Danzig, Thorn and whatever other territories they could: their chosen means was to encourage Polish 'patriotic' indignation against Russia, to foment internal disorders, which they would exploit to secure their aims. When, in October 1788, a new Sejm met, it gloried in an orgy of virulent russophobia. The appalled king, who had a good inkling of the Prussian game, was unable to prevent emotions from running amok. In what amounted to a constitutional coup, the Sejm took over the running of the country. Egged on by Prussia, it repudiated the 1773–5 settlement and guarantees.

Russia's distractions – the Turkish war, combined with a war with Sweden between July 1788 and August 1790 – allowed the Poles to conduct a prolonged debate as to how the state should be reformed. For the great majority, there could be no pushing back of the clock to the fat times and constitutional anarchy of Augustus III's reign, although there also remained powerful individuals who hankered precisely after this. The offer of an alliance from Prussia (designed to reassure the Poles as to Prussian intentions), and successful insistence that the Russians should desist from using Polish territory as a transit route to the Balkan front helped convinced the 'Four Years Sejm' that the era of humiliations was over. The new parliament set about dismantling much of the constitutional machinery put in place after 1773; it voted to increase the army from around 18,000 to 100,000 – but only too late did it give serious consideration to paying for it. Patriotic fervour, not political calculation, carried all before it. Events in France, of which the uncensorable press kept the public fully informed, added to the general excitement. Even the hitherto largely passive townsfolk of Warsaw – whose population during the Sejm exceeded 100,000 – began actively joining in the politics. Something like a true 'public sphere' of uncontrolled conversation and debate across the spectrum of the literate emerged, focused on the capital. It was possible to publish just about anything. The jovial clergyman Franciszek Jezierski, in his *Miscellany of words alphabetically arranged* of 1791, even tore apart Rafał Leszczyński's much-loved late seventeenth-century soundbite (which had so impressed Rousseau he used it in his *Social Contract*), 'Malo periculosam libertatem quam quietam servitutem' – 'I prefer dangerous liberty to tranquil slavery'. It was nonsense – a nation which survived, no matter how oppressive its government, still had the chance to reform; a nation which lost its liberty would lose everything. Even a few years earlier, no one would have dared utter such sentiments in a society which did indeed seem to place 'freedom' above self-preservation.

The most important achievement of the dizzy years of 1788–92 was the experience of unprecedented rule-by-parliament. Poniatowski's reign had been a harsh political school. For all the brutality which accompanied them, the Sejmy of 1764, 1766, 1767–8, 1773–5 and 1776 hammered home a new principle: that parliament could and should legislate; and that it was for the rest of the country to follow. For two centuries or more, the *szlachta* had been unwilling to learn these lessons themselves. Now, others had inculcated them. The Four Years Sejm was the culmination of this process of forced political education, as a political elite discovered that it could create new administrative bodies, vote new taxation, take diplomatic and political initiatives – that it could do more than simply defend old privileges, that it could govern. If old phobias of royal absolutism survived, some politicians at least came to appreciate that there was more to politics than the long-established keeping of the phantom power of monarchy in check.

The sense of freedom provided by the temporary lifting of the Russian protectorate was not always well used. Garrulity ruled in the debates, as individuals showered the assembly with pet projects and the Sejm and its sub-committees tried vainly to cover all aspects of government activity. So matters might have gone on, had not the opposition to Stanisław August split: between those who wanted genuine reform, even enlightened social policies, and those who merely wanted a return to the status quo of Augustus III's reign. It was the former who mended their fences to the king; and it was in collaboration with him that, on 3 May 1791, in a legitimist *coup d'état*, they sprang a new constitution on Poland: a curious

DZIEŃ TRZECIEGO MAYA MDCCXCI

21   Jean-Pierre Norblin's sketch of the oath to the Constitution of
3 May, 1791.

hybrid of royal hopes for a more vigorous monarchy and a more
effective parliament, with checks and balances to curb any despotic
tendencies. The two sacred cows of the *Rzeczpospolita*'s history
were slaughtered: the *liberum veto* was abolished and, even more
remarkably, elective monarchy was rejected. This last issue gave
rise to the most heated and prolonged debates, in and outside
parliament. Only the most resolutely obstinate were prepared to
defend the veto. On the other hand, 'free' royal elections had, for
two centuries, been mythologized into the most effective mech-
anism for the restraining of kingly pretensions. In practice, they
had proved a disaster. Almost every royal election had been the
occasion for internecine strife and an opening for foreign interference. Gradually, the sheer volume of polemic in favour of
hereditary kingship let a reluctant nobility be coaxed into some
appreciation of this. A dynastic throne was offered to Augustus III's
grandson, Frederick Augustus III of Saxony. The English principles

of ministerial accountability and monarchic irresponsibility were adopted. New central commissions, reflecting an obsession with a Montesquieu-inspired conception of the separation of legislative, executive and judicial branches, were introduced.

Townsmen were given limited rights of participation in the Sejm in matters directly affecting commerce. Poland's politically active 'bourgeoisie' was still very weak and largely confined to Warsaw. More thoughtful souls among the *szlachta* were keen to play up its potential role for the future. Townsmen settled gratefully for what they were given. The Sejm never got around to proper consideration of the place of Poland's many Jews, despite their prominent commercial role. They had a vibrant culture of their own, but they continued to remain outside the political framework. Peasants were given little, beyond a vague commitment to the state's legal protection – but even this was a major turning-point after almost three centuries of letting noble landowners have their way over their serfs. On the other hand, peasants migrating to Poland were assured of their personal freedom. The conservative nature of the so-called 'Statute of Government' of 3 May was reflected in the treatment of religion, which had for so long dogged the Polish–Lithuanian enterprise. Catholicism was declared the ruling faith; freedom of worship 'according to the laws of the land' was promised, but 'apostasy' from Catholicism was prohibited. It was only very grudgingly that subsequent legislation allowed the Uniate metropolitan a seat in the Senate. The changes promised far more than was delivered – but they were radical enough to alarm both Russia and Prussia: only struggling Austria welcomed the Third of May Constitution, for its policy-makers hoped that a revived Poland might be turned into an ally against Prussia.

The new constitution was fêted throughout Europe: in Paris, because it carried the promise of even backward Poland joining the revolutionary bandwagon; in London, because it was not French and the Polish minister produced a nicely honed translation which made it appear almost English. Of course, the constitution sealed Poland's fate. The Saxon Elector did not dare take up the offer of the throne. Russia could not tolerate such a show of defiance in its vassal. As soon as the Turkish war was over, in May 1792, over 90,000 troops poured across the frontier, overwhelming the untried Polish army. The Prussians refused to honour their defensive alliance on the grounds that they had not been consulted over the new constitution. In St Petersburg, half a dozen Polish malcontents proclaimed that they had set up a confederacy in the border village of Targowica, in defence of Polish liberty. It was true – 'Targowica' (a political insult which has lost none of its venom even in the twenty-first century) was the last gasp of the 'Liberty' that the Third of May Constitution tried to redefine. Yet the many for whom the Third of May was a step too far could not but despise the diehards who invoked the empress's protection.

Targowica's leadership embarked on an orgy of score-settling and self-enrichment. Poniatowski's accession to the Confederacy, encouraged by his own ministers, in the hope that he could restrain its excesses, brought him only an opprobrium from which his memory has not yet recovered. It was clear within weeks that, even backed by Russian troops, the Targowica confederates were utterly incapable of providing effective rule in Poland-Lithuania.

The solution was simple: another Partition. Catherine's latest lover, Platon Zubov, and his friends were all too eager to enrich themselves with the Polish Ukraine. The empress herself had gone fully native and decided that it was her historic mission to reunify the old Rus' lands, so many of which still lay inside the *Rzeczpospolita*'s borders. Prussia could scarcely wait for a deal: since April 1792, it had been supporting Austria in the war against revolutionary France, in the belief that the democratic rabble who had taken over would provide easy pickings. Instead, in September, that rabble turned back the Prussians at Valmy. A humiliated Frederick William looked to Poland for 'compensation' for his trouble. Behind the back of the Austrians, who were committed to defending their possessions in the Netherlands against the French, the Prussians and the Russians signed a second treaty of Partition in St Petersburg on 23 January 1793. Catherine would take an enormous slab of land between the Dvina in the north and the Dniester in the south. Frederick William would acquire a triangle of territory between Silesia and East Prussia. A little buffer-state would be left – for how long? Prussian troops began to enter Poland on 24 January, without even waiting for news of the agreement to be confirmed.

The brutal pantomime of the 1773–5 Sejm was repeated at the parliament summoned to the Lithuanian town of Grodno (Warsaw was deemed too subversive) in June 1793. Consent to the cessions and a new constitutional package, formally reducing Poland to the status of a subservient Russian ally, was extracted from the assembly by the end of September. The rump state of some 4 million inhabitants remained under a Russian occupation which few doubted could be anything other than a prelude to final partition. In desperation, some Poles looked to revolutionary France for support; some even dreamed of a genuinely national uprising. General Tadeusz Kościuszko, who had played a distinguished role in the war of American Independence (on the colonists' side), had good connections in France and had given sterling service against the Russians in the unhappy war of 1792, was chosen to head the insurrection. The rising itself was precipitated by a wave of Russian arrests and proposals to scale back the Polish army – demobilized men were to be pressed into Russian service. It began in Kraków on 25 March 1794. Even after Kościuszko's tactical victory over a small Russian force at Racławice on 4 April, it should have been rapidly snuffed out by the more numerous Russian veterans. But the news of the victory electrified Poland – not since Sobieski had the Poles won a set-piece encounter against a foreign army. Warsaw rose in bloody revolt and expelled the Russian occupiers. Wilno followed suit. Frederick William II, scenting easy victory, joined the Russians. Their combined forces defeated Kościuszko at Szczekociny in June. The Prussians went on to take Kraków but the siege of Warsaw which they undertook with the Russians ended in failure. Lack of heavy artillery, mutual mistrust and an uprising in his newly annexed Polish lands caused Frederick William to break off his operations in early September.

Kościuszko hoped that if the peasantry could be rallied to the cause of independence, revolutionary France might be persuaded to lend its assistance. But unless centuries of serfdom were overturned, the peasantry would never furnish enthusiastic support. Equally, Kościuszko could not fight without the *szlachta* and few of these were prepared to welcome the overturning of the only social and economic system that they knew. They wanted an independent

22   Poland that has disappeared. Two views of the Lubomirski palace in
Równe (now Rivne), Ukraine.

(a) The sketch by Napoleon Orda (1807–83) shows the palace, built in
the 1720s by one of the greatest aristocratic families of Poland, the
Lubomirskis, as it was in the early 1870s. Orda spent some three years
travelling around the territories of the partitioned Commonwealth,
making sketches of buildings and monuments in an attempt to keep a
sense of Polish national spirit alive.

(b) The photograph shows the same palace, as it was in 1925. Its location
placed it in some of the most bitterly contested lands between Russian and
Austrian forces during the First World War, when it served as an Austrian
hospital. It was devastated in 1920 during the Polish–Bolshevik war, and
destroyed by fire in 1927. Now nothing remains.

Poland, but very few could imagine a free peasantry. Peasant support did, indeed, play a key role at the battle of Racławice – but Kościuszko could at best only admonish, cajole and plead with landowners to reduce peasant obligations. His Proclamation of Połaniec of 7 May 1794, declaring all peasants personally free and cutting back their labour services, was largely a dead letter. As for revolutionary France, it offered revolutionary rhetoric, but nothing else.

It was to anticipate the arrival of Russian reinforcements under General Suvorov that, on 10 October, a badly outnumbered Kościuszko attacked General Fersen's corps at Maciejowice, southeast of Warsaw. Kościuszko's army was defeated; he was captured. On 4 November, Suvorov's troops stormed the poorly fortified suburb of Praga, across the Vistula from Warsaw. Around 10,000 people were massacred. Warsaw capitulated the following day. The Rising was over.

This time, Vienna would not miss out. It had begun to send troops across the Polish border in June. Catherine was now ready to include the Austrians. On 3 January 1795, Austrian and Russian diplomats signed a fresh treaty of Partition in St Petersburg, carving up what remained, and assigning a share to Prussia. Russia, once again, took the greatest share. The Austrian portion, smaller than Prussia's, was economically far more valuable. Prussia's would include Warsaw – which would now become a frontier town – but it would have to disgorge Kraków. Catherine was determined to make it quite clear to her allies that it was by her grace and favour that scraps of Poland were being thrown to them. Not that the Prussians were grateful – their relations with Austria had deteriorated so much during their joint offensive against France that the two powers were on the verge of war. It was not until 24 October that a furious Frederick William agreed to accept what he had been given and to hand Kraków over to the Austrians. Prussia was too exhausted to do otherwise.

Since the *Rzeczpospolita* no longer existed, parliamentary ratification of the recent proceedings was irrelevant. On 25 November 1795, Stanisław August Poniatowski signed an act of abdication. He died in St Petersburg on 12 February 1798. On 12 January 1796, a tripartite convention between Russia, Austria and Prussia in St Petersburg insisted on 'the need to abolish everything which can recall the memory of the existence of the kingdom of Poland'. The experiment in noble-democracy was over, a resounding failure. What lived on was the resentment of a noble-nation which, despite being torn apart, still felt itself a coherent unity and which, in its final years, had experienced a new pride in cultural and political resurrection.

PART II

POLAND, AFTER 1795

4

Challenging the partitions, 1795–1864

Poland's cultural and civic revival during the reign of Stanisław August Poniatowski, impressive as it was, was unable to save the Polish state from annihilation in 1795. If anything, by challenging Russia's domination, the Polish reformers had precipitated the very disaster they were desperate to avoid. One can only speculate whether greater patience would have enabled a compliant Poland to survive intact into the nineteenth century under the watchful eye of Empress Catherine's successors, or whether the Napoleonic wars would have dragged Poland, in any case, into some disastrous international quagmire. One way or the other, it is difficult to imagine the Poles escaping unscathed from the upheavals of the Napoleonic period.

Be that as it may, from 1795 until the end of the First World War the extensive lands of the former Polish-Lithuanian Commonwealth remained politically divided and under foreign rule. This long period of partition, punctuated with several heroic but unsuccessful bids for independence, did not destroy Polish high culture or many of the traditions and values of the *szlachta*, out of whose ranks was to emerge the modern Polish intelligentsia, or indeed the Roman Catholicism which distinguished most Polish-speakers from Protestant Prussians and Orthodox Russians, if not Catholic Austrians. Nevertheless, the different patterns of political, economic and social development of the separate parts of historic Poland were to accentuate regional differences, while the emergence of several mutually exclusive ethnic and linguistic nationalisms was to add a further twist to the complex issue of national identity. The answers to the questions 'Who is a Pole?' or 'What is Poland?' would be very different in 1918 from those given in the last decades of the eighteenth century. Not surprisingly, the recreation of a Polish state after 1918 was to be no easy task.

As things stood in the mid-1790s, Poland's prospects were very bleak indeed. For many of its political and intellectual elite their once free and glorious republic, like the great polities of the ancient world, had disappeared for ever; many educated Poles doubted at first whether their nation could survive without a state. The Austro-Prussian-Russian convention of January 1797, removing the very name of Poland from official usage, seemed only to confirm such a pessimistic verdict. The leaders of the movement of national regeneration of 1788–94 had to flee abroad or languished in prison: Kościuszko in St Petersburg until 1796, and Kołłątaj in the Austrian fortress of Olmütz until 1803. All attempts to renew armed resistance within Poland between 1796 and 1798 were likewise brutally crushed. At the same time, many men of property felt that to save their fortunes they had little choice but to adapt to the new political realities and to swear fealty to their new masters. Two young Czartoryski princes were sent as supplicants to the Russian court in the hope of recovering their family's sequestrated estates; the court of Berlin succeeded in winning over Prince Antoni Radziwiłł, who even married a Hohenzollern princess, and Prince Józef Poniatowski, the nephew of Poland's last king, who settled down to a life of revelry in Prussian-occupied Warsaw. By the same token, many Galician aristocrats established fine residences in Vienna.

While delighted to receive such submissions from the Polish aristocracy, the three partitioning powers pursued contrasting policies towards their vast ex-Polish territories in the immediate post-1795 period. Although in her propaganda Catherine II had claimed that she was recovering the lost lands of old Kievan Rus', Russia lacked the more sophisticated bureaucratic machinery of her Germanic neighbours to embark on a thorough policy of russification in a region that was markedly different from the old Muscovite lands. Much of the distinct social order of the western *gubernii* (governorships) of the Russian Empire was to remain unchanged for many decades: the local Polish-Lithuanian landed gentry retained many of its social and legal privileges, and some vestiges of local self-government. Polish schools continued to function, as well as the Lithuanian legal system which had been in operation in the eastern part of the Commonwealth since the sixteenth century. Nor did the Russian authorities do anything to alleviate the conditions of the serfs, whose labour exactions were even increased. This suited many landowners, especially in the southern (Ukrainian) districts, who looked with glee at the attractive prospects of exporting their grain through Odessa, the newly founded Russian emporium on the Black Sea. Only in the area of religion did Catherine attempt to strengthen the 'Russian' character of these lands: most of the Greek Catholic Ukrainian peasants were obliged to return to the Orthodox fold. In the former Grand Duchy of Lithuania, where Catholicism had struck deeper roots, this policy was abandoned by Tsar Paul. The resulting contrast between the Catholicism (both Roman and Uniate) of the Lithuanian-Belarusian north and the Orthodoxy of the Ukrainian south, where social tensions were also more acute, was to contribute markedly to the shaping of very different regional attitudes to the Polish national movement in the Russian Empire in the nineteenth century.

In the Polish lands acquired by Prussia in 1793 and 1795 the Hohenzollerns introduced a centralized and highly staffed system of administration and the Prussian legal system (*Landrecht*); consequently, many noble privileges were respected but the serfs did acquire a degree of protection against seigneurial exploitation. The Polish secondary school system was largely dismantled and German-language education was promoted. Easy credits in Berlin banks and the prospect of handsome profits from grain exports via the Baltic ports helped to mollify the local Polish landowners' feelings of national resentment, although in the long run many estates would be ruined by high mortgages and would fall into German hands. In Austrian Poland the centralized Josephinist system of administration which had been introduced in 'Old' Galicia in the 1780s was now extended to 'New' Galicia acquired in 1795. The amorphous Polish noble estate was reclassified on the Austrian model into a titled hierarchy, the Polish school system was abandoned, and censorship introduced. The Polish university in

Kraków was turned into a German-Latin institution. On the other hand, sentiments of loyalty to the Habsburg emperors were encouraged among the peasants of the two Galicias by the easing of labour burdens and the granting to the serfs of some property rights. Although all three partitioning powers imposed a twenty-year period of military service on their serf conscripts (a burden that had not existed in the largely demilitarized Polish-Lithuanian Commonwealth), Austrian military discipline was the least harsh.

The three partitioning governments placed the Roman Catholic Church under tight state supervision. Nor did they spare the large Jewish population from heavy taxation and bureaucratic controls: in Galicia, for instance, the Jews were obliged to adopt German surnames, while in Russia (which had acquired half of the Commonwealth's Jewry) they were confined to their area of settlement, the so-called Pale of Jewish Settlement, and were later subject to a misguided and ultimately unsuccessful physiocratic policy to force them out of their artisanal and innkeeping trades into farming. Many of Poland's towns were also afflicted by the economic dislocation brought about by arbitrary frontier changes; after a period of vibrant growth in the 1770s and 1780s, when its population reached 100,000, Warsaw now found itself reduced to a half-deserted Prussian frontier town.

Despite the shock of the final Partition and the resignation of many aristocrats and notables in favour of a quiet life, 1795 proved not to be the end of Polish yearnings for independence. The long legacy of nobiliary republicanism contrasted starkly with the absolutism of Poland's conquerors, and the national awakening of the reign of Stanisław August Poniatowski could not simply be obliterated from the minds of Poland's elite. The presence across the length and breadth of the former Commonwealth of hundreds of thousands of petty noblemen, many unsophisticated yet fiercely proud of their former status as free citizens, was also to provide a reservoir of future freedom fighters – soon to be exposed to the intoxicating message of Romantic nationalism. The long period of continuous international instability generated by the French Revolution and the Napoleonic wars also provided many Polish patriots with opportunities to challenge the post-partition status quo in their homeland.

Initially Polish national aspirations were kept alive mainly by exiled patriots, many radically minded, who sought the assistance of the French Republic for their cause. About 20,000 Poles, many of them Austrian conscripts taken prisoner by the French, were to serve in the Polish legions formed in Italy under French aegis and commanded in a spirit of egalitarianism by Generals Henryk Dąbrowski and Karol Kniaziewicz. The legend of their exploits against the Austrians and Russians between 1797 and 1800 was to inspire many future Polish generations, while their hymn 'Poland has not perished while we live', a mazurka with Józef Wybicki's words of defiance against Poland's oppressors, eventually established itself as the modern Polish national anthem. The radicals also launched several clandestine organizations in Poland itself, such as the Society of Polish Republicans, which linked the cause of national independence with that of serf emancipation and dreamt of introducing a French-style constitution in a restored Poland.

In the immediate term the radical patriotic cause was a failure. The Polish exiles in Paris were divided, the conspirators at home lacked wide support, while the French Republic under the Directorate lost its initial revolutionary ardour. Bonaparte's rise to power dismayed Kościuszko and other Polish democrats. The Polish legionaries' dream of marching through Austria to liberate Poland was finally shattered when France concluded peace with Austria and Russia in 1801, and when Bonaparte cynically dispatched 5,000 Polish legionaries to reconquer Haiti. The freedom fighters had been transformed into an instrument of colonial repression; few of them were ever to see Europe again. Kościuszko's proposal of 1800 for waging a peasant-backed guerrilla war in Poland, without any foreign aid, against the armies of Austria, Prussia and Russia was, in the circumstances, sheer quixotic fantasy.

The disenchantment with Republican France and the consequent return to Poland of many exiles (although not of Kościuszko) only strengthened the hand of those who saw better prospects for preserving Polish national identity through legal cultural activity. The Warsaw Society of the Friends of Learning, established in 1800, gathered some of Poland's leading scholars and writers; it aimed at making Polish a major language of scholarship and one of its leading lights, the lexicographer Samuel Bogumił Linde, was to publish between 1807 and 1814 the first modern dictionary of the Polish language. At the same time in Puławy Princess Izabela Czartoryska founded a museum devoted to the glorification of Poland's past.

The greatest Polish hopes, however, came to be associated with Alexander I, Russia's tsar since March 1801, who privately condemned his grandmother's treatment of Poland, and professed 'liberal' political views. At Alexander's side was his close friend Prince Adam Czartoryski who had been sent to Russia to recover his family's estates. Confident that an honourable Russo-Polish reconciliation, underpinned ideologically by sentiments of Slavonic solidarity, was possible under Alexander, Czartoryski accepted high office from his imperial friend. As curator of the Wilno (Vilnius) educational district from 1803, Czartoryski presided over the reform of the university of Wilno which stood at the apex of an extensive network of Polish-language secondary schools in Russia's ex-Polish *gubernii*. Tsar Alexander's recognition of the supremacy of Polish nobiliary culture in his western territories militated against the russification of this area but also of course did nothing to promote the literary development of the local non-Polish tongues; this role was left to individual patrons, such as Józef Giedroyć (Giedraitis), the bishop of Samogitia, who with his circle promoted the use of the Lithuanian language as a literary vehicle. The university of Wilno became a beacon of Polish academic life and by far the largest university in the Russian Empire. Within its walls were to study many eminent figures in Polish culture, such as the Romantic poet Adam Mickiewicz and the historian Joachim Lelewel. Little wonder that for many Polish-Lithuanian noblemen Russia appeared the most tolerant of the three partitioning powers.

More controversial was Czartoryski's record as director of Russia's foreign policy from 1804 to 1806. His vision of Alexander as a crusader for a new just and moral European order, in which Poland would be restored in dynastic association with Russia, appealed to the young tsar's vanity and idealism, but collapsed in the face of harsh political realities and the tsar's own indecisiveness. Russia's attempt in 1804–5 to draw Austria and Prussia into an anti-Napoleonic coalition could hardly be reconciled with Czartoryski's scheme of despoiling those states of their Polish provinces.

The defeat of the Russian and Austrian armies at Austerlitz in December 1805 undermined Czartoryski's influence in St Petersburg and brought about the end of his ministerial career. And by the end of 1806 the situation in the Polish lands was dramatically reversed by another twist of fate: Napoleon's victorious campaign in 1806 against Prussia which brought the French army into Prussian Poland.

As the Hohenzollern state collapsed under Napoleon's blows, Berlin's Polish provinces erupted in a widespread national uprising. The appearance of the former legionaries Dąbrowski and Wybicki in the van of Napoleon's army revived earlier hopes of French assistance that had been so cruelly dashed in 1801. Tsar Alexander joined the fray on Prussia's side, and the war dragged on. Napoleon therefore authorized the creation in Prussian Poland of an administration run by local Poles that would maintain social order and provide him with additional fighting men and supplies. After much soul-searching, Prince Józef Poniatowski was persuaded by Murat to accept the command of a resurrected Polish army to fight alongside the French. Prince 'Pepi', the playboy of Warsaw, had taken the first step that would turn him into a national hero and the most chivalrous symbol of Polish military valour in the Napoleonic period.

The creation of a *de facto* Polish government with a regular conscripted army (numbering over 30,000 men by June 1807) in western Poland was an accomplished fact, but its future prospects depended entirely on the outcome of the war. The battle of Friedland on 14 June 1807 finally established French superiority and obliged Alexander I to sign a compromise peace treaty with Napoleon at Tilsit on 7 July. Most of Prussia's Polish lands went to form the so-called 'duchy of Warsaw'; Russia annexed the district of Białystok and undertook to join the Continental System against Britain; and Danzig was restored as a free city. In October 1809, following a brief war between France and Austria, in which the Polish army gave a good account of itself, the duchy was enlarged at Austria's expense: Vienna had to surrender about half of its gains in the partitions, including Kraków and Lublin.

The duchy of Warsaw was undeniably a French satellite, harnessed to and exploited by the Napoleonic war machine; 20,000 of

23 Napoleon bestowing a constitution on the duchy of Warsaw. This allegorical painting by Marceli Bacciarelli (1731–1818) depicts the event which occurred on 22 July 1807 in Dresden where the emperor had summoned leading Polish notables, including the venerable Stanisław Małachowski (sixth from the left), the former speaker of the Great Sejm of 1788–92. Napoleon ignored the proposals brought by the Polish delegation and proceeded to dictate his own version in one hour. The constitution was nonetheless an effective adaptation of the French model to Polish realities. Bacciarelli was court painter to Stanisław August Poniatowski and remained active in Polish cultural life to his death.

its troops participated in Napoleon's inglorious attempt to sub-
jugate Spain, and nearly 100,000 Polish soldiers accompanied the
Grande Armée into Russia in 1812. The duchy had to accept a
constitution dictated by Napoleon, a French-style centralized
administrative system staffed by professional bureaucrats, and the
Napoleonic legal code. On the other hand the duchy's creation
shattered the mould of the partition treaties and reawakened hopes
of national revival. Although it comprised a mere fifth of old
Poland and only 30 per cent of its population, the duchy did
contain within its post-1809 borders the Polish heartland:
Poznania, the cradle of Poland's medieval statehood with the
ecclesiastical centre of Gniezno, and the two historic capitals of
Warsaw and Kraków. The elevation to the ducal title of King
Frederick Augustus of Saxony, the nephew of Augustus III of
Poland, and the restoration of a bicameral Sejm and provincial
dietines (*sejmiki*) represented a gesture to Polish tradition. The
duchy's large army instilled civic virtues in its officers and soldiers,
while its exploits revived military values in Polish society and
inspired a cult of Napoleon that would survive in Poland into the
twentieth century. The duchy's uhlans, with their distinctive square
caps (the *czapka*) and their red and white pennants, became a
model for the lancer regiments of many European armies; and
despite its appalling human losses in 1812, the duchy's army had
the satisfaction of returning from Russia with all its standards and
artillery pieces intact.

The Napoleonic regime, backed by the duchy's rationalist aristocracy, also injected modern elements into Polish society. The
Napoleonic Code abolished serfdom, introduced legal equality and
personal liberty for all inhabitants, and permitted civil marriage
and divorce, to the horror of the episcopate. Some non-nobles
could now vote, sit in the Sejm, and hold office, while the
Voltairean education minister Stanisław Kostka Potocki expanded
elementary schooling. All this contributed to the growth of a
professional intelligentsia and the narrowing of the gap between
the *szlachta* and the urban middle class. But there were also
compromises with Polish 'feudal' traditions: the landed nobility
obtained full property rights to all manorial land and all former
serf allotments, while the now 'free' peasants were reduced to a

Map 6   The duchy of Warsaw, 1807–15.

landless class of tenants still obliged to perform the corvée. The Jews were barred from buying land and had their political rights suspended for ten years, on the grounds that they were not yet fully assimilated into Polish society.

Polish traditionalists and republicans resented Napoleon's authoritarianism, and the Continental System accentuated further the structural weakness of Polish agriculture. Nevertheless, in contrast to Spain or Germany, the national movement in Poland became associated with Napoleon, who by 1809 had forced two of the partitioning powers to relinquish a large proportion of their Polish possessions. Tsar Alexander's belated attempts to lure the Polish leadership in Warsaw away from the Napoleonic alliance with tempting political and territorial offers failed; his half-baked schemes to restore a Grand Duchy of Lithuania as a rival to Napoleonic Poland fared no better. The Polish imbroglio inevitably contributed to the rapid deterioration of Franco-Russian relations between 1810 and 1812. The duchy's leaders welcomed the war of 1812: the restoration of the Kingdom of Poland was solemnly proclaimed on 28 June and the recovery of Russia's ex-Polish lands was regarded as certain, although in Lithuania there was a cautious rather than an enthusiastic response to the French invasion.

Napoleon's disaster in Russia shattered Polish hopes and illusions. It was now Tsar Alexander's turn to be the arbiter of Poland's future, although to avoid weakening the new anti-Napoleonic coalition he initially refrained from making public his ambition to restore a Polish kingdom under his rule. In these ambiguous circumstances Prince Józef Poniatowski felt he had no choice but to stay at Napoleon's side; he died a hero's death while covering the French retreat with his troops at the decisive battle of Leipzig (16–19 October 1813). Immediately after Napoleon's abdication on 6 April 1814, Alexander openly laid claim to the duchy of Warsaw, took the remnants of the Polish army under his protection, and authorized a reform committee in Warsaw to prepare the ground for a Romanov kingdom of Poland to which, he intimated to the Poles, he was willing in due course to add the western *gubernii*. Although pro-Napoleonic sentiments remained strong in the duchy, many of its notables, actively encouraged by Czartoryski, accepted the tsar's professed magnanimity as their country's only hope. Even Kościuszko, that paragon of patriotic virtue, briefly left his Swiss exile to offer his services to Alexander.

The final outcome of the Congress of Vienna (1814–15) fell dramatically short of what had been Polish hopes and expectations. However, it was simply not possible in 1815 to restore an independent Poland with the frontiers of 1772. It was the Poles' misfortune that the continental powers which had finally toppled Napoleon happened to be the same states that had partitioned Poland. It was also plainly unrealistic to expect Russia to surrender the conquered duchy of Warsaw as well as all its gains in the partitions of Poland on the very morrow of its greatest military triumph since Peter the Great. At the same time, the Napoleonic presence in eastern Europe had revived Polish national aspirations to such an extent that it would have been difficult to restore stability in this region without some concessions to the Poles. Among the peacemakers it was Tsar Alexander who appreciated this most, and recognized that Russia's security in the west would be increased by winning over the distraught Poles to his side. A constitutional Poland under his sceptre could also provide a pilot project for the reforms he still contemplated for the Russian Empire. On the other hand, Alexander's insistence on having a free hand in arranging the future of a Polish state under his control met with strong international opposition and dominated the diplomatic struggles at the Congress.

Metternich and Castlereagh, the Austrian and British foreign ministers respectively, both feared the extension of Russian power in central Europe under whatever guise and would have preferred a simple partition of the duchy of Warsaw. In the end they had to accept most of Alexander's Polish demands, although the tsar had to compromise by relinquishing his claims to Poznania, Toruń (Thorn) and Kraków. As a result the so-called Congress Kingdom of Poland emerged 30 per cent smaller than the duchy of Warsaw. Indeed the lands of the former Polish-Lithuanian Commonwealth remained fragmented after 1815 in a complex mosaic of six political–administrative units: Austria retained 'Old' Galicia; the contested city of Kraków became a republic under the protection of the three eastern powers; Prussia held on to West Prussia (its original gain of 1772) and received Poznania as the quasi-autonomous duchy of Posen; Russia's Polish lands also consisted of two

'Congress' Kingdom of Poland, 1815 ('Vistula Land' after 1874)

Grand Duchy of Posen (Poznania), 1815–49

Galicia (included Kraków after 1846)

Free City of Kraków, 1815–46, then annexed by Austria

Chełm (Kholm) *guberniya* detached from the Kingdom of Poland in 1912 and incorporated in the Russian Empire

Polish–Lithuanian Commonwealth, 1771

The Pale of Jewish settlement in the Russian Empire, 1791/1804–1917

✂ Major battles in 1831

International borders 1815–1914 (except for Kraków)

COURL

Memel

Danzig · Königsberg

EAST PRUSSIA

POMERANIA

Stettin

WEST PRUSSIA

BERLIN

Thorn

Ostrołęka ✂

Gniezno

Płock

Poznań (Posen)

WARSAW ✂ Grochów

Kalisz

Łódź

Oder

SAXONY

Breslau

SILESIA

Radom

Lublin

Częstochowa

Kielce

Oppeln

Dąbrowa Basin

Upper Silesia

Vistula

Rzeszów

Kraków

GALIC

Teschen (Cieszyn)

Przem

Zakopane

AUSTRIA

Warta

P R U S S I A

(AUSTRIA–HUNGARY AFTER 1867)

Map 7   Partitioned Poland, 1815–1914.

regions with a different status, the western *gubernii* of the Russian Empire and an integral part thereof, and now the new autonomous Congress Kingdom of Poland. Little did the Polish patriots appreciate that, unlike the short-lived arrangements of 1795, the international frontiers established across Poland in 1815 were to last for a century, with the minor exception of Kraków.

Alexander must take most credit for salvaging a Polish state out of the ashes of Napoleonic Europe, yet his Polish kingdom owed much to its Napoleonic origins in terms of its size, its institutions and its legal system; Alexander retained the Napoleonic Code. Exhausted and war-weary, the Polish leaders accepted the new order and slipped easily into positions of authority under their new ruler. Indeed, all that Alexander had told them in 1814–15 led them to expect further acts of generosity from their tsar-king in whose exclusive gift remained both the new kingdom's constitution and its envisaged eastward extension. Intellectuals such as Stanisław Staszic and politicians like Czartoryski and the former radical Horodyski saw in Russia a defender of Polish national interests, and openly espoused sentiments of Slavonic solidarity. For all its limitations the settlement of 1815 was a marked improvement on that of 1795. In respect of their national rights, the Polish elite under Russian domination were to enjoy more favourable conditions between 1815 and 1830 than at any other time of the long partition period. No amount of Romantic nostalgia for the Napoleonic era could obscure the fact that the duchy of Warsaw, groaning under military exactions, stood on the shifting and ultimately perilous sands of the Napoleonic order. In 1815 the Great Powers explicitly recognized the Polish nationality throughout the area of the former Commonwealth, and took a number of steps to give an institutional expression of these rights not only in Alexander's share of Poland but also in Prussia's duchy of Posen, and even, although heavily watered down, in Austrian Galicia. In many areas Polish education was maintained, and scholarship and cultural life in general flourished. The decade and a half after 1815 also witnessed some economic development.

In 1815 Tsar Alexander was still the darling of many liberals and patriots. In November he granted to his Polish kingdom what appeared in the context of Restoration Europe an advanced liberal

24 Emperor Alexander I and the foundation of the university of Warsaw in 1816, by an unknown painter (1850). Alexander I presents the foundation charter of the university to its first rector W. A. Szweykowski. With the exception of his father Tsar Paul I, Alexander I was the only Russian ruler in the modern period who permitted the development of Polish-language education in the western *gubernii* of the Russian Empire, and encouraged it after 1815 in the 'Congress' Kingdom of Poland. In 1804 he contributed 500 ducats to the publication of Linde's dictionary of the Polish language. The university of Warsaw was closed in 1831 and re-opened in 1862–9, after which it functioned as a Russian institution until 1914. The proposal to erect a monument in Warsaw in Alexander's honour, endorsed by the Polish Sejm in June 1830, was never implemented.

constitution. With its elected Sejm, wide franchise and extensive civil rights, the Congress Kingdom represented a stark contrast with the autocracy of the Russian Empire to which the Kingdom was united 'for ever'. Yet the deficiencies of the new constitutional order reflected well Alexander's narrow interpretation of 'liberalism'. The Sejm was denied all control over the budget and over the army, which became a major drain on state finances, and rarely met in the 1820s. Other mechanisms for the supervision and control of Alexander's Polish kingdom were created. The post of viceroy went to the obedient ex-Napoleonic general Józef Zajączek and not to the independent-minded Czartoryski; the erstwhile liberal and now cynical toady Nikolai Novosiltsev became the tsar's personal extra-constitutional overseer of the Kingdom, while Alexander's ill-tempered and brutal brother Grand Duke Constantine was given command of the Polish army and of the large Russian force stationed in the Kingdom. In 1819 preventive censorship was introduced. Disappointing also were Alexander's tantalizing but ultimately unfulfilled earlier promises to attach the western *gubernii* to the Congress Kingdom, one of the main attractions for the Polish elite of the Russian connection. Likewise, the treaty provisions for a free trade zone across the Polish lands proved unworkable; a customs barrier was established between Russia and the Kingdom, which also had to contend with high Prussian and Austrian tariffs.

The reactionary trend after 1819 in the internal and external policies of the so-called 'Holy Alliance' of the three eastern powers was to press heavily on their respective Polish provinces. The resulting restrictions were primarily of a political nature and were not aimed at 'denationalizing' the Poles; indeed, by twentieth-century standards they were very mild. Nevertheless, they were perceived by many contemporaries as inimical to the Polish national cause. The most vivid public expression of discontent in the Congress Kingdom came from a small group of enterprising gentry liberals led by the Niemojowski brothers from the western province of Kalisz. Their campaign in defence of the constitution prompted Alexander to warn the Polish Sejm in 1820 against the 'abuse' of liberty, and to authorize Constantine to use any means to maintain order in the Kingdom. The Sejm was not convened until 1825, when its debates were also closed to the public. The reactionary trend was supported by the Kingdom's episcopate and its native conservative champions of 'Altar and Throne'. The remaining representatives of the ideals of the Enlightenment came under direct attack; in December 1820 the anticlerical S. K. Potocki was replaced as education minister by the obscurantist Stanisław Grabowski. Decrees against secret societies led to the dissolution of masonic lodges which Alexander had himself once encouraged to promote ideas of social and cultural improvement and Russo-Polish reconciliation. Now also outside the law were clandestine patriotic societies committed to education and national reunification, which had grown since 1817 under the cover of masonic forms, and which attracted Napoleonic veterans, young officers and university students, many of poor *szlachta* backgrounds. Their first martyr was Walery Łukasiński, an army major, who was arrested in 1822 and who eventually spent most of his remaining forty-four years in a fortress dungeon outside St Petersburg. Reluctant to seek careers in the tsarist civil service and facing limited job prospects at home, the large student body in Wilno proved to be a particularly fertile ground for early Romantic ideas, but then faced the wrath of the authorities. Members of the Society of Philomats in Wilno, including Adam Mickiewicz, the most promising Romantic poet writing in Polish, were exiled into the Russian interior. In 1823 Czartoryski was replaced as curator of the Wilno educational district by Novosiltsev, nicknamed 'the Herod of Lithuania' for his brutal interrogation of the students.

Much of Polish public opinion took a dim view of the retreat from 'liberalism' during Alexander's last years. There was disappointment in many quarters when Alexander's successor in 1825, Nicholas I, further integrated the western *gubernii* with the rest of the Russian Empire, thereby dashing hopes that the Kingdom might be enlarged in the east. The trial in Warsaw, in 1828, of members of the revived National Patriotic Society for their contacts with the Russian Decembrists further damaged the already uneasy Polish–Russian relationship. Tsar Nicholas was furious when the Polish Senate, in its capacity as the Kingdom's High Tribunal, could not quite bring itself to condemn the conspirators' ideal of national reunification and acquitted the defendants of high treason. Only Russia's involvement in a new Turkish war in 1828–9 prevented the outraged Nicholas from overriding the Senate's verdict and bringing about a major constitutional crisis.

To appease his Polish subjects, Nicholas attended a formal coronation ceremony in Warsaw in May 1829, presented Warsaw with Turkish guns from Varna (the place of death in 1444 of the crusading Polish king Władysław Jagiellon), and agreed to summon the practically defunct Polish Sejm in June 1830. Even so, Nicholas found the role of constitutional monarch not at all to his taste; it had to be politely explained to him that the rejection of a government bill (in this instance to abolish civil marriages) was not unusual in a parliamentary system and was not intended as an affront to majesty. Grand Duke Constantine's behaviour also improved in the late 1820s; he felt increasingly at home in Warsaw with his morganatic Polish wife, and even espoused Polish irredentist aspirations in the east.

Sober minds well appreciated that the Kingdom did not need irresponsible patriotic antics but a period of calm. Particularly conscious of the need for political stability and economic consolidation within the strict limits of autonomy prescribed by St Petersburg was Prince Ksawery Lubecki, a former civil governor of Wilno and from 1821 to 1830 the Kingdom's energetic and hardheaded finance minister. He balanced the Kingdom's chaotic budget through rigorous taxation, initiated the creation of a land credit society and of the Bank of Poland, and even launched a modest programme of state-encouraged industrial development. This period also witnessed the emergence of Łódź as the centre of the Polish cotton industry, while a favourable tariff treaty with Russia in 1822 opened Russia's vast markets to the Kingdom's manufactures. Lubecki's fiscal burdens were felt most keenly by the peasantry whose conditions did not improve in what continued to be a difficult period for agriculture. Little was done to endow peasants with leaseholdings on state lands and even less on privately owned estates, while the eviction of peasants by private landlords acquired alarming proportions, despite the examples set by Czartoryski, who introduced generous tenancy terms on his Końskowola estates, and by Staszic, who created a large peasant co-operative near Hrubieszów. Peasant discontent only grew as the number of landless peasants in the Congress Kingdom reached 800,000 by 1827, with obvious damage to the cause of national solidarity. There was likewise no Polish consensus for improving the status of the Kingdom's 300,000 Jews, who continued to be deprived of full civic rights.

The other region of historic Poland endowed with extensive autonomy in 1815 was the small republic of Kraków, which obtained a liberal-aristocratic constitution and also retained the Napoleonic legal system. The three Protecting Powers interfered in the 1820s in Kraków against liberal agitation and student conspiracies, but the republic managed to survive until 1846. The status of the republic's peasantry was to be for many years the most advanced in all of historic Poland. Electoral rights and security of tenancy holdings did much to encourage early political and national consciousness of the rural population, in stark contrast with the peasants of Austrian Galicia. As a free-trade entrepôt Kraków also benefited from commerce with Silesia and the Congress Kingdom and witnessed some early industrial activity on its territory; the first steam engine installed anywhere in Poland appeared here in 1817.

Prussia's ex-Polish lands presented a more complex picture. Roughly equivalent in size to modern Belgium, the duchy of Posen had a mixed population of nearly 800,000 in 1815, of whom the Poles represented about two-thirds; in the city of Poznań the Polish and German elements were roughly even. Although the Prussian *Landrecht* replaced the Napoleonic Code, Polish was recognized as the main language in the administration, the courts and the schools, and Prince Antoni Radziwiłł was appointed viceroy. In practice, Poznania's degree of autonomy remained limited but the Prussian authorities, well aware of the pull of the Congress Kingdom, avoided alienating the Poles and dealt leniently with illegal patriotic societies. In terms of rural property rights, the Prussian government brought Poznania in line with the land reform operational in the rest of the Prussian monarchy since 1811; the landed nobility retained most of the land, but the process of creating a substantial class of prosperous peasant farmers was now set in motion.

Unlike in Poznania, no significant institutional or administrative concessions were made to the Polish nationality in West Prussia (formerly Polish Pomerania held by Berlin continuously since 1772), to which were added Danzig and Thorn. In West Prussia, Polish-speakers (including the Kashubians) equalled the Germans numerically, but the towns were predominantly German and the landed class was becoming increasingly so. In 1824 East and West Prussia were amalgamated into a single province, while the restoration of Marienburg (Malbork) castle, begun in the 1820s, was intended to express the 'idea' of the Teutonic Order and of German Prussia. There were even further intricacies on the linguistic and religious map of the eastern marches of the Hohenzollern state: the Protestant Masurians of East Prussia and much of the Roman Catholic country folk of Upper Silesia spoke Polish dialects yet their regions had never belonged to the Polish-Lithuanian Common-wealth. Both communities were to witness the gradual emergence of Polish national consciousness, of a highly distinct regional flavour, as the century wore on.

Of the three eastern powers it was Austria which made the fewest concessions to Polish nationality after the Congress of Vienna. Corresponding in size to three-fifths of the Congress Kingdom and with an almost identical population of 4.25 million (in 1830), Austrian Galicia continued to be administered by an imperial governor in Lwów (Lemberg) and a German-speaking bureaucracy. Austrian law continued to operate, while a strict censorship and a loyalist church hierarchy further reinforced the political status quo. Wealthy landowners dominated the largely ineffectual provincial assembly. The province was both economic-ally underdeveloped and financially exploited by the imperial government. It was only Austria's concern with Russian successes against the Turks in 1828 and 1829 that prompted Vienna to woo Galicia's nobles with a series of linguistic and cultural concessions. And despite a degree of government protection, the serfs of Galicia, whether Roman Catholic Polish-speakers in the west or Uniate Ukrainian-speakers in the east, saw no further improvement in their condition.

It would be too one-sided to regard developments in Russia's share of Poland from 1815 to 1830 solely in terms of violations of Polish rights and a drift towards unavoidable conflict. Despite its many defects and lack of sovereignty, a Polish state in the form of the Congress Kingdom was able to function in relative stability for fifteen years, twice as long as the Napoleonic duchy of Warsaw. Warsaw's status as a capital was enhanced by the construction of several imposing neo-classical buildings, such as the Great Theatre and the Bank of Poland, and of new palaces, churches, squares and avenues. The unveiling of Thordwaldsen's statue of Copernicus in 1830 served as a reminder of Poland's contribution to science and universal civilization. Three Polish universities functioned in this period: in Wilno, in Warsaw (founded by Alexander I in 1816) and in Kraków. Warsaw also acquired an Institute of Music (1821), a Polytechnic Institute (1828) and other specialist centres of professional training. Despite various restrictions imposed in the elementary sector in the 1820s, the Polish-language schools of the Congress Kingdom and of the Wilno educational district remained an impressive phenomenon by the standards of eastern Europe. In the realm of literary and philosophical ideas there was also much cross-fertilization across the borders, despite the irritating interference of censors.

At the same time the intellectual ferment generated by the influence of western Romanticism and of German idealistic philosophy encouraged the younger generation in the Kingdom and in the western *gubernii* to challenge the essentially rationalist political and ethical values of the old Polish elite. The appeal to heroic action and defiance against all odds, so vividly expressed in Mickiewicz's 'Ode to Youth' (1820), was given a further subversive twist in his poetic drama *Konrad Wallenrod* (1828), set in medieval Lithuania during the wars with the Teutonic Knights, in which duplicity was justified in the name of patriotism. The Romantic concept of the nation as a moral community yearning towards its self-fulfilment was advocated by the radical literary critic Maurycy Mochnacki. Democratic ideas too were fomented at the university of Warsaw by the popular history lecturer Joachim Lelewel, who had been expelled from Wilno in 1824 for his radicalism. The myth of Napoleonic military glory and the advent of Romantic nationalism made the vision of a reunited Poland even more painfully at variance with the narrow confines of the post-1815 settlement. Thoughts soon turned into action.

On 29 November 1830 in Warsaw a conspiratorial group of junior officers, fired by Romantic dreams of Polish independence and inspired by the political upheavals of that year in western Europe, launched an armed insurrection against Russian domination. It was a reckless and inept affair. The attempted assassination of Grand Duke Constantine was bungled and only some units joined the rebels. However, the seizure of the arsenal and the distribution of 30,000 rifles among the city's population transformed the situation. All Poles in positions of higher authority in Warsaw condemned the revolt, while Lubecki and Czartoryski,

25   Portrait of Poland's greatest Romantic and poet, Adam Mickiewicz
(1798–1855), painted in 1828 by Walenty Wańkowicz (1799–1842).
Born near Nowogródek (Navahrudak in modern Belarus) in historic
Lithuania and educated at the university of Wilno (Vilnius), Mickiewicz
spent most of his life in exile, first in Russia and later in France. His poetry,
as well as his lifelong commitment to the cause of liberty, profoundly
shaped the Polish Romantic mind. With his fellow Romantic poet Juliusz
Słowacki he lies buried next to the kings of Poland in the cathedral of
Wawel in Kraków. He is also highly regarded as a national poet in
Lithuania and Belarus. Mickiewicz's patriotic sentiments (evocatively
expressed in his epic *Pan Tadeusz*) were associated with the former multilingual Grand Duchy of Lithuania and would be alien to the narrow ethnic
nationalisms, whether Polish or Lithuanian, that emerged after 1863–4.

two very different political temperaments but now acting together to save Poland's limited gains of 1815, even urged Constantine to use force against the rebels. To their dismay he refused, and left the restoration of order to the Polish authorities. Desperate to avoid a breach with Nicholas and to tame the fires of the insurrection, the government co-opted the respected Czartoryski and the popular Napoleonic veteran General Józef Chłopicki. Against it arose a new self-styled Patriotic Society, led by the radical Lelewel and the fiery orator Mochnacki, committed to widening the insurrection. In Warsaw the situation was getting out of control while more units outside the city joined the rebels. Further government re-shuffles and Constantine's departure from Warsaw failed to restore order, and the government felt obliged to summon the Sejm.

Any hope that the Sejm would restrain public opinion failed; moved by a wave of patriotism, it endorsed the insurrection as 'an act of the Nation' and on 20 December appointed the reluctant Chłopicki 'dictator'. Paradoxically, Chłopicki hated all disorder and was eager to achieve a reconciliation with the tsar-king, but Nicholas refused to negotiate or to make any concessions that might have appeased Polish opinion. On 17 December he offered an amnesty but demanded unconditional capitulation. Unable to deliver what Nicholas wanted and unwilling to crush the rising, Chłopicki resigned on 18 January 1831. Little could now prevent an irrevocable break with Nicholas. On 25 January, after two months of indecision, the Sejm deposed Nicholas by public accla-mation. By this act the Sejm broke with legality and defied the treaty of Vienna which had sanctioned the Kingdom's union with Russia. Polish claims that Alexander's and Nicholas' violations of the constitution justified the deposition were essentially flawed.

There now ensued an internal struggle over the nature, methods and aims of the insurrection. To prevent the ultra-patriots and the radicals of the Patriotic Society from seizing power, moderate conservatives like Czartoryski felt that they had no option but to assume the leadership of the insurrection. The five-man National Government elected on 30 January by the Sejm included Lelewel but was presided over by Czartoryski, who acquired special respon-sibilities for foreign policy. Furthermore, on 8 February, the Sejm declared that Poland would remain a hereditary constitutional

26 The battle of Grochów, fought on 25 February 1831. Painted in 1887, and improved in 1928, by Wojciech Kossak (1856–1942), the scene depicts the 4th regiment of the line of the Polish army in action. General Chłopicki, the overall Polish commander, can be seen on horseback in civilian dress. Observing the battle on the Russian side was Grand Duke Constantine, who had commanded the Polish army in 1815–30 with brutal discipline. He expressed perverse but understandable delight at seeing 'his' soldiers perform so well.

monarchy and that only the existing Sejm had the authority to elect a new king. While the radicals wanted a 'people's war' against Russia, the moderate leadership hoped that a successful military campaign would force Nicholas and the Great Powers to revise the clauses of the Vienna treaties relating to Poland. Secretly, Czartoryski was even willing to retain a loose dynastic link with Russia. He was anxious to reassure the governments of Europe, especially Austria and Prussia, that the Polish revolution was national, that its aim was the Kingdom's independence, and that it was in no way socially subversive. Yet the force of events extended Polish war aims. The spread of the insurrection to the western *gubernii* of Russia compelled the Sejm, in another act of defiance against the treaty of Vienna, to pass a bill in May 1831 incorporating that vast area into the Polish state. Nicholas in the meantime had resolved that he would reduce the Kingdom's autonomy, while to surrender to the full territorial demands of the Poles would be tantamount to relegating Russia from the ranks of the Great Powers. The Poles were now left with no alternative but to fight and win a war with Russia.

The well-trained Polish army, which reached 80,000 effectives, gave a good account of itself. On 25 February Chłopicki halted the Russian advance on Warsaw at Grochów, the largest land battle fought in Europe between Waterloo and the Crimean War. A string of subsequent Polish successes in the spring alarmed St Petersburg, but the defeat of the indecisive General Skrzynecki at Ostrołęka on 26 May turned the scales of the war against the Poles. Commanded by the experienced campaigner Paskevich, the Russian army was able to cross the Vistula near the Prussian border and approached Warsaw from the west. The prospect of defeat led to vicious street unrest in Warsaw in mid-August and to recriminations within the National Government. Czartoryski's suggestion that the Poles should seek Austrian protection infuriated Lelewel and the radicals who now pressed for the creation of an egalitarian republic. The government resigned and full power was finally conferred on one man, General Jan Krukowiecki, who restored order. But by then it was all too late. Conscious of the ignominious behaviour of the Targowica Confederacy in 1792, the Polish civilian and military leadership refused to capitulate to the tsar and went into exile.

The glaring differences in resources between Russia and the landlocked Congress Kingdom were bound to tell eventually on the war's outcome, yet there were specific failings on the Polish side. The Poles lacked political unity during the early stages of the insurrection. Some of their leaders were doubtful about their chances of success, while the 200-man Sejm retained effective control of the war effort and deprived the National Government of real power. On balance, the Polish high command showed less initiative than Marshal Paskevich. The rising also lacked wide social support. No imaginative attempt was made to win over the peasant masses; even a modest government bill to enable peasants on crown lands to purchase their own freeholds was rejected by the Sejm in April. And for all its respect for the social order, the Polish leadership failed to win any effective international support. The enthusiasm for the Polish cause among the public of Britain, Germany, and especially France was widespread. Casimir Dela-vigne's impassioned song 'La Varsovienne' was sung in Paris in March 1831 to the stirring music by d'Auber, and rapidly acquired in translation a prominent place in the repertoire of Polish patriotic songs. Across much of Germany resounded songs (the so-called *Polenlieder*) in praise of the valiant Poles. Yet nothing could sway the governments into action. The cabinets of Berlin and Vienna remained neutral but essentially hostile, while the British and the French were preoccupied with acute domestic problems and were at loggerheads over the Belgian Question.

The cost of defeat for the Poles was disastrous; not only did the mirage of a large independent Poland dissolve into thin air but most of the limited gains of 1815 were also lost. Nicholas I formally respected the Vienna treaties by retaining the Kingdom as a separate administrative and legal unit, but he abolished the consti-tution, the Sejm and the Polish army. The university of Warsaw was closed down. Excluded from a general amnesty were the original conspirators, all members of the Sejm and of the National Government, and all exiles. Paskevich, now created 'prince of Warsaw', remained an all-powerful viceroy with a permanent army of occupation. In 1833 martial law was introduced, and a vast citadel-prison was built to overawe the restive city.

The end of the Kingdom's statehood encouraged Prussia and

Austria to rescind some of their concessions to the Polish nationality. In 1833–4 the three partitioning powers mutually guaranteed
their respective Polish possessions and committed themselves to the
suppression of all revolutionary activity. The 'Holy Alliance' was
back in business. Even the papacy, committed to the preservation
of the international order, condemned the insurrection. In the
western *gubernii* the local insurgents had to endure hard labour,
servitude in the tsarist army, and the loss of their property. The
closure of the university of Wilno (except for the medical and
theological faculties) and of the entire network of Polish schools
was a tragic blow to Polish culture, yet only the beginning of the
region's further russification.

With the collapse of the insurrection in 1831, about 10,000
Polish exiles, including much of the Kingdom's political, military
and cultural elite, headed west, mostly to France. They promoted
among their hosts an idealized vision of Poland as a heroic victim
of tsarist tyranny and did much to promote russophobia among
western liberals and radicals. In the west the exiles were also free to
assess the causes of their failure and to discuss and prepare various
plans for their country's future salvation. Indeed, the next decade
and a half witnessed among the 'Great Emigration' an extraordinary flowering of Romantic literary creativity and of political
and social thought which was to exert a deep impact on Polish
national consciousness. Of the exiled bards the greatest was
Mickiewicz. In his *Books of the Polish nation and Polish pilgrimage* (1832) he called on the exiles ('the soul of the Polish nation') to
prepare for 'a universal war for the freedom of peoples', and gave
expression to his messianic vision of Poland as the 'Christ of
Nations' whose resurrection would bring about the religious
regeneration of mankind. In his lectures at the Collège de France
between 1840 and 1844 Mickiewicz was to develop his subversive
attacks on the existing European order, drawing on himself inevitably the opprobrium of the French authorities. The poet Juliusz
Słowacki considered nations as spiritual categories that should be
led by revolutionary spiritual elites. While endorsing the ideal of
national self-determination, the conservative Zygmunt Krasiński
was disturbed by the notions of popular sovereignty advocated by
Mickiewicz and Słowacki, and in his *Undivine comedy* (1835)

presented an apocalyptic vision of the destruction of the old social order by 'the hungry and the poor'. Mickiewicz's revolutionary eschatology was also attacked by Cyprian Norwid, the last of the great philosophizing poets of the Romantic period, who was to warn against raising patriotism into an 'unjustified religion'.

What emotionally united all the poets and all the exiles was the music of Frédéric Chopin: from the powerful 'Revolutionary' *étude* (op. 10 no. 12 in C minor), in which the composer was believed to express his anguish on hearing of Warsaw's fall in September 1831, to his preludes, mazurkas and *krakowiaks* which conveyed sentiments of yearning for the distant homeland. More than the written word, it is Chopin's music that remains the purest and the most universally accessible expression of Polish Romantic feeling. It is extraordinary how this frail and sickly man, who never lifted a sword or gun in the national cause, is revered to the present day as a sacred national icon.

The political and ideological disputes that had raged in Warsaw during the insurrection acquired even greater intensity in exile in a climate of mutual recrimination. Within the wide spectrum of émigré political groupings, the most prestigious was that led from Paris by Prince Czartoryski, whose support for a modern constitutional monarchy based on a propertied and educated electorate attracted moderate conservatives and liberals. As a statesman of international renown, Czartoryski cultivated unofficial links with the governments of Britain and France and established across Europe an extensive network of agents. At first he concentrated on defending Poland's limited rights as defined by the treaties of 1815, a legalistic position tactically justified to win international support but condemned by many of his less restrained fellow exiles. Two conditions, Czartoryski sensibly argued, had to be met for a Polish national uprising to succeed: it had to coincide with a major European war between Russia and the Western Powers, and it had to enjoy wide peasant support, which could only be gained if the nobility voluntarily endowed the peasants with their own landholdings. The vital lessons of 1831 had clearly been learnt, not that they brought independence any nearer. In 1840 Czartoryski adopted a more independent policy by using his agents to weaken Russian influence in the Balkans and to promote the cause of nationality in general. He also persuaded the papacy to modify its originally negative stance towards Polish nationalism.

Despite his relentless defence of the Polish cause, the majority of the exiles turned their backs on the aristocratic Czartoryski and sought more radical if equally fruitless solutions. While Czartoryski considered the traditions of the *szlachta* as the essential ingredient of Polish national values, Lelewel found theoretical inspiration for his collectivist brand of democracy in his romanticized pseudo-historic accounts of primitive Slavonic communes in pre-Christian Poland. With his associates from the Patriotic Society Lelewel put his hopes in the early overthrow of the continental autocracies by the *carbonari*; he joined 'Young Europe', the international revolutionary republican brotherhood led by Giuseppe Mazzini. The efforts of Lelewel's emissaries to rekindle the flames of insurrection in Russian Poland not only failed but also provoked the tsarist authorities to weaken even further Polish and Catholic influence in the western *gubernii*. In 1839 the Greek Catholic Church with its 2 million mostly Belarusian-speaking adherents was formally absorbed by the Russian Orthodox Church. In 1840 the Lithuanian legal code, the last functioning institutional link with the old Polish-Lithuanian Commonwealth, was replaced by Russian law, and in the south-western (Ukrainian) *gubernii* Governor-General Bibikov zealously implemented the policy of reducing the legal status of the petty *szlachta* to that of 'one-dwelling peasants'.

As the conspiratorial work of Lelewel's Young Poland fizzled out in the late 1830s, it was replaced as the main left-wing rival to Czartoryski by the more realistic and larger Polish Democratic Society, founded in Paris in 1832. The Democratic Society called for the removal of all social privileges, and for the inclusion of all social groups within a modern democratic nation of equal citizens. After bitter internal wrangles most of the democrats acknowledged that the participation of the *szlachta*, with its tradition of political and personal liberty, was essential for the recovery of independence; at the same time they insisted that the peasants had to acquire full property rights to their holdings without the payment of any indemnity. After 1840 the Polish Democratic Society was run from Versailles by a five-man directorate; its most outstanding strategist was Wiktor Heltman, who had already been involved in student conspiracies in 1817. The Democratic Society's critical but ultimately conciliatory approach to the nobility and its acceptance of private property as the basis of society was not shared by one of its splinter groups, the Commune of the Polish People formed in Portsmouth by exiled non-commissioned officers and soldiers. Drawing eclectically on all schools of French socialist and democratic thought, and inspired by Lelewel's theories of primitive Slav communalism, the Commune called for the overthrow of the nobility, the introduction of collective landownership, and the rejection of western industrialization. Isolated from the majority of the exiles and weakened by internal feuds, the populists were soon to learn how poorly the cause of agrarian socialism was to fare in Poland.

It was clear by the 1840s that all active émigré groups in various degrees accepted the involvement of the peasantry in the national struggle as a precondition of a successful insurrection. It was an urgent matter since it was feared that the partitioning governments would improve the peasants' lot and thereby rob the peasants of the material incentive to join the national cause. At the same time it needs to be borne in mind that the Polish radicals and democrats saw in the Lithuanian-, Belarusian- and Ukrainian-speaking serfs of the western *gubernii* future equal citizens of a democratic Polish nation embracing all the lands that had constituted the Polish-Lithuanian Commonwealth in 1772. In that sense they identified Polish territorial claims in the east with the universal cause of liberty. Whether this generous vision had any mileage within the complex and increasingly confrontational ethnic, religious and social realities of that region remained to be seen.

It is worth noting at this juncture that not all men of talent who found themselves outside Poland in this period remained in Europe or were always directly involved in politics. Ignacy Domeyko, a geologist and railway builder, contributed much to the economic and educational life of Colombia and Chile, while Paul Edmund Strzelecki was a pioneering explorer in Australia and named that country's highest peak after Kościuszko. For those educated Poles who did not have to choose exile, and who eschewed political agitation or revolutionary conspiracy, there remained some scope

27 'Organic work' in action: the Cegielski factory in Poznań (Posen). Established by the industrialist Hipolit Cegielski (1813–1868) in 1855, the factory produced agricultural equipment and machines, and contributed to the modernization of agriculture on Polish-owned farms in Poznania. Cegielski also helped to create a Polish-language press and promoted Polish cultural life under Prussian rule. In 1849 he served as deputy to the Prussian parliament. The photograph dates from 1883.

for legal economic and cultural activity within the limits set by the governments of the partitioning states. It was in Poznania that political and material conditions were most favourable in the 1840s for all such work of social improvement, which became known in Polish as 'organic work' (*praca organiczna*). Prussian rule mellowed under the liberal-minded Frederick William IV, and it was possible for the philanthropist Karol Marcinkowski to launch a variety of practical initiatives in the fields of education, commerce and the crafts. A conceptual framework for this activity was provided by the eminent Hegelian philosopher August Cieszkowski, who endorsed modern scientific and bourgeois civilization. Modern agricultural methods also raised the productivity of noble-owned estates and peasant farms in Poznania. The increased cultivation of the potato, in western and then central Poland, added a much welcomed nutritional boost to the peasants' staple diet of brown bread and vegetables, especially the ubiquitous cabbage. Industry and commerce continued to make impressive inroads in the Congress Kingdom in the 1830s and 1840s, especially in textiles and railway building; the Warsaw–Vienna railway, financed by private investors, was completed in 1848. Many of the Kingdom's substantial landowners accepted the necessity of modernizing the retarded rural economy; the case was growing for commuting peasant labour dues into money rents, and even for introducing a land reform on the Prussian model. It is noteworthy that it was in Russian-occupied Wilno in the early and mid-1840s that Stanisław Moniuszko, the creator of the Polish national opera, wrote and produced some of his earliest works. In Galicia, however, backward social conditions and the absence of committed activists militated against 'organic work'.

Against this background of gradual economic improvement, wealth creation and political realism, the scheming exiles and revolutionaries seemed at times to be a peripheral element in the daily lives and concerns of their fellow countrymen. For all their zeal the different Polish movements for national and social liberation had clearly failed by 1840 to overthrow the foreign yoke: there was no great European war nor was there a great rising of the peoples of Europe. Yet this did not deter further attempts to challenge the political and social order in Poland; Czartoryski continued with his propaganda and the exiled Polish Democratic Society set about restoring an underground network across Poland in the early 1840s. While the programme of the Democratic Society was potentially relevant in the more advanced Poznania, the ground in Russian and Austrian Poland was less fertile for modern democratic ideas. Yet it was there that a new generation of impatient radicals set to work. Henryk Kamieński and his nephew Edward Dembowski, two 'penitent' noblemen, espoused the cause of a peasant revolution and of a 'people's war' as the only solution to Poland's national and social predicament. Dressed as a peasant, Dembowski wandered through the villages of Galicia preaching his revolutionary gospel, only to realise that his listeners were more interested in property rights than in rural socialism. He duly felt obliged to modify his message, but his call for action found a response among the leadership of the Democratic Society which was also encouraged by the existence in 1844 of a populist conspiracy led by Piotr Ściegienny, a revolutionary parish priest in Lublin province.

The continuing rumbles of discontent in the villages of Galicia and of the Kingdom were interpreted by the democrats as evidence of an imminent revolutionary outburst that had to be channelled in the national cause. There was no time to waste. The directory of the Democratic Society in Versailles coordinated plans for a national insurrection throughout Poland for 1846. The forces of the partitioning states were to be destroyed piecemeal by a mass peasant army at the head of which was to stand the 32-year-old émigré Ludwik Mierosławski, in whom the democrats recognized a rare but so far unproved strategic genius. Even Czartoryski, unable to halt the revolutionary movement yet desperate to prevent an internecine class war, urged the nobility to participate. But the agitation of the democrats and populists among the peasantry was nothing less than playing with fire; their failure to appreciate the deep social and cultural divisions in large areas of the Polish countryside was soon to be borne out in a horrifying and tragic fashion.

Mierosławski and his associates were betrayed to the Prussian police before any action could begin in Poznania; the Russians too quickly foiled the conspiracy in the Kingdom. Conditions were more favourable in the Republic of Kraków, where the free and

propertied peasants rallied in support of the democratic revolutionary government established in February 1846, which Prince Czartoryski recognized out of patriotic solidarity. In the western half of
Galicia, however, the gulf between the patriotic and democratic
ideology of the insurgents and the class antagonism of the semi-
serfs ended in catastrophe. The Polish-speaking Catholic peasants
turned against the rebels and their liberal gentry sympathizers in an
orgy of killing and destruction. Dembowski, who joined the
Kraków revolution, was killed by the Austrians while leading an
unarmed religious procession from the city on 27 February in a
desperate bid to win over the Galician peasants. Having manipulated the peasants' fury in suppressing the insurrection, the
Austrian government then forced them back to their villages, and
to their feudal duties. The Republic of Kraków, the last island of
Polish freedom, was annexed by Austria, with Russian and
Prussian consent and despite British and French protests. The
mirage of national and social solidarity burst in the aftermath of
the Galician jacquerie. While the authorities mopped up what was
left of the revolutionary network, many landowners came to the
conclusion that they would have to seek government protection of
their economic and social interests. At the same time Tsar Nicholas
moved briskly in 1846 and 1848 to reduce the danger of a peasant
explosion in his Polish lands and to lessen the influence of the
Polish nobility there; in the Kingdom he granted security of tenure
to the peasants, and in the western _gubernii_ he placed firm limits on
the seigneurial exploitation of the serfs.

Just as the events of 1846 exposed the gross unreality of a
'people's war', so too did the ideal of the brotherhood of nations
founder on the rocks of conflicting nationalisms during the revolutions that gripped much of continental Europe in 1848 and 1849.
Russian Poland remained sullenly quiet in 1848–9 as Nicholas I
tightened his repressive controls. Elsewhere, however, in exile and
at home many Polish patriots were galvanized into action by the
revolutionary wave that seemed to herald the collapse of absolutism in Prussia and Austria, and of the international order that
sanctioned the subjugation of their country. Mickiewicz threw
himself body and soul behind the cause of revolutionary internationalism in Italy and France; Mierosławski was released from

prison in Berlin and set to work to organize a Polish army and administration in Poznania, where the poet Słowacki also arrived to lend encouragement. Alluring prospects of an alliance between the new Liberal government of Prussia and the Poles, supported by the French Republic, against Russia proved short-lived. In the end Berlin was not willing to go beyond the division of Poznania into two ethnic areas and when this was rejected by the Poles the Prussian army restored full control in April and May 1848. The initial support, in March, of the German Pre-Parliament in Frankfurt for Polish independence evaporated in July in acrimonious arguments over Germany's future eastern border; only a handful of radicals remained true to German solidarity with Polish national aspirations. In Paris, on 15 May, thousands of workers, to the cry of 'Vive la Pologne!', invaded the National Assembly. Lamartine spoke movingly in Poland's favour, but the French Republic dared not risk waging a major war for Poland's liberation.

Memories of the tragedy of 1846 were all too recent in Galicia and the response of the local Poles to the Viennese revolution in March 1848 was initially cautious and limited to a petition for autonomy for the province. In a separate attempt to win over the peasants to the national cause, the Polish national committees in Kraków (reinforced here by members of the Democratic Society) and in Lwów invited the landed nobility voluntarily to abolish labour dues on Easter Sunday. They were outmanoeuvred by the Austrian governor Stadion, who pre-empted the Polish leaders by first announcing the end of the corvée in the Emperor's name on Easter Saturday, and then bombarding Kraków into submission on 26 April. Continuing revolutionary ferment in Vienna in May 1848 and the spread of nationalist uprisings in Italy and Hungary encouraged the Poles to rally again. This time a 20,000-strong national guard was created; there was even talk of Galicia becoming a kind of Piedmont, an independent Polish centre from which would proceed the liberation of the rest of Poland.

By now, however, Polish aspirations clashed in the east of Galicia with those of the young Ukrainian national movement, focused around the Uniate Church, which demanded imperial protection against the Poles and the division of Galicia along ethnic lines. In the summer and autumn of 1848 the imperial authorities showed considerable powers of recuperation: they exploited all inter-ethnic conflicts, and found that many peasants, now emancipated and free from the corvée, showed limited support for national movements led by the gentry and the intelligentsia. Province after province fell to the imperial forces, which eventually in November restored full control over Galicia. About four thousand Polish fighters managed to escape across the Carpathian mountains to join the Hungarians, who still defied the Habsburgs. The Polish generals Józef Bem and Henryk Dembiński, veterans of the 1831 war against Russia, were given high commands; Bem was eventually appointed overall commander of the Hungarian army. At this juncture the Habsburgs turned to St Petersburg for help. Implacably hostile to the national awakening in central Europe and to any developments that might raise the hopes of his ungrateful Polish subjects, Tsar Nicholas willingly obliged and in May 1849 dispatched a Russian expeditionary force under Field-Marshal Paskevich, the conqueror of Warsaw in 1831. Within three months the Hungarians were crushed and thousands of exiles, including the Poles, had to flee into Ottoman territory.

The Polish contribution to the revolutions and wars of liberation in Italy, western Germany and Hungary in 1848–9 did more than justice to the Polish patriots' internationalist slogan of 'For Your Freedom and Ours', but the national rivalries in Poland and elsewhere also revealed that the Romantic belief in the brotherhood of Europe's nations was mostly wishful thinking. In the long run the events of 1848–9 did contribute to the strengthening of Polish national consciousness. The brief revolutionary period witnessed the blossoming of unfettered journalism and public debate in both Prussian and Austrian Poland. The willingness of the emancipated peasants of Poznania to rally to the national cause was profoundly telling, and helped in due course to shape the sturdy Polish nationalism of that region. And even in Silesia the social upheavals of 1848–9 reawakened among the Polish-speaking peasantry an attachment to their mother tongue. By the same token, the end of serfdom in Galicia was to begin the lengthy process of integrating the Polish-speaking peasants there into a wider Polish community. In the eastern part of that province Ukrainian national feeling was to prevail.

On the other hand, the contrasting experiences in the separate parts of Poland in 1848–9 only accentuated the already pronounced regional differences between them. The partition frontiers appeared as firmly drawn as ever. Inevitably, the influence of the émigrés plummeted; many educated Poles in Poland now resented the claims of the exiles to guide the nation's destiny. In the years that followed, the advocates of non-revolutionary methods gained the upper hand in the Prussian and Austrian parts. Conservative Polish deputies attended the Prussian parliament, established in 1851, while the appointment in 1850 of a Polish viceroy in Galicia, Count Agenor Gołuchowski, encouraged the loyalism of the Galician aristocracy to the Habsburgs.

The outbreak in 1854 of the Crimean War, in which Britain, France and Turkey challenged Russian ambitions in the Balkans, appeared at first to be Providence's answer to the lengthy prayers of the dejected Polish exiles, who promptly raised a variety of armed formations to fight against Russia. Mickiewicz, the embodiment of Polish Romantic defiance, himself arrived in Constantinople to help the military effort, only to be struck down by cholera. However, by agreeing to sue for peace in 1855, the new tsar Alexander II successfully deflected the British and French threat to widen the conflict to embrace the Polish Question, which was excluded from the agenda of the Paris peace conference of 1856.

At the same time the era of reforms that Alexander II launched after the debacle of the Crimean War could not ignore Russia's Polish lands. An amnesty for political prisoners, the suspension of military recruiting, the opening of a medical academy in Warsaw, and the appointment of the conciliatory Prince Gorchakov as viceroy in the Congress Kingdom all heralded a much-welcomed political thaw, which also coincided with a period of vigorous economic growth. Police controls were eased and restrictions on public activity lifted. In 1858 Count Andrzej Zamoyski, the largest landowner in the Kingdom, was permitted to launch an Agricultural Society which attracted the old established landed nobility as well as landowners of recent bourgeois, including Jewish, origin. While initially concerned with the urgent issue of agrarian reform, the Agricultural Society became in effect the national forum for moderate opinion in the Kingdom, a kind of substitute Sejm. The cause of peaceful modern progress was also promoted by Leopold Kronenberg, Warsaw's most influential banker and industrialist, and a Jewish convert to Calvinism, who associated himself closely with Zamoyski.

Among Warsaw's intelligentsia, voices could also be heard calling for the introduction of accountable local government and for wider social reform, including Jewish emancipation and the abolition of peasant labour dues. More alarming for the tsarist authorities was the growing receptivity of the younger generation to radical ideas and to Polish Romantic literature, which became more accessible in the new freer climate. The anticipation of change was encouraged by the authorized debate on peasant emancipation in Russia, and by the achievement of Italian and Romanian unification between 1859 and 1861. From his exile the indefatigable yet reckless Mierosławski resumed his urgent call for an early national insurrection which would pre-empt the tsar by offering a generous land settlement to the peasants in the Kingdom and especially to the serfs of the western *gubernii*.

The Russian authorities, faced with the growing ferment in the Kingdom in 1859–60, found themselves in an awkward situation characteristic of authoritarian imperial regimes that embark on liberal reform; repression would only inflame Polish patriotic feelings while concessions would only encourage the Poles to ask for more. Demonstrations became increasingly frequent in Warsaw. In October 1860 stink bombs were let off in the Great Theatre at a performance attended by Tsar Alexander, Emperor Franz Josef of Austria and the prince regent of Prussia. The singing of patriotic songs in churches and in the streets heightened popular feelings. In early 1861 events took an alarming turn. In response to the tsar's February decree emancipating the serfs of the Russian Empire, the Agricultural Society in Warsaw formally called on 26 February for the granting of full property rights to the Kingdom's peasant leaseholders. A series of demonstrations was violently dispersed and in one instance Russian troops fired on the crowd, killing five people. The tsar, with one eye on improving relations with Napoleon III, offered to introduce limited cultural and administrative concessions in the Kingdom, but also resolved to crush all unrest and to curtail all independent political initiatives.

On 27 March Marquis Aleksander Wielopolski was appointed head of a revived department of religious and educational affairs in Warsaw. Wielopolski was a conservative patriot who had participated in the anti-Russian uprising of 1831 but who, under the impact of the horrors of the Galician jacquerie of 1846, had accepted the necessity of collaboration with Russia. Now in 1861 he saw himself as a man of Providence who believed he could restore to the Kingdom a measure of its lost autonomy while at the same time keeping at bay all the restless and subversive elements in Polish society. Unfortunately, his strategy also entailed the dissolution on 6 April of the Agricultural Society and of the City Delegation, two institutions which enjoyed considerable moral authority in the city. The crowds that gathered in Castle Square on 8 April to protest against the authorities' actions displayed patriotic and religious emotions of an unparalleled intensity; many of those present continued to pray on their knees as Russian troops fired into the crowd killing over 100 people. Public opinion was enraged, collaboration with the tsarist authorities was discredited, and a state of national mourning was declared; the women of Warsaw, of all social ranks, wore black for the next two years. Many of the city's Jews, encouraged by the chief rabbi Beer Meisels, also joined the protest movement. In towns across the Kingdom and even in the western *gubernii*, vast congregations attended patriotic religious services. Significantly enough, much of the countryside remained aloof from the outburst of patriotic grief, preferring to agitate against labour dues, which Alexander finally replaced with cash payments in October.

The stick-and-carrot policy was not abandoned. The promised local authority elections, in which only 25,000 persons qualified to vote, took place in the autumn of 1861. But the new viceroy Lambert introduced martial law and banned all public gatherings, some of which had been highly symbolic and provocative, such as the celebration of the anniversary of Poland's union with Lithuania or the quasi-royal funeral of the popular archbishop of Warsaw Fijałkowski. On 11 November, the anniversary of Kościuszko's death, crowds again poured into Warsaw's churches. This time Russian soldiers entered the churches and proceeded to arrest thousands of worshippers. In a dramatic gesture against this

28   The closure of the churches, painted by Artur Grottger (1837–67) in 1861. All places of worship were closed in Warsaw as a protest against Russian soldiers arresting worshippers on 11 November 1861. Patriotism and religion made a powerful combination in Russian Poland in the run-up to the insurrection of 1863. Like many Polish artists of his generation, Grottger focused on patriotic themes, making the insurrection his major subject in a series of symbolic paintings. He had studied at the Vienna Academy before returning to Kraków. The painting is kept today in the Muzeum Narodowe (National Museum) in Wrocław.

profanation, the ecclesiastical authorities of all faiths ordered the closure of all the city's Catholic and Protestant churches and of all its synagogues. Wielopolski resigned and left for St Petersburg.

All this played into the hands of conspiratorial radical groups, now styled the 'Reds', who embarked on preparations for an uprising. Links were established with radical officers in the tsarist army while Mierosławski's followers, trained in Italy with Garibaldi's blessing, slipped into the Kingdom. Zamoyski, Kronenberg and other moderate 'White' leaders remained bitterly hostile to such adventurism, and concentrated on mobilizing Polish and foreign opinion in favour of the peaceful extension of Polish national rights. In mid-1862 events seemed to favour their cause. The government's relations with the Catholic Church were eased by the appointment of a new archbishop of Warsaw, while Wielopolski's dignified and sensible arguments finally persuaded Alexander II to restore to the Kingdom much of its lost self-rule. The tsar's liberal-minded brother Constantine was appointed viceroy, and all non-military matters in the Kingdom were placed in the hands of a civilian government led by Wielopolski, who immediately proceeded with some badly needed social and educational reforms. The compulsory commutation of labour dues into rents was a step forward, although it did not satisfy peasant demands for land and did not bridge the gulf between the nobility and the peasantry. The Jewish population finally obtained equal legal rights. The university of Warsaw and a network of Polish schools were restored.

There was, however, no extension of political liberties, and Wielopolski's unpopularity did little to enhance the objective attractiveness of the reform package. If anything, the youthful Reds, led by Jarosław Dąbrowski, stepped up their revolutionary preparations: the rudimentary structures of an underground state were put into place under the direction of a Central National Committee, a secret paramilitary force was raised, and plots were hatched to assassinate the viceroy and Wielopolski. Many young Catholic clerics found themselves drawn to radical beliefs akin to modern liberation theology. The position of the Whites, unwilling to alienate public opinion by co-operating with Wielopolski yet not wishing to give the Reds any advantages in the patriotic stakes, was becoming increasingly difficult. In September 1862, in an attempt to seize the patriotic high ground and to marginalize the Reds, Zamoyski proposed to Grand Duke Constantine that the western *gubernii* should be reunited with the Kingdom and that the 1815 constitution should be restored in its entirety, with the Sejm and a separate army. The tsar exiled Zamoyski for his audacity, but thereby weakened the influence of those Poles who wished to avoid an uprising. The middle ground in Polish politics was fast disintegrating.

The conspirators, led by the 22-year-old Stefan Bobrowski and the 28-year-old Zygmunt Padlewski, were planning to strike in the spring of 1863. However, their hand was forced when Wielopolski ordered, on 14 January 1863, the round-up and conscription into the tsarist army of 12,000 urban youths known to the police for their radicalism. With one surgical cut Wielopolski hoped to destroy the Reds in the middle of the winter when conditions were least favourable for an insurrection. To the consternation of many of their fellow conspirators in the provinces, the Red leadership decided to act. On 22 January 1863 the Central National Committee proclaimed itself the 'Provisional National Government', and declared war on Russia for the liberation of all of Russia's Polish lands within the limits of 1772. The insurgents initially had at their disposal merely 6,000 poorly armed men, mostly urban workers, artisans and impoverished nobles, against a Russian army of 100,000 in the Kingdom and a further equal number in the western *gubernii*. Most men of property looked aghast at the sheer irresponsibility of the young Reds.

The self-styled National Government hoped to lessen the disparity between the forces by winning over the mass of the peasantry to the struggle. To this end it issued a decree granting the peasants full property rights to all their holdings, and promising rewards in the form of land to all landless peasants who joined the insurrection. In mid-February Mierosławski, aspiring to become the Polish Garibaldi, was back in Poland as 'dictator'. The initial peasant response to the uprising was generally favourable but muted. The insurrection turned into a guerrilla war in which no more than 30,000 insurgents at any one time pitted themselves with little more than shotguns and scythes against the largest army in Europe. Yet despite their enormous military superiority and their early victories over Mierosławski's units, the Russians were unable to stamp out the insurgents whose hit-and-run tactics proved highly effective in the forests of Poland and Lithuania. Wide expressions of public sympathy in the West, and official British and French diplomatic protests to St Petersburg, only encouraged the insurgents in their illusions that foreign intervention would save their cause; as a result, support for the rising spread within Poland to groups hitherto opposed to the armed struggle. The Whites could not stomach Mierosławski and some were unhappy about the anonymous character of the National Government, but they were persuaded to join the insurrection when command was assumed by the moderates Marian Langiewicz and later Karol Majewski. The insurrection engulfed much of Lithuania and western Belarus but not the Ukraine, while numerous volunteers crossed the border from Poznania and Galicia.

In April 1863 the tsar's offer of an amnesty was rejected and the rising entered a more bitter phase. Alexander II dismissed Wielopolski, and replaced Grand Duke Constantine as viceroy with Field Marshal Berg, whose harsh methods emulated those of Mikhail Muraviev, the governor-general of Vilna, whose pitiless repression in the east earned him lasting notoriety in Polish patriotic tradition as 'the hangman'. The Reds took the reins of the National Government and responded with their brand of terror, deploying a security corps of so-called 'stiletto-men' against Russian officials and their Polish collaborators. Desperate to prolong the struggle until the spring of 1864, in the hope that France might yet intervene, the insurgents elected a new leader in October 1863: Romuald Traugutt, an experienced professional officer from the tsarist army who had resigned his commission in 1862 and who had proved his mettle as a guerrilla commander in the woods and marshes of Polesie. Traugutt's political sympathies lay with the Whites, but he infused the underground state with a renewed determination to survive; the insurrectionary army was reorganized and a unified military and civilian command created.

But the tide of events was turning against the insurgents. They were unable to establish effective control over any sizeable region of Russian Poland and were thus unable to implement systematically their land reform. The tensions between the Whites and the Reds weakened Traugutt's authority. The vocal support for the Polish cause of the Russian radicals Herzen and Bakunin, and of the Russian revolutionary organization 'Land and Will' produced limited practical benefits. Indeed, most of Russian public opinion, including many liberals and Slavophiles, rallied against the Poles in a powerful outburst of indignant patriotism. And once again the international situation, so vital a factor in the Poles' calculations and hopes, proved unfavourable. Austria and Prussia, in league at the time over the Danish problem, both adopted a hostile attitude to the Polish insurrection; Bismarck even offered to help the Russians against the rebels. Cut off from the rest of Europe, the Polish insurgents soon learnt that all the expressions of support and sympathy from Paris, London and elsewhere were a cruel deception. There was to be no European Congress to discuss the Polish issue, let alone any military intervention on their behalf.

In early March 1864 the tsarist authorities made a bold stroke to outmanoeuvre the National Government in the struggle for the hearts and minds of the peasants. The liberal Russian reformer N. N. Miliutin had finally persuaded the tsar that to offer the peasants the same property rights as those promised by the revolutionary government would do more than anything else to restore Russian control in the Kingdom. Indeed, following Tsar Alexander's generous decree of 2 March on land reform, support for the insurrection in the Polish countryside began to slacken as the peasants turned to securing their new rights. Traugutt and his associates were arrested in April and executed on 5 August 1864, by which time the remaining flames of insurrection had been largely snuffed out. The last insurgent unit, led by the radical priest Stanisław Brzóska, held out in Podlasie until 1865.

For those thousands of insurgents who were spared the gallows, there awaited the long march to penal servitude in Siberia. Landowners who had sympathized with or supported the uprising faced fines or the confiscation of their property. Yet another Polish generation paid the price for a heroic but ultimately doomed attempt to challenge the Partitions. However, it was a remarkable feat that the uprising managed to last for eighteen months against such overwhelming military odds. The insurgents proved to be an elusive and tenacious foe. From its hideouts in Warsaw the National Government was able to function under the very noses of the tsarist police, and in the countryside its secret agencies played hide-and-seek with the Russian army. In many areas landowners and peasants paid a 'national tax' and offered supplies to the insurgents who, although often surrounded and defeated, would quickly reform and resurface with fresh volunteers. The secret underground state that operated over much of Russian Poland in 1863–4 was an extraordinary phenomenon in the history of nationalism in nineteenth-century Europe. In the words of Viceroy Berg, it had been 'a truly devilish conspiracy'. But it could not hold out indefinitely against an army of nearly 400,000 men (half of the entire Russian land forces) which flooded the tsar's Polish lands, and especially with the demoralizing absence of any foreign intervention. Increasingly harsh reprisals and finally the tsar's gesture to the peasants also took their toll. Yet through its endorsement of the peasant cause, the insurrection had prompted the tsarist authorities to offer to the Kingdom's peasantry a far more generous deal than that contemplated by Wielopolski or indeed offered by the tsar to the peasants in Russia proper.

It now remained to be seen whether the peasants of Russian Poland would become the grateful and loyal subjects of their imperial master in St Petersburg, or whether, with their immediate economic demands satisfied, they would find a common national identity with their fellow countrymen. The international order that emerged after 1864 also represented a watershed in the history of the Polish struggles for independence. With the rise of Bismarckian Germany as the major power on the continent of Europe, and the consequent eclipse of France, all Polish illusions of western help died. The era of Romantic insurrections had come to an end. Nevertheless, the memory of the heroism and sacrifice of 1863–4 and the sense that a great injustice had been done were to leave a bitter and potent legacy.

5

An era of transformation, 1864–1914

The crushing of the insurrection of 1863–4 dealt what seemed to be a final and fatal body blow to the cause of Polish independence. A new wave of exiles, as defiant but not as illustrious as their predecessors of 1831, sought sanctuary in the west. Militant radicals amongst them joined the cause of international socialism, and many went to fight, and perish, on the barricades of the Paris Commune. The moderates set about devising no less unrealistic plans to preserve the national cause. Some of their ideas and activities were to germinate in the long run into vigorous socialist and nationalist movements within Poland, but at the moment, with every year that passed, the Polish Question as an international issue faded more and more into the distant background. The Russo-Turkish war of 1877–8 and the resulting Eastern Crisis raised a few desultory hopes, only to dash them. Indeed, the 1870s and 1880s witnessed a reinvigorated campaign by both the Russian and Prussian authorities to weaken still further the Polish character of their respective shares of old Poland. It was ironically in Austria, which had been least well disposed to Polish national aspirations in the early decades of the century, that Polish fortunes were to improve.

The distinct administrative status of the Congress Kingdom was much reduced, and Russian was imposed as the language of administration and of the courts. In 1874 that ill-fated creation of the Congress of Vienna was even formally renamed 'the Vistula Land' (Privislansky Kray), and the office of viceroy was abolished.

Censorship and strict police controls became the order of the day, and steps were taken to weaken the influence of the nobility among the Kingdom's peasantry. In the western *gubernii* the purchase of land by individuals of Polish or Catholic origin and the public use of the Polish language were forbidden. The Poles' sense of political impotence was further reinforced when two important liberal reforms, introduced in the 1860s in the rest of the Russian Empire by Tsar Alexander II, were not extended to any of the ex-Polish lands. These were the *zemstva*, elected district councils with extensive responsibilities for health, education and the economic infrastructure; and secondly, the jury system in the law courts. On the credit side, however, Polish conscripts into the tsarist army were at least able to benefit from Miliutin's humane army reforms which ended the system of twenty-year military servitude.

The active involvement of the Roman Catholic clergy in the recent uprising brought upon the Church increased restrictions, in both the Kingdom and the western *gubernii*. Most monasteries were closed, and surviving ones were forbidden to admit new members. A fifth of all Roman Catholic parishes in Lithuania and Belarus were dissolved. Protesting bishops were deported, with the result that by 1870 all but one of the Kingdom's dioceses were unoccupied. The surviving Greek Catholic diocese of Chełm in the south-east of the Kingdom was compelled to return to Orthodoxy in 1875; troops were used to whip the reluctant villagers into submission. An agreement between St Petersburg and the papacy in 1882 brought only limited respite to the Church in Russian Poland.

The Kingdom's educational system was not spared either. In the mid-1860s Russian became the obligatory language of instruction in all secondary schools, followed by all elementary schools in 1885. In 1869 a Russian-language university was opened in Warsaw to replace the closed 'Main School'. The humiliation experienced in 1878 by the young Maria Skłodowska (later Curie), and her fellow pupils, when instructed by a government school inspector to recite the Lord's Prayer in Russian and then to enumerate from memory all members of the imperial family, was a characteristic feature of those years.

The distinct status of Prussia's ex-Polish provinces was also eroded. Poznania and Danzig Pomerania (West Prussia), which had not been included in the German Confederation of 1815, were now fully integrated within the new Germany after 1871. German was finally established as the exclusive language of local administration, the courts and, by 1887, of all schools, with the notable exception of religious instruction. Nothing was now left of earlier Polish hopes for the creation of a Polish university in Poznań. Bismarck was not a modern-style German nationalist, and initially considered Polish-speaking peasants capable of loyal service to the Prussian state. But he was adamant that Polish aspirations to statehood were fundamentally incompatible with Prussian and German state interests, and that Polish nationalism, represented primarily by the nobility and the clergy, was on a par with Catholicism as a centrifugal force hostile to the new Reich. Bismarck's attempt in the 1870s to subordinate the Roman Catholic Church to the German state and to limit its influence in society, the so-called *Kulturkampf*, acquired in the east a distinctly anti-Polish character. In the Poznań-Gniezno archdiocese most remaining monasteries and convents were dissolved, and between 1873 and 1877 30 per cent of the parishes were deprived of their priests by police arrests. The ultramontane Archbishop Ledóchowski was imprisoned for two years and was then obliged to leave for Rome. Yet the unintended outcome of the *Kulturkampf* in the east was the strengthening of the links between religion and nationality, most unexpectedly in Upper Silesia. In response to growing nationalist demands within the Reich to strengthen even more the German character of the Prussian east, Bismarck created in 1886 a special fund to buy out Polish-owned estates with the aim of distributing the land among German settlers. Except for a short conciliatory period towards the Poles under Chancellor Caprivi between 1890 and 1894, when the government needed the support of the Polish deputies in the Reichstag, the resulting struggle over land added yet another dimension to the persistent nationality conflict in the east.

The policies of the Austrian government towards its Polish subjects in the latter part of the nineteenth century provided a sharp contrast to developments in Russia and Prussia. Major defeats at the hands of France and Prussia, in 1859 and 1866 respectively, weakened the Austrian Empire and obliged Vienna to make constitutional concessions. The creation of a partly representative

Council of State and of regional parliaments in the early 1860s led in 1867 to the more thorough transformation of the empire into the Austro-Hungarian Dual Monarchy. Inhibited by still vivid memories of the jacquerie of 1846 and apprehensive about the Ukrainian national revival, the predominantly conservative Polish leadership in Galicia contented itself with a limited degree of autonomy within the Austrian half of the Dual Monarchy.

In return for loyalty to Austria, control of Galicia's internal affairs was gradually transferred to the local Polish elite. Until 1918 the posts of viceroy and of the minister for Galicia in the Viennese cabinet were both held by Poles. A narrow class-based franchise ensured a landed and middle-class domination of the provincial Sejm in Lwów, and of the Galician representation to the central Austrian parliament. Between 1877 and 1889 there were no peasant representatives in the provincial Diet, and only a handful of Ukrainians. A number of Polish aristocrats held high office in Vienna: Count Alfred Potocki and Count Kazimierz Badeni served as Austria's prime ministers in 1870–1 and 1895–7, respectively; Count Agenor Gołuchowski (the elder) was interior minister and minister of state from 1859 to 1860, while his son served as foreign minister between 1895 and 1906. Polish national culture was allowed to flourish; after 1870 the Polish language was restored in the administration, the courts, the schools and in the two universities of Kraków and Lwów. The hitherto passive Catholic hierarchy in Galicia acquired a more pronounced national character and greater freedom of action: in 1879 the patriotic Albin Dunajewski was nominated archbishop of Kraków, and in 1890 was elevated to the cardinalate. Kraków emerged as the centre of the Polish world of art, to be dominated for three decades by Jan Matejko, whose vast historical canvases portrayed a glorified and dramatic vision of Poland's past. Compared to what had existed before, and to what was happening in Russian and Prussian Poland, these were substantial political and cultural benefits; yet they did not quickly bring commensurate economic and social progress to what remained for decades a backward province of the Austrian Empire.

The new realities within Poland and across Europe as a whole compelled many educated Poles to reassess critically their nation's predicament and its prospects for the future. The first and most vigorous intellectual and historical condemnation of the futility of political Romanticism and of the tradition of armed insurrections came in 1869 from a group of erstwhile freedom fighters, now prominent intellectuals in Kraków: the historian Jan Szujski and the literary historian Stanisław Tarnowski. In Szujski's memorable phrase, *liberum conspiro* (the freedom to conspire) was an anarchic and destructive principle on a par with the old *liberum veto*. To this was added, in the late 1870s, a scathing critique of Poland's past by the influential historian Michał Bobrzyński. Known in Poland as the 'Stańczyks', with reference to Stańczyk, a sixteenth-century court jester, they endeavoured to influence Polish public opinion in the spirit of political realism, hard work and social conservatism. The essential unity of Polish culture had to be promoted, ran their message, but politically the Poles had little alternative but to accept 'tri-loyalism', or co-existence with their three respective governments. It was a position easier to adopt under the Habsburgs' tolerant rule in Galicia than under the strict tsarist regime in Warsaw; nevertheless, to many conservative men of property across Poland tri-loyalism offered a prudent way of coming to terms with difficult political realities.

The futile heroism of the insurrectionary tradition was also condemned in the 1870s by the Positivists of Warsaw. Drawing heavily on the values of western rationalism and empirical philosophy, and on the tradition of 'organic work', they called on the Poles to focus on strengthening the economic, social and cultural sinews of the nation. Modern European civilization had to be the way of the future, not impractical dreams. The leading Positivists, such as the journalist and publicist Aleksander Świętochowski, the novelists Bolesław Prus and Eliza Orzeszkowa, or the poet Adam Asnyk, offered in their work a realistic and anti-obscurantist approach to social problems which did much to promote the cause of progress in their country. One of the main achievements of the Positivists was a clandestine 'flying university', founded in 1886, offering rigorous academic courses in Polish. By the 1880s, however, it was becoming clear that industrialization and urbanization, especially in Russian Poland, were creating social divisions and tensions rather than the social harmony and national unity of which they dreamt.

The latter objectives were most successfully promoted in Poznania where Polish landowners, artisans, peasants and priests found common ground in the defence of their faith, their land and their nationality against German nationalist pressure. Economic co-operatives and self-help educational societies, many led by priests, flourished. Over a thousand Polish libraries, mostly of a religious and moralistic character, operated in Poznania and Silesia. The Polish-owned Peasant Bank, founded in 1872, had 125,000 members by 1910. In 1888 the Poles of Prussia even founded a Land Bank to counteract Berlin's policy of buying out Polish landowners. The strong sense of nationality of the Poznanian peasants was not only a reaction to the *Kulturkampf* but also a reflection of the advanced level of civilization in Prussia's Polish lands. The emergence in Prussian Poland of a modern, highly productive system of agriculture owed much to the early Prussian land reform which had favoured the creation of economically viable large and medium-sized farms. It was also encouraged by the demand for food in Germany's expanding industrial cities, by the German government's protectionist tariffs on agricultural products, and by the construction of a dense railway network throughout Prussia.

The pace of economic development and social change during the last four decades of the nineteenth century was markedly different in each of the regions of partitioned Poland. In the former Congress Kingdom the tsarist land reform of 1864 had created an uneven patchwork of reduced landed estates and numerous small and fragmented peasant holdings. Agricultural productivity here was much lower than in Poznania. Indeed, the entire rural sector was badly hit by the agricultural slump of the 1880s. In contrast to the wealthier aristocracy, many landowners among the lesser gentry did not survive the crisis and drifted into the urban professions and into the growing ranks of the intelligentsia, which retained many of the gentry's cultural values and genteel habits. Among the peasants, too, the more robust coped, but many had to sell their uneconomic holdings (most were under 15 hectares in size) and seek new jobs or join the armies of seasonal labourers that criss-crossed this part of Europe at harvest time. On the other hand, there was a striking

29 Weaving hall of Karl Wilhelm Scheibler's cotton mill in Łódź, the 'Manchester of Poland'. The importance of Łódź as textile centre dates from the 1820s. The abolition of the customs barrier between Russia and the Kingdom of Poland in 1850 and the arrival of the railway in 1866 stimulated the city's economic expansion. By the 1870s, the German-born Scheibler (1820–81) was the leading mill-owner in Łódź, and his textile business the largest in the Russian empire. The dynamic, acquisitive and socially divided world of Łódź, with its Polish, German and Jewish inhabitants, was recreated in the novel *Ziemia obiecana* (*The promised land*) (1898) by Władysław Reymont. Two film versions of the novel have been made, one in 1927 and one in 1974 by Andrzej Wajda.

growth of industry, of towns and of railway construction, even if modest by English or German standards. The population of Warsaw, now an important metallurgical centre, doubled between 1864 and 1890 to nearly half a million and reached over 760,000 in 1910; that of Łódź, which attracted much German capital and which directed much of its vast textile production to Russia and the Far East, increased spectacularly from 28,000 in 1860 to 410,000 in 1910. Coal-mining expanded in the Dąbrowa basin near the Silesian border. The proportion of the urban population of the Kingdom grew from just over a fifth of the total in 1872 to about a third in 1909, by which time the value of industrial production exceeded the agricultural. In economic terms, the former Kingdom had become the most advanced region of the Russian Empire.

Much less developed was Galicia with its dense patchwork of small and frequently subdivided peasant holdings, its abject rural poverty and its socially conservative elite. Until 1890 the province remained in debt to the central government in Vienna and was burdened by indemnity payments to landowners following the peasant emancipation of 1848. It trailed far behind industrialized Teschen Silesia as well as other western regions of Austria. At the beginning of the twentieth century, out of a population of 7.3 million, Galicia had no more than 60,000 industrial workers. Its only significant industrial activity was the extraction of oil (over 5 per cent of world production in 1909) around Borysław and Drohobycz in the south-east. Economic expansion did accelerate after 1890, and the cities of Lwów and Kraków reached a respectable size by 1910, with 207,000 and 174,000 inhabitants respectively.

The last decades of the nineteenth century witnessed substantial demographic growth across Poland, with the resulting mass exodus of poor peasants to the industrial areas of Westphalia and subsequently overseas, mainly to the United States and Brazil; about 2.5 million peasants are estimated to have left the ethnic Polish lands between 1870 and 1914. By 1914 the number of Poles in the United States stood at about four million; they had their own schools and churches, and represented at that stage the largest immigrant community from central Europe. The Polish character of large parts of Chicago in the first half of the twentieth century

30   Marie Curie-Skłodowska: a Nobel prize-winner, photographed in
1913 in Birmingham. After training herself in chemical analysis in the
laboratories of the Museum of Industry and Agriculture in Warsaw, she
left to study in Paris where she graduated in physics and mathematics. In
1895 she married the physicist Pierre Curie. In 1898 she discovered two
highly radioactive new elements, polonium and radium. She was twice
awarded the Nobel Prize: in 1903 (together with her husband and
Antoine Henri Becquerel) for physics, and in 1911, alone, for chemistry.
She always maintained close contact with her native country, and was
instrumental in the establishment of the Radium Institute in Warsaw in
1932.

owed much to this early wave of job-seeking emigrants. In the absence of adequate cultural and educational institutions, especially in Russian Poland, many talented Poles of gentry or middle-class background also left to make careers abroad. Joseph Conrad (Korzeniowski), Ignacy Paderewski and Maria Curie-Skłodowska (see opposite) provide three most eminent examples. To these one could also add the names of two future presidents of Poland: Gabriel Narutowicz, an expert on hydroelectricity, and the chemist Ignacy Mościcki, both of whom acquired their professional reputations in Switzerland. By the same token, numerous Polish engineers made their fortunes in the Russian interior and Siberia where their Polish origins were not a liability. Nor did his national background prevent Wacław Niżyński (better known as Vaslav Nijinsky) from making a glittering career as a star of Russian ballet. And even among Poles sentenced to exile in Siberia and the Russian Far East there were scholars who contributed to the scientific knowledge of those distant lands: Benedykt Dybowski classified the fauna of Lake Baykal, while Bronisław Piłsudski (Józef's brother) conducted anthropological studies on Sakhalin.

The western *gubernii* of the Russian Empire retained a predominantly rural character, although the coming of the railways did stimulate economic activity. Nevertheless, rural over-population took its toll here too; nearly a quarter of the ethnic Lithuanian population emigrated, mostly to the United States, between 1864 and 1914. Belarus, with its poor soil and extensive forests, remained most backward; among the isolated and self-sufficient marshland communities in Polesie primitive conditions continued well into the twentieth century. In the Ukraine west of the river Dnieper, substantial Polish landed fortunes managed to survive; their owners, such as the Potockis or the Branickis, had the scope and resources to modernize their estates and to develop ancillary food industries, especially the highly profitable refining of beet-sugar. Until 1917 Kiev was home to a large and thriving Polish intelligentsia.

Economically, the separate zones of what had once been the Polish-Lithuanian Commonwealth were moving in different directions and according to different rhythms. The growing dependence of Poznanian agriculture on the German market and of the

31   A scene of peasant life in Polesie. The photograph was taken in 1938, but it reflects a way of life that had changed little since the late nineteenth century. Much of Polesie, perhaps the most backward part of the lands of the former Polish-Lithuanian Commonwealth, consisted of marshland fed by the river Prypet and its tributaries. The region's rural inhabitants were mostly Orthodox and spoke Belarusian. They would most probably refer to themselves as 'tutejsi' – 'we who live here'. Illiteracy here still amounted to well over 70 per cent in 1914.

Kingdom's industrial sector on the Russian market integrated those regions with the German and Russian economies. The railway systems constructed across Poland in the nineteenth century reflected this vividly. Warsaw's long circuitous railway links with Poznań, Kraków and Lwów were hardly those that would have been built had Warsaw been the capital of a united Poland. Only with Wilno was a direct line established in 1862 as part of the Warsaw–St Petersburg railway. The railway networks continued to grow, but even as late as 1914 only three mainline and three secondary rail routes crossed from Prussia into Russian Poland. A cursory glance at a map of the Polish state railways today clearly highlights the dense network in the areas that had belonged to the German Reich before 1918.

Against this background of economic and social change it is difficult to be precise about the degree and extent of the Polish-speaking peasantry's national sentiments. A complex set of regional factors was at play here. While military service, especially in the Austrian army, had some influence in inculcating loyalty to the three empires among young male Poles, official Prussian and Russian hostility towards Catholicism and the Polish language, not to mention a misguided tsarist campaign against the wearing of national dress, had the opposite effect. The migration of thousands of peasants into the towns also affected cultural and social mores. The peasants brought with them traditions of rural religiosity and in turn were exposed to the patriotism of the urban artisans and to the ideas of the early socialists. The end of serfdom and the growing awareness through education and literacy of a wider world beyond the village community were undoubtedly key factors in shaping the peasants' consciousness. Yet there were unusual contrasts in this respect. In Prussian Poland primary education was compulsory and illiteracy was virtually eliminated by 1900, but all schools used German as the language of instruction; nevertheless, evidence of an emerging Polish identity could be observed even among the Kashubians of Danzig Pomerania who started electing Polish deputies to the Reichstag. In Russian Poland, government-sponsored primary education was in Russian, but the provision of schooling at all levels remained woefully inadequate; at the end of the nineteenth century illiteracy levels there still hovered about the 65 per cent mark. The teaching of the Polish language, in both Prussian and Russian Poland, became the activity primarily of voluntary and autodidactic educational societies sponsored by private philanthropists and by socialist and nationalist parties. By the early 1900s such secret teaching embraced about a third of the Kingdom's population. In aristocratic and well-to-do families, and among the intelligentsia, the written language was taught at home by the ladies of the house or by tutors. At all levels of society effective counter measures were deployed against the onslaught of cultural germanization and russification.

Only Galicia enjoyed a formal system of primary education in Polish, even though as late as 1900 it was available to only about 30 per cent of the province's children; in the case of Ukrainian youngsters the proportion was even lower. A major government-sponsored expansion of village schooling under viceroy Bobrzyński between 1908 and 1913 did lower illiteracy levels to below 50 per cent. Galicia's extensive national and political freedoms (universal male franchise was introduced in Austria in 1907), its Polish-language schools and newspapers, and opportunities of partici-pating in public life all helped to nurture a sense of a Polish identity among the rural population. The memoirs of Jan Słomka (1842–1927), the first written by a Polish peasant, who described the evolution from serfdom to constitutional government in Galicia, provide a vivid illustration of this process.

Just as feelings of national consciousness were spreading among wider sections of the Polish-speaking population, so similar devel-opments could be observed among other ethnic groups inhabiting what had been the eastern half of the former Commonwealth. In due course, the new national movements in the east, led by the native clergy and the emerging local intelligentsias of peasant descent, acquired a political character; they rejected the concept of the old multicultural Commonwealth and challenged the con-tinuing Polish social and cultural supremacy in the east. The earliest strides in this direction had been made by the Ukrainians of eastern Galicia where, in conditions of relative freedom under Austrian rule, their cultural and learned societies gave evidence of impressive vitality. Conservative clerical leaders among the Galician Ukrain-ians initially favoured closer bonds of affinity with Russia, but in the 1880s they were successfully challenged by a younger radical group, inspired by the writer Ivan Franko, which espoused the cause of an all-Ukrainian national identity, clearly distinct from Russians and Poles alike. Many Polish and Ukrainian communities existed peacefully side by side under Habsburg rule, but the Polish domination of Galicia's public life and the prevalence of Polish-speaking landlords in eastern Galicia accentuated inter-ethnic and class resentments and eventually contributed to bitter mutual antagonism. A Ukrainian literary and cultural movement also emerged in the Russian Empire in the 1840s; its chief ideologist was Mykola Kostomarov and its leading bard Taras Shevchenko. A single Ukrainian literary language, based on the dialects of the Poltava and Kiev regions, was eventually adopted by Ukrainian writers and publicists on both sides of the Austro-Russian border.

The tsarist government was not only uncompromisingly hostile towards all Polish-inspired secessionism, but it also adopted a negative attitude to the awakening of other local national cultures in the western borderlands of the Russian Empire. The Ukrainian language, for instance, was banned from Russian schools in 1863, and from printing and publishing in 1876, as was the case with Belarusian. The existence of these Slavonic languages was denied by Russian officialdom; indeed, their encouragement was seen as part of a Polish conspiracy to weaken the Russian nation. Discriminatory restrictions against the Lithuanian language, which is not a Slavonic tongue, were less severe, but the tsarist authorities insisted, until 1904, that the Lithuanian language could only be printed in the Cyrillic alphabet. However, they could not effectively prevent the illegal distribution from East Prussia of Lithuanian-language publications printed in the Latin alphabet and vigorously expressing a new linguistically based Lithuanian national identity. The most important journal was *Auszra* (Dawn), edited by Jonas Basanavičius and Jonas Šliupas. In 1863–4 most ethnic Lithuanians had sided with the Poles against tsarist despotism, but the paths of the two nationalities began to diverge soon after that. Indeed, the new Lithuanian national revival, despite its indebtedness to Polish Romanticism and the support of several eminent bi-cultural bishops and writers, acquired strong anti-Polish characteristics, born out of a resentment towards the cultural polonization of most of the *szlachta* and of the educated classes in the former Grand Duchy of Lithuania. The modest beginnings of a Belarusian literary revival, based largely on Polish models and even encouraged by local Polish patriots as a means of resisting Russian influence, could also be observed in this period. The pattern of inter-ethnic relationships in the western *gubernii* was complicated by social, linguistic and religious factors. While the Roman Catholic faith tended to reflect Polish cultural orientation in Belarus and in the Ukraine, it was the linguistic divide, and not religion, that came to distinguish modern Lithuanians from Poles or polonized Lithuanians.

The world of the Jewry of the former Polish-Lithuanian Commonwealth was also changing. In the Congress Kingdom the process that had begun with the emancipation decree of 1862 continued; many able, better-off and enterprising Jews left the confines of their traditional religious and cultural communities to

32 Feast of the Trumpets – Jewish New Year. Painted by Aleksander Gierymski (1850–1901) in 1884. Orthodox Jews singing and praying on the banks of the Vistula in Warsaw. Gierymski, a realist painter sensitive to the effect of strong light, painted many memorable scenes of Jewish life. In the background a steam train crosses the Kierbedź railway bridge.

play a full part in the Gentile world. Indeed, in large urban centres cases of assimilation into the upper bourgeoisie and the intelligentsia were not uncommon, the most prominent examples being the banking and industrial families of the Kronenbergs, the Blochs and the Poznańskis. Assimilation could also be observed in Galicia, especially in Kraków and Lwów, where Jews were granted equal civil rights after 1867. On the other hand, large numbers of poorer Galician Jews sought a better life by migrating to Vienna. In Poznania most Jews gravitated towards German culture, and indeed left for Germany proper. In the western *gubernii*, where about 40 per cent of the urban population was Jewish, secularized Jews were increasingly drawn to Russian culture, despite the continuation there of a wide range of tsarist restrictions on Jewish life.

The expansion of industry and trade, and the rising proportion of Jews in the towns of the Kingdom also accentuated the economic rivalry between Gentile and Jewish shopkeepers, pedlars and all sorts of middlemen, and added a further dimension to popular anti-Jewish sentiments. These were also fuelled by the arrival there in the 1880s of thousands of russianized Jews (the so-called 'Litvaks') fleeing poverty and pogroms in western Russia, and by the emergence of an exclusive ethnically based Polish nationalism. The hopes that Gentile and Jew would act together in the cause of civil rights and of national liberation, so strong in the Kingdom from 1861 to 1864, burnt much less brightly as the century wore on, although they did continue in the Polish socialist movement and among the progressive intelligentsia. Jewish emigration, especially to the New World, grew apace; over a million Jews left the lands of the former Commonwealth between 1870 and 1914. The extraordinary diversity of the Jewish world was further accentuated in the late 1890s by the rise of two rival secular political movements: Zionism, with its vision of Jewish statehood, and the socialist Bund, which set out to embrace the large Jewish working population of the Russian Empire.

As elsewhere in central and parts of eastern Europe, new ideological and political movements were emerging in Polish society: socialism, modern nationalism and agrarian populism. A new generation of radicals took up the mantle of the exiles of 1864 and challenged the Polish elites who had sought some form of accommodation with the prevailing political realities. Although these movements were eventually to acquire a mass and pan-Polish dimension, they also possessed their own specific regional characteristics, reflecting the different conditions under Russian, German and Austrian rule.

Modern Polish socialism, which appeared in the 1870s, drew not only on the inspiration of Marx and Engels but also on the native Romantic insurrectionary tradition and the revolutionary potential of Russia's militant populists (the Narodniks). From the start there were tensions between the movement's national and internationalist objectives. The early socialist Bolesław Limanowski, who was based in Geneva, favoured the former; Ludwik Waryński, who in 1882 founded the first Marxist group on Polish soil, stressed the primacy of the latter. Waryński's organization was quickly broken up by the tsarist police and the focus of Polish socialist activity moved abroad. In 1892 in Paris the Polish Socialist Party (the PPS) was formed, soon to be led by the conspiratorial Józef Piłsudski.

Just as the earlier generations of radicals hoped to mobilize the peasants in the struggle for independence, so now Piłsudski saw in the growing industrial working class of Russian Poland a revolutionary instrument with which to overthrow tsarist rule. Central to this was the presupposition that socialism could only be achieved in an independent and reunited Poland, which would be open on a voluntary basis to all its historic national groups. This met with the bitter opposition of those doctrinaire Marxists, like Rosa Luxemburg, who rejected the cause of Polish independence as fundamentally incompatible with the supranational nature of socialism, and running in the face of capitalist development which had bound the Kingdom economically to Russia. In 1893 Luxemburg and her associates formed the rival Social Democratic Party of the Kingdom of Poland (the SDKP); in 1900 it was given a new lease of life, largely through the efforts of Feliks Dzierżyński (Dzerzhinsky), as the Social Democratic Party of the Kingdom of Poland and Lithuania (the SDKPiL). In terms of size the PPS was to have a marked advantage over the SDKPiL, with 50,000 members compared to 30,000 in 1906; but it was clear that Polish socialism was bitterly divided. It is ironic that Piłsudski and Dzierżyński, who both experienced tsarist repression in their youth and whose personal careers were to lead in totally different directions, both came from gentry families in Lithuania. The two socialist parties were to remain unreconciled over the 'national question'; and even within the PPS tensions between the party's social and national objectives would surface repeatedly. And although Rosa Luxemburg was a secularized Polish Jewess from Zamość, the establishment in 1898 in Russia of a distinct Jewish socialist party, the Bund, was a further reflection of the problematic relationship between socialism and nationality in eastern Europe.

Whether in its German or its Polish variety, socialism failed to strike deep roots in Prussian Poland. In Poznania the number of industrial workers was small, and the association of Polishness with Catholicism was too strong. In Upper Silesia the large industrial labour force (numbering about 360,000 in 1900) tended to vote for the German Catholic Centre Party until the 1890s. The advanced system of social security introduced in the 1880s by Bismarck also lessened material deprivation and class tensions in the German east. Socialism made a little more headway in Galicia, where it tapped into the local radical traditions. The socialist party was able to function legally in Austria and adopted a gradualist non-revolutionary programme of extending workers' political and social rights. But socialism in Austria had to contend with the monarchy's complex nationality problems which brought about the movement's fragmentation into autonomous linguistic-ethnic components. The most outstanding among the Polish socialists in Galicia was Ignacy Daszyński, a talented orator and future parliamentarian; among the Ukrainian socialists it was Ivan Franko and Mykhailo Pavlyk.

However significant the rise of socialism in Poland, there existed in Polish society even more powerful nationalist undercurrents which could be tapped and profitably manipulated by a modern nationalist party. The potential attraction of nationalist sentiments was reflected, for instance, by the enormous popularity of Henryk Sienkiewicz's historical *Trilogy*, published between 1883 and 1888. Although himself not a nationalist, Sienkiewicz's swashbuckling epic, set in the seventeenth century during Poland's difficult wars against rebellious Cossacks and invading Swedes and Turks, provided a powerful Romanticized vision of Poland's past which was to leave its mark on the historical consciousness of subsequent Polish generations. Strong anti-German sentiments were also given vent in Bolesław Prus' *Placówka* (The outpost) of 1885 which dealt with the rivalry of Polish and German peasants over land, and in Sienkiewicz's medieval tale of conflict with the rapacious Teutonic Knights (*Krzyżacy*, 1890).

The origins of the modern Polish nationalist movement can be traced to the clandestine Polish League founded in Geneva by the émigré Zygmunt Miłkowski, a veteran of the 1863–4 insurrection, and to the secret youth organization 'Zet' created by Zygmunt Balicki in Kraków, both in 1887. Miłkowski's nationalism, however, contained too many liberal elements to be acceptable to Warsaw's hard young nationalist activists such as Roman Dmowski. The movement was renamed in 1893 the National League and then, in 1897, the National Democratic Party (nick-named in Polish the 'Endecja'). Dmowski and his associates attacked the political passivity of the Positivists, the tri-loyalism of the conservatives, as well as all manifestations of the 'sentimental patriotism' and 'false doctrinaire humanitarianism' of the Romantic era. New strategies were needed if the Poles were to survive under foreign rule in the age of imperialism and *Realpolitik*. Without abandoning the dream of independence, the National Democrats focused on pragmatic but effectively organized political action, and developed a nationalist ideology that owed much to the new ideas of Social Darwinism. A naturalist by education, Dmowski was attracted to the idea, best expressed in his book *Thoughts of a modern Pole* (1902), that a struggle for survival existed among states and national groups, and that conflict had a vital functional role in strengthening the identity and resilience of a nation. The ethical values of the individual, Balicki argued in turn in his *National egoism and ethics* (1903), had to be subordinated to the collective national interest.

By moderating their early social radicalism, which had initially alarmed many wealthy Poles, the National Democrats made impressive strides in the Kingdom, winning considerable middle-class and artisan support. Their skilful propaganda campaigns and educational activities in the countryside also brought them many peasant adherents, just as their gymnastic societies and youth organizations attracted many youngsters. By emphasizing their opposition to socialism, the National Democrats were able to attract many members of the Catholic clergy, although in the Kingdom the party's relationship with the Church was not always harmonious. The National Democrats saw in the recently united and economically dynamic German nation a greater threat to the Poles than the sluggish empire of the tsars. The anti-German stance of the ND party also enabled it to extend its influence in Poznania and among the industrial workers of Upper Silesia where the local ND leader Wojciech Korfanty attained prominence. The ND attitude to the non-Polish nationalities in the east, especially to the Ukrainians in Galicia, was uncompromising: they had to submit to cultural and linguistic polonization or had to prove their own claim to nationhood in an uneven political and economic battle with the Poles. Hardly surprisingly, anti-Semitism became a key element in the ND ideology. The Jews were depicted not just as a prominently visible alien religious-cultural entity, but also as an economic and elemental threat, all the more menacing through their influence on Polish intellectual life, to the creation of a strong integrated and ethnically based Polish nation. It was all a categorical repudiation of the early Romantic vision of a pluralist Poland bringing freedom to all its national and ethnic groups, and as such horrified Polish conservatives and left-wing democrats alike. Nevertheless, the National Democrats were to succeed in inculcating xenophobic attitudes among numerous Poles who were at this time acquiring a semblance of political awareness and a sense of their national identity.

The modern Polish populist or peasant movement made its gradual appearance in Galicia in the mid-1870s. Much of the early leadership was provided by Stanisław Stojałowski, a priest with a considerable flair for demagogy who tried to instil among the peasants of Galicia the virtues of self-reliance, economic cooperation and civic patriotism. The sight of Stojałowski entering Kraków in 1883 at the head of a 12,000-strong peasant rally to commemorate the bicentenary of Sobieski's victory over the Turks outside Vienna must have amazed anyone still remembering the jacquerie of 1846. But Stojałowski's methods soon met with the strong disapproval of state and church authorities alike, and his influence waned. More lasting proved the efforts of Bolesław Wysłouch, an exile from Russian Poland, who as a student in St Petersburg had been associated with Russian populists and later with Polish socialists in Warsaw, and who had since settled in Lwów. In his journals, in the late 1880s, Wysłouch attacked the conservatism of the Stańczyks and outlined the vision of a prosperous, fully politicized and nationally conscious peasantry as the basis for a future democratic Polish state that would embrace all ethnic Polish lands and which would recognize the national rights of the Ukrainians and of other peoples in the east. With his indefatigable wife Maria and his talented follower Jan Stapiński, Wysłouch launched his political peasant party in Rzeszów in 1895. Although its anticlericalism brought it into conflict with the Catholic Church, the new party successfully entered Galician political life, and gradually widened its ambitions; in 1903 it adopted the title of the Polish Peasant Party (the PSL).

The response of the Catholic Church to the new social conditions and to the accompanying ideological ferment varied in the different regions of the country. As already indicated, the *Kulturkampf* had strengthened the link between Polishness and Catholicism in Prussian Poland. In Galicia the Church's privileged position in public life and its long hostility to independent political action among the peasantry militated at first against the emergence of a priest–peasant solidarity of the Poznanian type. Although the clergy here were heavily involved in the rural temperance movement, it was only during the first decade of the twentieth century that the Church hierarchy modified its negative attitude to the populist movement.

Despite a welcome general thaw in tsarist policy towards the Kingdom after the accession of Tsar Nicholas II in 1894, the scope for open social and educational work by the Church in Russian Poland was hampered by the authorities until 1905. Considerable help to the rural and urban poor was provided by worker-nuns, who wore ordinary clothes, lived privately or at home, and thereby concealed their membership of officially banned religious orders. The Church's involvement in social work was encouraged by Pope Leo XIII's encyclical 'Rerum Novarum' (1891) which recognized the rights of workers to form trade unions and to receive fair pay. It was a belated but significant response by the Vatican to the problems of modern industrial society and to the threat of godless socialism. Out of this arose in the Polish lands a Church-sponsored Christian political-social movement which promoted social harmony; it struck roots especially in Prussian Poland and, not surprisingly, was to find much common ground with the programme of Dmowski's National Democrats.

The outbreak of the Russo-Japanese war in February 1904 and the Russian Revolution of 1905 brought out in sharp relief the political and social divisions in the Kingdom; like an X-ray, the Revolution illuminated starkly the new realities that had arisen in Russia's Polish lands since 1864. All political groupings expected some benefits for Poland from Russia's discomfort in the Far East. Conservative elements among the Kingdom's wealthy classes formed a Party of Realistic Politics, and hoped that their public loyalty to the tsar would be rewarded with religious, linguistic and legal concessions. Dmowski's NDs hoped for a fair degree of autonomy. The PPS, on the other hand, as the inheritor of the Romantic insurrectionary tradition, started preparations for an uprising. To seek assistance against Russia Piłsudski even travelled to Japan, only to discover that Dmowski had preceded him there and had helped to dissuade the Japanese from sponsoring a Polish revolt against Russia. Nevertheless, Piłsudski did return with some funds and arms to equip PPS fighting squads. Tension continued to grow in the Kingdom. The war disrupted trade, brought a fall in industrial production, and increased unemployment. The situation was exacerbated by a poor harvest and widespread opposition to the mobilization for the Russian army. Demonstrations became more frequent, and PPS squads started regular shoot-outs with the police. News of 'Bloody Sunday' on 22 January 1905, when tsarist troops fired into a procession of unarmed workers outside the Winter Palace in St Petersburg, electrified opinion throughout the Kingdom, which was soon paralysed by a month-long general strike of industrial workers. Students and pupils boycotted Russian schools and demanded the restoration of Polish in educational institutions. The peasants, increasingly aware of their nationality and responsive to political militancy, also agitated for the wider use of the Polish language in public administration.

In April 1905 the tsarist government introduced religious toleration and rescinded some of the restrictions on the use of local
languages. Worker protests, inspired by the socialist parties, continued regardless. Even agricultural labourers stopped work and
demanded higher pay. In June an armed workers' uprising gripped
Łódź, resulting in the loss of hundreds of lives. An all-Russian
railway strike in October led to a general strike throughout the
empire, plunging Russia further into revolutionary chaos. Disorder
spread in the Kingdom, and the scale of terrorist attacks on tsarist
officials and policemen approached that of 1863. The gulf between
the militant PPS and the pragmatic NDs widened as a result, and
then degenerated into mutual hatred. The NDs condemned the
unequal struggle against the tsarist regime as grossly irresponsible,
and formed their own worker organizations and fighting squads to
oppose the socialists. The revolution in Russian Poland was
turning into a civil war. The conservative Realists and the Catholic
hierarchy, led by the archbishop of Warsaw Wincenty Popiel,
increasingly felt obliged to look to the tsarist government for the
preservation of the threatened social order. Tsar Nicholas II's
October Manifesto, promising political liberalization and the
introduction of a Russian parliament (the Duma) gave heart to the
NDs and to the Realists in their hope that the restoration of a
Polish administration would calm tempers in the Kingdom and
weaken the forces of socialism; it was a calculation very reminiscent of Wielopolski in the early 1860s. But the Russian authorities
were not prepared to make any substantial political concessions to
the Poles; a delegation of ND and Realist leaders returned empty-
handed from St Petersburg. On 11 November martial law was
introduced in the Kingdom. Political polarization in Russia continued as the future of the revolution hung in the balance. On the
heels of the workers' uprising in Moscow in December, the PPS
made another armed bid to overthrow the tsarist regime in the
Kingdom, and to transform the revolution into a national uprising.
But events were slowly turning in favour of the authorities.

The Russian army, which in the main remained loyal to the tsar,
proceeded to crush the remaining pockets of resistance within the
Russian Empire. Moderate elements in the Kingdom, as in Russia
proper, remained willing to participate in the new constitutional

order promised by the tsar. Fissures emerged within the PPS: between the young left-wingers ready to seek benefits for Poland within a wider revolutionary settlement in Russia, and the 'elders' under Piłsudski, with his paramilitaries, who continued to press for an independent socialist Poland. In November 1906 the PPS formally split into the 'Revolutionary Fraction' under Piłsudski, and the 'Left', which then gravitated to the SDKPiL, hostile as ever to independence. Piłsudski reorganized his fighters, who continued their terrorist attacks throughout 1907, until the futility of the internecine killings between the PPS and the NDs made both sides see sense.

None of the political parties operating in the Kingdom gained their full objectives during the revolutionary turmoil. Tsarism had survived, the Kingdom's status was not altered, and martial law remained. The animosities and hatreds exacerbated by the revolution left their poison in Polish society. On the other hand, 1905 did bring about important benefits to the Poles under Russian rule. Workers' pay and conditions improved, trade unions were legalized, and a vigorous co-operative movement was able to mushroom. The lifting of many restrictions on political, social and cultural life, and on the public use of the Polish language was welcomed by the Poles, especially in the western *gubernii* where they were again allowed to buy land. A 'Polish Circle' of fifty-five deputies, dominated by the NDs and led personally by Dmowski, was to sit in the Duma. Dmowski had every intention of using his team in parliamentary horse-trading to win further benefits for the Poles, playing a role not dissimilar to Redmond's constitutional Irish Home Rule party in Westminster. There is also no doubt that the dramatic events of 1904–7 heightened the political awareness of wider sections of the urban and rural population, and gave encouragement to the radicals. On the other hand, for many men of property and for many Catholic clergymen the attraction of the National Democrats, as a force against socialism and all revolutionary methods, grew.

The failure of Edward Ropp, the bishop of Wilno, to create a broad Catholic front embracing Poles, Lithuanians and Belarusians demonstrated that new national loyalties were also at work among the population of historic Lithuania. Lithuanian political agitation in 1904–5 had won concessions for the use of the Lithuanian language in primary schools and in village administration. There were unmistakable stirrings among the Belarusians, the least advanced of the nationalities in the east, who were allowed to publish their first newspaper *Nasha niva* (Our Soil) in both Latin and Cyrillic script. Among Ukrainian radical activists in the Russian Empire there was even less interest in a Polish connection, and most preferred to co-operate with their larger Russian counterparts, especially the pro-peasant Socialist Revolutionaries and the Russian Social Democrats.

The ripple effects of the 1905 revolution in the Kingdom reached Galicia with some force, encouraging the left-wing parties to attack the conservative-dominated constitutional order. Demands for democratizing the Austrian electoral system were successful: in 1907 universal male suffrage was introduced for elections to the central Austrian parliament in Vienna. But there were strings attached. The NDs, who had established themselves as a major party in Galicia in 1905, secured the continuation of Polish influence in east Galicia by the creation there of two-member constituencies. Further attempts to abolish the class-based system of electoral colleges in elections to the Galician Sejm in Lwów were bogged down until 1914 in complex political horse-trading, made all the more acrimonious by the rise in Polish and Ukrainian nationalist passions. In 1908 the viceroy, Count Andrzej Potocki, was assassinated by a Ukrainian student, while in 1913 his moderate successor, the history professor Michał Bobrzyński, was forced to resign by an ND-led campaign for promoting reconciliation between the two communities. In 1913 the NDs succeeded in splitting the peasant movement, winning over its right wing (PSL-Piast) led by Wincenty Witos. The left-wing peasant group now veered towards Piłsudski's pro-independence socialists. It was yet another contributory factor to the continuing polarization of Polish politics in a period that witnessed increasing international tension over the Balkans and ominous talk of a general European war.

How the Poles should react to the growing likelihood of a conflict between Austria-Hungary, supported by Germany, and Russia inevitably came to prey on Polish political thinking. Several

33   A hunting party in the Grodno *guberniya*, 1908. Local Polish gentry gather at Wężowszczyzna, the home of Stanisław Żórawski, east of Grodno (today Hrodna in Belarus). Despite tsarist repression during the nineteenth century, about 60 per cent of land in historic Lithuania was still in Polish hands in 1914. The world of the Polish and polonized aristocracy and gentry in this area finally came to an end with the Soviet invasion in 1939.

conflicting strategies emerged, based on different geopolitical calculations and ideological preferences, and shaped by contrasting experiences of life in Austrian and Russian Poland. Many of Galicia's conservatives and democrats, acutely conscious that only in Austria did the Poles enjoy full political and cultural freedoms, favoured the so-called 'Austro-Polish Solution'; in the event of war, the former Congress Kingdom would be attached to Galicia, to form the third component of a triune Austro-Hungarian-Polish state. However, the increasingly enlivened political and intellectual climate in Galicia also encouraged more adventurous concepts. The Young Poland (Młoda Polska) movement in literature and the arts, of which the most outstanding and original representative in Kraków was Stanisław Wyspiański, issued a neo-Romantic challenge to the complacency and conservatism of Galicia's traditional elite. The impact of Wyspiański's dramas, with their blend of mystical visions and national myths, was electrifying. In his historical play *November night* (1904), set in Warsaw in 1830, Wyspiański utilized the Greek legend of Demeter and Persephone to produce a powerful poetic expression of faith in Poland's rebirth. The acquisition in 1905 by the Galician authorities of the former royal castle of Wawel (the 'Polish Acropolis'), hitherto used as an Austrian army barracks, and its subsequent restoration to its former glory, was not without symbolic significance.

It was therefore hardly surprising that it was in Galicia, where he had moved in 1908, that Piłsudski found many students and youngsters responsive to his charismatic appeal and ready to join his paramilitary riflemen formations which he was able to organize with the tacit approval of the Austrian military authorities. Piłsudski's flirtation with Marxism was coming to an end; he was now studying Napoleon and Clausewitz, and preparing for the moment when he could assume the mantle of Poland's military liberator. The riflemen's role was enhanced when they were recognized as the military wing of a broad pro-independence association, formed in 1912. This included representatives of most of Galicia's left-wing parties and PPS-controlled groups in the Kingdom. In the event of war, Piłsudski's 10,000 riflemen were to fight alongside the Austrians, but above all they were to promote an uprising in Russian Poland and, ultimately, to provide the nucleus of a future Polish army. In such a climate the influence of the internationalist left was weakening across Poland.

Diametrically opposed to Piłsudski stood Dmowski, who argued in 1908 that German imperialism, and not tsarist Russia, posed the fundamental threat to the survival of the Polish nation. He considered it unlikely that an independent Polish state would emerge out of a major European war; the most realistic solution, in the short run, was the reunification of all Polish lands as an autonomous unit under the tsar. Dmowski's appeal for Russo-Polish reconciliation, and his endorsement of neo-Slavism (with its emphasis on the equality of all Slavs) echoed some of the ideas of Adam Czartoryski a century earlier. And like Czartoryski, Dmowski discovered that it was not easy to win over to his 'realistic' programme either Russian officialdom or indeed many of

34   Stanisław Wyspiański (1869–1907). Self-portrait, 1902. Playwright,
poet, painter, designer of furniture and textiles, and an innovator in the
graphic arts, Wyspiański was the most outstanding and versatile artist of
the neo-Romantic 'Young Poland' movement in literature and the arts.
Creator of modern Polish drama, his plays drew on tragic episodes in
Polish history and on ancient Greek myths. Wyspiański's artistic life was
closely associated with the city of Kraków.

his own fellow countrymen. The Russian government under the
premiership of Stolypin and his successors was at that very moment
pursuing nationalist policies against many of the minorities of the
western borderlands, including Jews, Finns and Poles. If anything,
the behaviour of the Russian authorities was a slap in Dmowski's
face: in 1907 the size of the Polish representation in the Duma was
cut by two-thirds, and appeals for Polish autonomy were rejected.

In 1911 local elected councils (*zemstva*) were finally introduced in the western *gubernii*, but on the basis of a restricted franchise that favoured ethnic Russians; Russian officials were also given disproportionate voting rights in the municipal councils introduced in the Kingdom in 1913. And 1912 proved to be a particularly bad year for Russo-Polish relations: the region of Chełm was detached from the Kingdom and incorporated administratively and legally into the empire as a new Russian *guberniya;* the Russian state purchased the Warsaw–Vienna railway and dismissed many of its Polish employees. The recently completed Orthodox cathedral of St Alexander Nevsky, in the very centre of Warsaw, already provided a monumental symbol of Russia's domination of the 'Vistula Land'.

In such circumstances, Dmowski's geopolitical calculations seemed to make little sense. Many of his disenchanted younger and more radical followers seceded from the NDs and gravitated towards Piłsudski. To counter this serious haemorrhage from his movement, Dmowski turned increasingly, from 1911 onwards, to anti-Semitic propaganda. His call for an economic boycott of Jewish shops met with a favourable response among large sections of the Kingdom's lower middle classes, although it alienated enough voters for him to lose his seat (representing Warsaw) in the 1912 Duma election. Yet for all their reverses the NDs remained the largest political movement in the Kingdom, with tentacles reaching far beyond, and with a claim to a monopoly on Polish patriotism.

Dmowski's anti-Germanism found an exceptionally fertile soil in Prussian Poland, where the German–Polish struggle over land and language resumed with extra vigour after 1902. The former was graphically illustrated by the case of the peasant Michał Drzymała, who defied a 1904 law restricting the right of the Poles to build on newly purchased land, by living in a circus caravan which he had wheeled onto his plot of land. Drzymała lost his case, but not without a legal battle that went on for many years and ended in the Prussian supreme court. Berlin's policy of promoting German settlement in the east was not always as successful as expected, with many Germans in the east even preferring to move to seek better-paid industrial jobs in western Germany. The Poles managed to hold on tenaciously to the land they had, but in the long run their prospects seemed grim: among the estate-owners and the upper bourgeoisie of Poznania and Danzig Pomerania (West Prussia) the German element was already dominant, while a government bill introduced in 1908 authorized for the first time the compulsory purchase of Polish-owned estates.

Other forms of administrative pressure were also deployed. First came the replacement of Polish with German as the language of religious instruction in primary schools. The large-scale resistance of pupils and parents, which lasted from 1901 to 1906, was eventually broken by the use of the cane, fines and even imprisonment. Numerous towns and villages received new German names, and in 1908 restrictions were placed on the use of Polish at public gatherings. Extra numbers of German civil servants and teachers were directed to Poznania, giving that province the highest ratio of state officials to the size of the population within the Reich. It was all a boon for the NDs whose influence increased in most Polish cultural and social organizations of Prussian Poland. The NDs came to dominate the Polish Circle of parliamentary deputies in the German Reichstag, and in 1912 voted against further credits for the German naval programme. The ability of the NDs to establish an active and co-ordinated political presence in all parts of Poland and in the parliaments of the three occupying empires was a remarkable achievement.

Nothing could disguise the fact that as 1914 approached the lands of the former Commonwealth were deeply divided by conflicting political preferences, ideological values and ethnic loyalties, as well as profound economic, social and legal disparities brought about by the simple fact of partition and the integration of the ex-Polish lands within three very different empires. No region of what could be considered 'Poland' was exclusively homogeneous in terms of nationality, religion or speech: there were numerous Germans in the west and north-west, large highly diversified Jewish communities in the centre and the east, and of course substantial non-Polish populations in the east. Different historical experiences accentuated local identities and created different regional flavours of Polishness. With its largest concentration of Polish-speakers, and with its traditions of conspiracy and insurrection centred on

Warsaw, the primacy of Russian Poland was unquestioned. It was here that Polish Romanticism and Positivism first appeared as well as Polish socialism and modern nationalism as mass movements. Yet despite its largely archaic social order, Galicia's role as the centre of free political and cultural expression could not be underestimated. Here conspirators and exiles from Russian Poland could find refuge; here Poles of both sexes from all parts of the partitioned country could study in Polish universities; here great national anniversaries, such as the 500th anniversary of the Polish victory over the Teutonic Knights at the battle of Grunwald (1410), could be publicly celebrated. Here too the Poles gained the widest experience of parliamentary government (of a specific Austrian variety) and developed a native class of professional civil servants and educationalists which would play a crucial role in independent Poland after 1918. In their turn, the Poles of Prussia were economically hardened and socially disciplined through their exposure to and confrontation with Prussian rule.

The trappings of modern civilization, in the shape of electric trams, luxury hotels, telephones (first introduced in Warsaw and Łódź in 1883), or Parisian fashion, could be observed in all major cities of partitioned Poland. The cinema too was making inroads in the provinces. On the other hand, in the central and eastern regions there were overcrowded urban slums in which Gentile and Jewish families eked out a miserable daily existence. There was poverty and disease in the countryside. The ratio of one doctor per 800 people in the larger towns and one per 30,000 in the rural districts is just one indicator of the deep contrasts in the former Kingdom. In fact, an unmistakable civilizational faultline could be traced between the more advanced territories of the German Reich and those within the Austrian and Russian Empires. In terms of levels of literacy, agricultural and industrial productivity, urban infrastructures, and the general standard of living, Prussian Poland outclassed the other regions. At the same time it was in Prussian Poland that clerical and National Democrat influences were strongest; ironically, it was also in Poznania that the percentage of the Jewish population was the lowest of all regions of historic Poland.

The different standards and quality of public administration in the three parts of Poland also helped to shape different cultures of civic behaviour. In Russian Poland the wholesale evasion of government rules and regulations, as an expression of contempt for the tsarist regime, was proverbial; it was a habit that was to weigh heavily on life in restored Poland after 1918. In one anecdote among many, a Jewish merchant living near the meeting point of the three empires complained that German customs officials never took bribes, that the Russians always did, and that with the Austrians it was never quite certain. Different lifestyles also generated popular inter-regional prejudices; jokes abounded about 'Galician misers', about 'dopey Poznanians', or about Warsaw's notorious 'tricksters'. The mutual distrust between the neighbouring industrial communities of Upper Silesia (in Prussia) and the Dąbrowa basin (in Russian Poland) continues to be reflected to the present day in the intense hostility between the football clubs of the two regions.

Yet for all the regional and social differences, there were also strong cohesive cultural forces at work. Despite the absence of a Polish state, Polish national consciousness had spread widely since 1864 among the Polish-speaking sections of the urban and rural population. The growing emphasis on an ethnic-linguistic national identity meant, however, that Polish cultural influence was on the retreat in the east, that it was consolidating in the centre, and that it was making some gains in the west. On the eve of the First World War about 15.5 million Polish-speakers occupied a relatively compact area of settlement in the basin of the Vistula and Warta rivers, and along the upper Oder. A further 1.3 million lived in eastern Galicia, constituting a third of that area's population, and perhaps 2 million Poles lived scattered along the length and breadth of Russia's western *gubernii*, with a substantial concentration in the Wilno area.

The Poles' distinct sense of nationality was fostered by extensive cultural bonds which transcended the state frontiers and reached wider sections of society. A single literary language and a common literary tradition, dating back to the sixteenth century, linked all educated Poles, irrespective of where they lived. Poems, novels, plays and works of scholarship criss-crossed the borders. In one way or another literacy was growing among the masses. A vivid example of the existence of a single Polish reading public was the

35   The Teatr Miejski (Municipal Theatre) in Lwów (L'viv) in Galicia.
Built in 1897–1900, it was one of the most modern theatres in
contemporary Europe, and was one of the great centres of Polish drama
in the early twentieth century, although it never equalled Kraków in this
respect. Among the better-known actors and actresses who made their
debut or appeared on its stage were Ludwik Solski and Helena
Modrzejewska (known as Modjeska in the English-speaking world).
The photograph dates from the early 1940s, during the Nazi occupation
of eastern Galicia.

simultaneous serialization in 1911 of Sienkiewicz's best-selling
adventure story *W pustyni i w puszczy* ('In desert and wilderness')
in Polish-language newspapers of Warsaw, Wilno, Poznań and
Lwów. The lives of great poets and writers were celebrated with
festivities in the major cities of Austrian and Russian Poland: in
1898, on the centenary of his birth, statues of the great Romantic
bard Adam Mickiewicz were erected in Warsaw, Kraków and
Lwów. The Polish universities and other institutions of higher

36 Our Lady of Ostra Brama (Aušros Vartų Madona) in Wilno (Vilnius). The icon was painted by an unknown local artist around 1620–30, and was probably based on a sixteenth-century Flemish print. The cult of the Ostra Brama Madonna started in the second half of the eighteenth century, and has since spread throughout Poland, Lithuania and Belarus. The Madonna is venerated by Roman and Greek Catholics, and Orthodox alike.

learning in Kraków and Lwów attracted and brought together students from all parts of Poland. Journalists, physicians, scientists and musicians attended professional gatherings spanning all regions of the country. The impressive development of historical scholarship and scientific research; the existence of a diverse press and of a lively theatre scene; the emergence of a native cinematography; the musical accomplishments of Karol Szymanowski and of Ignacy Paderewski; the literary achievements of Henryk Sienkiewicz (Nobel Prize in 1905), of Stefan Żeromski, or of Władysław Reymont (Nobel Prize in 1924), not to mention the bohemian artistic milieu of Kraków, all provide compelling evidence of a creative cultural vibrancy during the two decades or so before 1914.

And despite the Roman Catholic Church's potentially divisive leanings towards the National Democrats, traditional Catholicism played an important integrating role in Polish society, still predominantly rural and in the main conventionally pious. Without belittling the existence of well-established but relatively small Polish-speaking Protestant, Moslem or Armenian communities in some areas of the country, it was Roman Catholicism which highlighted most Poles' difference from the predominantly Protestant Prussians and Orthodox Russians, not to mention the unassimilated bulk of the Yiddish-speaking Jewish population. Polish hymns and carols, religious festivals, and the intensely moving atmosphere of the Christmas Eve supper held in most Polish homes all promoted powerful emotional bonds. These were reinforced at a popular level by the annual participation of hundreds of thousands of people from all parts of Poland in pilgrimages to the shrine of the Black Madonna in Częstochowa, to that of Our Lady of Ostra Brama (Aušros Vartų Madona) in Wilno, and to many other lesser centres of Marian devotion.

In the realm of culture Poland certainly existed, although very few ordinary Poles realistically expected the early arrival of reunification and independence. As the clouds of war gathered over Europe in July 1914, few contemporaries could have foreseen the extensive human losses, the large-scale material destruction, and the unexpected political vicissitudes that this disparate nation would soon experience.

6

Independence regained and lo͜s͜,
1914–1945

The outbreak of the First World War created an unprecedented situation in the Polish lands. For the first time since the destruction of the old Polish-Lithuanian Commonwealth the three partitioning powers (or their successor states) were now at war with each other: on the one side Germany and Austria-Hungary (the Central Powers), and on the other Russia in alliance with France and Great Britain (the Entente). Some patriots in the previous century had considered that an independent Poland could only emerge out of a great European war. Yet there was nothing inevitable about Polish independence. Although both sides in the war were to make general appeals to their Polish populations, for neither of them was Polish independence initially a war aim. However, by the end of 1918 the core of an independent Polish state had come into being, made possible by the unexpected collapse of the three eastern empires, and by the readiness of the Poles to exploit this advantageous situation.

The outbreak of the war found the Poles bitterly divided. The anti-Russian Piłsudski was the first to act, anxious to establish a distinct Polish military presence in the war with Austrian permission. The incursion of his riflemen into the former Kingdom in August 1914 ended in a fiasco; the local population was unmoved by the appeal to rise against the Russians. As a result Piłsudski had to submit his legions to stricter Austrian control. The legions' subsequent exploits against the Russians on the Galician front were to sow the seeds of a legend which was to elevate Piłsudski to the

.us of Poland's man of Providence. But at the turn of 1914–15 ᴧsudski's cause seemed unpromising. Not only were the National Democrats hostile to Piłsudski's anti-Russian campaign but they also welcomed the manifesto of the Russian commander-in-chief Grand Duke Nicholas Nicholaevich of 14 August 1914 which called, albeit in vague and semi-religious language, for a reunified autonomous Poland under the tsar. Indeed, the prevailing mood of the population in the Kingdom was at first pro-Russian. The Russians even created a volunteer Polish force of their own to counteract Piłsudski's legions.

The first year of the war brought no significant political gains for the Poles, but much suffering and destruction. Conscripted in their hundreds of thousands into the three fighting armies, the Poles found themselves killing each other for the tsar and for the two kaisers. The eastern front ran across historic Polish lands, whose economic resources were ruthlessly exploited by the warring sides. The occupation of the whole of the former Kingdom by the Central Powers in August 1915 altered the situation dramatically. The century-old Russian occupation of Warsaw ended, while Dmowski and the leadership of the ND and of the Realist parties left for Petrograd; there they continued their thankless task of lobbying the tsarist government to declare itself more resolutely on the issue of Poland. Frustrated by the lack of progress, Dmowski left Russia in November 1915 to campaign in Britain and France. In the meantime the Germans embarked on wooing the Poles of the Kingdom with significant concessions: the use of the Polish language was permitted in local government, in the courts, and especially in education, and a Polish university and polytechnical institute were reopened. The idea of a Habsburg kingdom of Poland was briefly floated in Vienna, but the Austrians finally gave way to Berlin's proposal for a small puppet Polish state under German control which could provide the German war machine with Polish cannon-fodder. On 5 November 1916 the German and Austrian emperors issued a decree proclaiming the creation of a Polish constitutional monarchy. This kingdom still had no fixed borders and no monarch, while its Provisional Council of State was granted merely consultative powers. Nevertheless a breakthrough had been made. Piłsudski agreed to head the new kingdom's military department, but insisted that the formation of a regular Polish army had to be conditional on the creation of a genuine Polish state. This the Germans were not prepared to accept at this stage.

Although ousted from their Polish lands, the Russians were encouraged by the western allies to respond to the German initiative. On 1 January 1917 Nicholas II announced as a war aim the restoration of a free and reunited Poland in union with Russia. The bartering for Poland's future took a further step when the February Revolution toppled the Romanov dynasty. Both the Petrograd Soviet and the Russian Provisional Government, encouraged by the Polish liberal Aleksander Lednicki, declared their support for an independent Poland, but left the issue of borders to a future Russian Constituent Assembly. The Provisional Government not only permitted the Poles in Russia to organize their own military formations but also agreed to the creation of a Polish army in France to fight on the side of the Entente. Now that their Russian ally had publicly endorsed Polish independence, both France and Britain no longer felt restrained in their attitude to the Polish Question and recognized Dmowski's Polish National Committee (established in Paris in August 1917) as an 'official Polish organization'.

While the prospect now appeared of Poland becoming, at least on paper, a member of the Entente, the realities in the country were still determined by the Central Powers. The refusal of Piłsudski and most of his legions to take an oath of 'military brotherhood' with the armies of the Central Powers ruined Berlin's plan to raise a 'polnische Wehrmacht', and obliged the Germans to raise their bids in the Polish stakes. Piłsudski was imprisoned for his defiance, but on 12 September 1917 the Central Powers bestowed on their Polish Kingdom the equivalent of 'home rule': a three-man Regency Council was created with powers to appoint a government with full control of educational and judicial affairs, as well as a partially elected legislative body. There was still no king. On the Regency Council sat three highly respectable figures: the archbishop of Warsaw Aleksander Kakowski, Prince Zdzisław Lubomirski and Count Józef Ostrowski. But no sooner had the Regency Council been established when the political and military landscape in eastern Europe went through another convulsion brought about by

37   The Polish National Committee in Paris, 1918. Roman Dmowski is
seated in the centre front. On the left is Count Maurycy Zamoyski, the
largest landowner in Poland, and on the right is Erazm Piltz, a conservative
politician and publicist who had lived in St Petersburg. The Committee
acted as the official Polish delegation at the Peace Conference at Versailles
where it pressed for the weakening of German power in the east. Although
Dmowski was one of Poland's leading political figures, he only held high
office once, as foreign minister in 1923.

the Bolsheviks' seizure of power in Petrograd and their readiness to
sign a separate peace with the Central Powers. As the former
Russian Empire disintegrated, German priorities and tactics in the
east changed, to the marked disadvantage of their puppet Polish
Kingdom. Berlin recognized Ukrainian and Lithuanian statehood,
while the Austrians also agreed to create out of eastern Galicia a
separate imperial Ukrainian crownland within the Dual Monarchy.
The treaty of Brest-Litovsk with Bolshevik Russia, signed on
3 March 1918, confirmed the total victory of the Central Powers in
the east. In view of Berlin's aims to extend the eastern frontier of
the Reich into formerly Russian Poland, it was clear that what

remained of the Polish Kingdom would end up as little more than a dependency of a German-dominated *Mitteleuropa*.

Poland's fate did not rest, however, entirely in German hands. The energetic campaigns led by Dmowski and Paderewski on both sides of the Atlantic in the cause of Polish independence were having a marked impact on governments and public opinion alike. The inclusion of the demand for the restoration of an independent Poland with access to the sea in Woodrow Wilson's Fourteen Points of January 1918 was highly significant. The treaty of Brest-Litovsk, which took Russia out of the war, and the failure of the great German offensive in the West in March to May 1918 removed whatever reservations the Entente Powers had with regard to Poland. On 3 June 1918 the restoration of an independent Poland was officially endorsed as a war aim by the Entente. Not that the Poles were passively awaiting developments: an anti-German Polish army in Russia was 30,000 men strong, while the Polish army in France under General Józef Haller attracted thousands of volunteers, many from Polish communities in America, and fought alongside the western allies in France.

With the evident exhaustion of Germany and Austria-Hungary, and with the growing prospect of independence, the struggle for political power in Poland resumed with intensity between the pro-independence left and the National Democrats. The NDs, however, only brought ridicule on themselves by an inept attempt to seize power from the Regency Council which was in any case trying to wriggle out from German tutelage. The situation was further complicated by the disintegration of Austria-Hungary at the end of October. Local Poles took control of parts of Teschen Silesia and of western Galicia. In Lublin a pro-independence left-wing People's Republic, led by the socialist Daszyński and supported by Piłsudski's allies, was proclaimed on 6–7 November as a rival to the Regency Council in Warsaw. Workers' councils appeared in the Dąbrowa basin and other industrial centres. The outbreak of revolution in Germany, the creation of a socialist government in Berlin on 9 November, and the all-important decision of the German garrison to evacuate Warsaw removed the remaining obstacles to independence. In December the Poles of Poznania took up arms and wrested the control of their province from the Germans.

The three empires that had ruled Poland in 1914 were no more; the unbelievable had happened. But a single Poland still had to be created out of the disparate regions and out of the conflicting political and social forces that were now in the open. Piłsudski's return from German captivity on 10 November provided the catalyst for the dramatic events of the following days. His role proved providential. His legendary exploits as a fighter for national freedom, his left-wing background yet his readiness to rise above party factionalism, and his sixteen-month spell in German captivity had earned him wide support among a population desperate to escape wartime privations yet euphoric about the imminence of independence. On 11 November the German troops in Warsaw allowed themselves to be disarmed. On the same day (celebrated since as Poland's Independence Day) the Regency Council appointed Piłsudski commander-in-chief of its armed forces. Three days later, before dissolving itself, it conferred on Piłsudski the authority of head of state with almost dictatorial powers. On 18 November the People's Republic in Lublin recognized Piłsudski's authority, while the new head of state nominated the socialist Jędrzej Moraczewski to lead a left-wing government. Piłsudski's position was very strong: it had been sanctioned by the conservative Regents and enjoyed the undisputed support of the pro-independence socialist and peasant parties. To win even wider popular support for the reborn state, Moraczewski's government introduced a wide package of social reforms and welfare measures, and an eight-hour working day; it also promised compulsory land reform. Yet all was not harmony. The NDs resented Piłsudski's authority, and the predominantly ND-run administration in Poznania still refused to recognize the left-wing government in Warsaw. The SDKPiL and its allies, who merged in December 1918 to form the Communist Workers' Party of Poland, refused to recognize Polish independence altogether, and put their faith in local workers' councils and the imminence of a Bolshevik-led universal revolution.

Industry was paralysed and over four-fifths of industrial workers were unemployed, communications were severely ruptured, agricultural production had fallen dramatically, and poverty and malnutrition stalked the land. About 400,000 Poles had perished while serving in the three imperial armies. The new state, which now consisted of the former Congress Kingdom and western Galicia, also faced the burning and intractable issue of frontiers. Fighting raged for control of Lwów (L'viv) with the West Ukrainian Republic which had established itself in eastern Galicia. The situation in the borderlands between Poland and Russia was ominously fluid as the Red Army advanced west in the wake of the German forces retreating from Russia (in accordance with the November 1918 Armistice provisions), and as local national movements laid conflicting claims to the region. The precise delimitation of the boundary between Poland and Germany had to await the decision of the Versailles peace conference.

The Entente Powers still recognized the Paris-based and ND-led Polish National Committee, and not the government in Warsaw, as Poland's official representation. It was clearly apparent to Piłsudski that national unity, so vital if Poland was to exert any effective influence at the peace conference, could only be achieved by a compromise with the NDs, and consolidated by early democratic parliamentary elections. In an inspired move to ease internal tension, Piłsudski replaced Moraczewski with the eminent pianist Paderewski, who was highly respected by the NDs, as head of a non-party government of experts. The elections of January 1919, based on universal suffrage and proportional representation, produced a fragmented but relatively evenly balanced Sejm (parliament). Just over a third of the seats went to the NDs, who emerged as the single largest grouping, while about 30 per cent each went to the centre (including the peasant PSL-Piast led by Wincenty Witos) and to the Left (including the left-wing peasant parties and the socialists). The communists' appeal for a boycott of the elections was largely ignored.

On 20 February the new Sejm adopted the so-called 'small' constitution modelled on that of the French Third Republic: ministers were to be responsible to the Sejm which also elected a head of state with very limited powers. Piłsudski retained the latter post which was now shorn of effective constitutional authority; his position as commander-in-chief, however, gave him considerable influence. Indeed, the creation of a large national army within months of independence was a remarkable early achievement. In late February the restored Polish Republic was finally recognized by France, Britain and Italy. It now faced the daunting task of securing its frontiers.

Poland's western borders and its access to the sea proved to be the most contentious territorial issue at the Versailles peace conference. Dmowski's extensive claims were challenged by Lloyd George and had to be modified. The treaty of Versailles (28 June 1919) transferred outright to Poland Poznania and most of Pomerania along the lower Vistula (West Prussia), providing Poland thereby with direct if narrow access to the Baltic Sea. Some compromises had to be made: Danzig (Gdańsk), Poland's natural and historic port but with an overwhelmingly German population, became a Free City under the League of Nations and within the Polish customs area; plebiscites were to decide the future of Upper Silesia and the southern part of East Prussia.

In the south-east the Poles destroyed the West Ukrainian Republic and occupied eastern Galicia, and thereby confirmed in the minds of many local Ukrainian patriots that Poland was the main enemy of their nation. But since the Ukrainian cause enjoyed some Entente support at the peace conferences, the province's future was by no means a closed issue. Of even greater magnitude and complexity was the question of the future western frontier of Russia, still in the throes of a civil war. The Entente, especially France, hoped in 1919 for a White victory which would restore France's earlier anti-German alliance with Russia. The NDs too, in line with Dmowski's earlier geopolitical thinking, believed in the possibility of an accommodation with a non-Bolshevik Russia. In his turn Piłsudski refused to support the Whites, whose traditional nationalism appeared more anti-Polish than the internationalism of the Bolsheviks.

There existed two conflicting visions of Poland's role in the eastern lands of the former Polish-Lithuanian Commonwealth with their complex mosaic of intermingling nationalities and religions. Overall, Polish or polonized Roman Catholics, landowners, various professionals, as well as *déclassé* petty nobles and peasants, were in a minority here, but were important economically and socially. The narrowly nationalistic NDs called for the outright annexation of Lithuania, most of Belarus and western Ukraine, areas which they considered could be effectively absorbed within a unitary Polish state and assimilated in terms of national identity. Piłsudski's patriotism, on the other hand, was not based on modern ethnic criteria but owed much to the traditions of the former multi-ethnic Grand Duchy of Lithuania. He felt that there existed a rare historic opportunity to achieve wider regional security under Polish leadership against a resurgent Russia by creating an extensive east European federation, encompassing ethnic Poland, the Baltic states, Belarus and the Ukraine. While Polish and Lithuanian nationalists rejected any federalist structures in favour of nation states, a federalist concept for the lands of Lithuania and Belarus was favoured by an important section of the Polish-speaking elite (the so-called 'Regionalists') of the Wilno region and by some Belarusian national activists. In April 1919 Polish forces expelled the Bolsheviks from Wilno and Minsk, providing Piłsudski with two of the building blocks of his large eastern federation. But it was clear that Piłsudski's so-called 'Jagiellonian Idea', with reference to the vast Polish-Lithuanian realm of the late Middle Ages, could only be achieved by war against Bolshevik Russia. Despite ND opposition and the misgivings even of his left-wing allies, but in the light of Bolshevik intentions to transport their revolution to the West, Piłsudski won approval for his plan. Consequently, while retaining the contested east Galicia, Poland recognized the independence of the Ukraine, and formed a military alliance with the Ukrainian government of Symon Petliura which was battling against the Red Army.

The Poles and their Ukrainian ally launched their offensive on 25 April 1920; on 7 May they entered Kiev. But the euphoria proved short-lived. The Poles had underestimated Bolshevik strength and overestimated popular support in the Ukraine for Petliura. Bolshevik forces under Tukhachevsky counter-attacked in the north while the cavalry army of Budenny struck in the south. Numerous former tsarist officers, enraged by the Polish attack, rallied to the cause of 'National Bolshevism'. The Poles had to retreat. It was now Lenin's turn to implement his grand vision; over the corpse of 'bourgeois Poland' the Red Army was to bring the proletarian revolution into the heart of Europe. In the van of the Red Army travelled a committee of Polish communists, including Felix Dzerzhinsky, all set to bolshevize their country.

Map 8   Rebirth of the Polish state, 1918–23.

Rewja w Stucku 24/8. 1919   x Bogusław Załęski

38   Polish cavalry in Slutsk in Belarus, August 1919.

In the face of a possible disaster, the Polish government sought Entente mediation in the war and reluctantly accepted the so-called Curzon Line (named after the British foreign secretary) as a provisional demarcation line in the east, corresponding roughly with the eastern limit of the former Congress Kingdom. The Bolsheviks ignored the proposal and continued their advance towards the Vistula. Across western Europe and in Germany workers and trade unions protested against Polish 'aggression'. The workers and peasants of Poland did not, however, rise to welcome the Red Army. If anything, the threat of godless Bolshevism generated an outburst of patriotism. On 24 July an all-party Government of National Defence was formed in Warsaw under the premiership of the peasant leader Witos and with the veteran socialist Daszyński as deputy. Its radical programme of land reform helped to neutralize Bolshevik propaganda. Thousands of volunteers, including students and schoolboys, rallied to the colours as the Bolsheviks approached Warsaw. It was not the French military mission under General Weygand, whose unhelpful advice was ignored, which turned the tide of the war, but Piłsudski's bold counter-attack on 16–18 August from the south against the over-extended Bolshevik lines east of Warsaw. That Polish cryptographers were able to read much of the Red Army's radio signals gave the Polish High Command a decisive advantage during the battle; they were also able to jam Bolshevik radio communications, broadcasting for this purpose extracts from the Book of Genesis in Morse Code. And in the last great cavalry battle of modern warfare, involving 20,000 horsemen on each side, Budenny's army was destroyed near Zamość. The Bolshevik rout was confirmed by a subsequent Polish victory on the Niemen river in September.

Not since Sobieski's triumph outside Vienna in 1683 had Polish arms met with such success; but the so-called 'Miracle on the Vistula' was a close-run thing. What the impact of a Soviet victory in 1920 would have been on the much-troubled societies of Germany and western Europe can only be speculation. The Poles like to think that in 1920 they saved Western Civilization from the Bolshevik hordes. In one sense they certainly repaid some of their debt for the Entente's victory over Germany which had made Polish independence initially possible in 1918. The Polish–

39 A Polish armoured train, *The General Sosnkowski*, during the
Polish–Bolshevik war, 1920. The long struggle for Poland's frontiers in
1918–22 witnessed the rapid growth of the Polish Army, from 6,000 men
in November 1918 to 600,000 in autumn 1919, reaching 900,000 in July
1920. The integration in one army of officers and non-commissioned
officers who had only recently served in different and even opposing
armies was no mean feat. Unlike the trench war on the Western Front
during the First World War, the war between reborn Poland and Bolshevik
Russia from 1919 to 1921 was one of considerable mobility over a vast
area of eastern Europe, and involved large numbers of cavalry and even
armoured trains.

Soviet war ended with the peace of Riga of 18 March 1921. It
established a frontier well to the east of the now infamous
'Curzon Line', but closer to the limit envisaged by the assimi-
lationist National Democrats; the Polish delegation at the peace
talks was dominated by Stanisław Grabski, a National Democrat
opposed to Piłsudski's federalism, who declined the Bolshevik
offer of Minsk. The National Democrats were very conscious that
their electoral position would be weakened by the inclusion of any
more ethnic minorities in the east. At Riga the Poles also abandoned their Ukrainian allies. Piłsudski's federal scheme, for which
so much blood had been shed, lay in ruins. By the same token,
Bolshevik ambitions of a European revolution had been checked.
In Moscow the idea of Socialism in One Country was born, while

Lenin's New Economic Policy represented a partial compromise with capitalism.

While fighting for its very survival against the Bolsheviks in the summer of 1920, the fledgling Polish state was unable to press its territorial claims effectively in southern East Prussia, where the Polish-speaking Mazurians, whose national identity was still indeterminate, voted overwhelmingly to remain in Germany rather than risk inclusion in a Bolshevik Poland. At the same time the Czechs obtained the Entente's recognition of their occupation of the disputed industrial region of Teschen (Cieszyn), a move that was to damage Polish–Czech relations during the rest of the inter-war period. The violent Polish–German dispute over Upper Silesia, one of the main industrial areas of central Europe, was not resolved until October 1921 when, following a plebiscite, the League of Nations divided the region: Poland obtained only 29 per cent of the territory but 46 per cent of the population and most of the mines and industrial plants. Polish Upper Silesia was to enjoy considerable regional autonomy in the inter-war period.

The city of Wilno (Vilnius), which the new Lithuanian state claimed as its historic capital but whose population was predominantly Polish- and Yiddish-speaking, was seized in October 1920, with Piłsudski's unofficial authorization, by allegedly mutinous local Polish units. But Piłsudski's proposal for a bi-cantonal Lithuania (including Wilno) in a federal association with Poland was rejected both by the Lithuanians and by the Wilno regional assembly which voted in January 1922 for simple incorporation into Poland. The old multilingual Grand Duchy of Lithuania could not be recreated in an age of ethnic nationalism. Unreconciled to the loss of Wilno, the Lithuanians established a provisional capital in Kaunas, and insisted until 1938 that a formal state of war existed with Poland. Polish attempts in the 1920s to create a Baltic security zone were to suffer as a consequence.

It was only in March 1923 that the Conference of Ambassadors in Paris, acting as the executive organ of the Allied Powers, finally recognized Poland's eastern frontiers. The struggle for the frontiers had lasted for over four years, almost as long as it took to achieve a final settlement in the lands of the former Ottoman Empire. Poland's inter-war borders were no more unfair than many of those redrawn elsewhere in central and eastern Europe. Most Poles now found themselves within a Polish nation-state; nevertheless, national minorities constituted nearly a third of Poland's population of 27 million in 1921. While the western border corresponded roughly with the ethnic-linguistic division (and with Poland's pre-partition frontier), that was mostly not the case in the east, where strategic considerations were paramount. What was more worrying was that Poland had emerged as a sizeable independent state only because of the temporary weakness of Germany and Russia. Only with Latvia and Romania was Poland to maintain good neighbourly relations throughout the inter-war period. The failure of both Poland and Czechoslovakia, who remained divided over Teschen and over their very different strategic priorities, to form an alliance in the inter-war period was, in retrospect, highly unfortunate. Security against Germany was provided, for the time being, by a French alliance of February 1921, but no major power was committed to defending Poland in the east. Poland's sovereignty was also restricted by international treaty obligations with regard to the legal rights of its national minorities. The net result of the struggles of 1918–21 was that the Poles came to distrust the Great Powers while acquiring an exaggerated belief in their own military capabilities.

A new constitution, adopted in March 1921, symbolized the consolidation of the Polish Second Republic, but also introduced what was to prove an unwieldy system of parliamentary government. Fearing Piłsudski's return to power, the NDs prevented the creation of a strong presidency. In their turn, the left-wing parties secured the introduction of proportional representation in parliamentary elections to prevent the domination of the NDs, who were the largest party. But since the Polish parliamentary scene was composed of at least eighteen parties, it was a recipe for unstable coalition government. A wide range of civil rights and political and religious freedoms was guaranteed as well as the sanctity of private property; it was clear that the land reform, so eagerly adopted in 1920 and so important in a country in which a third of all peasant holdings were under two hectares in size, was going to be a limited affair. On the other hand, the advanced social welfare provisions of 1918 were retained.

A kind of normality began to return after the political and military upheavals of the war years. The outburst of patriotic feelings in 1920 and the start of post-war reconstruction did much to dampen the earlier social tensions. The authority of the new state was also increasingly felt in most areas of national life as the previously disparate regions of the country were gradually re-integrated administratively and economically. A vigorously expanded national system of education and a national army provided two important foci for the cultivation of a supra-regional national identity. Yet the new state lacked a well-established tradition of constitutional government, while within its new borders there still functioned four different legal systems. The inheritance of three different railway systems also hampered communications. The collapse and loss of the Russian market forced Poland's industry to reorientate itself to the highly competitive markets of the west. The strong regional differences, in terms of contrasting levels of economic and social development and popular literacy, remained, and were further accentuated by the existence of national minorities.

The largest minority, concentrated in the south-east and numbering over 4 million, were the Ukrainians, many of whom retained strong aspirations for their own statehood. The idea of autonomy for eastern Galicia had been mooted since 1919, but the fact that nothing was to come of it had damaging results for inter-ethnic relations. Indeed, in the early 1920s Ukrainian nationalists waged an underground war against the Polish state. Ukrainian nationalism was to have a serious destabilizing impact on political life in inter-war Poland. Among the 1.5 million Belarusians there was social unrest. As for the Germans, many thousands had left Poland by 1921, but there remained a scattered yet economically and socially important German minority of nearly 1 million; those in the ex-German regions resented their separation from the Reich. In 1921 Poland's highly diverse Jewish population numbered about 2.2 million, of whom well over four-fifths used Yiddish as their mother tongue. While Polish national aspirations were alien to most Jews, some of whom were even hostile to Polish independence, many members of the Jewish intelligentsia were willing to co-operate with the Polish state. Assimilated Jews could be found among the ranks of Polish patriots, for instance the eminent

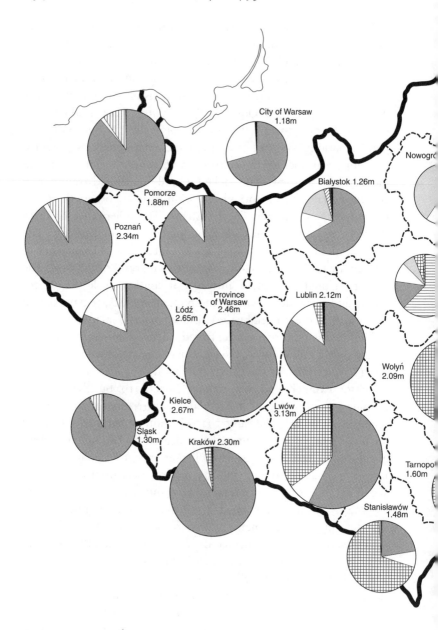

Map 9   Inter-war Poland: a land of many nationalities and faiths.
Source: *Petit annuaire statistique de la Pologne 1939* (Warsaw, 1939).

Wilno 1.28m

dek 1.06m

Polesie 1.13m

Nationalities according to language (Polish 1931 census):
Each pie-chart on the map represents a province (*województwo*) with its population in millions. The City of Warsaw enjoyed the status of a separate province. Divisions of the pie-charts represent percentages.

Key

	Polish
	Ukrainian
	Yiddish
	Belarusian
	'Local'
	German
	Russian
	Lithuanian
	Others

All of Poland (31.92m)

Notes

1. Ukrainian includes Ruthenian (*ruski*) which was a separate category in the census.

2. Yiddish includes Hebrew which was declared by 7.8% of the Jews, although few of them would have used it in daily life.

3. 'Local' was declared as their mother tongue by 707,000 Belarusian-speakers in Polesie.

Religious affiliations 1931

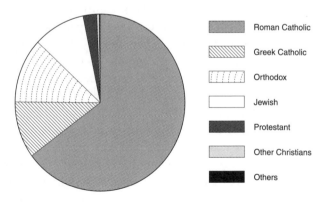

	Roman Catholic
	Greek Catholic
	Orthodox
	Jewish
	Protestant
	Other Christians
	Others

n Szymon Askenazy who from 1920 to 1923 represented at the League of Nations. On the other hand the anti-Semitism propounded by the NDs did much to poison Jewish–Gentile relations, and only increased among many young Jews the attraction of communism (Jews were to constitute about a third of the inter-war Polish Communist Party) and of Zionism. The Jewish contribution to Polish life, however, whether in medicine, law or literature, was to be enormous in the inter-war period. The poet Julian Tuwim and the writer Bruno Schulz provide just two examples of a remarkable Polish–Jewish cultural osmosis.

With the achievement of independence, Polish writers, poets and artists were freed from the obligation to fight for the national cause. Some remained involved in politics, as apologists for Piłsudski and the legend of his legions, or as commentators on the lives of ordinary working people, but others embarked on the search for new forms of expression. Among the most creative were the lyrical poets of the 'Skamander' group who tackled exotic, sexual and surreal themes; amongst them stood out the painter, playwright and novelist Stanisław Ignacy Witkiewicz, known simply as Witkacy.

With the end of the national emergency of 1920–1 the NDs renewed their struggle for political domination. They toppled Witos' centre-left government in June 1921, and consolidated the forces of the right in the so-called Christian Union of National Unity, but failed to secure a majority in the parliamentary elections of November 1922. The defeat of the ND candidate in the presidential election a month later and the victory of Professor Gabriel Narutowicz, made possible by the support of the parties of the left and the centre and of the National Minorities Bloc, drove the NDs to fury. On 16 December an ND fanatic assassinated the president-elect. Only narrowly did Poland avoid an outbreak of the kind of wider violence that was raging at the time in Germany, Italy and Spain. The murder of Poland's first president brought no immediate gains to the shamed NDs, who felt obliged to draw back and meekly accept the appointment of a strong government under General Władysław Sikorski and the election as president of the veteran socialist Stanisław Wojciechowski.

The National Democrats had to acknowledge that to achieve 'a government of the Polish majority' they would have to make concessions. In May 1923 they reached a compromise agreement with Witos' centrist peasant party Piast, the second largest grouping in the Sejm, and assumed office in a coalition government led by Witos. In return for the ND offer of support for a moderate land reform, PSL-Piast moved to the right and endorsed the NDs' programme to restrict the rights of the national minorities, and to reduce Piłsudski's influence by subordinating the army to a Ministry of War. Piłsudski thereupon resigned as chief of the General Staff. But the centre-right's success was blighted by the impact of the economic depression that had started in March. Inflation wreaked general havoc. In practical terms, a peasant who had borrowed funds from the state in 1919 to buy twelve horses was able to repay his debt in August 1923 for the equivalent of one kilogram of meat. Social distress grew as well as the number of strikes, from which Piłsudski's hawks and both the constitutional and revolutionary left hoped to benefit. In an atmosphere of mounting tension, accompanied by terrorist outrages, Witos' government decided to act against the left; in October it placed striking railwaymen under military discipline. A general strike on 5 November, initiated by the socialists, led to bloody confrontations with the army and the police. Witos' government lost its parliamentary majority when Piast split over the proposed land reform, and resigned in December.

The prospect of political and economic disaster brought the main parties to their senses. The moderate non-party government that took office in December under the stern Władysław Grabski was empowered by the Sejm to restore financial stability and to come to grips with the escalating inflation; between June and December 1923 the value of the Polish mark had fallen from 71,000 to 4.3 million to the US dollar. Grabski's policy of financial retrenchment, coupled with the rigorous collection of taxes, put brakes on inflation and restored confidence. In April 1924 a new currency, the Polish złoty, was introduced. But the effectiveness of Grabski's reforms was blunted by a disastrous harvest in 1924 and the damaging tariff war started in early 1925 by Germany, with which Poland conducted half of its trade.

Indeed, associated with the German economic offensive against

Poland was Gustav Stresemann's avowed intention of recovering some of the territories lost to Poland at Versailles. For General von Seeckt, the commander of the German army since 1919, the destruction of hated Poland was the ultimate objective. Already alarmed by the willingness of Weimar Germany and the USSR to co-operate at Rapallo in 1922, the Poles now observed with nervous concern the weakening of French influence after the Ruhr crisis and the international rehabilitation of Germany with a permanent seat on the Council of the League of Nations. The inviolability of Germany's western border, guaranteed at Locarno in October 1925 by the west European powers, was not extended to Germany's eastern frontier. Neither an arbitration treaty with Germany nor a much diluted Franco-Polish mutual assistance pact could conceal the reversal suffered by Poland.

At home, Grabski's government succeeded in other important areas of national life. In 1925 construction began of a new port and city in Gdynia which, unlike Danzig, was situated on sovereign Polish territory, and of a railway between Gdynia and Upper Silesia to facilitate the export of Polish coal. In February 1925 state–church relations were regularized with the signing of a Concordat which granted considerable privileges to the Roman Catholic Church in return for a government say in episcopal appointments, and for the recognition by the Vatican of Poland's new state boundaries. A moderate land reform, passed in December 1925, provided for the annual transfer of 200,000 hectares, on a voluntary basis and over a ten-year period, from large landed estates into peasant ownership. The government also came to grips with Soviet-inspired agitation along the long eastern frontier by creating a special border force and by encouraging the settlement of military colonists, although the latter were often deeply resented by the local non-Polish populations. Indeed, official policy towards the national minorities was hardening. A law of 1924 promoting bilingual schools led to a drastic reduction of single-language Ukrainian schools in eastern Galicia; another law in the same year banned the use of the Ukrainian language in governmental agencies.

In November 1925 the renewed economic crisis overwhelmed Grabski's administration. Alarmed by the prospect of yet another

40   The new Polish port of Gdynia in the 1930s. From a fishing village of a thousand souls in 1921, Gdynia expanded to a city of 120,000 people in 1939. In the mid 1930s it overtook Danzig (Gdańsk) as the main port for Poland. In 1938 nearly four-fifths of Poland's total trade (in tonnage) and over three-fifths (in terms of value) went by sea. The so-called 'Polish Corridor' to the Baltic Sea was of vital economic importance for the inter-war Polish state.

political crisis and by the mutinous rumblings among Piłsudski's followers in the army, the main parties patched up their differences in a grand coalition government under the even-tempered Aleksander Skrzyński, a distinguished diplomat and recent foreign minister with no formal party affiliation. But the days of Poland's young parliamentary system of government were numbered. A sense of disillusionment with the political order was growing, exacerbated by financial scandals and by a lack of consensus for dealing with the continued economic difficulties. Matters came to a head after Skrzyński's resignation on 5 May 1926 and the failure of the president to recreate Grabski's non-partisan administration. As a result the peasant leader Witos returned to office on 10 May at the head of a centre-right cabinet. But memories of Witos' disastrous administration of 1923 were still very fresh. Piłsudski now took it upon himself to save the country from what he saw as a contemptible breed of corrupt and bickering politicians. From his country retreat in Sulejówek outside Warsaw he marched on the capital on 12 May at the head of rebel army units. At a dramatic meeting on the Poniatowski bridge over the Vistula, President Wojciechowski rejected Piłsudski's unconstitutional demands for a change of government. After three days of fighting between Piłsudski's men and government troops, both the president and Witos agreed to resign. A railwaymen's strike, inspired by the socialists, prevented pro-government reinforcements from reaching Warsaw. Piłsudski's coup was welcomed by all the non-communist left, by Poland's industrialists, and by wide sections of the population, including many Jewish organizations. Only in ND-dominated Poznania were there mass protests. There were specific Polish causes and features of Piłsudski's 1926 coup, but it does provide another instance of the fragility of parliamentary institutions in much of continental Europe after the First World War.

Piłsudski had no wish to assume a public role as a dictator, preferring to deploy lesser figures to carry out his ultimate objective of introducing strong presidential government in Poland. The overawed and humiliated Sejm legalized the coup. Piłsudski's choice, the former socialist and eminent chemist Ignacy Mościcki, was elected president by the National Assembly. Kazimierz Bartel, another professor of no party affiliation, was to serve intermittently

41 The 1926 coup. Marshal Piłsudski (fourth from left) crosses the Poniatowski bridge into Warsaw on 12 May 1926, in the company of loyal officers, to confront President Wojciechowski. 'For me', declared the Marshal, 'the legal road is closed.' He had hoped that a military demonstration would suffice to topple Witos' centre-right government. The fighting that ensued cost 379 lives.

as prime minister until 1930. Until his death in 1935 Piłsudski retained control of the army as minister of war and as the General Inspector of the Armed Forces.

Piłsudski's coup was carried out in the name of Sanacja, a term used in the sense of restoring 'health' to the body politic, and which gave the name to the political regime that continued until 1939. With its emphasis on discipline, anti-corruption and loyalty to the state, the Sanacja hoped to appeal to a wide cross-section of the population, including the national minorities. Significant if limited steps were taken in 1927 to abolish some anti-Jewish restrictive laws from the tsarist period which were still in operation in ex-Russian Poland. And in Volhynia, under governor Henryk Józewski, considerable efforts were made after 1928 to foster a Ukrainian patriotism that would be compatible with Polish statehood; little ultimately came of this but it was enough to increase

Stalin's suspicions of Polish intentions towards the Soviet Ukraine. Formally Poland retained a multi-party parliamentary system, but the constitution was modified in August 1926 by the augmentation of the president's powers to dissolve parliament and to rule by decree, and also to determine the state budget. With no political party at his disposal, the marshal exerted his authority indirectly through his faithful followers within the parties of the centre and the left, and those promoted in the armed forces and the civilian administration. Not wishing to be beholden to the left, and determined to weaken the right, Piłsudski skilfully engineered a rapprochement with the conservative elements in Polish society: aristocratic landowners, industrialists and even the once hostile Catholic Church.

Piłsudski's regime was further strengthened by the marked improvement of the Polish economy between 1926 and 1929. The pace of cultural life also quickened, whether measured by the expansion of the press and periodicals, or by the number of radios, which increased from 120,000 in 1927 to 246,000 in 1930. Elementary education expanded with extra vigour, and social security provisions were further extended. Considering Poland's very modest economic base of 1921 these were noticeable improvements. Yet while the demand for agricultural products brought substantial gains to the peasantry, the 1925 land reform was inadequate to resolve the acute problem of rural over-population, especially in the south of the country. Alleviation continued to come in the form of large-scale emigration to the Americas, and especially to France, which alone received 320,000 Polish immigrants between 1925 and 1930; most headed for the coal-mines in the region of Lille, where their descendants still represent France's largest Polish community. The existence of only 30,000 passenger cars in 1930, representing one-ninth of Germany's car ownership on a per thousand of population basis, provides a telling index of Poland's relative poverty. The cost of maintaining Poland's armed forces, which consumed 35 per cent of total state expenditure in 1929, continued to be an unavoidable burden on a country in a precarious geopolitical position.

Conditions were now ripe for Piłsudski to consolidate his regime. Despite his aversion to party politics, the marshal realized

Jadwiga Smosarska
w filmie „Ziemia Obiecana"
Wytw. „SFINKS".

42   One of the great stars of the inter-war Polish cinema: Jadwiga
Smosarska (1900–71) in a still from the 1927 film *The promised land*
(*Ziemia obiecana*) (see plate 29). Between 1919 and 1937 she appeared
in twenty-five films, and also frequently played on stage. She was typical
of many of her generation in that the war forced her into exile, in her case
in the United States. She revisited Poland on several occasions after 1958
before returning for good in 1970.

that he needed a formal pro-government political grouping in the
Sejm. The resulting Non-Party Bloc of Co-operation with the
Government (BBWR), formed in early 1928, embraced individuals
of diverse ideological standpoints; its two guiding principles were
service to the state and loyalty to the marshal. Although the 1928
election saw the effective eclipse of the National Democrats and of
Piast, the BBWR won only a quarter of the parliamentary seats,
not enough to push a revision of the constitution through the Sejm.
A long war of attrition now began against the opposition in the
Sejm.

To browbeat the Sejm into submission, the marshal deployed a
variety of intimidatory tactics, including placing in office hard-line
'colonels' from among his coterie of close ex-legionary followers.
The public declaration in July 1929 by Walery Sławek, the most

ambitious of the colonels, that 'it is better to break the bones of one deputy than to bring machine guns into the streets', well reflected the incipient threat of violence. Determined to restore full parliamentary democracy, the parties of the centre and the left formed an alliance in September 1929; their cause was facilitated by the impact of the Great Depression, which by mid-1930 had brought a painful end to the recent years of relative prosperity. With the virtual paralysis of parliamentary government, the centre-left embarked on a campaign of mass public demonstrations, starting in Kraków on 29 June 1930. But it underestimated the marshal's readiness for a final confrontation.

On 25 August 1930 Piłsudski personally assumed the premier-ship, announced new elections for November, and on the night of 9–10 September had the opposition leaders, including Witos, arrested and incarcerated in the fortress of Brześć (Brest Litovsk). Thousands of opposition activists were detained. The inability of the centre-left to establish a common front with the National Democrats, the communists and the national minorities prevented the creation of a broad movement of resistance to the regime. The elections of November 1930 finally yielded an absolute parliamentary majority of 55.6 per cent of the seats to the BBWR. The centre-left alliance altogether managed to muster only 21.9 per cent, while the NDs tailed far away with 14 per cent. The victory of the Sanacja was such that Piłsudski could afford to pass the premiership back to Sławek and to leave the country on a three-month rest cruise to Madeira.

In the meantime the Great Depression was making ever deeper cuts in the Polish economy. By 1932 industrial production had fallen to 54 per cent of the 1929 level, and in 1933 nearly a third of the industrial workforce was unemployed. The steep fall in agricultural prices brought severe hardship to the peasants. The regime's initial response to the crisis was a deflationary economic policy aimed at maintaining the value of the złoty, and the tightening of political control over the judiciary, local government and academic institutions. The arrested opposition leaders were tried in Brześć between 1931 and 1933 and either jailed or, as in the case of Witos, obliged to leave the country. A 'camp of isolation' was established at Bereza Kartuska in 1934 for the most militant critics of the regime: communists, right-wing extremists and Ukrainian nationalists.

The Sanacja under Piłsudski was a secular authoritarian system of government of a non-fascist type. The government did try to mobilize mass support for the regime, but large areas of national life remained outside its direct control: opposition political parties, many trade unions, a host of social, cultural and sporting organizations from the co-operative movement to the scouts, much of the economy and the press (although subject to limited censorship), as well as the country's many religious denominations with their charitable societies. Many of the old *szlachta* values of individualism and personal liberty remained deeply ingrained in many areas of Polish culture. The creation of a strong modern state did, however, open a multitude of careers to the intelligentsia: in the civil service, in education, or in the armed forces. Responses to the new political realities among the intellectual and artistic elite varied. Some writers, like Julian Kaden-Bandrowski, the father of the Polish political novel, endorsed the Sanacja; others, such as Witold Gombrowicz or Julian Tuwim (especially in his scathing poem 'The ball in the Opera' written in 1936), responded with acid satire. The greatest asset of the Sanacja was of course Marshal Piłsudski himself, with his brusque manner, simple lifestyle, and heavy-handed paternalism. Until his death from cancer in May 1935 he concentrated on military and foreign affairs and left the day-to-day business of government to his colonels.

Essentially Poland was still a pluralist society. Nevertheless, the scale of the Great Depression obliged the authorities to consider increasing state intervention in the economy. Some of the opposition parties, even those with a democratic pedigree, now veered towards more radical collectivist solutions to Poland's problems. In 1931 the main peasant parties united to form a single Polish Peasant Party (PSL) of 100,000 members, which adopted as its programme the expropriation, without compensation, of private landed estates. In its turn, in 1934 the PPS called for the nationalization of the major branches of the economy, and even endorsed the principle of 'the dictatorship of the proletariat' as a temporary necessity. Needless to say, the communist KPP gained new followers. The Christian Democrats, weakened by desertions to the government camp, turned towards ideas of Catholic corporatism. The National Democrats, relying increasingly on the Gentile lesser bourgeoisie, moved even further to the right; in 1932 the elderly but still active Dmowski launched the so-called Camp of Greater Poland with 250,000 members, only to see it banned by the government the following year. The appeal of fascism and of anti-Semitism was most pronounced among young radical NDs, who in 1934 formed the 'National-Radical Camp' (ONR), from which emerged the distinctly totalitarian ONR-Falanga under Bolesław Piasecki. The grim warnings coming from Witkacy, the leading 'catastrophist' writer, about eastern totalitarianism and about the creation by contemporary civilization of a 'socially perfect, mechanized man' seemed particularly apposite in the new anti-democratic and anti-liberal climate sweeping the continent in the 1930s.

On the other hand, the Roman Catholic episcopate, led since 1926 by the calm but resolute Cardinal August Hlond, distanced itself from its earlier pro-ND tendencies. Despite the Church's good relations with the state, Hlond publicly criticized the authoritarianism creeping into government policy in the 1930s. Indeed, this period witnessed the revitalization of Polish Catholicism and the rise of the Church's moral prestige across a broad spectrum of the Polish population. The parochial system was reformed and expanded; seminaries were improved. The growth of lay Catholic organizations, such as Catholic Action and the so-called 'rosary brotherhoods', involved many millions of faithful, mostly in the rural areas; membership of Christian trade unions exceeded membership of those of the socialists. The introduction of religious instruction in schools, the creation of a Catholic university in Lublin, the appointment of inspired university chaplains, and the Church's concern for the easing of social tensions helped to weaken the anticlericalism that had been widespread among the left-wing and liberal intelligentsia before 1918, and promoted the emergence of a new open-minded Catholic intelligentsia. All this provided the roots of the Church's resilience during the ordeals that were to face it and the nation after 1939.

In the meantime, Poland's continuous search for security presented new problems, new opportunities and new traps. In July

1932 Poland signed a non-aggression treaty with the USSR which strengthened Poland's hand in responding to Hitler's rise to power. Indeed, the ideological enmity between Nazi Germany and the USSR militated against the 'spirit of Rapallo' and encouraged Piłsudski, through his new foreign minister Colonel Józef Beck, to develop a policy of 'balance' with regard to Poland's two dangerous neighbours. Increasingly apprehensive about the reliability of the French alliance and sceptical about French plans for an eastern security pact, Piłsudski decided on a direct resolution of all Polish–German problems. In his turn, Hitler was eager to separate the Poles from the French. The ensuing Polish–German non-aggression treaty of January 1934 ended the tariff war, but equally raised French fears about Polish intentions. Piłsudski was under no illusion about Poland's vulnerability; confidentially he predicted in 1934 that Poland had gained perhaps four years of breathing space in its relations with Germany.

In view of Piłsudski's rapidly declining health and the growing political radicalism in the country, the Sanacja moved to give a new legal framework to the post-1926 system of government. A new constitution, introduced in April 1935, emphasized the primacy of the state and endowed the president, who would now be elected by a small electoral college, with enormous powers. By the same token the powers of the Sejm were reduced, while a subsequent electoral law abolishing proportional representation nearly halved the number of deputies, and gave the authorities a major say in the selection of parliamentary candidates. The election of the Senate ceased to be by universal and direct voting.

Marshal Piłsudski did not live long enough to assume the new-style presidency, which had been the original idea. Despite the highly controversial nature of his regime, Piłsudski's death on 12 May 1935 was deeply felt by the majority of the population who recognized his enormous contribution to the struggle for independence. But his death deprived the ruling elite of its main focus of unity. President Mościcki, hitherto an obliging executor of Piłsudski's wishes, refused to surrender his office to Sławek, envisaged as Piłsudski's successor; rejecting the advice of the colonels, Mościcki appointed General Edward Rydz-Śmigły as head of the armed forces. The elections of 1935, boycotted by over half of the electorate, further accelerated the divisions within the Sanacja. Two distinct groupings emerged: one centred around President Mościcki and the distinguished economist Eugeniusz Kwiatkowski which laid emphasis on efficiency and professionalism in government, the other of a more military and authoritarian flavour around Rydz-Śmigły. A compromise between the two in May 1936 resulted in the creation of a surprisingly stable caretaker administration under the malleable General (and ex-physician) Felicjan Sławoj-Składkowski which survived until the outbreak of war in 1939. Although lacking the necessary political talents, Rydz did not abandon his ambition of stepping into Piłsudski's shoes. In November 1936 he was promoted to the rank of marshal, and in 1937 his followers formed a new highly centralized political party, the Camp of National Unity (Ozon), with a strong nationalist and anti-Semitic programme. This attempt to appeal to the right backfired on Rydz, who had to moderate his tone; too many of Piłsudski's followers, including the Mościcki group, were horrified by this betrayal of the dead marshal's essentially non-extremist ideals. Thereafter even Ozon softened its line.

The failure of the Sanacja to win wider popular support was vividly portrayed by the continued political agitation and social turmoil in the country which was only slowly emerging out of the Depression. During 1936 and 1937 the police responded violently to large-scale outbreaks of strikes by industrial workers and peasants. On the other hand, the opposition parties were too divided to organize an effective common front against the Sanacja. The National Democrats, still the largest party in the country, refused to have any dealings with socialists and freemasons, and spent most of their energies on anti-Semitic outrages and internecine leadership struggles for the succession to Dmowski (who was to die in January 1939). As a result only a small, if eminent, group of centrist politicians, including Sikorski, Witos and Paderewski, was involved at the inception of the 'Morges Front', named after Paderewski's Swiss residence. The socialist and peasant parties refused to collaborate in a 'Democratic Front'. The prospect of a 'Popular Front', launched by the Comintern in Moscow in 1935 to unite all European left-wing and democratic parties against fascism, fared little better in Poland; in 1937 Stalin put to death most members of the Polish Communist Party (KPP) residing in the USSR, and in 1938 dissolved the entire organization on charges of Trotskyism. Furthermore, in 1937–8 over 100,000 Soviet Poles (half of them from the Soviet Ukraine) were summarily executed on his orders.

The Great Depression, and the political and nationalist radicalism it encouraged, accentuated the problems of Poland's national minorities. The Greek Catholic (Uniate) Church under the outstanding leadership of Metropolitan Sheptyts'kyi, the extensive Ukrainian co-operative movement, and moderate Ukrainian political parties strove through legal means to protect Ukrainian cultural and economic interests. The horrors of Stalin's collectivization in the Soviet Ukraine had also dissolved any attraction the USSR might have exerted on Poland's Ukrainians. However, despite some conciliatory gestures made by the Polish government in the mid-1930s, instances of official anti-Ukrainian discrimination only hardened the bitterness of the increasingly assertive Ukrainians. Nationalist paramilitary groups, some trained in Germany, turned to terrorism to undermine Polish rule. The social and material position of Poland's Jews also deteriorated in the 1930s. Polish nationalist groups encouraged peasants to boycott Jewish shops and organized anti-Jewish demonstrations at the universities. Some professions imposed restrictions on Jewish membership, while the government even endorsed unrealistic plans for Jewish emigration. The Zionist movement also promoted Jewish emigration to Palestine, although, of the 400,000 Jews who left Poland between 1921 and 1937, only about a third headed there. Nevertheless, by 1937 Polish Jews constituted 40 per cent of the mandate's Jewish population. The growth of Nazi influence among Poland's German minority further compounded nationalist tensions in the country. Discreet attempts to seek a reconciliation with Lithuania, endorsed by the Lithuanian-born Piłsudski, gave way after his death to a hardening of official Polish attitudes towards the Lithuanian republic, still resentful of the loss of Vilnius (Wilno) and still refusing to establish normal diplomatic relations with Warsaw.

The most constructive undertaking of the Sanacja in this period was the new interventionist economic policy inaugurated in 1936

43   Peasants harvesting near Nowy Sącz in southern Poland, 1936. It was
in the south of the country that the greatest fragmentation of holdings
existed; in 1921 four-fifths of all holdings there were less than five hectares
(12.5 acres) in size. In the whole of Poland in 1939 there were only 2,000
tractors, compared to 30,000 in France. Note the scythe with a pitchfork
attachment.

by Kwiatkowski, deputy prime minister and minister of finances
since 1935. The most important element in his four-year state
investment plan was the establishment of the Central Industrial
Region (COP) in the most over-populated and strategically secure
area between the Vistula and the San rivers. The construction of
hydroelectric power stations, of aircraft, rubber and motor vehicle
factories, of chemical plants, and of a new industrial centre at
Stalowa Wola was to make possible the modernization of the
armed forces, due to be completed by 1942. Further investment
plans envisaged the modernization, by 1954, of Poland's communications, agriculture and education. Already in 1938 Poland's
industrial production and real industrial wages well exceeded those
of 1928; its per capita national income was now similar to that of
Spain.

By 1939 an entire generation had been brought up for whom national independence was the norm. After the long period of partitions, the different parts of the country had been quite successfully reintegrated, government institutions and the civil service functioned effectively, and the process of unifying the legal system was far advanced. The railway network had been expanded; several shipping lines and a national airline 'Lot' had been created. Higher and secondary education was still limited but of a good standard, and many Polish scholars and academics, especially mathematicians, gained international renown; popular illiteracy, still mostly evident in the eastern provinces, had been reduced from 33 to 15 per cent; mortality rates had been cut by half; the infrastructures and appearance of most towns had been improved; and by 1939 wireless ownership had reached 1 million. Overall, however, living standards were still modest, and in the countryside hidden unemployment affected an estimated 5 million people. The nationalities issue also remained as intractable as ever; Polish officialdom continued to perceive the nationalist aspirations of the minorities as a threat to the integrity of the Polish state.

However impressive the early fruits of Polish economic *étatisme*, Poland had neither the means nor the resources, nor the totalitarian controls, ever to achieve economic or military parity with either of its two big neighbours. In 1937 Polish steel production was 1.5 million tons, that of Germany 19.8 million, and of the USSR 17.8 million. And time was running out. While Warsaw considered the USSR temporarily weakened by Stalin's purges of the Red Army, Poland's international position became increasingly vulnerable as a result of Hitler's blatant policy of overthrowing the Versailles system, and the irresolute response to the dictators by Britain and France in their anxiety to avoid war. France's failure to challenge Hitler's remilitarization of the Rhineland in March 1936 undermined Foreign Minister Beck's confidence in the French alliance. However, Beck's sceptical attitude to collective security, and his attempt to strengthen Poland's position without unduly irritating Berlin, gave the misleading impression that Poland was acting in collusion with the predatory dictators. When Hitler annexed Austria in March 1938, Beck, with a veiled threat of war, forced Lithuania to establish diplomatic relations with Warsaw. Even more shameful was the manner and timing of Poland's annexation of Teschen (Cieszyn) in October 1938 from a prostrate Czechoslovakia which had been sacrificed at Munich by Britain and France in the greatest act of appeasement. Nothing was to come either of Beck's ambition to assert Polish influence over Slovakia and to establish, with Hungary and Romania, a middle-European bloc between Germany and the USSR. Nor did an improvement in Polish–Lithuanian relations in late 1938 lead to any wider Polish association with the Baltic States.

Germany's sights focused next on Poland itself. Initially Hitler's preferred intention was to turn Poland into a vassal state which would act both as a springboard for the conquest of *Lebensraum* in the USSR, and as an eastern screen should Germany first have to fight France. Poland's anti-communist record and anti-Russian traditions, the anti-Semitism of its right-wing parties, and even from a 'racial' point of view the strong Baltic and Germanic elements in its population qualified Poland in Hitler's eyes as a possible and useful ally. To establish Germany's domination over Poland, Berlin requested the return of Danzig, already controlled by local Nazis, and the creation of an extra-territorial highway and railway across Polish Pomerania (the so-called Polish Corridor); the Poles were also invited to join the Anticomintern Pact.

Hitler's occupation of Prague on 15 March 1939 and the destruction of the rump of Czechoslovakia proved to be a turning-point for Poland and for the Western Powers. Hitler's attempt to intimidate the Poles into subservience had the opposite effect, while the collapse of appeasement prompted Britain and France to show more resolve in checking Nazi expansion. On 26 March the Polish government politely but unequivocally declined the Führer's 'magnanimous' offer. Chamberlain's public declaration of support for Poland on 31 March was followed by a formal British guarantee on 6 April, which only stiffened Polish resolve to resist Hitler's demands. Hitler responded furiously by repudiating both the Anglo-German naval agreement of 1935 and the Polish–German non-aggression treaty of 1934. The *Wehrmacht* was now instructed to plan an attack on Poland. On 19 May France signed a military agreement with Warsaw, but France's commitment to launch 'the bulk of its forces' against Germany on the fifteenth day of a

German attack on Poland was hedged with political reservations. The Polish high command in its turn took the French assurances at face value.

The deterioration of international relations in 1938 and 1939 and the economic recovery had calmed political tensions within Poland and encouraged national solidarity. The election of November 1938, held under the restricted arrangements introduced by the 1935 constitution, and coinciding with the twentieth anniversary of independence, proved a success for the government, which gained more than 80 per cent of the parliamentary seats. The government rejected all suggestions for the creation of a coalition government of national defence on the 1920 model. Nevertheless, its decision to defend the country's sovereignty had the overwhelming backing of Polish public opinion.

Just as Poland had refused to be drawn into the German embrace, so it also remained highly suspicious of British and French efforts to include the USSR in an eastern 'peace front'. For the Polish government the Soviet conditions for such co-operation were unacceptable for they were equally tantamount to the loss of sovereignty. Moscow demanded the stationing of Soviet troops in eastern Poland, the dissolution of the Polish–Romanian alliance, and the limitation of the British guarantee to Poland's western frontier. In his turn, Stalin was deeply mistrustful of western motives, especially after Munich, and was keen to buy time. Placing imperial interests over ideology, Stalin opted for a deal with Hitler, who offered him more than the West. The secret clauses of the Nazi–Soviet non-aggression pact of 23 August 1939, revealed only in 1946 but denied by the USSR until 1989, provided for the joint division of eastern-central Europe and the partition of Poland.

Hitler now schemed hard to drive a wedge between Warsaw and the Western Powers in order to complete his victim's isolation. However, the failure of Franco-British talks in Moscow and the signing of the Nazi–Soviet pact removed the last obstacle to the conclusion, on 25 August, of a formal treaty of alliance between Britain and Poland. Hitler was momentarily unnerved, while the West persuaded the Poles to delay their mobilization in the hope of last-minute talks. Hitler did not really expect the West to fight for Poland; and in any case, in this game of double bluff, he was

44 Poland's state-of-the-art bomber, the PZL P.37 Łoś ('Elk'). With a maximum speed of 277 m.p.h., a range of 932 miles and a bomb load of 4,850 pounds, it compared favourably with the best medium bombers in service anywhere in the world. But the Poles had too few modern aircraft to face the Nazi and Soviet onslaughts in 1939. Only 180 of these machines were produced between 1936 and 1939. After the war, its designer, Jerzy Dąbrowski, was to work in the aircraft industry in Britain and in the United States.

willing to take the risk. Early in the morning of 1 September Germany unleashed the bulk of its forces against Poland. Two days later Britain and France declared war on Germany.

Poland would fight. Honour and national interest made the alliance with Britain and France, whose effective help had been promised and was expected, preferable to becoming a German satellite. The September campaign was an uneven struggle. The bitter resistance of the partly mobilized Polish armed forces could not alter the enormous superiority of the Nazi war machine in terms of men, modern equipment, mobility and firepower. While the Germans applied the new doctrine of *Blitzkrieg* with awesome effect, the Poles tried to defend their long and over-exposed frontiers. Yet the campaign was no simple walkover. The small Polish air force bravely harried the *Luftwaffe*, while from 9 to 12

September the Polish counter-attack on the river Bzura, west of Warsaw, mauled five German divisions. The Germans suffered a total of 50,000 casualties (more than in France in 1940) and lost 500 aircraft and over a thousand armoured vehicles. Polish military casualties numbered over 200,000, not to mention the civilian victims of indiscriminate German bombing, or the mass executions of Polish officials and civilians. The half-promised French general offensive in the west, which might have turned the course of the campaign, never materialized. Plans to create a redoubt in the south-east, along the Romanian border, were finally dashed by the entry of Soviet troops on 17 September, which sealed the Poles' fate. Warsaw did not surrender until 27 September, while General Kleeberg's Polesie Army held out against both Soviet and German forces until 5 October, the day on which Hitler presided over a victory parade in the Polish capital. A Nazi–Soviet agreement of 28 September divided Poland fairly equally along the rivers Narwa, Bug and San (the original plan had envisaged the line of the Vistula), although the Germans acquired the more populous and more developed regions.

The Polish state, in Molotov's words 'that hideous creation of the Versailles treaty', had yet again been wiped off the map. But for the Poles the war was by no means over. Tens of thousands of soldiers and airmen managed to escape via Hungary and headed for France; most of the Polish navy had earlier left the Baltic for British ports. The Polish government and high command refused to capitulate and sought refuge in Romania where, to their surprise, they found themselves interned. On 1 October, under French pressure, President Mościcki appointed Władysław Raczkiewicz, a moderate Sanacja politician, as his successor, while General Władysław Sikorski, a leading critic of the Sanacja, became prime minister of a broad coalition government-in-exile, residing in Paris and recognized by Britain and France. Constitutional legality was thus preserved. As commander-in-chief, Sikorski began the business of reconstructing a Polish army in France, and established contact with the resistance groups that were sprouting in occupied Poland. A quasi-parliamentary body, a National Council, under the nominal chairmanship of the elderly Paderewski and with representatives from all the main political parties, was also formed;

significantly enough, it included a Jewish Bundist member, but none from the other national minorities.

Both occupying powers focused their terror on the educated and ruling elite of the country, and, in the Nazi case, also on the Jews. The eastern half of Poland, except for the region of Wilno (Vilnius) which was handed over by the Soviets to the Lithuanians, was formally annexed by the USSR after bogus local plebiscites. Mass arrests took place of key figures in the Polish military, political and economic establishment, of civil servants and trade union leaders. All private and public enterprises were taken over; the press was shut down; and all Polish political, cultural and social organizations were dissolved. At first the Soviets made strenuous efforts to win over the local non-Polish populations by promoting the Belarusian and Ukrainian languages, by distributing confiscated landed estates among the peasants, and by extending the welfare system. Once effective control had been established, the Soviets launched an attack on all religions, dissolved all local autonomous organizations, including the highly developed Ukrainian co-operative movement, and arrested all local Ukrainian and Zionist leaders. Conscription into the Red Army was introduced, and in April 1940 Soviet-style collectivization was imposed. The entire population was now terrorized into obedience.

In 1940 and 1941 up to half a million people from all social classes and all ethnic groups, but mostly Poles and Jews, were deported from the Soviet-occupied territories to Siberia and Soviet Central Asia. Entire families, deemed in any way 'unreliable' by the Soviets, suffered this ordeal; scores of thousands were to perish in the inhospitable conditions of their places of exile or from forced labour in the Gulag. By mid-1941 many small towns of pre-war eastern Poland had lost much of their Polish character. The NKVD meted out special attention to captured Polish officers (regulars and reservists), civil servants, policemen and border guards. On orders signed on 5 March 1940 by Stalin and the Politburo, over 21,000 such prisoners were shot in April 1940; of these 4,000 perished in Katyn near Smolensk. For half a century, until Gorbachev's admission in April 1990, Soviet governments were to deny their responsibility for these atrocities. Yet while merciless to those he considered enemies of Soviet power, Stalin sought to recruit Poles, especially left-wing intellectuals, willing to co-operate with the USSR. This policy gained momentum after the unexpected defeat of France in June 1940 which left the USSR alone facing a Nazi-dominated European continent. In any confrontation with Germany, the Poles could be useful. In the autumn of 1940 the 85th anniversary of Mickiewicz's death was publicly celebrated in Lwów (L'viv), and in early 1941 the Comintern revived its Polish section.

Soviet terror was soon outstripped by its Nazi counterpart. The Nazi occupation lasted longer, it affected the majority of the Polish population (indeed, between 1941 and 1944 Nazi control extended to the entire area of pre-war Poland), and it took a heavier toll of life. A vast tract of western Poland, including Poznań and Łódź (renamed Litzmannstadt), was incorporated directly into the Third Reich, and its population classified according to crude and inconsistent 'racial' criteria. To affirm the German character of Upper Silesia and especially of Pomerania, two-fifths of their population were registered wholesale as 'German' (and therefore subject to military service) as opposed to 2 per cent carefully screened in the Wartheland. Those classified as 'Poles' were reduced to the status of a helot underclass, deprived of all property and of access to all but the most basic schooling, and subject to compulsory labour or deportation. In the Wartheland virtually all Polish Catholic churches, monasteries and charitable institutions were closed; in Upper Silesia and Pomerania German was enforced as the language of religious life. Patriotic Polish priests were either expelled, arrested or shot. The central part of Poland, administered separately by the Germans as the so-called General Government (to which east Galicia was added in 1941), was subject to a regime of terror, semi-starvation and ruthless economic exploitation. It became a dumping ground for all unwanted Poles and Jews from the lands annexed by the Reich. Most Catholic parishes were allowed to function in the General Government but under many restrictions. Polish Protestants were especially victimized by the Nazis. A policy of 'spiritual sterilization' brought with it an attack on Polish high culture: museums, libraries, universities, most secondary schools, and theatres were closed down, and the public playing of Chopin's music was forbidden. Only some primary schooling and limited technical training was permitted, while

Map 10   Poland during the Second World War, 1939–1944.

SCALE

| 0 | 50 | 100 | 150 | 200 | 250 | 300 | 350 km |
| 0 | | 50 | | 100 | | 150 | 200 miles |

LATVIA
(incorporated in
the USSR
1940–1)

REICHSKOMMISSARIAT

HUANIA
rated in the USSR 1940–1)

Kaunas

OSTLAND (1941)

Vitebsk

Dvina

Smolensk

KALININ

KATYN

Wilno
(Vilnius)

Suwalki

Niemen

Minsk

Grodno

Nowogródek
(Navahrudak)

U S S R

EZIRK
Białystok

LYSTOK
to Ostpreussen
1941)

Pinsk

Pripet

Brześć
(Brest)

OR
blin

Bug

Kowel
(Kovel)

JEK

REICHSKOMMISSARIAT UKRAINE (1941)

Kiev

KHARKOV

EC

Równe
(Rivne)

Dnieper

Lwów
(L'viv)

**DISTRIKT
LEMBERG**
(attached to
the G.G. in 1941)

TRANSNISTRIA
(to Romania 1941)

Dniester

ROMANIA

cheap entertainment was provided in the cinemas and through a so-called 'reptile' gutter press.

The incarceration in concentration camps in September 1939 of the staff of Kraków University was a foretaste of the fate awaiting the entire Polish educated class under Nazi rule. Indeed, a large proportion of the Polish intelligentsia and professional classes, including of course most of the Jews amongst them, perished through mass executions or in concentration camps: from 15 per cent of all teachers and 18 per cent of the Catholic clergy to 45 per cent of all doctors, 50 per cent of all qualified engineers, and 57 per cent of all lawyers. The rest of the Poles were treated as a slave workforce, 'ein Arbeitvolk'; from 1939 to 1944 about 2.8 million Poles were sent to Germany as compulsory labourers. About 200,000 Polish children with 'racially appropriate features' were removed from orphanages and from their parents in order to be brought up as 'Aryan' Germans in Nazi homes. And for every German killed in occupied Poland a hundred hostages were executed. Public hangings and shootings became commonplace in towns and villages. The Nazi 'Generalplan Ost' of April 1942 envisaged that the remaining Poles would eventually be scattered over the eastern wastes of conquered Russia as so much unwanted, racially inferior trash. All of Poland was to become a region of German settlement.

However vicious and costly in lives the Nazi treatment of Polish Gentiles was, the fate of the 'subhuman' Jews and Gypsies of Poland was to be catastrophically worse. Subject to mass killings and brutal maltreatment from the very beginning of the war, the Jews were herded into 400 sealed ghettos, where disease and hunger ravaged their inhabitants; the largest was the Warsaw ghetto with 450,000 people. After the German invasion of the USSR in 1941 the Nazis were able to get their clutches on the Jews of eastern pre-war Poland. At the notorious Wannsee conference in January 1942, the Jews of occupied Europe were condemned to total extermination. To implement this unprecedented act of genocide a whole system of death camps was developed in occupied Poland, the largest centres being Auschwitz-Birkenau (Oświęcim-Brzezinka), Majdanek and Treblinka. Here the inhabitants of the ghettos and Jews from all over occupied Europe were transported by the trainload. The uprising in the Warsaw ghetto in April and May 1943 was a hopeless but powerfully symbolic act of Jewish defiance against their oppressors. By the end of 1944 the Nazis had put to death about 90 per cent of pre-war Poland's Jewish population of 3 million, and had virtually wiped out a community which had been on Polish soil for centuries.

The reaction of Polish Gentiles to the fate of their Jewish fellow citizens during the Holocaust varied. On the dark side there were extortionists who exploited Jewish misfortunes, informers who betrayed Jews to the Nazis, and extreme right-wing nationalists even willing to kill Jews. The insidious influence of Nazi anti-Semitic propaganda, the introduction of the death penalty for anyone caught helping the Jews, the sight of mass executions, and the general atmosphere of terror gradually numbed the moral responses of many people, prompting indifference, fear for their own skin, and even fanning old anti-Jewish sentiments. Reports that some Jews in eastern Poland had welcomed the Soviets in 1939 also strengthened the widely held stereotype of 'Judaeo-communism' which had been promoted by right-wing parties before the war; such was the background to the massacres of Jews in Jedwabne and elsewhere by local Poles in areas the Germans had occupied during their invasion of the USSR in 1941. Contemporary accounts suggest that numerous Poles easily came to accept the dispossession of the Jews and their isolation in the ghettos. The observed willingness of many peasants to help the Jews, even in 1941, had definitely altered by the autumn of 1942. On the other hand, there were Gentile Poles willing to take the risk of offering sanctuary to the Jews, to which the Yad Vashem Institute in Israel today provides considerable testimony; religious convents were also able to save many Jewish children. Assimilated middle-class Jews had the best chance of survival outside the ghettos, while orthodox religious Jews, with their distinct dress and appearance, were the easiest targets for the Nazis. The influential Catholic writer Zofia Kossak-Szczucka condemned the genocide in no uncertain terms. In August 1942 the Polish Underground established a separate council (known by the acronym 'Żegota') for co-ordinating assistance to the Jews; this came in the form of money, false identity papers and safe places of refuge. The Polish

45 The Holocaust in art. *El Mole-Rachmim* from the series 'Kamienie krzyczą' ('The stones are screaming'), painted in 1946 by Bronisław Wojciech Linke (1906–62). 'El Mole-Rachmim' (God full of mercy) is sung at Jewish funerals and at the Day of Atonement. Except for the period 1939–46, Linke spent most of his working life in Warsaw. He deployed a powerful surrealist form of art to attack cruelty, meanness and hypocrisy.

government in London provided an initially incredulous outside world in June and December 1942 with details of the Nazi atrocities; the role of the courier Jan Karski, who provided much of this information, merits mentioning. In the circumstances, the saving of up to 45,000 Jews, including 12,000 within Warsaw itself until autumn 1944, could be seen as something of an achievement.

The absence of civilized norms of government during the Nazi occupation of Poland and the general brutalization of the population not only generated bitter Polish hatred of the Germans but created ripe conditions for the outbreak of other inter-ethnic conflicts, especially in the eastern areas of pre-war Poland where traditional social structures had already been destroyed by the Soviets in 1939–41. Polish underground fighters clashed with Lithuanian police units raised by the Germans and with Soviet-sponsored partisans. In 1943 terrible atrocities occurred in Volhynia, where local Ukrainian nationalists, many of whom had learnt their murderous craft during the Holocaust of Volhynia's Jews in 1942, set out to 'cleanse' the area of its remaining Polish population. The Poles retaliated, and so began a long brutal Polish–Ukrainian civil war which spread to other neighbouring regions. In the Belarusian-speaking districts nothing comparable happened, and in early 1944 many Belarusians in the Nowogródek region, fearful of the return of the Soviets, even joined the Polish 'Home Army'. But it was clear that the traditions of a multi-ethnic Polish state were largely erased during the Second World War.

The bestial nature of Nazi policies in Poland and the intensity of Polish nationalism ruled out any prospect of serious political collaboration with the Nazis; there was simply no scope for a Polish Pétain or a Polish Quisling. For General Sikorski's government there was no alternative but to continue the war effort. Polish troops displayed characteristic valour during the Allied expedition to Narvik in May 1940 and during the French campaign in which four Polish divisions took part. After the fall of France, the Polish government, with 20,000 soldiers, was evacuated to Great Britain. On the basis of the British–Polish treaty of 5 August 1940 Britain undertook to equip the remaining Polish armed forces which were to fight under overall British command. And in an attempt to break with Poland's pre-war foreign policy, the exiled Polish and

Czechoslovak governments signed in November 1940 a declaration
of intent for a post-war confederation between their two countries.
A Polish brigade helped to defend Tobruk in late 1941. Initial
British doubts about the competence of Polish airmen were rapidly
dispelled, and Polish pilots (numbering 10 per cent of Fighter
Command) showed their real mettle during the Battle of Britain
when they downed over 200 German aircraft, one-seventh of the
total. The Polish squadron 303, based at Northolt outside London,
was the highest-scoring fighter squadron in the air battle of 1940.
By 1944 the Polish air force in Britain comprised fourteen squad-
rons; its bombers took part in raids over Germany and its fighter
aircraft were active during the invasion of Normandy. The Polish
navy acquired additional ships, and participated alongside the
Royal Navy in most operations in the Atlantic and the Mediterranean. A particularly significant contribution to the Allied cause
was the transfer by Polish military intelligence to the French and
British, in August 1939, of a replica of the German 'Enigma'
machine, the coding system of which had been cracked by Polish
cryptologists. Out of this grew Station X at Bletchley Park, where
British cryptographers were able to decipher German military
communications; there is little doubt that this shortened the war.
Polish intelligence networks operated throughout occupied Europe,
including Germany, in north Africa and in the Middle East, and
provided London with vast amounts of valuable military and
industrial information. It is estimated that over 40 per cent of
reports from occupied Europe, many of great operational value,
came from Polish sources; they included details of the German
preparations for the invasion of the USSR and of subsequent
German troop movements to the east, as well as details of the
German V1 flying bomb and the V2 rocket project.

The Polish tradition of conspiracy and resistance, reinforced
now by the legacy of inter-war independence, found full expression
again. Diverse resistance groups began to emerge spontaneously as
early as September 1939; their activities were gradually co-
ordinated by General Stefan Rowecki, appointed commander of
the underground forces by General Sikorski in June 1940. By mid-
1944, when it reached its maximum size of 400,000 members, the
so-called Home Army (Armia Krajowa or AK) formed the largest

underground organization in the whole of occupied Europe; it embraced within its structure all Polish resistance groups with the notable exception of the smaller communist-led People's Army (AL) and the ultra-nationalist 'National Armed Forces' (NSZ). Although officers of the pre-war army who had evaded capture provided much of its cadres, the Home Army drew on all sections of the Polish population and represented a veritable citizen army on a scale hitherto unknown in Polish history. Its main area of activity was the General Government, but it also established sizeable units in the Wilno-Nowogródek region and in Volhynia. At first the AK concentrated on intelligence gathering, organizing propaganda, punishing collaborators, bandits and extortionists, and on organizing numerous acts of sabotage, especially along German lines of communication to the eastern front. It increased its military activity in early 1943, and, although woefully under-equipped, prepared for a nationwide insurrection in propitious circumstances.

The AK was the military wing of an extensive 'underground state' led since autumn 1940 by a Delegate appointed by the government-in-exile in London. The Polish Underground State was endorsed by the four main Polish political parties which continued to function clandestinely and which in February 1940 managed to overcome their pre-war rivalries to form a broad coalition committed to the creation of a genuine parliamentary democracy after the war: the Polish Peasant Party (PSL), the Polish Socialist Party (PPS), the National Party (SN) as the successor to the National Democrats, and the Catholic centrist Party of Labour (SP). The supporters of the pre-war Sanacja, humbled by the defeat of 1939, were mostly absorbed into the main resistance movement. Only the communists, who remained relatively inactive until the Nazi invasion of the USSR in 1941, and the right-wing extremists, dreaming of a nationalist one-party Poland, did not join the broad national coalition, nor recognize the authority of the Government Delegate.

Within the limits imposed by conspiratorial activity, the Underground State maintained the continuity of Polish statehood and carried out a remarkable number of the functions of a regular government. It possessed a civil service with quasi-ministries, a judicial system, and it promoted educational and cultural activities

as a counter-measure to the Nazi policy of debasing the cultural life
of the population. Clandestine university teaching and secondary
schooling took place in many cities and towns, at great risk to
those participating, and ensured the survival of a core of educated
people. Works of art were hidden; textbooks, journals and newspapers appeared off secret printing presses; banned Polish classics
were staged in covert dramatic theatres and at poetry readings.
Indeed, much of Polish organized cultural, social and sporting life,
from trade unions to the scouts, operated underground. Charitable
institutions allowed by the Germans, such as the Polish Red Cross,
also provided cover for conspiratorial activity. Street ballads,
mocking the Germans, helped to maintain popular morale, while
intentionally slow and shoddy 'tortoise' work in German-run
armaments factories damaged the Nazi war effort. German-
language black propaganda was also distributed in large quantities
among German troops in Poland.

The prospect of an early liberation of Poland was very bleak as
the Axis Powers extended their control of mainland Europe.
Britain by itself could not liberate Europe. It was the Nazi invasion
of the Soviet Union on 22 June 1941, and Hitler's ultimate failure
to destroy the USSR which dramatically altered the character of the
war in Europe; it also changed Poland's prospects, although not
necessarily in accordance with many Polish hopes. With the Japanese attack on Pearl Harbor in December 1941 the war became a
global conflict, the outcome of which would be decided primarily
by the USA and the USSR. The Poles were to make costly attempts
to recover their independence, but once again, as in 1814–15,
Poland's fate was ultimately to rest in the hands of the Great
Powers.

In the wake of the British–Soviet alliance of 13 July 1941,
Churchill pressed Sikorski to sign an agreement with the USSR (the
so-called Sikorski–Maisky treaty) on 30 July 1941: diplomatic
relations were restored, the Nazi–Soviet partition of Poland was
annulled, Polish prisoners in the USSR were freed, and a Polish
army was to be formed on Soviet territory. With all of pre-war
Poland now under Nazi occupation Stalin could afford to make
temporary concessions to the Poles. Sikorski hoped that a Polish
army, under the jurisdiction of the Polish government in London

and fighting on the eastern front alongside the Red Army, would help to liberate Poland, and that the USSR would respect Poland's future sovereignty. However, the absence of a precise Soviet commitment to respect the pre-war Polish–Soviet border split the Polish leadership and led to a government reshuffle which raised the profile of Stanisław Mikołajczyk, the leader of the Peasant Party (PSL). Nor was Stalin ultimately willing to nurture an independent Polish army that was being formed under the command of General Władysław Anders in Soviet Central Asia. Numerous Soviet bureaucratic obstructions, Moscow's refusal to recognize as Polish citizens all but ethnic Poles from eastern Poland, and finally the unexplained absence of thousands of Polish officers captured by the Soviets in 1939, all militated against Sikorski's strategy of co-operation with the USSR. The logical outcome was the evacuation of Anders' army of 70,000 men to Iran in the summer of 1942 to reinforce British and Commonwealth forces in the Middle East. With Anders left 40,000 emaciated civilians. Never before nor since during Stalin's rule were so many prisoners and detainees, with such personal knowledge of the Gulag, allowed to leave the USSR. However, tens of thousands of the original deportees remained behind in what the writer Józef Czapski, one of the freed prisoners, aptly labelled 'the inhuman land'.

Polish–Soviet relations continued to deteriorate just when the war on the eastern front, after Stalingrad, began to turn in Stalin's favour. Any Polish hopes that there might be a repetition of the outcome of the First World War were to be mere illusions. It is clear that, as a consequence of the Nazi attack on the USSR, Stalin had revised his earlier, inimical, views on Polish statehood; yet he was adamant that he would be the arbiter of the territorial and political configuration of a restored Polish state. Since the Polish government in London remained equally resolved in pressing for full Polish sovereignty and the restoration of the pre-1939 eastern border, there was ultimately to be no scope for a genuine compromise between the two sides. Stalin therefore set to work to create rival institutions to those of the Polish government in London and of the Polish Underground State.

To promote his influence within Nazi-occupied Poland, Stalin had already encouraged the establishment, in January 1942, of a revived Polish communist party under the modified name of the Polish Worker Party (PPR). Led after autumn 1943 by Władysław Gomułka, a Moscow-trained Polish communist, and by Bolesław Bierut, a former Comintern agent and member of the NKVD, the PPR not only refused to subordinate itself to the underground Government Delegature but began to lay a rival claim to represent the 'real' interests of the Polish nation. In early 1943 Stalin sanctioned the activities of a Union of Polish Patriots, led by Polish communists and fellow-travellers, the most eminent of whom was Wanda Wasilewska, the daughter of one of Marshal Piłsudski's closest associates, and the formation of a Polish army under Soviet control commanded by Colonel Zygmunt Berling, a former prisoner now willing to collaborate with the USSR. Into this army, which was to taste action at Lenino in Belarus in October 1943, flocked thousands of Poles who had failed to reach Anders. The discovery by the Germans of the mass grave with the corpses of 4,000 Polish officers at Katyn in April 1943, followed by Sikorski's request to the Red Cross to investigate, amid justified suspicions that the Soviets had perpetrated the atrocity, provided Stalin with an excellent opportunity to 'suspend' diplomatic relations with the Polish government on 25 April 1943.

The year 1943 brought further blows to the Polish cause. The death of General Sikorski in a still not fully explained air crash off Gibraltar on 4 July deprived the Poles of an internationally respected leader. Stanisław Mikołajczyk, the new prime minister, was shrewd and able but lacked his predecessor's authority, and was on bad terms with General Sosnkowski, the new commander-in-chief, who had opposed the Sikorski–Maisky treaty. Secondly, unknown to the Poles, at the Allied conference in Teheran on 28 November to 1 December 1943 both Roosevelt and Churchill expressed their broad agreement with Stalin's request that the Curzon Line should form Poland's future eastern border, thus leaving Wilno (Vilnius) and probably Lwów (L'viv) in Soviet hands, and that Poland should be compensated in the west at Germany's expense. For the Western Powers the Poles were a gallant and useful ally, but in the cold realities of the global Allied strategy after 1941, and at a time when the Red Army was bearing the brunt of the land fighting against Nazi Germany, the Soviet alliance was inevitably given precedence over Polish interests and sensibilities.

To weaken communist influence, the coalition parties of the Underground State announced their commitment, in August 1943 and March 1944, to a sweeping land reform and to the nationalization of the industrial base (although the nationalist SN was least keen on this part of the programme), the re-establishment of the pre-1939 eastern border, and territorial compensation from Germany for the human losses and material damage inflicted on Poland. What at this stage distinguished the non-communist Underground State and the crypto-communist PPR, which avoided any dogmatic posturing and presented itself in patriotic garb, was not so much the radical social and economic reforms advocated by both sides, but their attitudes towards national sovereignty, the frontier issue and the nature of future Polish–Soviet relations. The PPR attracted a variety of splinter groups from the peasant and socialist parties, but it remained for the moment a small player in Polish politics; its armed wing, the People's Army, was still only a fraction of the size of the AK. All this was to change with the approach of the Red Army.

In 1944 the Polish armed forces in the west were at last making a significant contribution to the Allied war effort: in May the Second Corps under General Anders stormed the heavily defended Monte Cassino and opened the road to Rome; in August General Maczek's 1st Armoured Division distinguished itself at the battle of Falaise, making possible the early liberation of Paris; while in September General Sosabowski's Parachute Brigade fought hard at Arnhem. All these men were fighting for Poland's freedom, but they were to be cruelly deceived by the wider course of events. The ground was rapidly slipping from under the government-in-exile. On the one hand Churchill pressed Mikołajczyk to come to terms with Stalin and to give way on the frontier issue; on the other hand, Stalin now demanded not only the explicit recognition of the Curzon Line but the exclusion from the Polish government of elements 'hostile to the Soviet Union', that is, the resignation of none other than President Raczkiewicz himself, General Sosnkowski, and other prominent ministers.

Nor was the Polish Underground State able to prevent Stalin,

46   Polish tanks in Normandy, early September 1944. Sherman tanks of the 24th Lancers of General Maczek's Polish 1st Armoured Division passing through the hamlet of Sommery, north of Rouen, in pursuit of the retreating Germans. The division's battle route took it from Caen, through Belgium and Holland, to Wilhelmshaven on the North Sea coast of Germany.

with his overwhelming power and ruthless methods, from imposing Soviet control on the ground. The attempt in the summer of 1944 to establish Polish authority in the former eastern territories of Poland in the path of the Soviet advance ended in tragedy. Initially joint action between the AK and the Red Army proved successful, as in the battle for the liberation of Wilno in July 1944. But once the front had moved on to the west, the Soviets arrested the local Polish leaders and demanded that the AK soldiers join the Soviet-sponsored Berling army; most refused and found themselves dispatched to the Gulag.

On 21 July 1944 the Red Army crossed the Bug river into what Stalin recognized as Polish territory. Yet even here he had no time for the independent Polish underground. On 22 July, in Chełm, a Soviet-backed Polish Committee of National Liberation (PKWN) laid its claim to be the effective government of liberated Poland. The PKWN announced its commitment to the democratic constitution of 1921, to radical reforms, and to Poland's expansion in the west at Germany's expense. It presented itself as a broad left-wing and democratic body of a Popular Front type, although none of the major Polish political parties was represented. Its chairman, Edward Osóbka-Morawski, was a hitherto unknown member of a socialist splinter group. Security, propaganda and military affairs were all controlled by communists. On 26 July the PKWN was installed in Lublin, from which it began to extend its authority within the areas occupied by the Soviet forces, and to conscript men for its armed forces.

In the summer of 1944 there were therefore two rival centres claiming authority in Poland. On one side, there was the non-communist Underground State with the AK, enjoying the support of most Poles, and owing allegiance to the legitimate Polish government in London, which was still recognized by the Western Allies; and on the other, the Soviet-sponsored PKWN which, despite its feeble roots among the Polish population, enjoyed the full material support of the Red Army and of the Soviet security forces in the creation of structures of government behind the Soviet front line.

The approach of the Red Army to Warsaw heralded the final tragedy of the Polish Underground State. On 1 August the AK in

Warsaw launched a wholescale attack on the Germans with a view to establishing an independent Polish administration in the city before the arrival of the Soviets. Expecting to seize control of the city from the retreating Germans within several days, the poorly equipped AK found itself fighting for two months. The Germans turned some of their most vicious units on the city. Desperate street fighting was accompanied by large-scale massacres of the civilian population. The Red Army halted its operations on reaching the Vistula, while Stalin delayed granting permission to Allied aircraft bringing supplies to the insurgents to use Soviet airfields. He simply had to wait while the Nazis annihilated the last Polish obstacle to his control of Poland. A late attempt by Soviet-sponsored Polish troops to cross the Vistula in September received little Soviet help, and failed.

While Paris was liberated in August with limited loss of life and little material damage, Warsaw was the scene of one of the most desperate and savage urban battles of the Second World War. The city's agony ended with capitulation on 2 October. Military losses on each side numbered about 17,000 killed, but up to 200,000 civilians also perished. The remaining population was driven from the city, which, in a barbaric act of vengeance, was then systematically destroyed; in Hitler's words, Warsaw was henceforth to be no more than 'a point on a map'. While the rising's heroism might have impressed on Stalin the strength of Polish nationalism, the heart of the Polish Underground State had been torn out and the AK effectively decapitated. The final concerted bid to assert Poland's independence had failed.

In the areas of Poland cleared of the Germans the PKWN deployed a carrot-and-stick policy. On the one hand, its security forces and the NKVD mercilessly hounded surviving units of the 'counter-revolutionary' AK; on the other hand, the PKWN moved deftly to win wider support among a sceptical population. The new, largely Soviet-officered Polish army, formed out of the fusion of General Berling's forces and the communist People's Army (AL), retained all the trappings of a national army. Indeed, this army was to expand to 400,000 men and was to participate in the subsequent Soviet drive into Germany and in the final assault on Berlin. Other gestures were made to patriotic sentiment. The authorities in

47   The Warsaw Rising, 1944. One can only speculate as to the fate of these young girls who, with many others, served as liaison officers for the Home Army (AK). To the present day, most Poles are united in their homage to the bravery of the fighters and the courage of the city in 1944. But they remain divided over the Rising's wisdom and objectives. The traumatic effect of the Rising's failure did much to instil greater political realism and restraint among the Poles when facing communist rule after 1945.

Lublin sponsored cultural activities, for which there was a powerful thirst after five years of occupation, and thereby attracted the collaboration of many actors and writers. And, in a highly effective move urged by Stalin to win over the rural poor to the emerging new political order (though the Underground State had been preparing similar legislation), a radical land reform of September 1944 inaugurated the distribution among poor peasant families of all private estates and farms with over 50 hectares (125 acres) of arable land; in 1944 alone over 100,000 such families benefited in this way, although most ended up with tiny holdings of under 3 hectares. The remaining aristocracy and landed gentry were hounded out of their ancestral homes.

Most of the cards were now neatly stacked in Stalin's favour: his control of Polish territory was growing every day, and he was now less interested in securing changes in the Polish government-in-exile than in using the PKWN as the basis for a new Polish government to which acceptable 'democratic elements' from the London government might be added. Although more concerned about Poland and more realistic in his attitude to the USSR than Roosevelt, Churchill felt that if genuinely free democratic elections could be built into a deal with Stalin then Poland, within new frontiers, could be assured of a degree of internal freedom. But ultimately, neither the United States nor Britain (increasingly dependent on its transatlantic ally) was prepared to damage their relations with the USSR over Poland. On the contrary, Roosevelt was anxious to secure Soviet help in the war with Japan and Soviet co-operation in the building of a new post-war order, symbolized by the creation of the United Nations Organization in 1945.

Having failed to secure his ministerial colleagues' agreement to Stalin's territorial and political demands, Mikołajczyk resigned from the premiership on 24 November 1944, taking the Peasant Party (PSL) out of the coalition government. For Stalin the games with the London Poles were over. On 31 December 1944, the PKWN declared itself the Provisional Government of the Republic of Poland; as such it received formal Soviet recognition in January 1945. The Polish government-in-exile, now led by the veteran socialist Tomasz Arciszewski, was still recognized by the United States and Britain, but to all intents and purposes it was no longer relevant in the settlement of the Polish Question. On 17 January 1945 Soviet-sponsored Polish troops entered the ghostly ruins of Warsaw.

At the end of the First World War Poland's western border had been decided with Polish participation at Versailles, while the eastern border had been secured after a victorious war with Bolshevik Russia. The scenario in 1945 was dramatically different; if anything, it resembled the settlement of the Polish Question at the Congress of Vienna in 1815. At the Yalta conference of February 1945 Stalin, Roosevelt and Churchill agreed to the establishment of 'a strong, free, independent and democratic Poland'; its eastern border was roughly to follow the Curzon Line, while in the west Poland was to obtain substantial but still unspecified territory from Germany. The western leaders also secured Stalin's agreement to broaden the Provisional Government in Warsaw with the inclusion of 'democratic leaders from Poland itself and from among Poles abroad'; this government would pledge to hold early and free democratic elections. For many Poles Yalta was the ultimate betrayal by their western allies. For the Western Powers it seemed, in the circumstances, a practical resolution of the Polish issue with plausible safeguards against the total Soviet control of Polish internal affairs. Mikołajczyk expressed his willingness to return to Poland on that assumption. It all depended, of course, on whether such free elections would take place and whether their results would be respected.

Two events in Moscow on 21 June 1945 demonstrated the new realities of power in Poland. In the Kremlin, Stalin graciously concluded a conference establishing the new Polish Provisional Government of National Unity. In accordance with the Yalta agreement, Mikołajczyk and five other non-communists joined a twenty-man cabinet dominated by the PPR and its allies, and led by the pro-Soviet socialist Osóbka-Morawski. Mikołajczyk was offered the agriculture portfolio and was made one of two deputy prime ministers, the other being the communist Gomułka. Meanwhile, a few hundred yards away, in the Hall of Columns of the trade union headquarters, the show trial ended of the sixteen military and civilian leaders of the non-communist Underground State, including the Government Delegate Jankowski and the last commander of the AK, General Okulicki, who had all been kidnapped by the NKVD outside Warsaw in March 1945. They were convicted, and in most cases imprisoned, on charges of belonging to illegal organizations and, what was most grotesque, of collaborating with the Germans. The tragedy that befell these men, and indeed many members of the now-dissolved AK, who for five years had struggled against the Nazi oppressors and more recently had defied Soviet designs on their country's independence, vividly symbolized some of the moral ambiguities of the Second World War. Indeed, between 1944 and 1947 some 50,000 Poles, mostly members of the AK and activists of the Underground State, were deported to the Soviet Gulag. On 5 July Britain and the United States finally withdrew their recognition of the Polish government-in-exile in London. It was to continue its phantom existence until

Map 11   Poland's 'move to the west', 1945.

1990, as a symbol of constitutional legitimacy, bearing witness before the world of the violence inflicted on its nation.

Of all the countries of Nazi-occupied Europe the Poles had fought the Germans the longest, and had suffered appalling human and material losses. It is estimated that Poland's total wartime losses (including both Gentiles and Jews) amounted to a fifth of the country's population. The Poles also had good reason to distrust the Soviets. Yet Poland's tragedy again was its geography. The country lay directly on the Soviet route to Berlin and to what was to become the Soviet zone of occupation in Germany; in that critical sense Poland was of greater strategic concern to the USSR than Hungary, Romania, or even Czechoslovakia, not to mention Finland. Soviet territorial demands from the latter three states were also relatively limited when compared to the Soviet annexation of over two-fifths of pre-war Poland. Despite the fears of some Poles, Stalin had no intention after 1941 of incorporating the rest of Poland as an integral part of the USSR, in contrast to the Baltic States. Nevertheless, Soviet imperial interests demanded that, even if allowed nominal statehood, Poland had to be under total Soviet control. Any resistance to Soviet domination therefore had to be quashed, while the admission of Mikołajczyk to the 'Provisional Government of National Unity' provided a democratic fig-leaf to cover the reality of communist control, and the price for western recognition.

At the Potsdam conference in July–August 1945, the United States and Britain reluctantly agreed to the Oder–Neisse (Odra–Nysa) Line as the western limit of Polish administration, prior to a final peace conference, and to the expulsion of the remaining German population in the areas under Polish control. Transferring to Poland extensive ex-German lands was bound to make Poland dependent on Soviet support in the face of any future German demands for the restoration of these lands. The non-communist Underground State had certainly envisaged some territorial acquisitions in the west at Germany's expense, but the push for the whole of Silesia and Pomerania as far as Stettin (Szczecin) came at first primarily from the pro-Soviet communist leadership which proudly proclaimed Poland's return to the frontiers of Piast Poland of the tenth century. With Stalin's blessing, and using the language of the pre-war nationalist National Democrats, Poland's communists endorsed the idea of a homogeneous nation-state within the new borders.

About 8 million Silesian, Pomeranian and East Prussian Germans, including those who had already fled before the Red Army and those who were now evicted by the Poles, paid a tragic price for the bankruptcy of Nazi dreams of *Lebensraum* in the east. Nazi ethnic cleansing in Poland was now reversed with a vengeance; so ended over seven centuries of German settlement east of the Oder river. In the place of the departing Germans there arrived in 1945–6 about 2 million settlers from central Poland and 1.5 million Poles uprooted and 'repatriated' from the eastern provinces annexed by the USSR. Most of the Polish population of Lwów (L'viv), for instance, found new homes in the largely ruined ex-German city of Breslau, now renamed Wrocław. Most of the Polish population of Wilno also moved into the new Poland; Vilnius was now to become a Soviet and Lithuanian city. A communist-run Ministry for the Recovered Territories had the monopoly of allocating to the new settlers former German homes and land, although half of the arable land there, which had belonged to great landed estates, was transferred to newly created state farms. Life in the new Polish 'wild west' was not easy at first as all sorts of looters descended on the ex-German lands during 1945 and 1946. Most of the so-called 'autochthonous' Polish-speaking inhabitants of East Prussia and former German Silesia were allowed to remain, but were discriminated against by outsider bureaucrats ignorant of local conditions; their future in communist Poland was not to be a happy one. Between 1945 and 1947 over 1.5 million Polish forced labourers and prisoners returned from Germany. Much of the new Poland in those years was like a vast railway station, with hundreds of thousands of people on the move.

The cause of Polish independence was not only weakened by the withdrawal of Western recognition of the Polish government-in-exile, but also by the demobilization by the British government of the Polish armed forces in the west; it was a painful blow for those Polish politicians expecting an imminent East–West conflict. Members of General Anders' 110,000-strong Second Corps, stationed in Italy , and composed largely of men and women from

pre-war eastern Poland, were particularly embittered by the war's
outcome. The existence of the Corps and of all the other Polish
armed formations in the west was now a source of political
embarrassment and a financial burden for the British government;
these units had also been swollen by Poles released from German
prisoner-of-war camps and by Poles who had been conscripted by
the *Wehrmacht* and who had changed sides at the earliest opportunity. However, although the new British Labour government
urged all Polish servicemen to return home (and indeed about a
half did so), it refused to hand over overall command of the Polish
armed forces in the west to the new pro-Soviet authorities in
Warsaw. Most of the remaining Polish forces were moved to Great
Britain; their ambiguous legal status was resolved by the creation
in 1946 of the Polish Resettlement Corps, a transitional non-
combatant unit in the British army, which was to prepare the
demobilized men and women for civilian life in Britain. In 1951
there were 136,000 Poles on British soil, of whom 49,000 were in
London, forming there the second largest ethnic minority until the
mid-1950s. Altogether, about 500,000 Poles chose political exile
and ultimately a new life in the west: primarily in Britain, North
America and Australia.

In Poland thousands of ex-AK guerrillas and other armed groups
hostile to the new regime continued a desperate struggle against
Soviet security forces and those of their Polish allies. But for
millions of ordinary Poles, exhausted, impoverished, mourning the
deaths of their loved ones, and forced to survive by barter or on the
black market, the end of the war naturally brought profound relief;
there was an overwhelming desire for reconstruction and for a
return to a normal everyday existence. The early pragmatism of the
new pro-Soviet government, with its appeal to many young radicalized peasants and workers, and to some intellectuals dreaming of
careers in the shaping of a better world, appeared to respond to
those expectations. At the same time, the presence of Mikołajczyk
and the legal activity of his large Peasant Party seemed to indicate
that the cause of freedom and democracy within Poland's imposed
borders might perhaps not be lost. In reality, however, the next few
years proved to be merely a transitional phase between one totalitarianism and another.

7

Communism and the Cold War, 1945–1989

Out of the ordeals of the Second World War emerged a new Polish state starkly different from the pre-war republic in terms of its territory, the size and composition of its population, its political and social order, and its relations with its neighbours. Poland's territorial losses in the east and its compensatory expansion in the north and west dramatically altered the country's shape and position on the map of Europe. The new Poland was 20 per cent smaller, but it was more compact and it had acquired a 300-mile-long Baltic coastline. Although much devastated, the ex-German lands were more developed than the provinces lost to the USSR. The demographic changes were also conspicuous. The new Poland had just under 24 million inhabitants in 1946, as opposed to 35 million in 1939, but it now contained an overwhelmingly ethnic Polish population. Death, displacement and dispossession had all but obliterated the country's pre-war political and social elite. With wartime material destruction estimated at two-fifths of its productive capacity, Poland was the most devastated country in Europe, comparable only to the ravaged Soviet republics of Belarus and the Ukraine. Accompanying this were malnutrition, acute shortages of housing, and the widespread incidence of tuberculosis and venereal diseases. The war had also left thousands of invalids and orphans.

The new Poland was also firmly under Soviet military and political control. All the key levers of power within the country rested in communist hands, while a Ministry of Public Security

48 A queue for water in ruined Warsaw, spring 1945. Although over 80 per cent of Warsaw had been devastated, many former inhabitants who had survived the Warsaw Rising of 1944 soon started to return to the city, despite the primitive conditions of existence. By July 1945 the population had reached nearly 400,000, a third of its pre-war size. The rebuilding of Warsaw was an undeniable achievement of the post-1945 regime.

directed by the NKVD-trained Stanisław Radkiewicz, and backed ultimately by the Red Army and the notorious NKVD itself, tightened its grip over the country. On the other hand, lacking genuinely popular leaders, the communist PPR was more than aware that it needed time to consolidate its position and to build up a mass membership. To mobilize the population in the awesome task of post-war reconstruction and to win for itself a degree of legitimacy, the regime had to make a broad patriotic appeal, not least by depicting the post-1945 frontiers, within which a purely Polish nation-state could at last be created, as representing a return to the original Poland of the Piasts. Furthermore, the decisions taken at Yalta and Potsdam demanded a limited gesture to pluralism. And so, while brutally destroying the remnants of the anti-communist underground, the Temporary Government of National

Unity pursued pragmatic and flexible policies in the realms of economic reconstruction, culture and religion.

All industrial enterprises employing over fifty workers per shift were nationalized in January 1946, but much economic activity, notably in the retail trade and in agriculture, remained outside direct government control. Indeed, the moderate *étatiste* proposals emanating from the newly created Central Office of Planning, where non-Marxist socialists and experts held sway, envisaged the continuation of a mixed economy. Current political issues were subject to strict censorship, but otherwise a broad range of publishing and artistic work, including films and radio broadcasts, was permitted. There was still no ideological supervision of teaching in the rapidly growing network of schools or in the hurriedly restored universities.

Although the 1925 Concordat was annulled by the government in September 1945, the Church recognized the need for compromise with the new political order. It retained full freedom of worship, and proceeded, not without a touch of triumphalism, with the creation of new parochial structures for the millions of Poles settling in the so-called 'Recovered Lands' and with taking over the ruined churches of the departing, mostly Protestant, German population. Indeed, as a result of the frontier and population changes, and for the first time since the fourteenth century, Poland was now an overwhelmingly Catholic country. The sufferings endured by the clergy and the patriotic and dignified behaviour of the Church during the war had enhanced the Church's status in Polish society and contributed to an even closer identification of the Church with the nation than had been the case before 1939. Little wonder that the authorities moved cautiously in their relations with the Church; the Stalinist Bierut even used the traditional formula 'So help me God' at his presidential inauguration in 1947.

However, the struggle for political power went on unabated, generating in many regions an atmosphere of insecurity and violence, even of civil war. Illusions that an armed conflict between the Western Powers and the USSR was imminent, and that it would reverse the Soviet domination of Poland, encouraged the survival until the end of 1947 of many armed anti-communist guerrilla groups or 'forest battalions'. Up to 30,000 people, mostly opponents of the new regime, perished in this internecine struggle. Anti-Semitic outbursts against Jews who had survived the Holocaust, the most notorious in Kielce in July 1946, were also a grim feature of this unsettled period. The Jewish background of some of the most prominent members of the new communist leadership exacerbated anti-Jewish feelings at the end of the war; disputes over ex-Jewish homes and property, which had acquired new occupiers, also aggravated inter-communal tensions. In these circumstances a large number of the remaining Jews opted for emigration. And in the extreme south-east of the country the forcible eviction of the local Ukrainian population, as part of the communist campaign to build a nationally homogeneous state, resulted in a brutal counter-insurgency campaign against nationalist Ukrainian partisans who waged a forlorn struggle against communist-led Polish and Soviet forces.

Far more dangerous for the PPR was the newly reconstituted Polish Peasant Party (PSL), led by Mikołajczyk; with its million members at the end of 1945 it was more than twice the size of the PPR. The PSL enjoyed widespread support in the villages and, in the absence of the main pre-war centrist and right-wing parties, it also became the focus for many elements in Polish society opposed to the communists. Conscious of its weakness, and desperate to avoid the kind of electoral disaster that befell Hungary's communists in November 1945, the PPR resisted Mikołajczyk's insistence on the free elections promised for Poland by the Yalta agreement.

Using intimidation, violence and electoral fraud, it took the communists just over two years to eliminate the PSL from public life. To delay an electoral contest the communists resorted to the ploy of a national referendum on 30 June 1946, with three questions relating to the abolition of the Senate, approval of the government's economic policies, and endorsement of the Oder–Neisse frontier. It was hoped that all voters would vote unanimously for the government propositions and thus endow the authorities with a degree of legitimacy. To assert their independence, the PSL recommended a 'no' vote to the first question; the anti-communist underground called for two or even three 'no' votes. The communists, who retained sole control of the electoral commissions, claimed that 68 per cent of the voters had endorsed all three of their proposals; the real figure, as revealed by confidential PPR records, was only 27 per cent. The falsification of the referendum result was to remain one of the most closely guarded secrets of the communist era. The final confrontation with the PSL occurred during the general election which finally took place on 19 January 1947. The PSL refused to join a single electoral list under PPR auspices, and stood as a distinct rival party. Thousands of PSL activists and over 100 PSL candidates were detained by the authorities; the number of polling stations was drastically reduced; over a fifth of the electorate was disenfranchized for alleged right-wing sympathies. A vicious propaganda campaign presented the PSL as stooges of the west. The officially announced outcome of the rigged election was hardly surprising: the PPR-led bloc obtained 80 per cent of the votes, and the PSL only 10 per cent. Recent fragmentary studies suggest that even with this heavy intimidation the PSL received between 60 and 70 per cent of the popular vote. The free elections promised at Yalta were little more than a farce. American and British protests had no effect, but the nature of the communist take-over in Poland contributed to the widening of the rift between the Western Powers and the USSR.

The new government formed in February 1947 (no longer 'provisional') was led by the pro-communist socialist Józef Cyrankiewicz, a flexible politician who was to survive as prime minister until 1970, while the key ministries continued to remain in communist hands. In October 1947 Mikołajczyk fled the country. The PSL was reduced to impotency and its rump taken over by communist sympathizers; in November 1949 it was formally absorbed into the pro-communist United Peasant Party (ZSL). Despite the inauguration of a superficially democratic 'little constitution' in 1947, effective power lay with the Politburo of the PPR, whose general secretary owed his position directly to Stalin.

On the political scene there remained for the communists the awkward problem of the Polish Socialist Party (PPS) whose wartime leaders, both in Poland and abroad, had little time for Soviet communism. Although the PPS had been reconstituted in Poland after the war under a left-wing faction which collaborated with the PPR, many rank-and-file socialists expected full equality for their party (whose membership exceeded that of the PPR until

1947) and the avoidance of sovietization. They hoped that Poland would retain a pluralism of autonomous social organizations, trade unions and co-operatives. Yet by associating themselves with the iniquities of the PPR and by co-operating with the PPR during the 1947 election, the PPS had allowed themselves to be tarred with the same brush.

In 1947 and 1948, in the ever-worsening climate of the Cold War, Moscow tightened its grip over its satellites. Not only were they obliged to abandon any involvement with the Marshall Plan but they were also forced to accelerate the adoption of the Soviet model of political, economic and social control. In 1948, after Stalin's split with Tito, steps were taken to eliminate all so-called 'Titoist' or 'nationalist' deviations within the communist parties of the Soviet bloc. In September 1948 Władysław Gomułka, the advocate of a milder 'Polish' road to socialism, was dismissed from his post as deputy prime minister and was replaced as secretary of the central committee of the PPR by Bierut. In December 1948 a thoroughly purged and browbeaten PPS agreed to unite with the PPR to form the PZPR (Polish United Workers' Party), under which appellation the communists were to rule Poland until 1989.

All of Poland's large pre-war political parties had either been banned, obliged to dissolve themselves, absorbed by the communists, or transmogrified into mere appendages of the PZPR; the latter were useful to demonstrate to foreigners as evidence of political pluralism. The PZPR had achieved hegemony. There was no room for any independent political or social movements in the 'brave new world' of Stalinist Poland in which the communist PZPR controlled all state institutions through the exercise of the patronage of jobs (the so-called *nomenklatura*) and the establishment of party cells at every level of public employment. For many opportunists and 'realists', often possessing little formal education, membership of the PZPR offered prospects of careers. In July 1952 a new constitution, amended personally by Stalin, enshrined the industrial workers as 'the leading class in society', and proclaimed the creation of the Polish People's Republic. Elections after 1952 became a collective ritual in which over 99 per cent of the electorate voted unanimously for a single list of candidates of the so-called Front of National Unity dominated by the PZPR. Consequently the Sejm was reduced to the role of a rubber-stamp on all Party decisions. The communist-controlled system of government was never to enjoy legitimacy based on a freely expressed and genuine democratic mandate.

A vast and repressive police and security apparatus (by 1953 numbering over 200,000 functionaries, or nearly sixfold the size of the pre-war police force) kept a vigilant eye on the population, which was intimidated by a continuous atmosphere of tension and fear, and mobilized in carefully staged public processions and other artificial expressions of joyful togetherness. Fear of informers stifled all free speech and corroded all natural social relations. Between 1945 and 1956 5,000 death sentences were passed for political reasons; half of them were carried out. Tens of thousands of people suffered longer or shorter periods of arbitrary detention; files were kept on nearly a third of all Polish adults. The judicial system, all trade unions, youth and student organizations, and the press came under Party control. Nor did Stalin trust the Polish army, whose native officer corps was purged and then in November 1949 placed under the command of the Soviet Marshal Rokossovsky, an appointment strikingly analogous to that of Grand Duke Constantine in the Congress Kingdom of Poland in 1815 to 1830. By the end of 1952 three-quarters of all active generals in the Polish army were Soviet citizens. At the same time the million or so Poles who had remained in the USSR following the border changes were deprived of their cultural and social organizations, and gradually of their parish priests and churches; only in Soviet Lithuania were some Polish-language schools allowed to function. Thousands of Polish prisoners continued to languish in the slave labour camps of the Gulag.

A Soviet-style planned economy was imposed. In 1950, Hilary Mine, the hard-line Stalinist chairman of the state planning commission who had already destroyed the private retail sector and deprived all co-operatives of their autonomy, launched the Six Year Plan, an ambitious programme of rapid heavy industrialization. Its triumphal showcase was the Lenin steel mill in Nowa Huta, a new 'socialist' town that was intended to dwarf the neighbouring ancient city of Kraków, that bastion of Polish conservatism. As international tension heightened during the Korean War, much of the industrial expansion, brought about at the expense of real wages and of consumption but accompanied by Stakhanovite propaganda, was geared to the production of armaments. Hundreds of thousands of young, mostly poor, peasants were uprooted from their village communities, lodged in workers' hostels at the industrial sites, and promised a share in a glorious proletarian future. Their often genuine enthusiasm was dampened by drunkenness, low productivity, and a sense of dislocation. The state provided a basic welfare system, although it favoured those who were economically active in the industrial sector at the expense of the elderly and the rural population. Nevertheless, the pre-war curse of unemployment seemed to have gone for good. For thousands of peasants and workers there was the prospect of social advancement in the new urban centres, and in the new vast economic and administrative structures created by the state; all this encouraged their loyalty to the new order and provided the regime with a growing core of supporters. But while industry mushroomed at breakneck speed, agriculture suffered. Having handed over to the peasants most arable land in 1944 and 1945, the communists began slowly in 1949 to enforce collectivization. By 1955 nearly a quarter of all arable land belonged to collective or state farms, although most of the latter were to be found in the still sparsely settled ex-German territories. Food production inevitably fell, which in turn led to compulsory requisitioning (especially in 1950 and 1951) and food rationing. The integration of the ex-German lands proceeded apace, although it would take many years before the new inhabitants there would begin to feel at home.

The methods of social engineering and Marxist indoctrination were applied also in educational policy and in the creation of a new intelligentsia. Youngsters from peasant and proletarian homes were encouraged, through positive discrimination, to enter higher education, while opportunities were narrowed for children with 'bourgeois' or 'reactionary' backgrounds. Syllabuses were revised in a Marxist spirit, many Soviet textbooks were translated for Polish use, and the teaching of Russian became compulsory in schools. All youths and young adults between the ages of 14 and 25 were drafted into Soviet-style pioneer and Komsomol organizations, while army conscripts received a two-year dose of ideological

49 Socialist realism: bringing culture to the masses. *Chopin's Polonaise in A-major in the forge of the Kościuszko steel mill*, in Chorzów, Upper Silesia. Painted in 1952 by Mieczysław Serwin-Oracki (1912–77). At the piano is the pianist Władysław Kędra who like other artists frequently performed in places of work. Until the construction of Nowa Huta in the 1950s, Chorzów possessed the largest steel mill in Poland.

instruction. Culture was made available to the masses on an unprecedented scale through the heavily subsidized expansion of publishing, of the cinema, the theatre and of concert halls. By 1957 Poland could boast twenty-seven symphony orchestras and nine major opera houses. But the content of this cultural diet was strictly controlled; anything deemed religious, anti-Russian or 'decadent' was excluded. In 1951 all university departments of English were closed, except in Warsaw, as potential centres of ideological contagion.

The main thrust of cultural policy as directed by the cultural commissar Włodzimierz Sokorski was socialist realism, defined many years later by Andrzej Wajda, one of Poland's most distinguished film directors, as the 'representation of reality not as it is, but as it ought to be'. Novels about the achievements of socialism, or about heroic workers who exceeded production targets and foiled the wicked schemes of imperialist spies and native counter-revolutionaries were the order of the day from 1949 to 1953. Poets and writers such as Zbigniew Herbert or Stefan Kisielewski, who refused to join the 'Stalinist choir', were pushed aside. The other officially approved theme in books and films was the horrors of the Nazi occupation. Academic research in the arts and social sciences had to bend to the ideological requirements of Marxism-Leninism; even in the sciences the Stalinist condemnation of the 'bourgeois' theories of genetics and relativity had to be endorsed. The first incisive attempt to analyse the illusions of the Polish intelligentsia and its vulnerability to Stalinism was provided by Czesław Miłosz in *The captive mind*, published abroad in 1953 after his defection to the West.

As the upholder of an alternative spiritual and ethical system of values and the only remaining autonomous all-national institution, the Roman Catholic Church could hardly escape the onslaught of Stalinist atheism. The fact that in 1949 Pius XII had threatened to excommunicate all Catholics who were members of communist parties, and that the Vatican had not formally recognized Poland's new western border and continued, until 1956, to recognize the exiled Polish government in London, provided convenient ammunition for attacking the Church. Despite an understanding between the Catholic hierarchy and the authorities in 1950 whereby the

50 General Władysław Anders visiting a resettlement camp for Polish refugees in Kelvedon in Essex, England, in November 1953. Imprisoned by the Soviets in 1939–41, Anders then commanded the Polish army in the USSR before leading the Polish Second Corps in the Middle East and Italy. The charismatic Anders became a living embodiment of Polish military valour during the Second World War and of the émigré cause after 1945. For the communist regime in Warsaw he was a hated symbol of reaction. He died in 1970 and is buried next to his soldiers who fell at Monte Cassino.

Church's loyalty to the state was rewarded with a degree of independent activity, many church-run organizations and charities were dissolved, religious activities were banned from schools, hospitals and the army, and church attendance was discouraged; priests and bishops were harassed. Diverse ploys were used to split the Church from the inside; schemes were even hatched to sever the Polish Church's links with Rome and to create a state-controlled national church. Bierut's grotesque plan to secularize Warsaw's skyline by cutting off all church spires was fortunately never implemented, but in 1951 there arose in the centre of the city a Palace of Culture and Science, Stalin's 'gift' to Poland and a towering symbol of Soviet domination.

The height of the anti-Church campaign was reached in 1953 when the state unilaterally assumed the power to control all church appointments and demanded an oath of loyalty to the state from all clergy. The new primate, Archbishop Stefan Wyszyński, eventually advised compliance but himself publicly and symbolically refused: 'We are not permitted to place the things of God on the altar of Caesar. Non possumus!' His resultant detention was followed by large-scale arrests of bishops and clergy, and the closure of numerous monasteries and churches. The leading Catholic weekly, *Tygodnik Powszechny* (Universal Weekly) of Kraków, was banned for refusing to publish a panegyric upon Stalin's death on 5 March 1953. While Wyszyński remained isolated in detention, the episcopate bowed in September 1953 to the state's demands.

As Stalinism tightened its grip on Poland, the Polish exiles in Great Britain, numbering some 150,000, maintained a veritable 'state in exile'. The exiled President Raczkiewicz continued in office, as did Arciszewski's government, still recognized by the Vatican, Spain and a handful of lesser states. Most pre-war political parties, and new political groupings, continued to operate in Britain and maintained branches around the world wherever Polish communities existed. Despite difficulties of life in exile and the exiles' physical dispersal across Britain, Polish cultural and social life thrived, bolstered by ex-servicemen's associations and by scores of social, educational and religious organizations. Something of the atmosphere of pre-war Poland was recreated in 'Polish London' by

Marian Hemar's satirical cabaret and institutions such as the 'Polish Hearth Club' in Exhibition Road. Journals, newspapers, scholarly works and wartime memoirs poured off émigré presses. The exiles waited for international changes that would favour their legitimist cause, and shunned anyone tainted with collaboration with the communists; this included Mikołajczyk, who arrived in London after his escape from Poland in 1947. Mikołajczyk soon moved to the United States where he secured the co-operation of the Congress of American Poles, the largest Polish organization in the USA; many Poles in France also followed his lead.

Just as the 'Great Emigration' of the 1830s and 1840s had warned the west about Tsarist despotism, so now the post-1945 exiles, regarded by some as the 'Second Great Emigration', promoted an awareness in the west of the dangers of Soviet communism and of the realities of Soviet atrocities. They scored a notable success when in December 1952 the US House of Representatives declared the USSR responsible for the Katyn massacre. The outbreak of the Korean War raised émigré hopes that the Polish issue would return to the international forum. The US government declined General Anders' offer to recreate a Polish army in the west, but it did draw a variety of exile groups into pro-American espionage activity; something which inevitably damaged the émigré cause. More constructive and long-lasting was American support for the Polish-language Radio 'Free Europe', established in 1952 and directed by Jan Nowak Jeziorański, a talented journalist and lobbyist, and a war-time courier between the Polish government in London and the Underground in Nazi-occupied Poland. Radio 'Free Europe' was beamed from Munich for nineteen hours every day and, despite extensive communist jamming, was widely listened to across Poland. The war in the ether became a major battleground of the Cold War. Ever vigilant for foreign spies and domestic counter-revolutionaries, the communist authorities remained on high alert against the activities of the émigrés and their organizations, and impeded contact between Poles living in Poland and their fellow countrymen abroad. Yet one thing, paradoxically, united the ideological and political foes: for while insisting on Poland's rights to its pre-war eastern border, the exiles called also for the international recognition of the Oder-Neisse Line as

Poland's western border and campaigned energetically against West German revanchism.

Needless to say, the world of exile politics was wrought with deep fissures. August Zaleski, a former foreign minister, succeeded Raczkiewicz as president-in-exile after the latter's death in 1947, but alienated the exiled socialists and the nationalist SN; he then refused to step down after the expiry of his term of office in 1954. A rival presidential body was created, the so-called 'Council of Three', consisting of General Anders, Tomasz Arciszewski (replaced after his death in 1955 by General Bór-Komorowski, the former commander of the Home Army), and Count Edward Raczyński, a highly distinguished diplomat and former Polish ambassador to the Court of St. James. The 'Council of Three' gained wide support among the exiles, while the position of the increasingly isolated Zaleski was further undermined when two of his 'prime ministers' decided to return to communist Poland. Launching a propaganda campaign among the Polish diaspora in 1955, the Polish communist authorities also set out to undermine the exiles' political role.

Despite its totalitarian features, Stalinist rule in Poland never became a clone of its Soviet model and avoided some of the excesses witnessed in other satellite states, such as the purge trials of communist leaders in Czechoslovakia and Hungary between 1949 and 1952. But the post-Stalinist political thaw was a slow process, limited at first to the PZPR. It started with discreet purges in 1953 within the Polish security apparatus. The defection to the West in December 1953 of Józef Światło, a high-ranking officer in the security police (the UB), and his revelations on the airwaves of Radio Free Europe in autumn 1954 about the iniquities of the UB, aroused widespread ferment within the Party. Scapegoats were sought for the now admitted illegalities of the security police. In December 1954 the Ministry of Public Security was restructured and its notorious chief Radkiewicz transferred, in a mild post-Stalinist manner of demotion, to the ministry for state farms. Gomułka, who had been under arrest since August 1951, was quietly released from jail. In January 1955 the central committee of the PZPR publicly condemned the repression of the Stalinist period. It proved increasingly difficult for the Party leadership to contain its internal critics, many of them young communists associated with the weekly *Po prostu* (Straight Talk) and a host of discussion clubs that appeared all over the country. An attack on socialist realism in literature was launched by Marek Hłasko, a young rebellious exponent of black realism, while the poet Adam Ważyk questioned the price paid for 'the great building of socialism' in his published 'Poem for adults'. Khrushchev's denunciation of Stalinism at the twentieth Congress of the Soviet Communist Party on 25 February 1956 was a clear message that the old style of repression had to go; in Poland and Hungary it provided a powerful boost for change.

The death of Bierut in Moscow on 12 March 1956 increased the pressure on the beleaguered Stalinists. It also provided the dispirited PZPR, now led by Edward Ochab, with a timely opportunity to break with the euphemistically labelled period of 'errors and distortions', for which Bierut could be blamed. But an amnesty for thousands of political prisoners could not by itself appease the growing demand for change. The lowering of the threshold of fear across the country and the continuing low living standards contributed to the outbreak of mass demonstrations in the city of Poznań on 28 June 1956. Crowds carrying national flags and singing religious hymns demanded 'bread and freedom'; security police and PZPR headquarters were attacked. Although quelled by troops with tanks, the protests in Poznań were a sharp warning that the communist system in Poland was facing a profound crisis. The participation of over a million pilgrims at the shrine of the Black Madonna in Częstochowa on 25–26 August 1956 to commemorate the 300th anniversary of the deliverance from Swedish invaders indicated that powerful national emotions were at play.

Within the Party, whose leaders had become isolated from the mass of the population, two rival strategies were proposed for dealing with the crisis. Advocates of reform called for the controlled liberalization of the system; the hardliners tried to channel discontent against scapegoats, including Jewish members of the now discredited security apparatus. Both groups were looking for a new leader with clean hands. Gomułka, the recently freed victim of Stalinist repression, appeared the ideal choice. The reformist grouping succeeded in winning over many workers and Party

51 The end of Stalinism. Władysław Gomułka, at the height of his
popularity, addressing hundreds of thousands of Varsovians on 24 October
1956. He appealed for an end to demonstrating and for a return to work.
'United with the working class and with the nation', he concluded, 'the
Party will lead Poland along a new path to socialism.' Gomułka's
popularity in October 1956 probably equalled that of Piłsudski in May
1920 and of Lech Wałęsa in 1980–1. Disenchantment was soon to follow.

intellectuals, and in making common ground with Gomułka. The
Party boss, Ochab, also wisely showed willingness to step down.
But Moscow was not consulted. And so when on 19 October 1956
the central committee of the PZPR met at its VIIIth plenary session
to resolve the internal crisis, Soviet forces stationed in Poland
started converging on Warsaw. The scent of a national revolution
was in the air and preparations were made for resistance. At that
juncture a furious Khrushchev, accompanied by most of the Soviet
leadership, made an unexpected appearance in the Polish capital.
But in a dramatic nocturnal talk, Gomułka succeeded in persuading
the Soviet leader that the undertaking of repairs would not undermine the principles of the system or deflect Poland from the road to
socialism. Mao Tse-Tung's support for Gomułka also carried
weight in Moscow. In a major speech on 20 October, Gomułka

attacked the Stalinist illegalities, the misconceived methods used in collectivization, and the excessive dependence on the USSR. On 21 October a new Politburo, with Gomułka as first secretary, was elected. While anxious to allay Soviet fears, Gomułka at the same time had to moderate the enthusiastic expectations of a population that saw in him a national leader against Soviet domination. The sobering effect of the brutal Soviet suppression of the Hungarian Revolution in November 1956 played well into Gomułka's hands. Hungary demonstrated to the Poles the limits of Soviet tolerance.

Poland remained within the Soviet bloc and the Party retained its monopoly of power. Yet the changes following Gomułka's appointment marked a radical break with the Stalinist past, and opened the road to a milder form of communist rule. It was a turning-point in the history of post-war Poland. Rokossovsky was deprived of the command of the Polish army and returned to the USSR, the security police was tamed, some of the worst Stalinist torturers were put on trial, and Party bosses were changed at every level. The most hated factory directors found themselves removed by the workers in wheelbarrows, while workers' councils were established in many factories as an antidote to rigid bureaucratic methods. Nearly all collective farms were dissolved. Cardinal Wyszyński was freed, his moral authority enhanced. A compromise was reached with the Church which in turn helped to restore stability within the country. Religious education returned to the schools and five Catholic deputies of the Znak group were allowed to sit in the Sejm. Gomułka successfully renegotiated in Poland's favour a number of military and economic agreements with Moscow; the USSR was no longer to buy Polish coal at paltry prices. The repatriation of over 200,000 Poles still detained in the USSR was secured. Foreign travel was eased, as was contact with Poles living in the west. In 1960 the USA granted Poland most favoured nation status in trade. The barriers between east and west were becoming more permeable.

Although the exiles were still capable of concerted action, such as the demonstration in London by 20,000 Poles in 1956 during the visit to Britain of the Soviet leaders Khrushchev and Bulganin, by the late 1950s the appeal of the 'state in exile' or the 'nation in exile' was beginning to wane among their rank and file; problems of daily life and the concern to preserve the Polish language and culture among their children were taking priority over politics. There were also consolations and even attractions of life in the west. Committed to the overthrow of communism, the émigré leaders found it difficult to adjust to the new realities in Poland. More imaginative proved to be the message coming from the Literary Institute outside Paris, founded by Jerzy Giedroyć, a political thinker of vision and something of an *enfant terrible* among the exiles. The monthly journal *Kultura*, which Giedroyć edited with his associate Juliusz Mieroszewski, proved to be the most influential Polish émigré publication of the entire Cold War period. Rather than call for the overthrow of communism, they thought in terms of its evolution, and set out to influence that process in Poland by an open-door approach. On the pages of *Kultura* appeared some of the best exiled writers, including individuals who had worked for the regime in Warsaw, such as Miłosz, as well as writers (under assumed names) living in Poland, and Russian writers banned in the USSR. *Kultura* also embarked on diffusing historical animosities between the Poles and their immediate eastern neighbours; it called on the Poles to accept the loss of Wilno (Vilnius) and of Lwów (L'viv), still regarded by most exiles as an inalienable historical and territorial legacy, in the name of reconciliation with the Lithuanians and the Ukrainians. *Kultura* discussed the Jewish issue, a subject largely ignored by Poland's officially sanctioned publications. Despite communist border controls, *Kultura* and its message reached numerous scholars and students in Poland, and was to have a formative influence on the new post-war Polish intelligentsia, and indeed among Poland's eastern neighbours.

In Poland Gomułka's regime acquired the qualified acceptance of much of the population, while the relative stability in the country obviated the need for preventive repression. In the field of culture, freed from ideological restraints, there was renewed vigour after 1956. The innovative musical compositions of Witold Lutosławski and Krzysztof Penderecki quickly acquired an international renown, while Andrzej Wajda's epic war films marked a breakthrough in the post-war Polish cinema. Sławomir Mrożek published his first satirical works, while Stanisław Lem began his long career as Poland's most famous science-fiction writer. New student cabarets introduced a breath of fresh air in the arts. Greater pluralism was tolerated in the academic world. Even Poland's Olympic successes in Rome in 1960 enhanced the country's reviving national pride. Poland was now effectively the most liberal country of the Soviet bloc, or as some wits put it: 'the most cheerful barrack in the camp'.

But there was only disappointment for those who expected further liberalization of the system. For all his courage in 1956, Gomułka remained adamantly hostile to revisionism, that is democratization within the Party and worker self-rule. In October 1957, the journal *Po prostu* was closed down, and in 1958 the workers' councils were dissolved and replaced by supine Party-led groups. The authorities' attack on revisionist communist intellectuals gradually widened into a general campaign to force all the country's writers and intellectuals to toe the Party line: in 1963 Mrożek left Poland, while the highly popular writer Melchior Wańkowicz, who had returned from exile after 1956, received a three-year sentence in 1964 for including in a private letter information 'liable to damage the interests of the Polish People's Republic'. In 1965 the young revisionists Jacek Kuroń and Karol Modzelewski, who had argued openly that the country's ruling class was the Party bureaucracy and not the workers, were expelled from the Party, to be followed the next year by the eminent philosophy professor Leszek Kołakowski.

Expectations of economic reform led nowhere. The retention of rigid planning, the continued emphasis on heavy industry, and Gomułka's incompetence in economic matters allowed only a modest improvement in living standards in the late 1950s and the 1960s. Polish agriculture continued to stagnate: obstacles were placed in the way of the modernization of private farming, while the highly subsidized state farms remained grossly inefficient. Food shortages, especially of meat, continued to plague the Polish scene for decades. And it was in the 1960s that the gulf between Poland's economy and standard of living and that of the countries of western Europe, even poorer ones like Spain, began to widen at a growing pace.

There was also a retreat from the concessions made to the

52   Cardinal Wyszyński at the Jasna Góra monastery in Częstochowa
during the celebration of the millennium of Christianity in Poland, 3 May
1966. Unlike the conservative Cardinal Mindszenty of Hungary,
Wyszyński was receptive to ideas of social and cultural progress, and was
politically more astute. He was slow, however, in implementing in Poland
the reforms of the Second Vatican Council. The Polish communist
authorities failed to break the moral authority of the Catholic Church
whose strength grew under Wyszyński's primacy. Many Polish Catholics
regarded Wyszyński as the 'interrex', the post held by the Primate between
two royal reigns in the old Polish Commonwealth.

Catholic Church. By 1961 religious instruction in schools had
ended and drastic official limits had been placed on the building of
new churches. The nadir in church–state relations occurred
between 1965 and 1966. In November 1965 Poland's bishops sent
a formal letter to the German Roman Catholic episcopate seeking
reconciliation between the two nations. While reminding the
Germans of Nazi atrocities in Poland, the letter also acknowledged
the sufferings inflicted by the Poles on the Germans. For Gomułka
this was an unacceptable interference by the Church in foreign
affairs, all the more resented since the communist authorities had
used the threat of West German revanchism as one of their key

arguments in defence of communist rule in Poland and of Poland's alliance with the USSR. But whatever points the government was able to score from the ensuing propaganda attack on the Church were lost the following year. The celebrations organized by the Church in 1966 to commemorate the millennium of Christianity in Poland (the baptism of Mieszko I in 966) confirmed the loyalty of the faithful to the Church. The authorities' attempt to hold rival celebrations of the millennium of Polish statehood introduced an element of theatrical farce and only weakened their standing among the population. Bruised, the communist party withdrew from any further direct confrontation with the Church, whose position in the country was gradually but remorselessly strengthened by the implacable Cardinal Wyszyński. In the late 1960s the Polish Church was even able to spare 800 priests, monks and nuns for missionary work around the world; a Polish cleric, archbishop Kozłowiecki, became the metropolitan of Lusaka in Zambia.

Within a year the country lurched into another phase of turmoil. For while Gomułka was able, for the moment, to silence the revisionists, a far stronger and more sinister threat was emerging within the Party apparatus in the form of an anti-intellectual communist grouping which was to make a bid for power by riding the nationalist tiger. Led by Mieczysław Moczar, the deputy minister of the interior and a shady wartime communist guerrilla fighter, the so-called 'Partisans' espoused a crude nationalism that was anti-German, anti-Ukrainian and anti-Semitic; they even offered a partial rehabilitation to former AK soldiers whose wartime record had been vilified by the communists since the war. The 'Partisans' targeted liberalizing pro-reformers within the Party, as well as 'cosmopolitan' writers and film-makers. The tensions within the Party between Moczar's Partisans on the one hand, and the remaining reformers on the other, came to a dramatic head in 1967–8. The condemnation of Israel and Zionism by the USSR and most of its east European satellites during the Arab–Israeli war of June 1967 was not shared by Poland's small number of Jews or indeed by many young Poles. Gomułka personally had no record of anti-Semitism (and his wife was of Jewish origin), but his public condemnation of Polish 'Zionists' who had rejoiced in Israel's victory as a potential 'fifth column' provided an excellent opportunity for Moczar and his followers to exploit anti-Semitism in their bid for power. In a climate of political hysteria, tantamount to a witch-hunt, old Party members of Jewish origin were expelled from their posts. An attack was also launched on the young radical revisionists (Kuroń, Modzelewski and the student activist Adam Michnik) whose support for Dubček's reform movement in Czechoslovakia further enraged the Party authorities.

The final push by the Partisans to topple Gomułka took place after students cheered all liberal and anti-Russian statements in Mickiewicz's play *Forefathers' eve* staged in Warsaw's National Theatre in January 1968. In an inept move of cultural censorship, probably inspired by Moczar to provoke disturbances, Gomułka ordered the play's suspension. The ensuing student protests, first in Warsaw and then in most university towns in March 1968, were met with a violent police response and thousands of arrests. All over the country, orchestrated demonstrations of hatred, endorsed by the Moczar-controlled press, were staged against 'Zionists', students and 'Stalinist criminals'. Protests against this came from the Church, the Union of Polish Writers, and the small Catholic Znak parliamentary group. Gomułka next tried to limit the wild anti-Semitism, but the damage was done: up to 20,000 people of Jewish descent, in the main fully assimilated and almost all belonging to the intelligentsia, and some non-Jewish intellectuals were pressured into leaving the country. Gomułka survived Moczar's onslaught, but serious damage had been inflicted on the international reputation of the communist regime in Poland. Indeed, the anti-Semitic campaign exposed the ideological hollowness of the Marxism propagated by the Polish communists. Gomułka's relentless hostility to all forms of revisionism, whether of the Polish or Czechoslovak variety, and a desire to maintain his credit in Moscow led him to support militarily (with 28,000 Polish troops) the Soviet-led invasion of Czechoslovakia in August 1968.

For the moment the Party apparatus was triumphant, but it had alienated an entire generation of young educated people by its brutal police methods and mendacious propaganda. Convinced that the communist system could not be reformed from within, the revisionists began to turn their backs on Marxism and to seek collaboration with non-Marxist student activists, Giedroyć's

Kultura in Paris, and the liberal Catholic intelligentsia. The deteriorating economic situation and continuing food shortages brought Gomułka no credit either. Nor did his apparent foreign policy success, in the shape of a treaty with the West German government of Willi Brandt on 7 December 1970, which recognized *de facto* Poland's post-war western border, enhance his domestic position.

Whatever self-satisfaction Gomułka's team may have felt at the signing of the treaty with Bonn evaporated a week later with the outbreak of strikes in the shipyards of Gdańsk and Gdynia. A programme of modest economic reform, intended to give some autonomy to factories and to introduce a system of wage incentives, went badly wrong when its first phase, a large increase in food prices, was introduced without warning on 12 December. It was a blow for many working-class families, who often spent about three-fifths of their budget on food. The timing of the measure, a fortnight before Christmas when Polish families make considerable and costly preparations for the festivities, was nothing short of crass stupidity.

The authorities' inept and bloody response to the strikes on the coast, especially the gunning down in Gdynia on 17 December of scores of workers on their way to work, led to a veritable workers' revolt across much of northern Poland. To economic demands was now added the demand for the creation of independent trade unions, in complete contravention of the Leninist principle that trade unions under communism were merely to serve as 'transmission belts' of Party orders to the masses. Faced with the prospect of a general destabilization of the entire country, Moscow agreed to the dismissal of Gomułka, taken ill after a mild cerebral stroke, and the appointment of Edward Gierek as first secretary of the Party on 20 December. As Party boss in Upper Silesia, Gierek had acquired a reputation for efficient management and had been the Party's rising star since 1968.

New strikes broke out in January 1971 and a general strike paralysed the port city of Szczecin on 23 January. Gierek's direct personal appeals to the workers of Szczecin and Gdańsk, his promises of reform and improvement of workers' living standards, and the freeing of detained workers, coupled with further personnel changes at ministerial and top Party level, finally helped to ease the situation. But it took a further strike by the textile workers of Łódź, a city much neglected by the authorities since the war, before the price rises were withdrawn on 15 February.

Although Gierek's team emerged from the crisis with some degree of public confidence, an end was put to all attempts to endow trade unions with greater autonomy. The workers remained cautious even if very much aware of their strength. The nationalist-communist Moczar, who had challenged Gomułka in 1968, was eased out of the interior ministry in the spring of 1971, after which Gierek skilfully kept ambitious colleagues away from the levers of power. Relations with the Church, now respected by the state as a key bastion of social peace in the country, improved. In June 1972 Pope Paul VI finally recognized the post-war ecclesiastical administration in the ex-German territories. There was a marked liberalization in cultural policy, especially evident in the realm of experimental theatre and in film-making. Repression was eased and government propaganda now emphasized the 'moral-political unity of the Polish nation'. The decision to rebuild the Royal Castle in Warsaw, which had been destroyed by the Nazis, was welcomed by Poles at home and abroad; Gierek's government was even able to attract some émigrés to co-operate in the fields of business and culture. On the other hand, the continuing emigration to West Germany of many Mazurians, Upper Silesians, and even Kashubians, who had been alienated from Polishness over the years by an insensitive administration, was a shameful indictment of the communist regime.

As for the London émigrés, it was only in 1972, after Zaleski's death, that their main groupings achieved a belated reconciliation. The succession of Edward Raczyński to the presidential office in 1979 restored some prestige to the exiled presidency. Outside this new bond of émigré unity remained the National Party (the nationalist heirs of Dmowski) who sought a more 'realistic' approach to Gierek's Poland and who continued to warn of German and Jewish intrigues in destabilizing the country. A great boost to the morale of the Poles in the United States was the appointment in November 1976 of the Polish-American scholar Professor Zbigniew Brzeziński, an expert on Soviet affairs, as President Carter's national security adviser, as well as the prominent role played in US political life by Senator Edmund Muskie, a Democrat presidential hopeful, and Klement Zabłocki, chairman (in 1977) of the Foreign Relations Committee of the House of Representatives.

The key to the early buoyancy of Gierek's regime was the rapid expansion of the economy, fuelled by western credits amounting to 24 billion dollars, and the introduction of modern technology with a view to increasing Poland's role in international trade. Gomułka's policy of economic autarky was abandoned. There was a marked improvement in the general standard of living. Emphasis was put on reversing the chronic housing shortage, and motor-car production under licence increased, notably of the Fiat 125p; between 1970 and 1980 car ownership grew from 450,000 to over two million. The easing of foreign currency restrictions gave many Poles access to otherwise rare western consumer goods. At the same time the state continued its heavy subsidy of housing, transport, holidays and of the health service, and it even brought independent peasant farmers within the social security system. Compulsory requisitioning of agricultural produce from the peasants, in force since 1945, finally ended in 1971. In the new climate of east–west detente, Gierek paid official visits to several western countries, including the USA, and in return was host in Warsaw to the French president Giscard d'Estaing, and the American presidents Nixon, Ford and Carter; the latter came in 1977, accompanied by Professor Brzeziński.

But Gierek's 'economic miracle' rested on flawed foundations. The centralized economy, run inefficiently by a privileged and venal Party leadership, still revolved round heavy industry which underwent no structural reform. Many of the investments were misdirected and indeed wasted. Many new Polish products intended for export proved to be of shoddy quality and failed to win foreign markets. External factors, such as the 1974 oil price rise (following the 1973 Arab–Israeli war) and rising western interest rates, compounded the economic difficulties. By 1974 the economy was overheating, inflation was growing, and there was a return of food shortages; in 1976 sugar was rationed. Gierek's honeymoon with the nation, whose consumer appetites had been whetted, was coming to an end. There were also serious squalls on the political

53 Comrade Edward Gierek, the ex-miner, meets the miners of
Rydułtowy in Upper Silesia, September 1974. Despite the disastrous
failure of Gierek's economic policies, an opinion poll of October 1999
found that most Poles who had reached maturity in the early 1970s as
well as those least well off in the Third Republic retained a favourable
image of the 'good times' under Gierek. Over 10,000 mourners attended
his funeral in Sosnowiec in August 2001. Yet the repayments of the debts
acquired under Gierek continue to rise, and will reach a peak of 4.3 billion
dollars in 2008.

front. As a price demanded by Moscow for Poland's greater
diplomatic activity, the government proposed in mid-1975 to
include in the text of the Polish constitution clauses stipulating that
the Party held the 'leading political role in society' and, in a
manner reminiscent of Poland's relations with Catherine the Great
in the eighteenth century, that the alliance with the USSR was
'permanent'. A campaign of indignation and protest, backed by the
Church, did not prevent the inclusion of the first amendment, but
did succeed in watering down the second. The socialist character of
the Polish state and the ideal of full collectivization were also
enshrined in the constitution. However, the whole affair consolidated a wide opposition movement, ranging from the Catholic

intelligentsia to the former communist revisionists, with significant implications for the future.

The government was further discredited when, faced with mounting foreign debts and growing inflation, it announced price rises on 25 June 1976. Widespread strikes and protests forced the authorities to back down. Although the authorities did not use firearms (unlike in 1956 and 1970), they meted out brutal punishments against the demonstrators. In September 1976 a Committee for the Defence of Workers (KOR) was formed which organized quick and effective material assistance to the victims of repression. KOR's early members came from diverse backgrounds, but among the most active were the former revisionists Jacek Kuroń and Adam Michnik, and the veteran socialist Jan Józef Lipski. Highly augural was the link which KOR provided between the intellectual opposition and the disaffected workers, something that had been lacking in 1968 and 1970 when both groups had fought their separate battles. In September 1977 KOR broadened its aims by becoming a permanent institution committed to the defence of human and citizen rights, and by stating as its aim the 'self-organization of Polish society'. Despite police harassment, KOR became an important focus for the opposition, publicizing acts of illegality committed by the state, and successfully assisting with the founding in 1978, in Gdańsk, of an independent (and of course illegal) trade union movement. Other dissident groups, some even demanding independence for Poland, also appeared.

In the less repressive climate of Gierek's Poland, and in marked contrast to the rest of the Soviet bloc, there was a burgeoning of unofficial cultural and publishing activity beyond the reach of the censor. The works of exiled writers like Czesław Miłosz, Witold Gombrowicz and Leszek Kołakowski, as well as translations of hitherto banned foreign writers such as Orwell, saw the light of day; outstanding among the illegal publications of authors living in Poland was Tadeusz Konwicki's *Minor apocalypse* (1979) with its entertaining yet disturbing caricature of life in People's Poland. A so-called 'flying university', drawing on the services of many academics and publicists, and very reminiscent of unauthorized teaching during the tsarist period, organized lectures in private homes on officially forbidden historical and political subjects.

Emigré publications and Polish-language radio stations abroad, especially Radio Free Europe in Munich and the Polish section of the BBC, also contributed to this effervescence of ideas. At the same time the relaxation on foreign travel and the spread of television (45 per cent of Polish homes possessed a television set in 1970) increased popular awareness of the ever-widening gulf between Polish and western living conditions. Dependent on western loans and being a signatory to the Helsinki Final Act of 1975 with its emphasis on human rights, the Polish government was unable to root out the vigorous and pluralist world of dissent which now flourished behind the increasingly sterile official political order.

The Catholic Church contributed significantly to the creation of a broad-based movement in defence of human rights, which embraced Catholic and secular intellectuals active in the opposition. The Church had already been strengthened by Cardinal Wyszyński's deft, yet relentless, extension of its influence as a mass organization firmly rooted in the national tradition. Its prestige soared to unexpected heights when Karol Wojtyła, the archbishop of Kraków, was elected pope on 16 October 1978, assuming the name of John Paul II. For the authorities, who had strongly disapproved of Wojtyła's robust support for evangelization, it came as a shock: 'By God's wounds, what are we going to do now?' Gierek was supposed to have exclaimed on hearing the news from Rome. The pope's triumphal pilgrimage to Poland from 2 to 10 June 1979, which the authorities did not dare to stop during a period of east–west détente, confirmed not only the adherence to the faith of the bulk of the Polish population, which turned out in hundreds of thousands to greet the pontiff, but also the enormous capacity for 'self-organization' of Polish society. The pope's frequent references to human and national rights, and his appeal for courage and for change did not fall on deaf ears.

The papal visit had a powerfully liberating impact on the national psyche at a time when, despite official propaganda to the contrary, the economic situation continued to deteriorate; in 1980 over four-fifths of Poland's income from exports went to service the foreign debt. Yet the scale and intensity of the strikes that swept across the country in July 1980, after the government had intro-

54   The Polish Pope. Karol Wojtyła, the archbishop of Kraków, inspects a guard of honour on his return to Poland as Pope John Paul II, 2 June 1979. On the left is Cardinal Wyszyński, and in the centre is Professor Henryk Jabłoński, the communist head of state. During his eight-day pilgrimage, six million Poles came out to greet the Polish Pope. Wojtyła's election to the pontificate and his visit had a catalytic effect on the country; it also boosted the morale of the Polish diaspora.

duced minor meat price rises in factory canteens, took the government and the opposition by surprise. And this time, unlike 1970 or 1976, the strikers did not pour out into the streets or attack local Party headquarters; they occupied factories and formed strike committees. Attempts to appease the strikers with pay rises and extra food supplies failed to stem the tide of protest. The creation of an interfactory strike committee in Gdańsk on 16 August under the chairmanship of Lech Wałęsa, a 37-year-old electrician, provided a model for similar committees in other coastal cities, and proved to be a turning-point. On 17 August the strike committee in Gdańsk issued its twenty-one demands, which included the right to organize independent trade unions, the right to strike, and the right to freedom of expression. Members of the political opposition offered their services as experts; individuals such as Tadeusz

55   Lech Wałęsa (with the giant pen) at the moment of signing the agreement which brought Solidarity into existence, in the Lenin shipyard in Gdańsk on 31 August 1980. On his immediate right is Mieczysław Jagielski, a deputy prime minister and member of the communist Politburo. Note the statue of Lenin, long since gone, in the right-hand corner.

Mazowiecki, a leading Catholic journalist, and Bronisław Geremek, a distinguished medieval historian and doughty nego-tiator, joined Wałęsa's team.

Yet again a large section of the Polish working class, created by the communist-led programme of post-war industrialization, turned against its bureaucratic masters. When on 26 August the strikes spread to the coal-mines of Silesia, Poland's industrial heart-land, the government had little choice but to negotiate with the strike committees. To his credit, Gierek rejected Soviet advice to use force against the strikers. On 30 and 31 August, in Szczecin and Gdańsk respectively, the floundering authorities capitulated over the central demand for independent trade unions. To con-solidate their position against any future government intrigues, the trade union leaders voted on 17 September to create a single national trade union called 'Solidarity'. Under the leadership of

Wałęsa, who displayed a shrewd political instinct, combined with dynamism and a sense of mission, Solidarity built up its internal democratic structures and became a magnetic focus for a wide range of protest groups. By mid-November it had 8 million members, roughly a third of Poland's adult population; a year later its membership exceeded 10 million. The discredited Gierek was removed from office on 6 September and replaced by Stanisław Kania, an experienced apparatchik.

The developments in Poland made the headlines around the world, while Miłosz's Nobel Prize for Literature in December 1980 also focused international attention on Polish affairs. In the west there was considerable sympathy for Solidarity which also enjoyed the support of the Polish pope. In Moscow and East Berlin there was horror and alarm. President Carter was briefed on the Polish situation by Brzeziński, and his threat of sanctions against the USSR, made to the Kremlin via the 'hot line' at midnight of 3–4 December 1980, may have dissuaded the Soviet leadership from ordering an imminent invasion of Poland. The likelihood of Polish resistance was probably another deterrent to a Soviet invasion which would have created a major international crisis. In any case, Moscow remained unyielding in its hostility, and leant heavily on the Polish authorities to crack down on Solidarity. For Solidarity was not an ordinary trade union; it was evolving into a mass social movement committed to the democratization of political life, the dismantling of the command economy, and the introduction of autonomous production units. Although its leaders were realistic enough to hold back from seizing political power (Kuroń described it as 'a self-limiting revolution'), an effective state of 'dual power' was emerging. By its very existence, Solidarity represented a challenge to the communists' monopoly of political control within Poland, and ultimately to the Soviet empire in eastern Europe.

Under Wałęsa's leadership Solidarity not only withstood the government's attempts to infiltrate its regional branches and to promote a split within its ranks but also grew in strength, most vividly demonstrated by the all-national four-hour general strike on 27 March 1981. In May Rural Solidarity of peasant farmers was legalized. The Polish authorities were not yet ready for a decisive confrontation. Indeed, under the impact of the euphoric expectations of greater freedom gripping the country, the Party itself was in turmoil and in a veritable state of decline. Of its 3 million members, about a third abandoned the Party altogether, while a further 700,000 members actually joined Solidarity. A reformist wing called for more democratic 'horizontal structures' within the Party, while the hardliners, encouraged by Moscow, urged decisive action against the 'counter-revolution'.

The Church's effective mediatory role in diffusing repeated crises between the authorities and Solidarity was temporarily blunted in May 1981 by the attempted assassination of the pope, probably instigated by the KGB, and by the death of Cardinal Wyszyński. The new primate Cardinal Józef Glemp did not have his predecessor's dominating prestige and had a hard act to follow. In any case, the day of reckoning was fast approaching, for the abnormal situation in Poland could not continue indefinitely. The appointment of the defence minister General Wojciech Jaruzelski as prime minister in February was an early indication that the Party leadership was bracing itself for action. Although of gentry origin and a young victim of Stalin's deportations, the aloof Jaruzelski was a loyal communist general with a long, successful military career behind him. At frequent meetings throughout the spring and summer of 1981, the Polish communist leaders assured the impatient Soviets of their resolve to end the crisis by their own means. At the extraordinary 9th Party congress in July, the first to be attended by democratically elected delegates, Kania succeeded in restoring some order within the Party. With the appointment in August of General Kiszczak, the head of military counterintelligence, as interior minister, the authorities accelerated plans devised earlier for the introduction of martial law.

The drastic deterioration of food supplies triggered off further wage demands and deepened the weariness of the population. The hardening of the authorities' attitudes radicalized many Solidarity activists. At its national congress, held in Gdańsk in September, Solidarity overwhelmingly endorsed an appeal of fraternity to the workers of eastern Europe and of the USSR; it was a romantic gesture that only served as a red rag to the Soviet bull. The gravity of the situation and the high stakes involved were reflected when, on 18 October, the central committee of the Party replaced Kania with Jaruzelski as first secretary. Control of the state and Party apparatus and of the country's armed forces now rested in one pair of hands. The failure of General Jaruzelski, Cardinal Glemp and Wałęsa to secure a national compromise at a meeting on 4 November, followed by Solidarity's announcement of a great demonstration in Warsaw for 17 December, and continuing Soviet pressure, forced Jaruzelski's hand.

During the night of 12–13 December 1981, in a well co-ordinated and efficiently executed operation, observed closely by the Soviet Marshal Kulikov, and involving most of the Polish army and all the security forces, martial law ('a state of war') was imposed over the entire country. To all intents and purposes it was a coup d'état: a so-called Military Council of National Salvation, headed by Jaruzelski, assumed supreme authority in the land. Taken by surprise, 6,000 Solidarity activists, including Wałęsa, were arrested and interned. Only in Wrocław was the local Solidarity leadership fully prepared for such an eventuality and avoided detention. All social organizations were suspended, and all factories, transport and communications militarized. Force was used to crush the strikes that erupted over the country, but largescale bloodshed was avoided; the worst incident was the killing of nine miners in the 'Wujek' coal-mine in Katowice. Within days the president-in-exile Raczyński broadcast to his fellow countrymen in Poland calling on them to keep their faith and hope; it was an echo of the broadcast he had made in September 1939 when serving as ambassador in London, and possessed a vivid historical dimension.

The military crackdown restored a semblance of public order and drove people back to work, but did little to resolve Poland's fundamental political and economic problems. The Solidarity leaders who had escaped detention rebuilt the movement's structures underground and prepared for a 'long march'. A propaganda war against the authorities was launched. Substantial amounts of printing and communication equipment, supplied by the CIA via American trade union organizations, was smuggled into Poland. Illegal 'samizdat' journals and books, many on historical and political topics banned by the authorities, rolled off secret printing presses. And it was fortunate that the call of some radicals to resort

to terror and sabotage was rejected by the Solidarity leaders and
strongly opposed by the Church. Wałęsa refused to be cowed by
the authorities, while his Nobel Peace Prize in October 1983
enhanced his international reputation and was a moral fillip to
Solidarity.

There existed in Polish society a widely felt respect for the army,
but Jaruzelski was unable to restore the badly damaged authority
of the Party, despite extensive efforts to the contrary. Periodic
amnesties were issued, Wałęsa was set free in November 1982 (but
treated only as a private citizen), the pope was allowed to revisit
his homeland again in June 1983, and martial law was formally
suspended in July 1983. During the course of 1983–4 a new
government-sponsored trade union was expanded as a counter-
attraction to the banned Solidarity. Of limited effect were gestures
to patriotic sentiment, such as the restoration of pre-war national
feastdays or the festive commemoration of the 300th anniversary
of King John Sobieski's victory over the Turks outside Vienna in
September 1683.

With the dissolution of most social-political organizations, the
role of the Church as the only publicly active autonomous focus of
national life expanded in a manner highly reminiscent of earlier
troubled periods in Polish history. Millions of people with Solidarity banners attended church services while the episcopate,
although not directly involved in the political opposition, intervened on behalf of the repressed. During his second visit to Poland
in June 1983, Pope John Paul II expressed his hope for the
relegalization of Solidarity to the 10 million Poles who came out
to greet him and during a long meeting with Jaruzelski called
for dialogue with the opposition. The murder of Father Jerzy
Popiełuszko, a vocal critic of the regime, in October 1984 by
agents from the interior ministry backfired badly on the government. Several hundred thousand people attended the funeral of the
martyred cleric, whose grave became a shrine.

By the mid-1980s there was political stalemate. Jaruzelski, who
believed that he had saved the country from civil war, economic
collapse and a probable Soviet invasion, curbed the advocates of
violent police methods and strove for moderation. But the government's inability to tackle the structural economic problems,

56 The bogeys of communist Poland. 'From the darkness of the middle ages: a crusade against Poland.' A propaganda poster in response to the imposition of US sanctions on Poland by President Reagan after the introduction of martial law; it includes a medieval Teutonic Knight and the former West German chancellor Konrad Adenauer, suitably attired. Hostility towards Germany, presented as Poland's greatest historical enemy, was a powerful, and probably the most widely accepted, element in the state ideology of the Polish People's Republic. Although a gradual change in public perceptions of the Germans started in 1970, the real watershed in Polish–German relations occurred in 1989/90.

compounded by the vast foreign debts ($40bn in 1988) and the west's unwillingness to advance further credits, not to mention US economic sanctions, continued to gnaw at the very sinews of national life. Industrial production and living standards continued to fall; prices rose; shops emptied; the state budget faced a dramatically growing deficit. Alarming effects of industrial pollution were observed in many areas of the country. Poland's prospects seemed hopeless and some half a million Poles, mostly young and enterprising, left the country or chose to remain abroad in this period. In 1986 the government released all remaining political prisoners but the Solidarity leadership, although no longer prevented from acting openly, refused to participate in a government-sponsored consultative assembly. Treated by visiting foreign politicians as the effective leader of the opposition and encouraged by the pope's third visit in June 1987, Wałęsa continued to insist on the restoration of political pluralism as a precondition for any all-national action to deal with the economic crisis.

Jaruzelski's government and the Party sought other measures to break out of the impasse without having to surrender their monopoly of power. A referendum, held on 29 November 1987, to seek the nation's endorsement of the government's hesitant attempt at economic reform, was a resounding defeat for the authorities. Nevertheless, the government refused to give way to Solidarity demands and responded with force against widespread strikes in April and May 1988. A second wave of strikes enveloped the country in August 1988. Fearing that the country was on the edge of an uncontrolled major explosion, the authorities drew back from reintroducing martial law.

Of decisive significance for the situation in Poland was now the dramatic reversal of the policy of the USSR towards its satellites. Forced by the stress of renewed military rivalry with the USA into a radical overhaul of the Soviet economic and political system, the new Soviet leader Gorbachev was no longer prepared to underwrite the unreformed communist regimes of eastern Europe. Disoriented by the changes in the USSR, and no longer able to justify a restoration of martial law as preferable to a Soviet invasion (as had been the case in 1981), the Polish communists now faced two stark choices: to maintain control by force over a restless population and a degraded economy, or retain some degree of power and the benefits of wider economic reform by an accommodation with the opposition which would secure for the regime popular legitimacy and international respectability.

In a televised broadcast on 26 August 1988 the interior minister General Kiszczak proposed 'round table' talks between the government and the opposition. Emerging as a level-headed politician, Wałęsa next succeeded in bringing to an end the strike campaign that was destabilizing the country. On 31 August Kiszczak met Wałęsa privately for the first time. Extremists in both camps opposed the talks, and it took five months of complex political manoeuvring before they got off the ground on 6 February 1989. It was only by threatening to resign that Jaruzelski and Kiszczak secured the consent of the central committee of the PZPR to the relegalization of Solidarity.

The deliberations of the 'round table' ended on 5 April with a compromise agreement which heralded extensive changes to the constitutional order. The offices of the president and the Senate, abolished in 1952 and 1946 respectively, were restored; the former was to be chosen jointly by the Sejm and the Senate, and the latter was to be elected on the basis of fully free national elections. Both the president and the Senate would exercise the power of veto over the Sejm in which 65 per cent of the seats would be reserved for the PZPR and its allies, while 35 per cent of the seats would be decided by a free electoral contest. Solidarity and Rural Solidarity were relegalized on 17 and 20 April, respectively.

The semi-free elections took place on 4 June 1989. Although boycotted by a sceptical third of the electorate, they were an overwhelming disaster for the Party and exceeded all expectations of the architects of the 'round table' agreement. In retrospect, the Polish elections of 1989 proved to be the first key move in the dismantling of the communist system in east-central Europe. All but one of the hundred seats in the Senate and all the free seats in the Sejm were won by the Solidarity-backed Citizens' Committee, while only five government-backed candidates passed the 50 per cent vote needed to secure the reserved seats in the Sejm. A second round of voting was therefore needed on 18 June to enable the pro-government parties to fill their guaranteed places. On 3 July

Gorbachev's envoy made the momentous announcement that Poland was free to determine the shape of its own government. In another compromise arrangement, Jaruzelski was elected president on 19 July; ten days later he resigned from the Party secretaryship. On the other hand, Wałęsa skilfully wooed the United Peasant Party (ZSL) and the Democratic Party (SD), hitherto communist-controlled parliamentary groupings but now eager to assert their independence, to prevent the creation of a coalition government led by General Kiszczak. On 19 August President Jaruzelski invited the respected Catholic intellectual Tadeusz Mazowiecki to form a coalition government. With the almost unanimous support of the Sejm, Mazowiecki became the first non-communist prime minister in what was still formally communist eastern Europe – and received a congratulatory telegram from Moscow. Wałęsa himself eschewed all public office for the time being. Although the PZPR retained the key ministries of the interior and of defence, in accordance with the 'round table' agreement and to reassure Moscow, its days as a 'Marxist-Leninist' party were over.

The forty-five-year period of communist rule in Poland cannot be simply dismissed as one in which nothing constructive or beneficial was achieved. And Poland's satellite status was certainly preferable to the fate of the Baltic States, which were incorporated in the USSR. But the forcible imposition of an ideology alien to most of its inhabitants, the cynical travesty of the concept of democracy, the decades of mendacity, the humiliating subservience to the USSR, and the sheer wastefulness of much economic activity all weigh heavily in any objective assessment of the communist legacy in Poland. In terms of living standards, communist Poland not only did not catch up with the west, but fell further behind. Impressive statistics of coal or steel production were no substitute for chronic shortages of basic goods. It now remained to be seen how Polish society, so long in a communist straitjacket, would respond to the sudden challenges of freedom and independence.

8

A new republic, 1989–

Although many hardline Solidarity supporters resented the lack of a clean break with the communist past and no settling of scores with the communists, the constitutional changes and the elections of 1989 are now generally accepted as marking the birth of the Polish 'Third Republic'. On 29 December 1989 Poland formally ceased to be a so-called 'People's Republic' and recovered the crowned white eagle as its emblem; references to the 'leading role' of the PZPR, to the Soviet alliance, and to socialism were expunged from the constitution. What made possible Poland's peaceful transformation in 1989–90 was the 'self-organization' of Polish society that had evolved since the 1970s and the self-restraint and sense of responsibility of the country's political leaders, whether communists or members of the former opposition. As a result a dangerous political vacuum was avoided and social peace was maintained. Indeed, the much greater political realism of the Poles in the second half of the twentieth century, as witnessed in 1956, in 1980–1, and now, marked a powerful contrast with the disastrous Romantic insurrections of the previous century and with the Warsaw uprising of 1944.

Mazowiecki's 'great coalition' showed exceptional energy in dragging Poland out of its economic marasmus. January 1990 saw the introduction of a wide-ranging programme of economic reform, the most radical in the whole of ex-communist Europe and prepared by the new finance minister Professor Leszek Balcerowicz. The resulting 'shock treatment' halted the galloping inflation and

propelled Poland fast towards a market economy, a process
assisted by the favourable re-negotiation of the country's vast
foreign debts and by financial assistance from western financial
institutions. The former dissident Jacek Kuroń, with his direct and
engaging manner, did much as minister of labour to allay popular
alarm at the painful social effects of the reform which by the end of
1990 had generated one million unemployed. The dismantling of
the socialist planned economy and the restoration of free enterprise
inevitably created social divisions. Ironically, many former communist officials and managers gained materially from the privatization of state enterprises, while many workers who had helped to
topple the communist system now found themselves the victims of
economic rationalization. The appearance of new well-stocked
shops ended the chronic shortages of the 1980s and began to alter
visibly the hitherto drab appearance of most Polish towns. The
location of the new Warsaw stock exchange in the former central
headquarters of the communist party added a nice touch of
historical irony.

   Unexpectedly liberated from the Soviet yoke, Poland was entering a new era in its history. During the decade following 1989 a
profound transformation of Polish political and economic life
occurred. A parliamentary democracy was established with a
popularly elected president and an accountable system of local
government; civil rights were restored; the death penalty was
abolished; and the armed forces were depoliticized. In cultural life
there was a move away from great political and ideological issues,
while Polish mass culture came under strong western influence. In
the realm of politics, the most striking phenomenon in the early
1990s was the disintegration of Solidarity as a broad social and
moral movement of protest. Mazowiecki hoped to retain Solidarity
unity and the 'round table' agreements during the difficult period
of economic transformation. Wałęsa on the other hand argued that
the collapse of the PZPR justified the acceleration of constitutional
changes. His subsequent presidential ambitions only deepened the
rift within the movement. The introduction in July 1990 of a
generous system of proportional representation in parliamentary
elections in its turn encouraged the proliferation of small parties.
By 1991 the bulk of Solidarity had fragmented into several rival

trade union organizations and a host of populist anti-communist and nationalist-Catholic groupings. Most remained suspicious of the free market economics propounded by Solidarity's liberal intelligentsia wing, represented by Mazowiecki and Geremek which, under the name of the Democratic Union (UD) and then the Freedom Union (UW), became the most successful post-Solidarity party.

The political parties of the communist era also underwent change. The communist PZPR dissolved itself in January 1990 and most of its members formed a disciplined social democratic party (SdRP) led by Aleksander Kwaśniewski, a young but experienced activist and sports minister in the last communist administration. In 1991 it allied itself with other left-wing groups to form the Left Democratic Alliance (SLD), still one of the most important parties in Poland today and, as heir to the PZPR, with considerable wealth and organization at its disposal. It is noteworthy that the post-communist left has respected the democratic process. The former pro-communist peasant party went through more traumatic up-heavals, but eventually in May 1990 linked with other peasant groupings and adopted its pre-1947 label of the Polish Peasant Party (PSL). Attempts to revive the historic Polish Socialist Party (PPS) have so far failed.

Wałęsa won the 1990 presidential election and chose to receive his insignia of office not from the outgoing Jaruzelski but from Ryszard Kaczorowski, the last president-in-exile, who travelled in person to Warsaw for this purpose, thus establishing a symbolic constitutional link with the legitimist successors of the pre-war Second Republic residing in London since 1945. Following Wałęsa's election the Polish government-in-exile dissolved itself, its historic mission completed. The way communism had ended in Poland and the territorial configuration of the Polish Third Republic were not exactly what the émigré leaders had been praying for, but no one could deny that Poland was again free. Yet there was no mass return of the wartime exiles; for many it was too late. Some notable individuals did take that step, such as Piłsudski's two daughters who had lived in Britain since the war. Yet many British-born professionals of Polish origin have elected to work in the country of their parents' birth. Some of the exiles from the first

Solidarity period have also returned. By the same token, the relationship between the Polish state and the many-million strong worldwide Polish diaspora, which had been poisoned during the Cold War by ideological differences and mutual suspicions, has inevitably altered for the better. There is greater and more fruitful contact today, and the Polish government supports Polish-language teaching in the diaspora, especially in the former USSR where Polish communities were often deprived of the possibility of cultivating their national and cultural identity.

The first fully free parliamentary elections since the Second World War, those that had been promised at Yalta in 1945, finally took place in October 1991. They produced a fragmented Sejm and a series of short-lived centre-right coalition governments betwen 1991 and 1993. The growing demands from the right for the 'de-communization' of public life and for the 'lustration' or purging of politicians who had collaborated with the communist security services, and Wałęsa's increasingly confrontational style and headstrong attempts to strengthen presidential authority all contributed to an atmosphere of political acrimony.

The parliamentary elections of September 1993, based on a reformed electoral system aimed at eliminating the smallest political groupings from the Sejm (5 per cent minimal threshold for parties) produced unexpected results. Despite winning over a third of the popular vote, the right-wing parties paid for their internecine divisions by being virtually wiped out from the parliamentary scene. The post-Solidarity liberals (UD) fared moderately well. But the largest number of seats went to the post-communist SLD (171 seats) and the peasant PSL (132 seats) who formed a coalition that survived until 1997. Wałęsa's narrow defeat in the 1995 presidential election at the hands of the more tactful and urbane SLD leader Kwaśniewski confirmed the ascendancy of the left, ironically at a time when the population was beginning to feel the benefits of economic reform.

The fragmented post-Solidarity right had to learn the lessons of its electoral disaster. Under Marian Krzaklewski, a 41-year-old cybernetician from Silesia, it consolidated itself into the so-called 'Electoral Action Solidarity' (AWS) and successfully entered the hustings in 1997, gaining 34 per cent of the popular vote and

57 President Aleksander Kwaśniewski ratifies Poland's treaty of accession to NATO, 26 February 1999. It is one of those ironies of Poland's history that an ex-communist and leader of the post-communist SLD was to lead Poland into NATO. The ceremony took place in the same hall of the Presidential Palace in which the Soviet-led Warsaw Pact had been created in 1955. On 8 October 2000 Kwaśniewski was re-elected president for a second five-year term in a landslide victory.

emerging as the single largest grouping in the Sejm. A coalition with the liberal Freedom Union (UW), led now by Balcerowicz, produced a centre-right government. The coalition of the two main post-Solidarity parties was not an easy one, but until the resignation of the UW ministers in May 2000 it did provide a degree of stability in Polish parliamentary life. Indeed, the AWS prime minister Józef Buzek, a chemistry professor, remained in office from 1997 until 2001, a record so far in the Third Republic. That Buzek was a Protestant was also a telling comment on the openness of the Polish political system. Unquestionably the single most significant event of Buzek's administration occurred on 12 March 1999 when Poland, together with Hungary and the Czech Republic, formally joined NATO. For the Poles, conscious of their country's vulnerability over the centuries, it was a major political and psychological breakthrough.

The status of the Roman Catholic Church, a powerful champion in the ideological struggle against communism and a key mediator in the transfer of power in 1989, remains high in Polish society. It is noteworthy that a quarter of all Catholic priests in Europe are Polish. The Church has also successfully lobbied for the tightening of legislation on abortion, one of the most explosive issues in Polish politics in the 1990s. Other events, however, have shown that in a democratic and pluralist Poland, the Church's political influence can no longer be taken for granted. The blatant intervention of the hierarchy and of many priests during the 1991 parliamentary election alienated many voters, including Catholics, and contributed to the victory of the left two years later. The episcopate's warnings failed to prevent both Kwaśniewski's presidential victory in 1995, and the endorsement by a popular referendum of a new liberal constitution in 1997. Yet as the Church comes to terms with the new Poland, a process eased by the long delayed ratification in 1998 of the concordat with the Vatican, it has encountered difficulties within its ranks in the form of 'Radio Maryja', the mouthpiece of a vociferous religious and xenophobic fundamentalism which has attracted many followers. The episcopate has not acted firmly against the radio, and there is concern that the Church is becoming excessively defensive and conservative.

Despite all the inter-personal rivalries and acrimonious political infighting of the last decade and a half, all the post-1989 governments have maintained a considerable degree of continuity in economic policy. After a short sharp recession in 1990–1 the Polish economy continued to expand until the end of the decade. Real incomes increased after 1994, foreign investment grew rapidly, and by 1998 inflation had fallen to below 10 per cent, securing thereby a stable currency. In the period 1993–9 the per capita GNP of the Polish population increased from 33 per cent to nearly 40 per cent of that of the European Union (and 60 per cent of that of Greece, the lowest then in that respect of all EU states). Private firms now produce over two-thirds of Poland's GNP. The pursuit of education and professional qualifications among the younger generation is a marked feature of the meritocratic nature of Polish society today.

However, the changes since 1990 have not been without pain for large sections of the population. The restructuring of heavy industry, especially coal mining, has proved difficult. The bankruptcy of the Gdańsk shipyard, the home of Solidarity, and its recent acquisition by the neighbouring Gdynia shipyard dramatically symbolized the ongoing transformation process. The great city of Łódź, once known as 'the Manchester of Poland', has ceased to be a major textile centre and has had to diversify its economic activity. Manual workers, and especially those on former state farms, have keenly felt a fall in real wages and in status. Fewer youngsters from peasant families now enter higher education. Indeed, the most backward sector of the economy remains agriculture with its low yields and small holdings. It is peasant farmers, still representing a fifth of Poland's labour force, who were most fearful of the country's move towards the European Union. High unemployment (15 per cent of the work force in 2001 and 20 per cent in 2003), housing shortages, underfunding of the public health and education services, and the growth of corruption and crime represent the bleaker aspects of Polish reality today. Many former owners (or their descendants) still await satisfactory compensation for property nationalized during the early years of communist rule. Yet for all its difficulties, Poland became, in the 1990s, one of the most stable and dynamic countries of the former Soviet bloc.

In the early 1990s Poland also found itself in the middle of a dramatic and historical upheaval in the geo-politics of the region. In the course of three years (1990–3) all three of Poland's neighbouring states of the Cold War era disappeared: the German Democratic Republic, Czechoslovakia, and the Soviet Union. They were replaced by seven new states: a united Germany, separate Czech and Slovak Republics, independent Lithuania, Belarus, and Ukraine, and the Russian enclave of Kaliningrad, wedged between Poland and Lithuania. Under the direction of the new foreign minister, Professor Krzysztof Skubiszewski, an academic (specializing in international law) of no party allegiance, Poland carefully and systematically asserted its interests as a newly independent state. Of central importance to Poland's security and future association with western structures was Germany, about to embark on re-unification. Despite a moving gesture of reconciliation and

Map 12   Poland and its 'new' neighbours, 1989–2005.

LITHUANIA
(indep. 1990)

t of
SIAN
ATION

VILNIUS •

PODLASKIE
Białystok
(29)

BELARUS
(indep. 1991)

SAW
RSZAWA)

IE

LUBELSKIE
• Lublin
(29)

• Rzeszów
KARPACKIE
(30)

UKRAINE
(indep. 1991)

GARY

═══════ Poland's boundaries since 1945

-------- New provincial (*Województwo*)
          boundaries introduced in 1999

POMORSKIE Names of the new provinces
           (*Województwa*) with administrative
           centres e.g. Gdańsk

(40) Average per capita income in each
      province as a percentage of the
      average per capita income in the
      European Union (1999)
      The national Polish average was 37%

▨ Provinces with 40% and above

□ Provinces with 30–39%

▨ Provinces with under 30%

■■■■ Boundaries of new states since
      1989, following the dissolution of the
      German Democratic Republic, the
      USSR, and Czechoslovakia

●●●●● Eastern external boundary of the
        European Union, 2004

peace between Mazowiecki and Chancellor Kohl in the former
palace of the von Moltkes in Krzyżowa (Kreisau) in Lower Silesia
on 12 November 1989, the Polish government and public opinion
remained nervous over the issue of Poland's western border;
indeed, during the following months Mazowiecki's government
even supported the continued existence, if temporary, of the
Warsaw Pact in order to avoid international isolation during the
next delicate stage in Polish–German relations. Although Poland
was excluded from the early phases of the so-called '4+2' Great
Power talks on Germany's future, American insistence that
Germany should be re-unified but within the existing external
borders of the two German states proved decisive. On 14 November 1990 Poland and united Germany finally signed a treaty in
Warsaw confirming the Oder–Neisse frontier; this was followed on
17 June 1991 by a treaty of friendship signed in Bonn. The issue of
the German minority in Poland, numbering some 300,000 and
whose existence had been denied by the communist authorities,
proved to be a short-lived irritant; the German minority was
granted representation in the Sejm and participation in local
government.

Voices raised in the German parliament in 1998 in support of the
property rights of Germans who had been expelled from Poland at
the end of the Second World War strained relations. On the other
hand the growing number of German visitors to Poland and the
activity of various Polish–German organizations promoting reconciliation (one of these was even the result of the initiative of a
descendant of Bismarck's) all helped to mellow some of the deeply
felt historical animosities. Co-operation across the Polish–German
border improved with the creation of Euro-regions, of a joint
university in Frankfurt on the Oder, and of a European School in
Gubin/Guben. By the end of the 1990s Germany was Poland's most
important trading partner and the largest contributor of foreign
investment, and had emerged effectively as the main champion of
Poland's integration with western institutions. Polish–German
relations had entered an era that would have been inconceivable a
generation or two earlier. Indeed, Professor Geremek, who had
served as foreign minister in Buzek's AWS-led government and who
since 2004 has been a Polish Member of the European Parliament,

did not hesitate in describing the reconciliation with Germany as 'one of the political miracles of the end of the twentieth century'.

Relations with Moscow did not only remain correct but improved dramatically with Gorbachev's official admission in April 1990 of Soviet responsibility for the 1940 Katyn massacre. Gorbachev's statesmanlike action marked a momentous watershed in Polish–Russian relations: the great lie and the unmentionable taboo of the communist period had been lifted. In June and July 1991 the Comecon, the Moscow-led economic association of communist states, and the Warsaw Pact were dissolved. During his visit to Warsaw in August 1993 President Yeltsin made a personal gesture of apology for Katyn and other Soviet acts of repression against the Poles; he also submitted details of two other mass killings of Polish prisoners which had taken place in 1940 at Starobelsk and Ostashkov. Agreements were signed in 1993 for the extension through Poland of a major gas pipeline and for the supply of Russian gas; that same autumn the last Russian troops left Polish soil. After the high point of 1993 relations cooled. The uncertainty of political developments in Russia during Yeltsin's illness, the revival of the communist party, the rise of the nationalists led by Zhirinovsky, the war against the Chechens whose cause won widespread sympathy in Poland, concern with dependence on Russian energy supplies, and finally the Russian campaign against Poland's membership of NATO all revived suspicions in Poland of the giant neighbour in the east. President Vladimir Putin's defence in May 2005 of the Soviet wartime record in eastern Europe was also badly received in Poland and in the Baltic States; some commentators have seen it as the Kremlin's response to Poland's (and Lithuania's) encouragement of Ukraine's 'Orange Revolution' in 2004. Be that as it may, diametrically opposed interpretations of the 1939 Nazi–Soviet Pact, of the Yalta conference, and of the nature of Soviet 'liberation' of central and eastern Europe in 1945, which jarred official Polish–Russian relations on the sixtieth anniversary of the end of the Second World War in 2005, are highly symbolic of deep disagreements still left by history. Ironically, it was the blossoming of unofficial trading across Poland's eastern border and the appearance of Russian bazaars in Poland in the 1990s, unthinkable during the 'internationalist' era of Soviet hegemony, that did most to enhance mutual knowledge of ordinary Poles, Russians and the other peoples of the eastern borderlands.

Poland was well prepared in 1989–90 for the dissolution of the Soviet Union: while maintaining official relations with the Soviet authorities in Moscow, the Polish foreign ministry also approached the governments of the individual Soviet republics. Indeed, Poland's case in securing the final recognition of the Oder–Neisse border was considerably strengthened by Warsaw's early and willing readiness to recognize the independence and territorial integrity of its eastern neighbours within their Soviet-era frontiers. In what was another ironic twist in Poland's recent history, the broad directives of post-communist Poland's policy towards its immediate eastern neighbours had been formulated in the 1970s and 1980s by the émigré Jerzy Giedroyć who had successfully redirected Polish political thought towards reconciliation with the modern nations of Lithuania, Belarus and Ukraine. It was largely due to the consistent pursuit of Giedroyć's vision by foreign minister Skubiszewski and his team of experts in 1989–93 that the collapse of communism did not re-ignite nationalist hatreds and irredentist conflicts along Poland's eastern border. Nor did Poland's communists and ex-communists play the nationalist card after 1989 in a bid to retain political influence – unlike the tragic cases of former Yugoslavia and post-Soviet Transcaucasia. Even before the dissolution of the USSR the Polish foreign ministry treated Lithuania, Belarus and Ukraine as emergent nation-states. The cultural rights of national minorities were to be protected by the mutual adoption of 'European standards', and not by frontier changes or blatant interference in the internal affairs of neighbouring states.

In December 1991 Poland recognized the independence of Ukraine – and was the first country to do so. Not threatened by any Polish revanchism, and supported by Poland's post-Solidarity elite, Ukraine's national movement 'Rukh' felt more confident in asserting its country's emancipation from Moscow. The constructive development of Polish–Ukrainian relations, confirmed by the treaty of May 1992, was all the more impressive if one bears in mind the horrific inter-ethnic slaughter and the ethnic expulsions of the 1940s. The joint declaration about reconciliation signed in Kiev in May 1997 by the presidents of Ukraine and Poland, Kuchma and

Kwaśniewski, led the way towards a 'strategic partnership' between the two countries. Poland had become Ukraine's main ally in Kiev's proclaimed orientation to the West. In 2000 a joint Ukrainian–Polish peacekeeping batallion was sent by NATO to Kosovo. The good relations maintained with Ukraine for over a decade enabled President Kwaśniewski to play a vital mediatory role during Ukraine's 'Orange Revolution' in November–December 2004.

Although Polish public opinion warmly supported Lithuania's bid for independence in 1990, it took much longer than in the case of Ukraine for Polish–Lithuanian relations to achieve normalization. Seeking historical continuity with Lithuania's medieval past and with the legacy of the inter-war Lithuanian republic, the new government in Vilnius adopted a negative attitude to their country's historic links with Poland; hostile administrative action was also taken against the Polish minority which had voiced separatist aspirations. Vilnius demanded that the Polish government should condemn the inter-war Polish 'occupation' of Vilnius (Wilno) as a condition of an inter-state treaty. Fortunately wiser counsels prevailed and the treaty of April 1994 focused on state interests and not on historic grievances; as it was, the Lithuanian parliament did not ratify it until October 1994. The late 1990s saw a marked improvement in mutual relations; under President Valdas Adamkus, a returned émigré from the United States, Lithuania began to perceive Poland as a useful link in its aspirations to join NATO.

The independence of Belarus, another former Soviet republic, was welcomed in Poland and a treaty was signed by the two states in June 1992. Since then the development of formal political and economic relations has been hampered by the consolidation in Minsk of an autocratic quasi-Soviet regime under Lukashenko. Concerned with the condition of the large Polish minority in western Belarus, Poland did not endorse international sanctions against Belarus in 1998. With Poland's entry into the European Union in 2004, Poland had to end the no-visa arrangements with Belarus and Ukraine, but offered free visas instead; Ukraine accepted and Belarus did not.

Relations with Poland's southern neighbour Czechoslovakia,

whose oppositionists had close personal contacts with their Polish counterparts, were cordial at first. Ghosts of history were buried when Poland offered fulsome apologies for the Polish occupation of Teschen in 1938 and for the military intervention against the 'Prague Spring' in 1968. On the other hand, neither Jaruzelski nor Wałęsa was able to establish a congenial relationship with the ex-dissident Czech leader Vaclav Havel. Following the dissolution of Czechoslovakia in 1992–3, the Czech Republic distanced itself from Poland in the hope of improving its prospects of joining the west. In 1997 the Czechs were told to join the queue with the other aspiring ex-communist states. Relations with Poland became correct but not overtly friendly. Warsaw's cool relations with Slovakia changed for the better with the election of a pro-western government in Bratislava in 1998.

Only with the end of communist censorship and the return of political freedom after 1989 was it possible to confront the darker aspects of Poland's recent past. Exposing communist and other crimes has been the work primarily of the Institute of National Memory (IPN), a non-political body (although not free of accusations to the contrary), which has access to thousands of secret police files. There has also been an attempt to re-evaluate the difficult history of inter-ethnic relations in Poland and of Poland's relations with its neighbours. The communist authorities had minimized the suffering of the Jews and focused on German and Ukrainian atrocities against the Poles. The recent open debate about the killing of Jews by local Poles in Jedwabne and elsewhere in 1941, or revelations about the maltreatment of Germans in the closing stages of the Second World War and during the post-war deportations generated heated arguments in the media and among public opinion, but have also revealed a willingness in many quarters to question taboos and to come to terms, in the spirit of truth and reconciliation, with the past. Official reconciliation with Ukraine has been successful, although painful memories and hostile stereotypes still linger at the popular level on both sides. The expressions of sympathy and support in Poland for the 'Orange Revolution' in Kiev in 2004 and the moving ceremonies of Polish–Ukrainian reconciliation held in June 2005 in Warsaw and at the Polish military cemetery in L'viv may bring beneficial changes. And the fact that former Polish Home Army (AK) soldiers and their wartime Lithuanian enemies are talking to each other is another encouraging phenomenon. In academia there has been real progress in treating Poland's eastern neighbours as equal nation-states; the publication by the Catholic University in Lublin, in Polish translation, of a series of histories of Lithuania, Belarus and Ukraine (former territories of the old 'Commonwealth of the Two Nations') by historians from those countries is a notable achievement. The Jewish festival held in the old ghetto in Kraków, participation in the annual 'march of the living' in Auschwitz, and the construction of a museum in Warsaw devoted to the history of Polish Jewry are further positive examples. It is also worth noting that since Poland joined the EU in 2004 numerous Israelis of Polish origin have applied for Polish passports. The myth of an ethnically homogeneous nation state created by the communists, and long flaunted as one of their historic achievements, has also been questioned. The existence of a German minority has been officially recognized although an attempt to secure the recognition of a separate Silesian national identity has met with opposition. There is a growing sense of a shared past in the lands which Poland acquired from Germany in 1945, and a departure from the rigid adherence to the 'Piast' origins of the 'recovered lands'. Nevertheless, Polish opinion is still unnerved by suggestions that former German owners might make claims under European law to their erstwhile private property now in Poland, and is ready to react in its turn with a litany of German wartime atrocities and acts of destruction. Chancellor Schroeder tried to reassure the Poles in this respect during his attendance at the commemoration of the sixtieth anniversary of the Warsaw Uprising of 1944, but the ghosts of the past have clearly not yet all disappeared.

The early years of the twenty-first century witnessed continuing turbulence in Polish political life (in 2004 there were over 100 registered political parties in the country) and the stalling of economic growth. On the other hand, the cause of Poland's membership of the European Union received a massive boost despite fears that foreigners (especially Germans) would buy up Polish land and despite some nationalist-clerical hostility towards 'Godless' western Europe. Of those who participated in the

Poland's European Union referendum 2003

Turnout of those entitled to vote (percentage by commune)

�as 59 – 76%	*Source:* Leszek Szewczyk, sociologist and economist, formerly of the Institute of Culture in Warsaw (1974–2002); editor of A. Wallis' *Atlas Kultury Polski 1946–1980* (Eco, 1994), and co-editor *Wskaźniki realizacji milenijnych celów rozwoju w polskich gminach* (UNDP Poland 2004)
46 – 59%	
21 – 46%	

Map 13a

national referendum in June 2003 on joining the EU, 76.8 per cent voted in favour.

The elections of September 2001 witnessed dramatic twists and turns in Poland's political kaleidoscope: nothing less than the implosion of Solidarity as a political alliance. Neither AWS nor its recent ally the liberal Freedom Union (UW) gained a single seat in

Poland's European Union referendum 2003

'Yes' vote for membership of the EU (percentage by commune)

77 – 92%

53 – 77%

12 – 53%

Source: Leszek Szewczyk, sociologist and economist, formerly of the Institute of Culture in Warsaw (1974–2002); editor of A. Wallis' *Atlas Kultury Polski 1946–1980* (Eco, 1994), and co-editor *Wskaźniki realizacji milenijnych celów rozwoju w polskich gminach* (UNDP Poland 2004)

Map 13b

the Sejm. The pendulum swung to the left: a coalition of post-communist SLD and the Union of Labour (UP) gained 41 per cent of the votes and, together with the Peasant Party (9 per cent), formed an administration under Leszek Miller, a member of the last communist Politburo but now a reformed advocate of modern European social democracy and of Poland's membership of NATO and the EU. Out of the defunct post-Solidarity parties there emerged new centre-right groupings: the 'Civic Platform' (PO) committed to reducing income tax and red tape, which scored 13 per cent of the vote, and 'Law and Justice' (PiS) led by the twins Lech and Jarosław Kaczyński who fought the election on an anti-corruption and anti-organized-crime ticket, and who scored 9.5 per cent. Possessing something of Christian-Democrat character, 'Law and Justice' attracted some of the anti-communist votes that used to go to Solidarity. In 2005 it is also calling for the overhaul of the constitutional order and the creation of a 'Fourth Republic' in the name of a 'moral revolution' which would break with the legacy of the 'round table' agreements of 1989, impose a further purge of ex-communists in positions of authority, and review all major cases of privatization of state enterprises since 1990. In many quarters there is a strong feeling that the break with communism has not been as thorough as it could have been, and that this has left a poisonous and debilitating legacy which will take years to get out of the system.

Two other significant parties, this time of a populist character, have also made a dramatic entry on the political scene. The 'League of Polish Families' (LPR), a Christian-nationalist party opposed to Poland's membership of the EU, which it regards as an instrument of German domination of the continent, won 8 per cent. Two of its leaders, Maciej and Roman Giertych, provide the LPR with a family link with the historic National Democrats. The most surprising newcomer was 'Self-defence' (Samoobrona), a radical party led by Andrzej Lepper, which scored 10 per cent. Casting himself as the protector of the poor against the country's 'thieving' political class, Lepper won the support of many Poles who had lost out from the post-communist changes since 1989. In early 2004 opinion polls suggested that 'Self-defence' enjoyed the support of about a quarter of the electorate. On the other hand, it alienated respectable opinion by its blatant disregard for parliamentary procedures, its abusive behaviour in the Sejm, and by its aggressive demonstrations and blockades across the country.

Miller tried to appeal to those Poles who sought stability and modernization, but his government faced difficult problems: shaky state finances and proposed cuts in public spending, falling foreign investments, continuing high unemployment, and erratic public support for the EU. In March 2003 the Peasant Party left the ruling coalition, leaving Miller with a parliamentary minority. In the absence of a creditable alternative candidate for the premiership, and buoyed briefly by the successful EU referendum, Miller continued in office, only to face new challenges. Two long and complex battles in 2003–4 over a new law regulating radio and television and over the reform of the ailing national health system brought to light serious cases of corruption; these badly tainted the government and further deepened public disillusionment with the ruling elite. In foreign affairs, Miller's government continued Poland's active role in NATO and tightened defence links with the United States. Poland actively supported the US-led invasion of Iraq in March 2003 and assumed control of one zone in the south of the country. Despite growing public unease about the presence of Polish troops in Iraq, Poland remains one of the most staunchly pro-American countries on the continent, and has earned a special place in Donald Rumsfeld's 'New Europe'. It is also the largest, by far, of the new member states of the European Union, and has already made an assertive impact on EU affairs, protesting with Spain against a planned new decision-making system that would end both countries' advantageous voting rights acquired at the Nice conference in December 2000, and calling with several other traditionally Catholic countries for the inclusion of a reference to united Europe's Christian legacy in the projected new European Constitution. Over Iraq and over the European Union Poland has found itself at odds with both France and Germany, but there are signs that this may be changing.

By the end of 2003 the increasingly unpopular SLD was in trouble, plagued by a constant stream of political scandals, and in March 2004 a splinter group defected to form the Polish Social Democracy (SDPL). Having secured Poland's formal entry into the EU on 1 May 2004, described by many commentators as a decisive date in Poland's modern history, Miller resigned as prime minister. His successor Marek Belka is an experienced politician and economist with a background on the left but independent of the SLD. His caretaker government of experts remained in office until September 2005. Renewed economic growth, increased foreign investments

1 maja 2004

POLSKA WRACA DO EUROPY

58 *Poland returns to Europe.* A self-mocking parody by one of Poland's leading cartoonists Andrzej Mleczko which appeared on the front cover of the weekly *Polityka* on 1 May 2004. Poland's terms of entry into the EU provide the country's farmers with only 25 per cent of the benefits of the Common Agricultural Policy (supplemented by a further 25 per cent from the Polish exchequer); they also restrict for five years the free movement of Polish labour to most EU states, except for the United Kingdom, Sweden and the Republic of Ireland. On the other hand, there is a 12-year restriction on the purchase of agricultural land in Poland by citizens of other member states. Between May 2004 and March 2005 nearly 100,000 Poles, from plumbers and builders to medical staff, have registered for work in the UK; most have taken 'hard-to-fill' jobs.

(8 billion pounds in 2004), and the overwhelmingly positive early effects of EU membership, especially on Poland's hitherto sceptical farmers, may yet erode the appeal of the populist parties and produce a 'yes' vote in favour of the proposed European constitution. Much will also depend on whether the centre-right can act together.

The year 2005 will also see the end of President Kwaśniewski's second and last term in office. Until recently, his record and reputation remained high, and his dignified and effective representation of Poland on the international stage was only strengthened by his constructive mediatory role during the 'Orange Revolution' in Ukraine at the end of 2004. In early 2005 there was still no clear successor to the presidential office, but in July of that year opinion polls suggested Włodzimierz Cimoszewicz, a former SLD prime minister and foreign minister and currently speaker of the Sejm, as the front-runner with Lech Kaczyński in second place. Cimoszewicz soon withdrew from the race, and Donald Tusk, a native of the Kaszub region near Gdańsk and one of the leaders of Civic Platform, emerged as Kaczyński's main rival. Although both Kaczyński and Tusk have a Solidarity pedigree, the former is stressing conservative national values and the importance of a strong state, while the latter represents a more liberal and free-market response to the nation's problems.

The death of Pope John Paul II on 2 April 2005 has deprived the Poles of their iconic 'guardian angel' in Rome. While it is too early for a conclusive evaluation of the Polish Pope's impact on his country, there is no doubt that in some areas his role has been profound. His first pilgrimage to Poland in 1979 did much to inspire the movement of liberation identified with Solidarity, while his appeal for moderation and dialogue contributed to the peaceful transition from communism. In the face of the still ambivalent attitude of the Polish Catholic hierarchy towards the European Union, the Pope's public endorsement of Poland's aspirations to join the EU did sway many Poles to vote 'yes' in the referendum of 2003. On the other hand, the Pope did criticize Poland's post-1989 transformation as too liberal and insufficiently based on Christian foundations. Not all of his teachings have been followed by Polish Catholics in their private and public lives, nor was he able to halt the gradual secularization of Polish society. Fierce electoral battles would be fought in Poland in the autumn of 2005, but during the month of April 2005 something of the spirit of Solidarity did briefly revisit the nation united in common grief.

At the beginning of the twenty-first century the 38.6 million inhabitants of Poland enjoy a degree of national freedom and national security which had been painfully denied to so many of their previous generations. The future of Ukraine and of Russia do remain areas of intense interest and even concern, but that Poland is at peace with all its neighbours, and in close partnership with most of them, is truly remarkable, given the history of the past centuries. Much has been achieved since 1989, and the possibilities of further development are great. The entry into the EU symbolized Poland rejoining the mainstream of European civilization, and confirmed Poland's re-emergence as a major actor in European politics – as it had been until the end of the seventeenth century and, too briefly and not entirely happily, in 1919–39. Yet many challenges face Polish society today, not least political corruption, the low quality of much political debate, the lack of confidence in many of the state's institutions, and a sense of apathy and exclusion of large sections of the population. The danger of populism is a cautionary warning of this. Whether membership of the European Union will in due course promote a greater sense of responsible citizenship, more equitable economic betterment and accompanying social harmony remains to be seen – and to be wished for.

POSTSCRIPT

Results of the parliamentary elections of September 2005: 'Law and Justice' (PiS) came first (with 26.8 per cent of the popular vote), 'Civic Platform' (PO) was in second place (24.2 per cent), and 'Self-Defence' in third (11.7 per cent). The previously ruling SLD dropped to fourth place with only 11.4 per cent of the vote. The final round of the presidential elections of October 2005 was won by Lech Kaczyński who gained 54 per cent of the votes cast; Donald Tusk came second, with 46 per cent.

Chart I   Polish rulers: the Piast dynasty

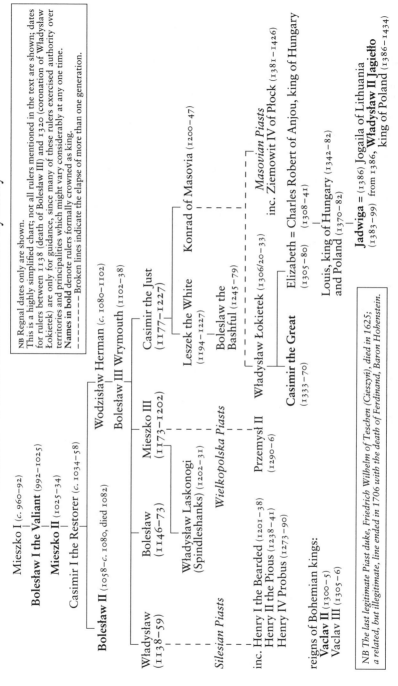

NB Regnal dates only are shown.
This is a highly simplified chart; not all rulers mentioned in the text are shown; dates for rulers between 1138 (death of Bolesław III) and 1320 (coronation of Władysław Łokietek) are only for guidance, since many of these rulers exercised authority over territories and principalities which might vary considerably at any one time.
Names in **bold** denote rulers formally crowned as king.
– – – – – Broken lines indicate the elapse of more than one generation.

Mieszko I (c. 960–92)

Bolesław I the Valiant (992–1025)

Mieszko II (1025–34)

Casimir I the Restorer (c. 1034–58)

Bolesław II (1058–c. 1080, died 1082)

Wodzisław Herman (c. 1080–1102)

Bolesław III Wrymouth (1102–38)

Władysław   Bolesław   Mieszko III   Casimir the Just
(1138–59)   (1146–73)   (1173–1202)   (1177–**1227**)

Silesian Piasts   Władysław Laskonogi   *Wielkopolska Piasts*   Leszek the White   Konrad of Masovia (1200–47)
                         (Spindleshanks) (1202–31)   (1194–1227)

inc. Henry I the Bearded (1201–38)   Przemysł II   Bolesław the   *Masovian Piasts*
Henry II the Pious (1238–41)   (1290–6)   Bashful (1245–79)   inc. Ziemowit IV of Płock (1381–1426)
Henry IV Probus (1273–90)

reigns of Bohemian kings: Władysław Łokietek (1306/20–33)   Elizabeth = Charles Robert of Anjou, king of Hungary
Vaclav II (1300–5)   (1305–80) (1308–41)
Vaclav III (1305–6)   **Casimir the Great**
                                                (1333–70)   Louis, king of Hungary (1342–82)
                                                                                                 and Poland (1370–82)

                                                                                                 Jadwiga = (1386) Jogaila of Lithuania
                                                                                                 (1383–99)   from 1386, **Władysław II Jagiełło**
                                                                                                              king of Poland (1386–1434)

NB *The last legitimate Piast duke, Friedrich Wilhelm of Teschen (Cieszyń), died in 1625; a related, but illegitimate, line ended in 1706 with the death of Ferdinand, Baron Hohenstein.*

Chart II   The Jagiellonian dynasty: kings of Poland and grand dukes of Lithuania

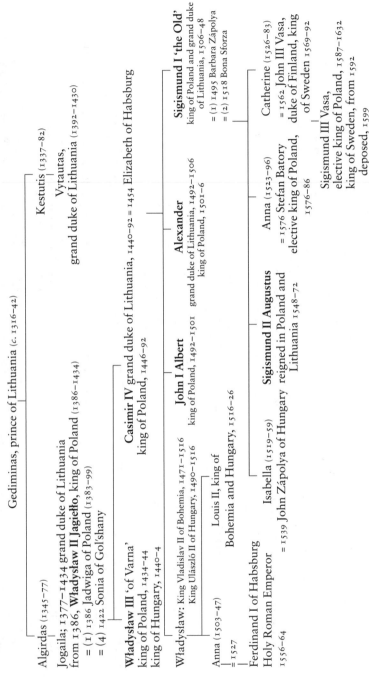

Chart III   Elective rulers of the Polish-Lithuanian Commonwealth (and others)

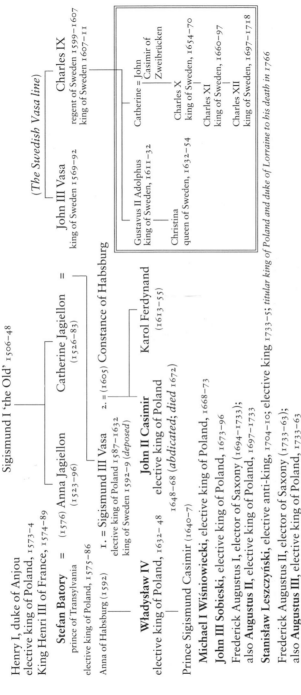

Chart IV Rulers of the partitioned Polish territories (regnal dates only are shown)

Romanov emperors of Russia (bearing the title of 'Polish king' after 1815)	The Habsburgs of Austria (Holy Roman Emperors until 1806; emperors of Austria 1804–1918)	The Hohenzollern kings of Prussia (also grand dukes of Posen after 1815; German emperors after 1871)	The Wettins of Saxony (electors of Saxony until 1806; kings of Saxony after 1806)
Catherine II 'the Great' (1762–96)	Maria Theresa (1740–80)	Frederick II 'the Great' (1740–86)	Frederick Augustus, duke of Warsaw (1807–15) (*abdicated*)
Paul I (1796–1801)	Joseph II (1765–90)	Frederick William II (1786–97)	
Alexander I (1801–25)	Leopold II (1790–2)	Frederick William III (1797–1840)	
Nicholas I (1825–55)	Francis (II) I (1792–1835)	Frederick William IV (1840–61)	
Alexander II (1855–81)	Ferdinand I (1835–48)	William I (1861–88)	
Alexander III (1881–94)	Francis Joseph (1848–1916)	Frederick III (1888)	
Nicholas II (1894–1917) (*abdicated*)	Charles I (1916–18) (*abdicated*)	William II (1888–1918) (*abdicated*)	

Heads of state, presidents, Communist Party leaders (1918–2005)

The Second Republic (1918–1939)

HEAD OF STATE

Józef Piłsudski (November 1918–December 1922)

PRESIDENTS

Gabriel Narutowicz (December 1922)
Stanisław Wojciechowski (December 1922–May 1926)
Ignacy Mościcki (June 1926–September 1939)

Governments-in-exile (1939–1990)
maintaining constitutional continuity with the Second Republic

PRESIDENTS

Władysław Raczkiewicz (September 1939–June 1947)
August Zaleski (June 1947–April 1972)
Stanisław Ostrowski (April 1972–April 1979)
Edward Raczyński (April 1979–April 1986)
Kazimierz Sabbat (April 1986–July 1989)
Ryszard Kaczorowski (July 1989–December 1990)

The Polish People's Republic (1944–1989)

HEADS OF STATE

President of the National Council (KRN)
Bolesław Bierut (November 1944–February 1947)

President and Chairman of the Council of State
Bolesław Bierut (February 1947–November 1952)

Chairmen of the Council of State
Aleksander Zawadzki (November 1952–August 1964)
Edward Ochab (August 1964–April 1968)
Marian Spychalski (April 1968–December 1970)
Józef Cyrankiewicz (December 1970–March 1972)
Henryk Jabłoński (March 1972–November 1985)
Wojciech Jaruzelski (November 1985–July 1989)

The Third Republic (since 1989)

BIBLIOGRAPHY OF WORKS
IN ENGLISH

GENERAL WORKS

Davies, N. *God's playground: a history of Poland*, 2 vols., Oxford: Clarendon Press, 1981; 2nd edn, 2005

Davies, N. *Heart of Europe: a short history of Poland*, Oxford: University Press, 1984

Jedruch, J. *Constitutions, elections and legislatures of Poland 1493–1977*, Washington, D.C.: University Press of America, 1982

Kloczowski, J. *A history of Polish Christianity*, Cambridge: University Press, 2000

Knab, S. H. *Polish customs, traditions and folklore*, New York: Hippocrene, 1999

Kridl, M. *A survey of Polish literature and culture*, The Hague: Mouton, 1956

Magocsi, P. R. *A history of Ukraine*, Toronto: University Press, 1996

Miłosz, C. *The history of Polish literature*, Berkeley: University of California Press, 1983

Prażmowska, A. J. *A history of Poland*, Basingstoke: Palgrave Macmillan, 2004

Subtelny, O. *Ukraine: a history*, Toronto: University Press, 1988

Wandycz, P. *The price of freedom: a history of east central Europe from the Middle Ages to the present*, London: Routledge, 1992

Zamoyski, A. *The Polish way: a thousand years' history of the Poles and their culture*, London: Murray, 1989

POLAND, PRE-1795

Barker, M. (ed.) *The military orders*, vol. I: *Fighting for the faith and caring for the sick*, Aldershot: Variorum, 1994

Bartlett, R. *The making of Europe: conquest, colonization and cultural change 950–1350*, Princeton, N.J.: University Press, 1993

Basarab, J. *Pereiaslav 1654: a historiographical study*, Edmonton: Canadian Institute of Ukrainian Studies, University of Alberta, 1982

Bogucka, M. *The lost world of the 'Sarmatians'*, Warsaw: Polish Academy of Sciences, Institute of History, 1996

Butterwick, R. *Poland's last king and English culture: Stanisław August Poniatowski 1732–1798*, Oxford: Clarendon Press, 1998

Carter, F. W. *Trade and urban development in Poland: an economic geography of Cracow, from its origins to 1795*, Cambridge: University Press, 1994

Christiansen, A. *The northern crusades*, London: Macmillan, 1980

Długosz, J. *The annals of Jan Długosz: Annales seu Cronicae incliti Regni Poloniae: an English abridgement by H. Michael with a commentary by P. Smith*, Chichester: IM Publications, 1997

Dolukhanov, P. M. *The early Slavs: eastern Europe from the initial settlement to the Kievan Rus*, London: Longman, 1996

Fedorowicz, J. K. (ed.) *A republic of nobles: studies in Polish history to 1864*, Cambridge: University Press, 1982

Fiszman, S. (ed.) *The Polish Renaissance in its European context*, Bloomington: Indiana University Press, 1988

Fiszman, S. (ed.) *Constitution and reform in eighteenth-century Poland: the Constitution of 3 May 1791*, Bloomington: Indiana University Press, 1997

Fletcher, R. *The conversion of Europe: from paganism to Christianity 371–1386 AD*, London: HarperCollins, 1997

Frick, D., *Meletij Smotryc'kyj*, Cambridge, Mass.: Harvard University Press, 1995

Friedrich, K. *The other Prussia: Royal Prussia, Poland and liberty, 1569–1772*, Cambridge: University Press, 2000

Frost, R. *After the Deluge: Poland-Lithuania and the Second Northern War 1555–1660*, Cambridge: University Press, 1993

Frost, R. *The Northern Wars: war, state and society in north-eastern Europe 1558–1721*, London: Longman, 2000

Fuhrmann, H. *Germany in the High Middle Ages c. 1050–1200*, Cambridge: University Press, 1986

Geremek, B. *The common roots of Europe*, Cambridge: Polity Press, 1996

Górecki, P. *Economy, society, and lordship in medieval Poland 1100–1250*, New York: Holme and Meier, 1992

Gudziak, B. A. *Crisis and reform: the Kievan metropolitanate, the patriarchate of Constantinople and the genesis of the Union of Brest*, Cambridge, Mass.: Harvard University Press, 1998

Hundert, G. D. *The Jews in a Polish town: the case of Opatów in the eighteenth century*, Baltimore: Johns Hopkins University Press, 1992

Hundert, G. D. *Jews in Poland-Lithuania in the eighteenth century: a genealogy of modernity*, Berkeley: University of California Press, 2004

Kamiński, A. S. *Republic vs. autocracy: Poland-Lithuania and Russia, 1686–1697*, Cambridge, Mass.: Harvard University Press, 1993

Kaplan, H. H. *The First Partition of Poland*, New York: Columbia University Press, 1962

Kirby, D. *Northern Europe in the early modern period: the Baltic world 1492–1772*, London: Longman, 1990

Knoll, P. W. *The rise of the Polish monarchy: Piast Poland in east central Europe, 1320–1370*, Chicago: University of Chicago Press, 1972

Kochanowski, J. *Jan Kochanowski: Laments*, trans. S. Heaney and S. Barańczak, London: Faber, 1995

Levine, H. *Economic origins of antisemitism: Poland and its Jews in the early modern period*, New Haven, Conn.: Yale University Press, 1991

Lord, R. H. *The Second Partition of Poland: a study in diplomatic history*, Cambridge, Mass.: Harvard University Press, 1915

Lukowski, J. T. *Liberty's folly: the Polish-Lithuanian Commonwealth in the eighteenth century*, London: Routledge, 1991

Lukowski, J. T. *The Partitions of Poland 1772, 1793, 1795*, London: Longman, 1999

Mączak, A., Samsonowicz, H. and Burke, P. (eds.) *East-central Europe in transition: from the fourteenth to the seventeenth centuries*, Cambridge: University Press, 1985

Manteuffel, T. *The formation of the Polish state: the period of ducal rule, 963–1194*, Detroit, Mich.: Wayne State University Press, 1982

Musteikis, A. *The Reformation in Lithuania: religious fluctuations in the sixteenth century*, Boulder, Colo.: East European Monographs, 1988

Pasek, J. Ch. *Memoirs of the Polish baroque: the writings of Jan Chryzostom Pasek, a squire of the Commonwealth of Poland and Lithuania*, ed. C. S. Leech, Berkeley: University of California Press, 1976

Polonsky, A., Basista, J. and Link-Lenczowski, A. (eds.) *The Jews in Old Poland*, London: Taurus, 1993

Rosman, M. *The Lords' Jews: magnate–Jewish relations in the Polish-Lithuanian Commonwealth during the eighteenth century*, Cambridge, Mass.: Harvard University Press, 1990

Rowell, S. C. *Lithuania ascending: a pagan empire within east-central Europe, 1295–1345*, Cambridge: University Press, 1994

Sedlar, J. W. *East central Europe in the Middle Ages 1000–1500*, Seattle: University of Washington Press, 1994

Segel, H. B. *Renaissance culture in Poland: the rise of humanism 1470–1543*, Ithaca: Cornell University Press, 1989

Subtelny, O. *Domination of eastern Europe: native nobilities and foreign absolutism, 1500–1715*, Kingston: McGill-Queen's University Press, 1986

Sysyn, F. E. *Between Poland and the Ukraine: the dilemma of Adam Kysil*, Cambridge, Mass.: Harvard University Press, 1985

Tazbir, J. *A state without stakes: Polish religious toleration in the sixteenth and seventeenth centuries*, New York: The Kościuszko Foundation, 1973

Zamoyski, A. *The last king of Poland*, London: Cape, 1992

Zank, W. *The German melting-pot: multiculturality in historical perspective*, Basingstoke: Macmillan, 1998

Żółkiewski, S. *Expedition to Moscow: a memoir*, London: Polonica Publications, 1959

POLAND, POST-1795

Abramsky, C., Jachimczyk, M. and Polonsky, A. (eds.) *The Jews in Poland*, Oxford: Basil Blackwell, 1986

Ascherson, N. *The Polish August: the self-limiting revolution*, London: Allen Lane, 1981

Bethell, N. *Gomułka, his Poland and his communism*, London: Longman, 1969

Brock, P. *Polish revolutionary populism: a study in agrarian socialist thought from the 1830s to the 1850s*, Toronto: University Press, 1977

Bromke, A. *Poland's politics: idealism vs. realism*, Cambridge, Mass.: Harvard University Press, 1967

Brown, J. F. *Surge to freedom: the end of communist rule in eastern Europe*, Durham, N.C.: Duke University Press, 1991

Brzeziński, Z. K. *The Soviet bloc: unity and conflict*, Cambridge, Mass.: Harvard University Press, 1971

Ciechanowski, J. M. *The Warsaw Rising of 1944*, Cambridge: University Press, 1974

Cienciala, A. M. *Poland and the Western Powers 1938–1939: a study in the interdependence of eastern and western Europe*, London: Routledge and Kegan Paul, 1968

Cienciala, A. M. and Komarnicki, T. *From Versailles to Locarno: keys to Polish foreign policy 1919–25*, Lawrence, Kans.: Kansas University Press, 1984

Curry, J. L. and Fajfer, L. (eds.) *Poland's permanent revolution: peoples vs. elites 1956–1990*, Washington, D.C.: American University Press, 1996

Czaplicka, J. (ed.), *Lviv: a city in the crosscurrents of culture*, Cambridge, Mass.: Harvard Ukrainian Research Institute, 2005

Davies, N. *White eagle, red star: the Polish–Soviet war 1919–1920*, London: Orbis Books, 1983

Davies, N. *Rising '44: the Battle for Warsaw*, London: Macmillan, 2003

Davies, N. and Moorhouse, R. *Microcosm: Portrait of a Central European City*, London: Jonathan Cape, 2002

Dawisha, K. *Eastern Europe, Gorbachev and reform, the great challenge*, 2nd edn, Cambridge: University Press, 1990

Dziewanowski, M. K. *The Communist Party of Poland: an outline of history*, 2nd edn, Cambridge, Mass.: Harvard University Press, 1976

Eile, S. *Literature and nationalism in partitioned Poland, 1795–1918*, Basingstoke: Macmillan, 2000

Eisenbach, A. *The emancipation of the Jews in Poland 1780–1870*, Oxford: Basil Blackwell, 1992

Fejto, F. *A history of the people's democracies*, Harmondsworth: Penguin, 1974

Fountain, A. V. *Roman Dmowski: party, tactics, ideology 1895–1907*, Boulder, Colo.: East European Monographs, 1980

Garliński, J. *Poland in the Second World War*, London: Macmillan, 1985

Garton Ash, T. *The Polish revolution: Solidarity*, London: Penguin, 1999

Gilbert, M. *The Holocaust: The Jewish tragedy*, London: Fontana/Collins, 1989

Gross, J. T. *Polish society under German occupation: the general gouvernement 1939–1944*, Princeton, N.J.: University Press, 1979

Gross, J. T. *Revolution from abroad: the Soviet conquest of Poland's western Ukraine and western Belorussia*, Princeton, N.J.: University Press, 1988; expanded edition, 2002

Hagen, W. W. *Germans, Poles, and Jews. The nationality conflict in the Prussian east, 1772–1914*, Chicago: University of Chicago Press, 1980

Hayden, J. *Poles apart: Solidarity and the new Poland*, Blackrock: Irish Academic Press, 1994

Howard, A. E. D. (ed.) *Constitution making in eastern Europe*, Washington, D.C.: Woodrow Wilson Center Press, 1993

Jaworski, R. and Pietrow-Ennker, B. (eds.) *Women in Polish society*, Boulder, Colo.: East European Monographs, 1992

Jedlicki, J. *A suburb of Europe: nineteenth-century Polish approaches to western civilization*, Budapest: Central European University Press, 1999

Jędrzejewicz, W. *Piłsudski: a life for Poland*, New York: Hippocrene Books, 1982

Kamiński, B. *The collapse of state socialism: the case of Poland*, Princeton, N.J.: University Press, 1991

Karski, J. *Story of a secret state*, London: Hodder and Stoughton, 1945

Karski, J. *The Great Powers and Poland 1919–1945: from Versailles to Yalta*, Lanham, Md.: University Press of America, 1985

Kaser, M. C. and Radice, E. (eds.) *The economic history of eastern Europe 1919–1975*, Oxford: Cleveland Press, 1986

Kenney, P. *Rebuilding Poland: workers and communists 1945–1950*, Ithaca and London: Cornell University Press, 1997

Kersten, K. *The establishment of communist rule in Poland 1943–1948*, Berkeley: University of California Press, 1991

Kieniewicz, S. *The emancipation of the Polish peasantry*, Chicago and London: University of Chicago Press, 1969

Kirby, D. *The Baltic world 1772–1993. Europe's northern periphery in an age of change*, London: Longman, 1995

Komarnicki, T. *The rebirth of the Polish republic: a study in the diplomatic history of Europe 1914–1920*, London: Heinemann, 1957

Korbel, J. *Poland between East and West*, Princeton, N.J.: University Press, 1963

Korboński, A. *The politics of socialist agriculture in Poland 1945–1960*, New York: Columbia University Press, 1965

Korboński, S. *The Polish Underground State 1939–1945*, Boulder, Colo.: East European Monographs, 1978

Kurczewski, J. *The resurrection of rights in Poland*, Oxford: Clarendon Press, 1993

Labedz, L. (ed.) *Poland under Jaruzelski*, New York: Scribner, 1984

Latawski, P. (ed.) *The reconstruction of Poland 1914–23*, London: Macmillan, 1992

Lepak, K. J. *Prelude to Solidarity: Poland and the politics of the Gierek regime*, New York: Columbia University Press, 1988

Leslie, R. F. *Polish politics and the revolution of November 1830*, London: Athlone Press, 1956

Leslie, R. F. *Reform and insurrection in Russian Poland 1856–1863*, London: Athlone Press, 1963

Leslie, R. F. (ed.) *The history of Poland since 1863*, Cambridge: University Press, 1980

Lipski, J. J. *A history of KOR: the committee for workers' self-defence*, Berkeley: University of California Press, 1985

Lucas, R. C. *Forgotten holocaust: the Poles under German occupation 1939–1944*, New York: Hippocrene, 1990

Markovits, A. S. and Sysyn, F. E. (eds.) *Nation building and the politics of nationalism: essays on Austrian Galicia*, Cambridge, Mass.: Harvard University Press, 1982

Micewski, A. *Cardinal Wyszyński: a biography*, San Diego, Calif.: Harcourt, Brace, Jovanovich, 1984

Olczak-Roniker, J. *In the garden of memory: a family life*, London: Weidenfeld and Nicolson, 2004

Olszewski, A. K. *An outline of Polish art and architecture 1890–1980*, Warsaw: Interpress, 1989

Paczkowski, A. *The spring will be ours: Poland and the Poles from occupation to freedom*, trans. by Jane Cave, University Park, Pa.: Pennsylvania State University Press, 2004

Polonsky, A. *Politics in independent Poland 1921–1939: the crisis of constitutional government*, Oxford: Clarendon Press, 1972

Polonsky, A. (ed.) *The Great Powers and the Polish Question 1941–1945: a documentary study in Cold War origins*, London: London School of Economics and Political Science, 1976

Polonsky, A. and Michlic, J. B. *The neighbours respond: the controversy over the Jedwabne massacre in Poland*, Princeton, N.J.: University Press, 2003

Porter, B. *When nationalism began to hate: imagining modern politics in nineteenth-century Poland*, New York: Oxford University Press, 2000

Prażmowska, A. J. *Britain and Poland 1939–1943: the betrayed ally*, Cambridge: University Press, 1995

Prażmowska, A. J. *Eastern Europe and the origins of the Second World War*, London: Macmillan, 2000

Prizel, I. and Michta, A. (eds.) *Polish foreign policy reconsidered*, New York: St Martin's, 1995

Raina, P. *Poland 1981: towards social renewal*, London: George Allen and Unwin, 1985

Ransel, D. L. and Shallcross, B. (eds.), *Polish Encounters, Russian Identity*, Bloomington and Indianapolis: Indiana University Press, 2005

Rothschild, J. *East central Europe between the two world wars*, Washington, D.C.: University Press, 1974

Rothschild, J. *Return to diversity: a political history of east central Europe since World War II* (2nd edn), New York and Oxford: Oxford University Press, 1993

Senn, A. E. *Lithuania awakening*, Berkeley: University of California Press, 1990

Snyder, T. *The reconstruction of nations: Poland, Ukraine, Lithuania, Belarus, 1569–1999*, New Haven and London: Yale University Press, 2003

Stachura, P. D. *Poland in the twentieth century*, London: Macmillan, 1998

Stachura, P. D. (ed.) *Poland between the wars*, London: Macmillan, 1999

Stehle, H. *The independent satellite: society and politics in Poland since 1945*, New York: Praeger, 1965

Stirling, T., Nałęcz, D. and Dubicki, T. (eds.), *Intelligence co-operation between Poland and Great Britain during World War Two*, London and Portland: Vallentine Mitchell, 2005

Stokes, G. (ed.) *From Stalinism to pluralism: a documentary history of eastern Europe since 1945*, New York: Oxford University Press, 1991

Sugar, P. F. and Lederer, I. J. (eds.) *Nationalism in eastern Europe*, Seattle and London: University of Washington Press, 1971

Sword, K. with Davies, N. and Ciechanowski, J. *The formation of the Polish community in Great Britain, 1939–1950*, London: School of Slavonic and East European Studies, 1989

Syrop, K. *Spring in October: the story of the Polish revolution 1956*, New York: Praeger, 1957

Thaden, E. C. *Russia's western borderlands 1710–1870*, Princeton, N.J.: University Press, 1984

Thomas, W. and Znaniecki, F. *The Polish peasant in Europe and America*, 2 vols., New York: Dover, 1958

Torańska, T. *Oni* ['Them']: *Stalin's Polish puppets*, London: Collins Harvill, 1987

Trzeciakowski, L. *The* Kulturkampf *in Prussian Poland*, Boulder, Colo.: East European Monographs, 1990

Walicki, A. *Philosophy and Romantic nationalism. The case of Poland*, Oxford: Clarendon Press, 1982

Wandycz, P. *Soviet–Polish relations 1917–1921*, Cambridge, Mass.: Harvard University Press, 1969

Wandycz, P. S. *The lands of partitioned Poland 1795–1918*, Seattle: University of Washington Press, 1974

Wiskemann, E. *Germany's eastern neighbours: problems relating to the Oder–Neisse Line and the Czech frontier region*, London: Oxford University Press, 1956

Wynot, E. *Warsaw between the world wars: profile of the capital city in a developing land 1918–1939*, Boulder, Colo.: East European Monographs, 1983

Zamoyski, A. *Chopin: a biography*, London: Collins, 1979

Zamoyski, A. *The forgotten few: the Polish Air Force in the Second World War*, London: John Murray, 1995

Zamoyski, A. *Holy madness: Romantics, patriots and revolutionaries 1776–1871*, London: Weidenfeld and Nicolson, 1999

Zawadzki, W. H. *A man of honour: Adam Czartoryski as a statesman of Russia and Poland 1795–1831*, Oxford: Clarendon Press, 1993

Zawodny, J. K. *Death in the forest: the story of the Katyn Forest massacre*, Notre Dame, Ind.: University Press, 1962

Zimmerman, J. D. *Poles, Jews and the politics of nationality: the Bund and the Polish Socialist Party in late Czarist Russia 1892–1914*, Madison, Wisc.: Wisconsin University Press, 2003

INDEX

355

CAMBRIDGE CONCISE HISTORIES

A Concise History of Mexico 2nd edition
BRIAN R. HAMNETT

A Concise History of New Zealand
PHILIPPA MEIN SMITH

A Concise History of Poland 2nd edition
JERZY LUKOWSKI AND HUBERT ZAWADZKI

A Concise History of Portugal 2nd edition
DAVID BIRMINGHAM

A Concise History of South Africa
ROBERT ROSS

Other titles are in preparation